BLOOD
GUN
MONEY

HOW AMERICA ARMS
GANGS AND CARTELS

IOAN GRILLO

BLOOMSBURY PUBLISHING
NEW YORK · LONDON · OXFORD · NEW DELHI · SYDNEY

BLOOMSBURY PUBLISHING
Bloomsbury Publishing Inc.
1385 Broadway, New York, NY 10018, USA

BLOOMSBURY, BLOOMSBURY PUBLISHING, and the Diana logo are trademarks
of Bloomsbury Publishing Plc

First published in the United States 2021

Bloomsbury Publishing Plc does not have any control over, or responsibility for, any
third-party websites referred to or in this book. All internet addresses given in this book
were correct at the time of going to press. The author and publisher regret any inconvenience
caused if addresses have changed or sites have ceased to exist, but can accept no
responsibility for any such changes.

ISBN: HB: 978-1-63557-278-0; eBook: 978-1-63557-279-7

Library of Congress Cataloging-in-Publication Data is available

2 4 6 8 10 9 7 5 3 1

Typeset by Westchester Publishing Services
Printed and bound in the U.S.A. by Berryville Graphics Inc., Berryville, Virginia

To find out more about our authors and books visit www.bloomsbury.com and sign up for
our newsletters.

Bloomsbury books may be purchased for business or promotional use. For information
on bulk purchases please contact Macmillan Corporate and Premium Sales Department at
specialmarkets@macmillan.com.

Everybody is a book of blood; wherever we're opened, we're red.

—CLIVE BARKER, *BOOKS OF BLOOD*

Leave the gun out of it. I can always hear the sound of money.

—RAYMOND CHANDLER, *THE BIG SLEEP*

CONTENTS

BLOOD
GUN
MONEY

1

The Guns of El Chapo

Freedom is beautiful.

—Joaquín "El Chapo" Guzmán, shortly
before his third capture, in 2016

————

Finally seeing El Chapo in the flesh, a few feet away from me, conjured mixed emotions.

Like many in the Brooklyn courtroom, I felt a rush being so close to such a notorious villain as Joaquín Guzmán, who is up there with Pablo Escobar and Al Capone as the most infamous gangsters of the last century. Not only journalists but fans and tourists had been queuing up to get a sight of the sixty-one-year-old from Mexico's Sierra Madre mountains and see his beauty-queen wife in the gallery. Only the first few dozen would make it into the courtroom, fifty more into an overflow room to watch it on screens, with the rest turned away, so people were arriving earlier and earlier to get in line. On that January 2019 morning, while the polar vortex sprinkled snow on New York, I arrived at four-forty A.M. and still only just made it onto a courtroom bench.

Guzmán was reaching the end of his three-month trial for trafficking cocaine, heroin, marijuana, and crystal meth, which federal prosecutors claimed had made him fourteen billion dollars. As he was so notorious, the prosecutors called an overkill of fifty-six witnesses, including fourteen of his former cohorts, employees, and lovers. The scariest was a Colombian drug lord known as Chupeta, who'd had plastic surgery so many times that his face looked like a rubber mask as he confessed to ordering a hundred and fifty murders. Other gripping testimony came from a computer buff who'd built Guzmán an encrypted cell phone network and then tapped the calls for the Drug Enforcement Administration, and a lover who described Guzmán jumping out of bed naked and running into a secret tunnel to evade capture.

Such tales made great television, and American networks were giving it broad coverage. A cable news reporter at the court told me that his editors liked the story because it provided a light touch from the divisive issues dominating media in the Trump era. Gun violence in the United States, from mass shootings to police killings, cut to the heart of the tribal politics gripping the nation. So did the migrant caravans of thousands of Central Americans arriving on the southern border. El Chapo, meanwhile, could be entertainment.

But seeing the short, stocky figure of Guzmán, in his finely pressed suit with his lively, wide-open eyes, also filled me with anger and sadness. I had been reporting on the drug violence in Mexico since 2001, after I moved there from Britain, and what I first saw as a thrilling tale of supervillains had morphed into a humanitarian catastrophe.

I found myself covering things I couldn't have imagined. I hit crime scenes across the country where gunmen would spray five hundred rounds at their prey, slaying bystanders and leaving pulverized bodies that began to color my dreams. Then I saw victims mutilated and decapitated, the rival cartels escalating the numbers of corpses they dumped in public as if they were playing high-stakes poker. In 2012, I found myself in a morgue in Monterrey, my nostrils filled with the stench of forty-nine bodies that had been left on a road, all with their heads, hands, and feet cut off.

Finally, I lost good friends to the bloodshed. Javier Valdez was a prolific and inspiring journalist from Guzmán's home state of Sinaloa who had penned eight books on the narco world. He generously shared his knowledge with me over long phone calls or longer drinking sessions in a cantina near his newspaper's offices. On May 15, 2017, he was leaving his office at midday when he was shot twelve times and died at the scene. "In the end, we are a big family of victims in this country," said his widow, fellow journalist Griselda Triana.[1]

The surreal stories of lovers and tunnels distracted from this colossal human cost. It may have been an exotic foreign villain in the dock, a man with such bizarre stories that there were already two Netflix dramas portraying him. But he was only one step away from those same wedge issues dividing America.

Many in the caravan at the southern border were fleeing mob violence. The same methods used to supply guns to gangs in American cities were used to arm cartels south of the Rio Grande. And the tragedy of innocent people being gunned down in senseless mass shootings across the United States was echoed in the tragedy of innocent people being murdered in equally senseless massacres in Latin America.

Guzmán was not only a drug trafficker. He had helped escalate the turf wars in Mexico into a brutal conflict that destabilized his country, part of the armed violence ripping havoc on Latin America and driving refugees to the U.S. border. He would be seen as a war criminal if it were to be understood as a war. And finally, after escaping from two "top security" Mexican prisons, he was facing justice that could put him away for life in an American supermax cell in the desert.

On my second day in court, Andrea Goldbarg, the assistant U.S. attorney for the Eastern District of New York, unleashed a grueling seven-hour closing argument to convict Guzmán. She showed a PowerPoint presentation explaining Guzmán's trafficking empire, replayed wiretaps of him plotting with gangsters and guerrillas, and went over some of the juiciest anecdotes his cohorts had said on the stand. Though it was grisly stuff, the long explanation became tiresome. Not only the jury of New Yorkers seemed to be struggling to keep attention; even the eyes of El Chapo himself were wandering.

Until she brought out the guns.

Prosecutors carried in a trio of AK-47s that had been seized from the Sinaloa Cartel in Texas and laid them in the center of the courtroom. As she came to the finale of her arguments, she pointed to the guns and then to El Chapo.

I had been seeing a lot of guns that week. I had flown to the trial from Las Vegas, where I'd been at the SHOT Show, the biggest firearms trade show in the world. It's just three miles from the Las Vegas Village concert venue, the site of the biggest mass shooting in recent U.S. history. The same models of Kalashnikovs that were in the courtroom were also on display at the SHOT Show, alongside bigger weapons like .50-caliber rifles, grenade launchers, and machine guns mounted on helicopters.

Goldbarg, who was born in Argentina and grew up in the United States, had built a career as a prosecutor going after Latin American gangsters. But El Chapo's trial was by far the biggest of her career, and the stakes were enormous. It was the culmination of a decades-long campaign by law enforcement to nail the top dogs in the narco world, and he had been billed as the ultimate kingpin. It might have looked an easy win, convicting a drug lord as infamous as Guzmán. But open goals are high-pressure shots.

The AKs were a physical way to illustrate that the short-suited Guzmán, who was calm and smiling in the courtroom, really was a bloodthirsty warlord. It wasn't the first time that prosecutors had shown off weapons. Just before Christmas, they wheeled out an entire haul of forty Kalashnikov-style rifles seized in El Paso, Texas, and linked by a witness to El Chapo and his Sinaloa Cartel. Some were made in Romania, others in Serbia, but all had been sold retail in the United States, where they were acquired by the narcos.

There to talk about the rifles was Curtis Williams, an officer from the Bureau of Alcohol, Tobacco, Firearms and Explosives, known widely as the ATF, the U.S. federal agency that polices the gun industry and leads the fight against gun crime. Williams walked around the courtroom with one of the Kalashnikovs, snapping open the folding stock, which made a member of the jury flinch.

The prosecutor cut in: "Can you just be clear: All these have been made safe, correct?"

"Yes," Williams replied.

The ATF's next witness, Max Kingery, went further and picked up a rocket-propelled grenade launcher, an RPG-7. El Chapo's defense lawyer William Purpura objected, saying, "It's really big. I'm looking at it."

Judge Brian Cogan overruled but said that Kingery had to be quick. "This is not a weapons show," he said. "This is a trial, okay."

There was another shudder from the jury. El Chapo's wife had brought their young twin daughters to court that day, and at the sight of the rocket launcher, she hustled them out of the courtroom.

In the coverage of the trial, the guns were a footnote, a colorful prop to support the main drama of a billionaire drug trafficker. But they are at the heart of their own momentous story, which I tell here.

This book is about America's "iron river" of guns, the millions of weapons that flow from the legal industry to the black market, feeding criminals across the nation and drug cartels across the continent. It follows this river from the corners of Baltimore to the battlefields on the border, the factories of Transylvania to the gun shows of Texas, and the gun vaults of Arizona to the jungles of the Andes. It delves into the twisted relationship between the illegal drug and gun trades, how they play off each other like angry lovers. It shows how this historic case of gun trafficking came to be and why attempts to stop it have failed so miserably. It looks at how weapons from the black market spill over to some of the terrorists and mass shooters spreading panic. And it asks how we can slow the iron river, or if we really have to face a world where anyone who wants to murder can have all the firepower they desire.

While guns are big in the news, American coverage is dominated by two main themes. On one side are the shootings at schools and nightclubs by "madmen," which have wrenched at the soul of the nation. On the other is the gun lobby's self-declared defense of law-abiding owners, linked to a wider culture war cutting through the country. But the cold fact is that illegal firearms are used in the vast majority of gun homicides in the United States as well as in Latin America.

The firearm black market has been surprisingly understudied considering its importance. Leaked weapons from the legal U.S. gun industry find their way to criminals in every U.S. state and 136 other countries. The guns are fired by killers who make the American continent the most homicidal one on earth, with forty-seven of the fifty most murderous cities, several in the United States. Despite the United States having the world's biggest economy and by far biggest military, cities such as Baltimore and St. Louis suffer homicide rates comparable to those in Latin American hot spots. The gun violence is in turn used to justify militarized policing, and the police murders of African Americans scar the soul of the nation—and threw it into turmoil in 2020. Wherever you stand on these issues, it's important to understand this gun trade.

At the heart of the iron river is the relationship between guns and drugs. The two fit together like a lock and key—boys with Glocks on the corner, inner-city cops kicking down doors to put drugs and guns on the table, and cartel killers carrying Kalashnikovs. But the mechanics of them are inverted. The illegal narcotics trade is huge, worth an estimated $150 billion a year in the United States alone and over $300 billion globally. The gun black market claims a fraction of that worth but provides a tool that allows gangsters to control those drug profits.

The two products are often bartered. And the prices of both go through crazy shifts dictated by the rules of the street. I unravel the "gun-onomics" over these pages by talking to the mobsters who sell them.

Guns from the U.S. retail market are of course not the only weapons in the hands of the continent's killers. I look hard at other sources, especially the "leakage" from corrupt security forces in Latin America, which are supplied by U.S. and European gun companies. I talk to one trafficker who conspires with Mexican soldiers to sell seized guns back to the crooks. But the United States has an estimated 393 million guns in civilian hands, more than the next twenty-five countries combined, and millions more are churned out every year.[2] From this arsenal, weapons pour across the hemisphere.

There is a painful paradox here. The United States lives with heavily armed criminals, and suffers the worst murder rates and highest number of police shootings in the developed world. But it still has relatively strong law enforcement that keeps organized crime in check. In contrast, Latin American countries suffer weak institutions that cannot contain the gun-toting gangsters. The weapons there fuel a hybrid of crime and war, a relentless conflict that confounds politicians and unleashes a refugee crisis.

Investigators have long divided gun trafficking into two areas: the deals between mobsters, seen as a domestic issue, and gunrunning over borders to war zones, seen as an international one. But this distinction is increasingly blurred, and America's iron river flows into these hybrid conflicts, or "crime wars," mixing with the arms from the charred Cold War battlegrounds.

The gun lobby is correct in pointing out that people who break the law to get firearms commit most murders. But then it has fought the policing of the gun black market, defending the loopholes and achieving crazy limits on law enforcement of firearms. The result is that it effectively defends the criminal market in guns used by cartels and corner hoods.

Part of this is explained by following the money. Gun companies profit from the black market like almost no other industry does. But digging into the gun business reveals wonky economics, and it is not as profitable as many would believe—or claim. Meanwhile, the National Rifle Association (NRA) makes money by selling a "gun lifestyle," and has transformed into a media machine in the culture war. And it profits from fighting a fundamentalist battle with no compromise. America's iron river is born out of the nation's unique, if mutating, gun culture.

Still, this book is not a rant against the Second Amendment or the right of law-abiding citizens to have guns. It looks at the measures that could reduce trafficking to criminals, while garnering wide support, and reduce the hundreds of billions of dollars of drug money financing gangs and cartels. As lawmakers and the wider society look for a new way forward on guns, drugs, and policing, it is crucial to understand the complexities of the black market. To forge effective enforcement, politicians have to hear from the dirty streets about how gangsters operate. The tales of crime bosses are not just food for Netflix but have become key to governance in the twenty-first century.

I tell the story of the iron river in twelve chapters, each focusing on a different angle linked to gun trafficking in the Americas. I trace the life of a gun from the factory to a Mexican murder scene; talk to men who bring firepower onto the corners of Baltimore; follow an undercover ATF agent who rode with bikers; track guns through the jungles of the Darién Gap; document the struggles in a Texas hospital ward after a mass shooting; and look at a drug cartel assembling its own AR-15s. To tell these stories, I talk to agents and traffickers, to gun sellers and peace activists, to presidents and protesters, to gunshot victims and gun shooters, to militiamen and murderers.

The iron river has sources and tributaries; it meanders into strange ground and bursts open like an estuary. Following the guns leads to all kinds of places: the ATF trace center in West Virginia working with bizarre restrictions, the Colombian war half a continent away, a factory in the Black Forest of Germany.

The tales are interwoven, with some of the same characters, and guns, floating between them. I trace the forces and institutions that have shaped them, from the development of gun technology to the parallel histories of the ATF and the gun lobby. They are not an A to Z of the continent's arms smuggling, as the web is too big and snarled. But they show different elements that together paint a portrait of the world's bloodiest racket—and of the flailing fight by law enforcement to stop it.

When prosecutors wheeled in the forty AK-47s to the courtroom, they called Max Kingery, the ATF's chief of firearms technology. Kingery explained how the gangsters convert the semiautomatic versions, which are sold in U.S. stores, into fully automatic machine guns.

"Simply drill a hole and install a single part," he said. "Five minutes total, you've got a very reliable machine gun."

Some gangsters will also switch to thicker barrels to withstand the heat of full-automatic fire. The cartels use the converted versions to spray the hundreds of bullets I saw at crime scenes in Mexico.

This talk of mechanics hits a central tenet of the modern black market, and of the gun debate. Potent rifles are wielded by guerrillas and cartels, mass shooters and terrorists. The daddy of these is the Kalashnikov, which, by a quirk of history, was forged in the Communist East and is now sold as a consumer product in the United States, and then smuggled to post-ideological battles in Latin America. I delve deeper into this history in the following chapter.

Eight of the ten counts against El Chapo were for drug trafficking. But count nine was for the use of firearms in furtherance of the conspiracy. This was fairly easy to prove. The prosecutor Goldbarg showed a photo of Guzmán posing in a bulletproof jacket with an AR-15 rifle. She displayed another picture of a diamond-encrusted .38 mm pistol with the initials JGL, those of his full name, Joaquín Guzmán Loera. And she reminded jurors of a witness who had described El Chapo personally shooting dead two captives as he shouted "*a chingar a su madre*," or "fuck your mother."

But then Goldbarg went further. She explained how Guzmán not only packed his own pistols, but also supplied guns to his army of hit men. This was where the stash of forty AK-47s came in. And this was just the tip of the iceberg. According to a ledger captured from a cartel safe house in the Mexican resort city of Cabo, El Chapo had been shifting guns by the thousands.

"The defendant did something like purchasing the weapons or distributing the weapons, not just for himself to use, but also for *sicarios* [hitmen] and pistoleros to use," she said. "It wasn't a bring-your-own-firearm situation. They had the firearms because the defendant purchased them.

"You saw numerous examples of this in the ledgers that were seized from Cabo. These notebooks had a shopping list for weapons. You can see that he's asking for fifty AK-47s, one thousand AK-47s, one hundred M16s; and then it says twenty-seven RPG-7s and AR-15s. That wasn't the only thing on his wish list. It has grenade launchers, bullets, and more . . . The defendant couldn't wage his wars without the tools of warfare like firearms."

By getting into this supply line of guns, Goldbarg was stepping into important but rocky territory. She was describing a gun-trafficking conspiracy. And indeed there was one. The Sinaloa Cartel didn't only provide a colossal amount of blow, enough for every American to snort a line. It was also a major player in arms trafficking.

The same trap cars that hide drugs going north over the U.S. border roll south with weapons. The same planes that carry cocaine out of South America haul guns in. As the cartel's drug trafficking has global reach, so its weapons networks run from the United States to Mexico to Colombia and beyond. They link up with criminals selling guns to American gangbangers as easily as they do with Latin America's corrupt security forces, and with guerrillas and paramilitaries designated as terrorists.

And the Sinaloa Cartel is just one of a range of outfits lugging guns over the Rio Grande. An array of smugglers ship weapons south, from a couple of guns in a trunk to a hundred weapons in a tractor trailer. This adds up to a phenomenal arsenal.

From 2007 to 2018, the ATF definitively traced 150,811 guns from criminals in Mexico to gun sellers and factories in the United States. Various stats are thrown around in this debate, but that is the most important concrete figure, which indisputably underlines the problem.

That would be enough guns to fuel an insurgency. And in a way they have. Cartels have killed thousands of police officers, soldiers, mayors, judges, political candidates, journalists, priests, and civilians. They have destabilized Mexico and stunted its growth.

The insurgent tactics really struck home when soldiers arrested the son of El Chapo, Ovidio Guzmán, in Culiacán, the capital of Sinaloa, in October 2019. Hundreds of gunmen took to the streets, blocking roads, battling with soldiers, and kidnapping officers. Some gunmen fired with immense .50 calibers, as terrified residents hid inside the schools where they were picking up their children. Faced with this terror, the Mexican government backed down and released Ovidio.

From 2007 to 2019, there were more than 277,000 murders in Mexico, according to the official count. Two-thirds of those killings were done with firearms. This period coincides with Mexican president Felipe Calderón launching a crackdown on cartels, which was supported by the United States, with helicopters and wiretap gear—and gun sales. U.S. factories supply both sides of the Mexican Drug War.

And these are only the guns they have captured and traced. Far more trafficked firearms are still out there and being used in cartel terror. We can never know the true scale of this traffic. But one study estimates more than two hundred thousand guns are trafficked over the border every year.[3] This led to Mexican law enforcement in 2020 estimating that 2.5 million guns had been smuggled over the border in a decade.

Even if it were a quarter of that estimate, it would be a matter of major concern. It's a historic case of gun trafficking into a highly violent conflict. Mexico has suffered a humanitarian catastrophe. And it doesn't help the United States to be living in a violent neighborhood, with Americans dying in Mexico and refugees heading north.

Guns also leak from Mexican police and soldiers. But all evidence indicates that the traffic from the United States, with by far the biggest gun market in the world, provides the bulk of the weapons to cartels. Of the 16,343 firearms that Mexico submitted to the ATF for tracing in 2018, 70.4 percent were definitively confirmed to have been made or sold in the United States.

I look in more detail at all the numbers later. One can make arguments that Mexican cartels will always find somewhere to get weapons. But there is no valid argument against the fact that right now they are getting a huge amount of guns from the United States.

It doesn't stop at Mexico. From 2013 to 2018, the ATF tracing center, located in West Virginia, tracked guns made or sold in the United States to 136 countries.[4] These include some of the most homicidal nations, such as Honduras, home of the biggest number of refugees arriving at the southern U.S. border.

Goldbarg talked about this. But the prosecutors did not actually charge Guzmán with gun trafficking, only with the use of weapons. The reasons why illustrate the enormous challenges in stopping the iron river as well as a scandal that plagues the ATF.

I was blown away when I found out the first reason: There is no specific law against gunrunning. Or to put it in another way, U.S. law has sharper teeth to go after drugs than after guns.

Agents hit cocaine traffickers with "conspiracy to traffic a controlled substance," the charge used against El Chapo and countless others in the war on drugs. This can pull in all those involved and put them in prison for decades. But it is harder to mount such a hard-hitting conspiracy charge against gun traffickers. As the Department of Justice states, "There is no federal statute specifically prohibiting firearms trafficking or straw purchasing."[5]

Instead, the law has dozens of smaller firearms offenses, such as "engagement in firearms business without a license," "knowing sale to prohibited person," and "knowing shipment or transport of a stolen firearm." There is also the Arms Export Control Act and a regulatory regime called the International Traffic in Arms Regulations, designed to oversee the legal arms-export business. But these are compliance measures, and offenses often lead to a telling-off or a fine.

This reflects the difference between drug trafficking, in which heroin and cocaine are illegal at all links in the chain, and gun trafficking, in which firearms divert from a legal industry.

Viktor Bout was the most infamous gunrunner in modern times, allegedly smuggling arms to Afghanistan, Angola, Sierra Leone, Rwanda, and the Democratic Republic of the Congo before he was caught in a sting, convicted in a federal court in New York, and sent to prison. But he was not charged specifically with gun trafficking, and instead faced counts including "conspiracy to kill U.S. nationals" and "conspiracy to provide material support for a designated terrorist group."[6]

Perhaps the wording of a charge is not paramount. If a dangerous criminal is in jail, they are in jail. But it does reflect priorities and have real implications in how prosecutors can make a case.

The second reason has to do with the biggest scandal in the history of the ATF, baptized "Fast and Furious" after the car-racing movies. In 2011, it was exposed that ATF agents watched almost two thousand firearms be trafficked to the cartels in Mexico without acting. The agents claimed they were trying to nail the kingpins rather than the small potatoes. But it blew up in their faces when gunmen shot dead Border Patrol agent Brian Terry and some of their weapons were traced to Fast and Furious.

In the following years, the Fast and Furious guns kept appearing in embarrassing places. Firearms made it into the hands of gangsters all the way down in Colombia. A .50-caliber rifle was seized in the last hideout of El Chapo when he was caught in 2016. And more keep showing up.

Federal prosecutors knew that the more gun charges they filed against El Chapo, the more his attorneys would try to open up this can of worms. And Guzmán would do life for the drugs anyway.

El Chapo's defense lawyer Eduardo Balarezo still tried to ask about Fast and Furious. But the prosecution shut it down, filing a motion "to preclude any questioning or reference to . . . Operation Fast and Furious." They argued that the fact a gun *walked* by the U.S. government ended up in a safe house of El Chapo's was "in no way relevant to this case" and that "the defense is attempting to use the well-known operation to place the government on trial."[7]

They didn't want the jury to hear about it. Or the public to keep hearing about it.

Fast and Furious cuts back to those divisive politics slicing through America. Many Democrats have long preached against gun trafficking. But Fast and Furious was a story owned by conservatives, outraged it happened under President Barack Obama, who wanted to harden gun laws.

It is indeed an important case that I look into in detail. And it reflects a wider problem of complicity between government agents and gun traffickers on both sides of the border.

Yet the issue of guns is not fundamentally about left and right—but about life and death. Most of us agree that hardened criminals shouldn't be armed. So why have the attempts to stop them been so ineffective?

Talking about guns triggers passionate emotions.

Especially in the United States.

Guns may be only machines in the end, tools that people can choose to use for good or bad. But few tools in the modern world inspire such passion for or against.

Obviously, when they are used to murder, they leave deep scars. Meanwhile, gun supporters argue that they are needed for self-defense, so their lives are on the line.

But perhaps it's also because they are such simple machines that wield such awesome power. With a light touch from the trigger finger, you can unleash the force to extinguish a human life. Including your own. This power fascinates, emboldens, and terrifies.

The issue is so explosive that even the words cause controversy. Terms such as "assault rifle" and "military-style weapon" spark furious debate even before you get to the argument over the definition of "terrorism."

The history of guns is intertwined with the fiercely debated stories of the United States. The traditional telling ties them to the winning of the West and the Revolutionary War to found the nation. More recent writers point out their use in the genocide of Native Americans, and by slave patrols and posses.

Gun politics gets into fundamental questions of our own era. There is the issue of how much the government should infringe on individual rights and, on the flipside, how much it is obliged to defend its citizens from armed attack. There is the concept of individual security versus the concept of collective security. And there is the integrity of the nation-state versus the efforts to find international solutions to humanity's problems.

This book is about gun trafficking, so this last point is key. Black market guns travel in secret compartments through checkpoints, in planes under the radar, and in tunnels under borders. They are often manufactured in one country, sold in another, and used to kill in a third.

The illegal gun trade is part of the dark underbelly of global capitalism that undermines national law enforcement, along with drug smuggling, human smuggling, and sex trafficking. These black markets make up a sizable chunk of the world economy, yet we struggle to make sense of them.

The coronavirus crisis of 2020 bought the world's ideological fault lines to the fore. On one side, the threat of the virus showed that we need collective solutions to the problems of our time. With millions thrown out of work and health systems under stress, the slogan sprung up that there are no libertarians in a pandemic.

On the other side, protesters went out across the United States flashing their firearms to demand the end of the lockdown. And gun sales soared, with people scared that society would break down and they would need firearms to fend off the marauding mobs.

When protests over the brutal police killing of George Floyd in Minneapolis filled the streets, and looting broke out in many U.S. cities, gun sales surged to new highs. Alongside the vast peaceful marches, there were undeniable problems of rioting. At the same time, cities suffered a sharp increase in criminal shootings, which gets back to the drug-gun black market. But there were also deep fears embedded by the stories that gun hard-liners had been telling since the sixties: that firearms are needed to fight the crime that comes from traditional values breaking down. The abundance of guns then helped turn the intense political divide into deadly street clashes.

I came into reporting on guns through covering Mexico's drug war and trying to figure out how criminals could destabilize a major country. For twenty years, I have been looking at the mechanics of the drug trade and wrestling with how it causes so much bloodshed. Writing a book on guns presented new challenges. While there is a mountain of literature on drugs, the specific coverage of the gun black market is surprisingly sparse.

I initially tried to understand gunrunning as a separate racket. But my reporting found that the illegal drug and gun trades in the Americas are thoroughly intertwined, like two noxious weeds tangled around each other. The links are true at all levels: from a heroin corner in Baltimore, to a biker clubhouse in Hollywood, to guerrillas in the coca fields of Colombia.

For at least a decade, writers have used the idea of an iron river to describe the vast flow of guns from the United States to Mexico. There was even a thriller with the title in 2011.[8] For even longer, politicians have talked about an "iron pipeline" of guns going from U.S. states with more liberal gun laws, including Virginia, Georgia, and North Carolina, to East Coast cities with stricter laws, especially New York, Washington, and Baltimore. However, these "waterways" are interlinked with gangsters crossing international borders as easily as they do state lines, and I use the term "iron river" more generally to refer to the broad flow of guns from the legal U.S. market to criminals across the continent.

It was also a challenge to navigate gun politics. Writing about drug cartels may sound scary, but most readers can sympathize with what I'm trying to do. Writing about guns, I walked into a controversy that tears through the United States; I had to come to terms with the behemoth of American gun culture.

I initially tried to look at the problem of the black market in purely criminal terms that avoided this debate. But that proved impossible. American gun culture helped forge the bizarre labyrinth of gun laws in which the black market thrives. And it cannot be dissected in only technical terms when the emotions are so heated.

As I followed the gunrunning, record years of mass shootings scarred America: Las Vegas in 2017, Parkland in 2018, El Paso in 2019. While the number of victims in these attacks is a fraction of crime deaths, the effect is gargantuan. The tragedy of children randomly murdered at school is beyond words, the psychological impact of terror devastating.

The weapons used in those particular tragedies were bought legally, while in some others, the shooters broke the law to get guns. But the nature of all the massacres was linked to the broader story I was looking at: the blur of crime and terror in the twenty-first century. While the motives are different, the techniques in the mass shootings echoed those in terror attacks in Europe. And the same AR-15s and AK-47s are trafficked to cartels.

The awakening of young people to this horror inspired me, as it did so many of us. The million-plus people in March for Our Lives reframed the debate and created a new opportunity to reshape how America—and in turn, the world—deals with guns. To find a new way forward, it is vital to understand how the black market works. But we also need to untangle the money in the legal industry and the pervasive gun culture behind it.

"Americans love guns."

I heard those three words time and time again to sum up American gun culture. And they are certainly true of a lot of Americans in a way distinct from people in most other countries. I traveled to Serbia, which is also considered a gun-loving nation, but discovered that gun control is now well enforced and gun advocates acquiescent. Yemen is another gun-loving country, but it is a tribal semi-failed state devoured by war.

The love is not true of all Americans, or even most. A Pew survey found that 30 percent of Americans own a gun, down from more than half in the 1970s. Still, 41 percent live in a home with a gun, and 72 percent have shot one.

The love takes many forms. Love of the sport, of shooting, getting better, mastering the art. Love of the hobby, of collecting old weapons, stripping them down. Love of the security.

When gun owners are asked why they have their weapons, the top answer, from 67 percent, is personal protection, according to the Pew survey.[9] There is a ferocious debate about whether guns really make you safer, given that they raise the chance of accident or suicide, or whether a shotgun is as much as you need to defend yourself against a burglar. And there are various factors behind why the United States suffers from more violence than Europe, but less than many countries in Latin America. But despite the debate, some hundred million Americans believe that their firearms are a necessary defense against crime.

American gun enthusiasts quickly point to another word—"freedom." It is the freedom to bear arms as defined in the Second Amendment, and the freedom that guns give to defend against crime and tyranny. The Pew survey found that three-quarters of gun owners say that the right to bear arms is essential to their personal freedom. And then there is the idea that armed Americans should be ready to rise up against a tyrannical government. While plenty of gun owners don't entertain this seriously, a significant number have it as an underlying credence.

This cocktail of passion and self-defense mixed with the political nature of the Second Amendment sharpens the edges of the gun debate. For hard-liners, it becomes a crusade embodied in a living struggle against predatory federal agents wanting to "take our guns." In such an environment, moderate gun owners are traitors, while zealots can go to the loony extreme of accusing crying parents of mass-shooting victims of being crisis actors.

I have talked to mild-mannered researchers who receive death threats, and I get plenty of angry messages myself for reporting on gun trafficking.

Still, the majority of gun owners don't fall on this extreme and simply want to pursue their passion and defend their family. Many have sophisticated, nuanced positions and are genuinely looking for better solutions. I hope this book can talk to many people with different views. It is a work of investigation, not preaching.

In any case, gun politics cuts strange ways. Law and order and locking up violent criminals was traditionally a rallying cry of conservatives, but for some this can be trumped by the crusade of gun rights. Concern about gangs, such as MS-13, is justified, but then where is the concern for how they get their weapons? Incidents of police unjustly shooting civilians rightly trigger national outrage. Incidents of gang members spraying bullets that kill children often don't garner the attention they deserve.

Gun culture is not static but has mutated over the decades. This change is most evident in the NRA, which began in New York in 1871 to teach straight shooting and only in the 1970s transformed into a militant group resisting any gun laws. Over the past two decades it has transformed again, forging a media empire that promotes a lifestyle, with millionaire executives and controversial accounting that has blown up into a crisis.

The NRA collects well from gun companies, which in turn benefit from the black market like almost no other industry. Some owners of firearms companies are loaded, and the industry has immense clout, shown in the elephantine influence of the gun lobby on Congress. Yet the gun business is nowhere as profitable as big tech, pharmaceuticals, or, indeed, illegal drugs. It does not provide that many jobs overall, and several big-name gun makers have gone through bankruptcies since 2000.

Individual gun sellers often struggle to make a living, and many are subsidized by their military pensions. Most gun shop owners are well intentioned and law-abiding. I talked to one who risked his life trying to stop gun trafficking. But there is also a small number of gun sellers who provide a huge amount of guns used in crimes.

"The desperation makes the criminal gun market much more important economically to the gun industry, and so that becomes a significant part of their customer base," Jonathan Lowy, chief counsel and vice president of the gun safety group Brady, tells me. "Even if it's not the direct customer base, it's the intended customer base."

The development of 3D-printed guns, hailed by libertarians, threatens to undermine the whole industry, as well as gun laws. But the dirty truth is that the affordable ones don't work, because the technology isn't there yet. The idea that 3D-printed guns have killed gun control is one of many myths in the gun story.

Another face of gun culture is criminals' love of guns. Violent offenders described to me how they were fascinated by the weapons, how guns give them a sense of power, of invincibility. Many referenced songs or movies that glorify Glocks and AKs, Uzis and 9 millimeters.

Tyree "Colion" Moorehead shot dead a man in Baltimore when he was fifteen. He explained the obsession with the steel.

"It's the fixation with guns, the movies, the sound, the grip, the power," he said. "It's too easy to kill with a gun. And it's too gangster."

My fear of gun violence is personal. In the two decades I have been living in Mexico, I have watched the bloodshed rise like a tidal wave, destroying too many lives and with them the broader hopes of the nation. I raise my family amid this fighting, which is a central preoccupation for all and begs real solutions.

This carnage is part of a regional murder epidemic that stretches through Central America down to Brazil and plagues the Caribbean. The total body count in Latin America has topped two million this century, driven overwhelmingly by gun violence. It's a cocaine-fueled holocaust that destabilizes whole countries and adds to a global refugee crisis.

At the same time, pockets of the United States suffer the same level of violence. Many parts of the country have certainly improved, and from the 1990s to the 2010s U.S. homicides dropped overall. But some U.S. cities have suffered their worst-ever bloodshed in the last decade. And this gun violence exacerbates the nation's core divisions over race and class, with American police morphing into militarized forces in supposed response to the gun deaths and armed drug dealers. In turn, amid protests against the police and pressures from the coronavirus lockdown, shootings surged in 2020.

It's such criminal violence that accounts for the majority of violent deaths in the world today, outnumbering conflict deaths by more than three to one in recent years. The fact that these murders are so concentrated in certain hot spots, especially in Latin America and a handful of U.S. cities, means that today's crime capitals can literally be more murderous than war zones, leading to inner-city youths rebaptizing their homes as Chi-raq, Drill-inois, and Body-more, Murder-land. The bloodiest cities in Latin America suffer homicide rates a hundred times higher than those of Western European cities.

I don't want to be alarmist; many parts of the world have historically little violence. But that doesn't provide solace to the people living in the hot spots, where the majority know someone who's been shot dead. And the issue of refugees impacts millions more, a factor in the convulsion of politics in the West.

Of course, there are various causes behind these contrasting levels of homicides, including corruption and inequality. But in the most murderous places, the gun black market is thriving and working in tandem with drug trafficking. To be clear on this central point: I am not blaming all the violence I portray in the book on guns, but guns are a factor.

It's not all a numbers game that depends on the sheer quantity of firearms. Some countries have more guns and fewer murders than others. But it is important whose hands the guns are in. When law-abiding citizens keep hunting rifles locked in safes, they don't leave human corpses. But when gangsters, guerrillas, and terrorists are armed to the teeth, they unsurprisingly commit a lot of murders. The big question is whether we can slow that iron river to them and reduce the body count.

As gun violence ravages the Americas, firearms are linked to the specter of terrorism in Europe. Fanatics used to hijack planes, but thanks to enhanced security at most airports, that has become near impossible. But they can have just as much impact walking into a disco with a Kalashnikov. The Paris attacks were the biggest mass shooting in Western Europe since World War II.

Gun terror attacks have also increased in the United States, including the white supremacist massacre in El Paso, the anti-Semitic attacks on Pittsburgh synagogues, and the Islamic State–inspired shooting in San Bernardino, California. And while atrocities in Vegas Village and Parkland, Florida, may not be political, the modus operandi and effects are almost identical. The horror has a ripple effect across society, leading to worries about whether your child will be hit by a bullet in school, and active-shooter drills. And this gets back to the central theme of the blurring of crime, terror, and war. In the early twenty-first century, certain potent rifles are used in all three.

The spread of guns to gangsters and terrorists around the world was long missed by policy makers. After World War II, everyone was petrified about nuclear bombs. Naturally, arms that can blow us back to the Stone Age should terrify us. But while the nuclear arms race reached a stalemate, it was the humble firearms that piled up the bodies—or were the "true weapons of mass destruction," as Rachel Stohl, who helped draft the United Nations Arms Trade Treaty, tells me.

In the Cold War, both the United States and the Soviet Union fed their allies with a steady diet of rifles. Guerrillas and governments alike realized they could cozy up to one of these sides to build their arsenal, and as Mao Zedong said, "Political power grows out of the barrel of a gun." In Latin America, governments and guerrillas aligned with the superpowers to fight bloody battles across the continent.

The problem of the hundreds of millions of guns, alongside handheld weapons such as grenade launchers, dawned on people only when the Cold

War ended and the weapons seeped into the hands of criminals and fanatics. Since then, a growing group of thinkers and advocates have been looking at the issue—or in their jargon, "the proliferation of small arms and light weapons."

Nobody knows the exact number of guns in the world today. But the best estimates come from the Small Arms Survey, a think tank based in Geneva. In 2018, the Small Arms Survey announced that the total number of guns on the planet had topped the one billion mark.

Each year, these guns are used to kill an estimated quarter-million people around the world. Almost two-thirds of those deaths are from firearms homicides or conflict killings, the rest from suicides and accidents. Many more people are shot and injured.

People are also stabbed, beaten, strangled, deliberately run over by cars, blown up by bombs, and poisoned. But in the early twenty-first century, guns remain the most popular method for humans to murder other humans.

Research into this proliferation is separated. On one side, investigators look at trafficking into war zones, which is mixed up with the more prosperous trade in bigger arms: tanks, fighter jets, helicopter gunships. This big-arms business has long been higher on governments' agendas—and better for their coffers. On the other side are the gun deals of criminals, seen as a domestic issue.

But these rackets are interlinked. The same factories produce guns used by gangbangers on American streets and rifles wielded by jihadists in Syria. In Latin America, cartel hit men have the same armaments as guerrilla forces, making their fighting resemble an insurgency. And many of today's guerrillas are more interested in crime than they are ideology.

The smuggling networks overlap. The Italian 'Ndrangheta delivered guns to the Islamic State. The Russian Mafia ran guns to Kurdish rebels. Mexican mobsters took guns to Colombian paramilitaries.

In covering the cartels, I became part of a scattered group of journalists looking at the mushrooming of organized crime amid the globalization after the Cold War. Two of the landmark books that identified this trend are *Illicit* by Moisés Naím in 2005 and *McMafia* by Misha Glenny in 2008. Since then,

a growing number of writers have added to the understanding of a phenomenon that is reshaping not only crime but also elements of politics and
economics in much of the world—in dangerous ways. Part of this landscape
is the rise of hybrid armed conflicts, or "crime wars."

The iron river followed in this book flows from the U.S. retail market into
these crime wars. It crosses from a domestic issue to an international issue,
which is one reason it has been so hard to deal with. But whether we like it or
not, the problems in our globalized economy are connected. The gun shows
of Texas lead to the crime scenes of Honduras, the gun shops of Georgia to
the corners of Baltimore, the gun factories of Germany to the mass graves of
Mexico. And across the world, we are united in having loved ones, and the
burning force in our lives to protect them from violence and death.

On a sunny June morning in rural North Carolina, I hand in my cell phone
to go into the Rivers Correctional Institution, a private prison for federal
convicts—a tiny corner of the vast U.S. penitentiary apparatus, with its more
than two million inmates. The rest of the visitors that day are women: wives,
girlfriends, mothers, and daughters, several from Mexico, one from Colombia.
It's a low-security facility, so we meet the prisoners without dividing glass
for a whole seven hours in a large room with numbered tables, vending
machines at the side, and games such as Scrabble to pass the time.

After a few minutes, the inmate I have come to see is brought in—a
stocky fifty-eight-year-old Mexican guy with a ponytail. He looks younger
than his years, a decade of being behind bars preserving his youth, he jokes.
I have many questions about cartel smuggling operations, and he is in a
privileged position to fill me in. For years, he flew planes for cartels, and
after he made millions, he bought several of his own jets and hired other
people to fly them.

He personally knows El Chapo, whom he worked with, as well as a who's
who of Mexican narcos. Ismael "El Mayo" Zambada, the head of the Sinaloa
Cartel, is godfather to one of his sons. He once bought a used plane that

turned out to be an ex-CIA jet, and when it was busted in Campeche, Mexico, with five and a half tons of cocaine, it sparked conspiracy theories. He kept on trafficking until DEA agents finally caught up with him in the Dominican Republic, where they snatched him and flew him to the United States. He is imprisoned under an alias he used, Luis Fernando Bertulucci, but his real name is Fernando Blengio. In the cartel world, he is known as "el Capi"—short for "the Captain."

Fernando is overloaded with information from a life in the trafficking underworld and says he wants to describe it so that the next generation can find a better way. He has enough stories for a book, and indeed would like to write one, he tells me. But I am looking specifically for the links between cocaine and gun smuggling and how his story fits in.

He describes flying planes packed with cocaine thousands of miles from Colombia, where it's worth under $2,000 a kilo, to northern Mexico, where it's worth ten times that. Organized crime is about maximizing profits, and those who rise high pursue the business side ruthlessly. It would be wasteful to fly down to Colombia with an empty plane, so the Mexicans filled it up with goods for their Colombian partners: tequila, riding saddles, and especially guns—which the Mexicans get easily from the United States.

The Colombian orders increased as the armed conflict in their country escalated in the nineties. They would ask for specific weapons, including Czech Škorpion submachine guns, .308 sniper rifles, Glocks, and, of course, AK-47s and AR-15s. "We took everything that these señores hankered for," Fernando says.

In one flight from Veracruz south to Colombia, Fernando flew over half a ton of guns, the equivalent of a hundred loaded AK-47s. This is not huge in global arms-trafficking terms. In 2018, the U.S. Navy busted a ship going to Yemen with a thousand AK-47s. But the cartels would move a lot of small planes all the time, so the total of guns being trafficked was considerable.

"Once, I flew in a convoy of twenty-seven planes," he said. "Imagine it. All going to the same destination. I was just one pilot in the convoy."

*   *   *

Eight hundred miles north in Maine, I find Billyjack Curtis, a former member of a prison gang called the Dirty White Boys. The forty-six-year-old with a shaved head talks in a broad Maine accent about bloody scrapes in jail cells and battling a heroin addiction. He spent close to half his adult life locked up and is now trying to keep off the drugs while fighting to feed his family.

Billyjack spent years running guns from Maine to Lawrence, Massachusetts, and exchanging them with Dominican gangsters for heroin and cocaine. The business was highly profitable, thanks to the elastic prices of both products on the black market. He could exchange a few wraps of heroin with a junkie in Maine for a $500 handgun and then take it to Lawrence and sell it the Dominicans for $1,000, which they gave him in more bags of heroin. That same smack would then be worth $2,500 when he drove back home and cut it up.

He also had a lucrative sideline in running ammunition, which he could buy in Walmarts in Maine and sell to the Dominicans for a dollar a bullet. He would have been rich—if he wasn't getting high on his own supply.

"I was living off the speedball. I would mix coke and heroin," he says. "I would use that around the clock. My main thing was to keep going and try and stack money. But you never stack enough money to pay for the lawyers."

Fernando and Billyjack are two of more than twenty men directly involved in gun trafficking I talked to for this book. And I also talked to drug sellers and smugglers, coyotes and contract killers.

When you hear the phrase "arms trafficker," you may imagine a devious billionaire kingpin riding on his yacht as he chalks up his sales to wars around the planet. Such supervillains have long existed in the popular imagination, even claiming their own subgenre in fiction, with recent portrayals in John le Carré's *The Night Manager* and by Nicolas Cage in *Lord of War*.

This image is inspired by real characters, going back to the mysterious Greek arms dealer Basil Zaharoff, who sold machine guns to rival powers in the late nineteenth century. More recently, the Russian Viktor Bout was portrayed as an authentic James Bond villain with his fleet of Soviet jets.

But behind these kingpins is a complex industry involving many people in many countries. Much of today's gun trafficking is done by a drove of smaller dealers, each moving weapons by the dozen rather than the thousand. That makes them harder to track and harder to stop.

Several of those I spoke to are in prison or have served time, while others are still on the street selling weapons. Various spoke on the record with their real names, including Fernando and Billyjack, and some gave me access to their case files. In some interviews, I have protected names to avoid incrimination or, in the case of those in Mexico, Honduras, and Colombia, the real risk of them being murdered if they are identified. However, all the quotes are verbatim from recordings; I would never be able to capture the vibrant speech from the projects of Baltimore to the barrios of Ciudad Juárez without the audio.

The criminals I talk to have committed bad crimes and contributed to rampant murder rates. But human beings are complicated, and most of them, even the assassins I talk to, can be easy to get along with, in contrast to their evil acts. I am interested in tracking their life stories, how they got involved in organized crime and how they see it, to make better sense of what is happening. This may be a tale about the cold metal of guns, but the characters breathe life into it.

People selling guns to murderers come from all nationalities and races—there are Bulgarian brokers, bearded bikers, border babies, Dirty White Boys, upper-middle-class Mexicans, poor Afro-Colombians, and U.S. hustlers from the projects, both Black and white. But the vast majority I found in the illegal gun business were men, which is why they dominate these pages. However, many of those fighting for change are women, as are some of the greatest writers on the subject, and tragically many of its victims.

When talking to gun traffickers, I tried to get as much out of them about the mechanics of the business—what are their "rules"? I use this to make sense of the logic of black market gun-onomics.

The black market is inextricably linked to the commercial gun industry. Most of the weapons in the hands of criminals and insurgents may have been bought illegally, but they were originally made in regulated factories. I look at how the people in the business view the links to the black market. There is perhaps no other industry in which such a sizable amount of the product ends up in the hands of criminals.

Each gun goes on its unique journey, from being forged to suppliers, shops, and buyers, sometimes crossing continents, into the hands of those who use it to kill. It is to one such a story, from the factory to the cemetery, that we now turn.

2

The Draco

I keep having the same unsolved question: if my rifle claimed people's lives, then can it be that I ... a Christian and an Orthodox believer, was to blame for their deaths? The longer I live, the more this question drills itself into my brain and the more I wonder why the Lord allowed man to have the devilish desires of envy, greed and aggression.

—MIKHAIL KALASHNIKOV, INVENTOR OF THE AK-47,
SHORTLY BEFORE HIS DEATH AT AGE NINETY-FOUR.[1]

Everywhere in the world people want guns. Everywhere.

—AUREL CAZACU, FORMER HEAD OF ROMARM,
ROMANIA'S STATE ARMS COMPANY

———

W e are shot! We are shot!"
It happens in a fraction of a second. You see the man raising his gun, his index finger using a fraction of his muscle power to press the trigger. You hear the distinctive bangs, not open like firecrackers but closed,

the sound of gas expanding inside metal. The bullets fly at more than two thousand feet a second, invisible as they slice through the air. The caps pierce your skin, plunge through your flesh. You could die imminently. Or be crippled. But you still have air in your lungs and manage to shout into a cell phone, calling for help.

"We are shot. We are shot . . . We've been shot and attacked on the highway."

As you are reading this someone just got shot. Someone, somewhere, is shot dead about every two minutes, and several times more are shot and injured. The last shooting could have happened anywhere on the planet. But there is a good chance it was in the Americas, the most murderous continent.

When it happened to Victor Avila, he was in Mexico, on a highway through the state of San Luis Potosí. But he was an American agent for Immigration and Customs Enforcement, operating south of the border.

"This is Victor Avila from ICE. We are shot! We are shot! . . . I am an ICE special agent."

The call was to the American embassy in Mexico City, routed to another U.S. agent, who calmly asked him to describe his exact location, to try to stay on the line. Hearing the recording of the message, the panic in Victor's voice, is chilling. But it also offers hope, the strength of a man fighting for survival.

The shooting was no more or less tragic than the thousands that happen every month in Mexico and are mostly unsolved. But thanks to a sprawling investigation, it allows us to track some of the guns used from their manufacture through a chain of sales overseas and across borders into the hands of the killers. That journey offers distinct insight into how the iron river pumps into Latin America.[2]

Victor Avila was born in El Paso on the banks of the Rio Grande, the son of Mexican migrants who crossed the river in the 1960s. He grew up with the typical identity questions asked by many on the borderlands between two great nations.

"It was a very unique situation to be born in a border town, speaking both English, Spanish, and both languages mixed together, the uniqueness of having to learn both cultures," he tells me. "I didn't realize until I was a little bit older, in my teenage years, how different it was compared to my cousins who lived in Mexico, how different they acted and how different their lifestyle was to mine, me living in El Paso. I never quite spoke the Spanish that they spoke, and I always spoke English with an accent, so it was always a difficult kind of identity crisis."

Victor comes across as reflective, underneath a tough law-enforcement inflection. After college, he became a parole officer, then a probation officer, before graduating as an ICE agent when the agency was formed in 2003.

Wedged into the sprawling post 9-11 Department of Homeland Security, ICE was charged with the broad mission of going after undocumented migrants in the interior and fighting human smuggling and contraband at the border. As it grew in size, it deported people in record numbers, throwing it into the heart of America's immigration row. In the heated rhetoric, protesters said it was a repressive institution that should be abolished, while hard-liners claimed it was defending America from invasion.

Less known is how ICE moved into investigating cartels, which not only were the biggest drug traffickers into the United States but also had diversified into human smuggling and sex trafficking. As mission creep set in, certain ICE agents began to work inside Mexico in competition with the DEA, dabbling in the espionage game against cartels. In an early case, ICE paid an informant code-named Lalo while he was helping bury the bodies of cartel victims. The scandal rose to the White House and forced out several agents. But it didn't stop ICE from expanding, doubling its budget in its first five years to top six billion dollars.

Serious and ambitious, Victor was less interested in the political turmoil around immigration than he was in trying to tackle organized crime. He built up intelligence on human trafficking gangs, those moving people for forced labor, including sex work. He also cracked the case of a corrupt Border Patrol agent, busting him and the gang he worked with.

In 2009, he was sent to Mexico City, cleared for diplomatic status, and took over the global initiative against human trafficking. He moved there with his wife, a fellow El Pasoan keen to travel, and their two young children. They arrived in the sprawling mountain capital of twenty million, with its imperious avenues, leafy bohemian suburbs, epic markets, and ramshackle slums.

"I loved Mexico City as soon as I landed there," he says. "Apart from a short period in San Antonio, one of my goals was to get out. Not just for me but for my kids. I really wanted them to experience a different world than the border city and the border culture."

By 2011, he had been working out of the U.S. embassy in Mexico City a year and a half, an accomplished agent, aged thirty-nine. Meanwhile, the Mexican Drug War hit new peaks. The period was especially explosive in the northeast of Mexico, the chunk of the country that runs up to East Texas and the Rio Grande Valley. Here, the crime army of the Zetas, commanded by Mexican special forces defectors, fought their old masters of the Gulf Cartel, sparking pitched battles with hundreds of gunmen blasting at each other on the highway that runs parallel to the Rio Grande.

The fact that such violence was happening right on the U.S. border was worrying officers in the Texas Department of Public Safety. Quietly, they had put gunboats on the Rio Grande, a senior officer told me, and on several occasions these exchanged fire with Zetas. The officials were concerned about how heavily armed the Zetas were, with many bearing Kalashnikovs, and some wielding rocket-propelled grenades.

Even within the standards of Mexico's conflict, the Zetas had acquired a reputation for brutality. Their worst atrocities included shooting dead seventy-two migrants who were traveling through Mexico, burning down a casino and killing fifty-two gamers and staff, and dissolving the corpses of hundreds of victims in steel barrels on a ranch. Amid this chaos, ICE decided to send Victor and fellow agent Jaime Zapata to drive directly through Zeta territory.

*   *   *

Thirty-two-year-old Jaime Zapata was another son of the borderlands, hailing from Brownsville, where he had grown up hunting and fishing with his father and four brothers. He was strong and tall, towering above Victor at almost six feet four, with long limbs and a jokey smile. Just a few years after dropping out of the University of Texas at Brownsville, Jaime was working for ICE in the Laredo office. The bosses sent him to Mexico on temporary assignment, while his fiancée stayed in Texas. He had been in the country only nine days, wandering the city and visiting the pyramids, when he got the marching orders.

On February 14, Victor and Jaime first met in the U.S. embassy after Victor had flown in from a conference on human trafficking. Late that afternoon, the ICE deputy attaché issued the sudden command: travel the following morning to meet agents based out of Monterrey, pick up surveillance gear, and ferry it back to Mexico City. That would mean driving hours through an area of significant cartel conflict. They would do the journey in an armored Chevrolet Suburban that Victor had been issued, worth $160,000, dark blue with diplomatic plates; ICE was confident that even the Zetas would not dare target a marked embassy vehicle.

You might think someone would advise against sending American agents in an expensive car through Zeta territory. You would be right. The month before, the State Department issued an internal warning about personnel road travel between the U.S. border and Mexico City because of an uptick in carjackings and shootouts.

When Victor heard the plan, he raised concerns with the deputy attaché. "Why don't they send this equipment through a diplomatic pouch or through the air or through a truck?" he said. "There are many ways of sending it."

The deputy attaché replied that he wasn't aware of security issues and that he wanted the agents to handle it personally. He needed the surveillance gear, which included wiretap devices and tracking equipment, by the end of the next business day. It was for a sting on cocaine-money laundering called Operation Pacific Rim. Victor accepted that he had no choice and finished paperwork late into the night, screwing up his Valentine's Day, and then got a few hours' sleep before a super-early morning.

When he woke, his young daughter was getting ready for school, and he hugged and kissed her.

"Where are you going?" she asked. "You just got home."

"Yeah. I'm going to be back today," Victor replied.

She spotted he wasn't in the attire he normally wore to the office.

"You are not wearing a suit. So you are going out of town," she said.

Maybe she sensed something was up. "Kids have a sense, an intuition, that sometimes we overlook," Victor tells me.

The two agents set off at six-thirty A.M., with Victor driving and Jaime in the passenger seat. American agents were not officially allowed to carry guns in Mexico, but under an informal agreement they took them anyway. They were behind the seat, hidden in the floor.

Burning rubber, they made it in five hours to the rendezvous point near the city of Matehuala, where they met the agents from Monterrey. The agents pulled up next to each other in identical armored cars and shifted the surveillance gear from trunk to trunk in three minutes. Without stopping for a chat, Victor and Jaime turned around and headed back south.

As they left, Victor noticed a lone Mexican federal police officer, supposedly directing traffic but clearly staring at them.

Victor slowed down, eyeballing the policeman. "What the fuck is this guy doing?" he said to Jaime.

He looked over and could tell Jaime was nervous. "Are you scared?" he asked.

Jaime nodded. "I'm scared."

"I'm scared too, man," Victor replied.

He put his foot on the gas and sped up for the long road ahead.

As their adrenaline subsided, Jaime and Victor spotted a Subway and decided to go in for a bite. Jaime, new in the country, was surprised they had the stores in Mexico.

"They've got almost everything they have in the U.S. here," Victor told him. "It's just a little different."

After plowing through the sandwiches, Victor told Jaime to have a try driving an armored car while he did some work. It takes practice maneuvering a vehicle with hundreds of kilos of extra metal, but Jaime took to it well, while Victor stuck his head in his phone, starting on the countless messages he had to answer.

They rode through semidesert that is home to peyote, the hallucinogenic cactus, and cleared the colonial silver city of San Luis Potosí. Two SUVs shot past them, packed with tough-looking faces, and Jaime spotted a rifle upright through the window. They immediately suspected they were cartel gunmen. And this was hard-core Zeta territory.

The SUVs sped out of sight, but then reappeared in the distance, driving slowly, blocking both lanes. Before the agents could react, the vehicles dropped back, one in front and one on the side of them. Then the front car slammed on the brakes, forcing Jaime to skid onto the shoulder. It was a maneuver known as a mobile roadblock, exactly what the agents themselves were trained to do.

The two SUVs skidded up beside them, and eight Zetas jumped out and surrounded the armored car, wielding Kalashnikovs, AR-15s, and handguns.

Which was when things got really screwed up.

Victor's car was fortified by the British arms company BAE Systems, which builds tanks and battleships, among other combat hardware. It should have been able to resist hundreds of bullets, even grenades. But when one of the Zetas tried the driver's door, it opened. The Chevy had been made with the commercial function that it unlocked when parked, and BAE hadn't changed this when it turned the Chevy into an armored vehicle for agents.

Jaime yanked the door back and slammed it shut, and both agents hit the lock buttons. But as they did, another button was touched, and Victor's window came down two inches, allowing the Zetas to stick two guns through. Victor pushed the window back up, but the guns were still getting in, now forced to point downward. He shouted they were American agents. Maybe the Zetas didn't hear. Maybe they didn't care.

They fired repeatedly into the Chevy. Victor, crouching, was hit three times, in the abdomen, thigh, and ankle. Jaime took six bullets, one ripping through the femoral artery of his left leg, another leaving a hole in his chest.

"I'm hit," Jaime said. "I'm shot."

The Zetas pulled the guns back after the volley, and Victor frantically pressed the button to shut the window, the smell of gunpowder thick in his nose. He managed to push Jaime's leg on the accelerator to launch the Suburban, only to have it crash a few yards ahead into the median strip on the highway. The Zetas fired away, unloading dozens more bullets. Most were bouncing off the armor, but some managed to pierce holes and ricochet into the trunk. Two of the Zetas got in a car and drove to the front of the Chevy. They jumped out and raised their rifles toward the vehicle.

Victor froze as he watched them fire the guns directly at him, only the bulletproof glass protecting him, terrified it would shatter. It felt surreal, like he was watching a crazy movie. Finally, they got into their SUV and left. He believed they thought he was dead.

After they had gone, Victor got on his cell phone and screamed for help. Which was when the message was recorded. "This is Victor Avila from ICE. We are shot! We are shot! We've been shot and attacked on the highway."

When the call reached the embassy, Victor's wife was there, on a temporary contract doing background investigations. She was right next to the agent who picked up the phone, and as the buzz erupted, it sank in that it was her husband who had been attacked. The agents called in everybody for help: Mexican federal police, soldiers, helicopter ambulances.

In the blood-filled Chevy, Victor grabbed his fellow agent.

"Jaime!" he said. "Look at me. Stay awake. Please don't die."

They stayed in the bloody car for forty minutes. By the time the medics arrived, Jaime was gone. He was the first American agent to be murdered on Mexican soil since the DEA's Enrique "Kiki" Camarena in 1985.

Jaime's life had ended on the arid plains of San Luis Potosí, and the story of the guns used to kill him was about to be uncovered. It's a tale that links the Soviet war machine to American consumers, and that illustrates how American gun sellers make millions from the murder fest in Mexico and how agents assigned to stop this trade became complicit in it. But it begins seven thousand miles from the site of murder, in the rolling hills of southern Europe, in the land called Transylvania.

More than a thousand mourners laid the body of Jaime Zapata to rest at his funeral in Brownsville, Texas, on February 22, 2011, a week after the shooting. Along with throngs of friends and family from his border community, many came in uniform—police, border agents, military. A black-clad trooper played a send-off tune on the bagpipes, and a group of six soldiers fired a salute of shots in the air.

Victor came in a wheelchair, still in pain and severe shock from the shooting. After being helicoptered away from the scene, he had been treated in a hospital before he and his wife and children had been whisked back to the United States, their belongings still in their Mexico City apartment. The cartels will often finish off victims who survive hits, even storming into hospitals, so ICE definitely wanted Victor stateside.

Victor got up from his wheelchair on crutches and hobbled over to place a single flower on Jaime's coffin, which was draped in the flag. Jaime's parents, his brother and sisters, and his fiancée hugged and kissed the coffin and wept uncontrollably while the cameras rolled.

Attorney General Eric Holder and Homeland Security Secretary Janet Napolitano gave speeches, looking at the parents and promising justice.

"Never let it be said that he died in vain," Holder said. "He was working to make two nations safer and our nation more secure for all of us . . . We must and will eradicate this scourge that took his life."

The son of Barbadian parents in the Bronx, Holder had become the first Black attorney general soon after Barack Obama had become the first Black president. Three years into the administration, this was not the only American agent killed in the line of duty who was on his mind. In December 2010, Brian

Terry, from the Border Patrol Tactical Unit or BORTAC, was shot dead in southern Arizona. Questions about the guns used in that murder were rattling the Justice Department.

Most murders in Mexico (almost 90 percent according to studies)[3] are never solved. But Washington put pressure on Mexico City at the highest levels over the Zapata killing. Security chiefs feared that if the assailants got away with it, then it would be open season to target American agents in Mexico—and everywhere else.

Sure enough, the very day after the funeral, Mexican soldiers raided a string of Zeta safe houses in San Luis Potosí and nabbed six suspects, including the alleged ringleader of the attack, a mustachioed man with a quiff known as "El Piolín" or "Tweety Bird," real name Julian Zapata. He happened to have the same last name and be the same age as his American victim. In the safe houses, the soldiers found a stash of guns, including variants of Kalashnikovs.

The motive for the Zetas hitting the ICE agents was unclear. U.S. and Mexican officials quickly came out with the story that it was a botched carjacking. Tweety Bird had orders from up the food chain to steal vehicles to use for other crimes, such as drive-by shootings, they said, and didn't notice the diplomatic plates.

But while this explanation may have been convenient for both governments, it had holes. Cartel operatives are taught to read license plates, routinely using spies to identify vehicles. It is a hard call that experienced gunmen, who could carry out a mobile roadblock, would not see it was a specially marked car. Victor himself told me it appeared like a hit, not a robbery.

"I know a carjacking when I see one. This was not a carjacking. They did not want this vehicle. They knew who we were. They had great opportunities to say, 'Holy shit, let's get out of here. They're Americans—we've messed up. *Vamanos*' [Let's go]. But they didn't. They decided, '*Nos vale madre*' [We don't give a fuck], or whatever, and we are going to kill them anyway."

Then there is the federal policeman they spotted right after the handover, a detail missed in the media coverage. Zeta operatives will often dress as police officers or have police on their payroll. If it had indeed been a cartel operative watching them, it again points to a calculated hit rather than a random carjacking.

The motive may have been connected to other events in the Zeta empire. At the time of the shooting, the DEA was going after the Zetas' supreme leaders in a sting operation. As part of this, several traffickers for the Zetas had become protected witnesses for the DEA and were feeding them information. The Zetas discovered the betrayals, and it led them to carry out a gruesome massacre in the city of Allende near the border. Perhaps it could also have provoked them to hit American agents, even those from another agency.

A key function of the ATF is to trace guns used in crimes. In the murder of Jaime Zapata, U.S. authorities wanted to investigate as much as they could themselves, wary of the links between Mexican officers and the cartels. So guns seized from the Zeta cell of Tweety Bird were given to ATF agents stationed south of the border.

Several of the seized weapons had the serial numbers scratched off, but the ATF restored them using etching and chemicals. Gun barrels, meanwhile, have grooves, known as rifling, to help spin the bullets straight forward. These grooves and lands (the flat parts in between) leave a unique set of marks on bullets, as the machining of each barrel is a little different. The firing pins also imprint a particular mark on the casings. Together, these make what ballistics experts refer to as the gun's fingerprint.

The ATF agents took over the casings from the Zapata crime scene and fired the seized weapons to compare the results. They found matches from the scene to two of the guns that they could trace through their serial numbers, identifying their journey from their manufacture into the hands of the Zetas.

One was a variant of a Kalashnikov known as a WASR-10, serial number 1981MF8477. The other was a more curious hybrid, an extremely short Kalashnikov, which could be technically considered a pistol, known as a

Draco, serial number DC-2777-10. Both were made by the Cugir Arms Factory, in Transylvania, central Romania.

———

Where does the life of a gun start? My first instinct was to look at the moment the weapons were forged in the factory from metal and wood. But as in any history, you find background that takes you further back through time. There is the moment the particular variants of Kalashnikovs were drawn up by the factory's gun designer. Then there is the question of why a factory in a backwater of southeast Europe was churning out weapons that turn up in conflict zones the world over. And to understand all this, we need to look at the fundamentals of gun history.

The origins of gunpowder stretch back over a thousand years to powder used for fireworks. The first bangs likely rang out in China, home of the first written evidence: A reference hails from as early as the Han dynasty in the second century A.D., when the alchemist Wei Boyang described how a mixture of three powders would "fly and dance."[4] By the ninth century, there are specific accounts of a black powder that mixes sulfur, saltpeter, and charcoal. As the centuries rolled on, Chinese fire lances, followed by hand cannons, slayed enemies on the battlefield.

By the early modern period, however, Europe overtook China as the center of firearms, with its matchlock guns using the first trigger devices, which evolved into wheel-lock guns and then into flintlock guns. Communities of gunsmiths emerged, financed by nobles, especially in kingdoms in what are now Germany, Belgium, and Italy but also reaching hubs in Birmingham, England, and Eibar, Spain.

The industrial revolution turned these gunsmiths into arms companies, with financing from the embryonic nation-states and their growing armies. The European powers carved out their global empires with guns, mostly made by a handful of coveted companies in their homelands. Firearms were shipped to Africa and traded for slaves, and shipped to the American colonies and sold to all sides.[5]

Following independence, gun production flourished in the rapidly industrializing United States, spurred on by eager inventors and orders from the U.S. Army Ordnance Department. After World War I, the Soviet Union emerged in the ashes of the Russian Empire and became a major player in gun tech. It would later help its ally in Communist China build its own supersize firearms industry.

Within the fury of the gun debate, people get angry about the words used to describe firearms. The term "assault rifle" engenders a particular controversy because of the attempts to ban them in the United States and other countries. Gun rights advocates claim there is no clear definition of what an assault rifle is—or as one told me, "My AR-15 never assaulted anybody." The term "military-grade guns" also sparks debate over what really is military grade.

In reality, it's tough to put the billion guns in the world into a set of boxes, and there is no universally accepted list of categories. All firearms can potentially be used to kill people. And the guns that military forces use vary over time and place. A Springfield musket was military grade in the American Civil War but would be laughed at on a battlefield today. Guerrillas often fight wars with a mishmash of weapons that soldiers would scorn.

Still, there is a massive difference between the power of certain firearms and the way they can be used to inflict mass casualties. Single-shot hunting guns are favored by sportsman but are not very potent in a gunfight.

The modern black market, meanwhile, mainly moves two types of guns. The first are handguns, defined by the ATF as those small enough to be fired by one hand (although people will use two to steady them). While they have limited range and capacity for ammunition, they can be easily concealed, which makes them useful to criminals, including hit men who sneak up and assassinate their victims at close range. They are used in many of the world's gang killings and in the majority of firearms homicides in the United States.

The second are rifles wielded by infantry soldiers and versions of them used by police forces or sold commercially. The most prominent are Kalashnikovs, the favorites of guerrillas and *sicarios*. Next are those used by the American army, the M16 and the newer M4 that is replacing it, and the semiautomatic versions, the AR-15s. The German G3 and Belgian FAL also make this hit list.

Knowing about the development of these automatic and semiautomatic rifles is key to understanding the rise of crime armies like the Zetas and the arguments over today's mass shootings.

In the late eighteenth century, armies fought with single-shot flintlock rifles, which were loaded from the top. They can be seen in the re-creations of British colonial soldiers in red coats standing in neat lines and taking turns to shoot and reload them, while making no effort to hide from enemy fire.

Machine guns shot their way onto the field with the Gatling gun, a monster of a firearm mounted on wheels that could spit hundreds of rounds per minute. Doctor Richard Gatling first designed his weapon during the American Civil War, but it wasn't widely sold until the late 1870s. It was quickly usurped, however, by the smaller and more efficient Maxim gun. When British colonial troops used Maxims to massacre rebels in Africa and India, Hiram Maxim boasted how his invention was excellent at "stopping the mad rush of savages."[6]

Automatic fire became handheld after World War I with weapons including the tommy gun. Retired brigadier general John T. Thompson developed his submachine gun for the military, where it was criticized for being inaccurate over distance on the battlefield. But it was beloved by trilby-wearing bootleggers, who didn't care about range when they showered caps into speakeasies.

"Armed with Tommy Guns, the gangsters of the Prohibition era were radically more violent than the criminals of yore," writes Adam Winkler in *Gunfight*, his landmark book on U.S. gun law.[7]

In 1929, Al Capone sent his thugs dressed as policemen to unload two tommy guns, along with a shotgun and a pistol, into seven members of Chicago's North Side Gang in the Saint Valentine's Day Massacre. Machine

Gun Kelly, Pretty Boy Floyd, and John Dillinger followed with the rat-a-tat-tat of automatic fire.

Toward the end of World War II, Germany crafted a more effective hand-held machine gun called the *Sturmgewehr*. This literally means "storm rifle," the origin of the term that became "assault rifle." Luckily for the Allies, the gun was made late and didn't get to enough soldiers before Germany was defeated.

The Soviet Union captured some *Sturmgewehrs* and shortly after created the firearm that revolutionized warfare: the Kalashnikov.

The Kalashnikov has been so successful that it's become the most common gun in the world, with over a hundred million of them spread around five continents. These are in fact a family of guns that are "Kalashnikov-style weapons," including the AK-47 and AK-74, some produced in Russia, and others from as far afield as China and Serbia.

They are recognizable for their shape, defined by the curved magazine, and the balance of black steel and polished wood. In Mexico, they call them *cuernos de chivo*, or "goat's horns." Easy to illustrate, the gun is found on T-shirts, in graffiti, and on a national flag (check out that of Mozambique). Amid the cult of the AK, some even call their kids "Kalash."

The AK's story is best told by C. J. Chivers in his meticulously researched *The Gun*. As he explains, the Kalashnikov solved various problems that gun designers had been grappling with for the ultimate infantry rifle. While the previous machine guns were forged in the industry of the capitalist West, the breakthrough Kalashnikov was crafted in the Communist East.

Credit was given to the young officer Mikhail Kalashnikov, who was just twenty-eight when the AK-47 was released in 1947. He is said to have won a competition to design a machine gun ordered by the dictator himself, Joseph Stalin. However, Chivers concludes that much of the design really hailed from the drawing rooms of committees inside the opaque Soviet superstructure. Elevating Kalashnikov was a way to promote the idea of entrepreneurial heroes within the system.

The genius of the Kalashnikov was its simplicity. It could be stripped down and cleaned by a child—and indeed would be by many, from the diamond mines of Africa to the opium fields of Mexico. It was incredibly durable, able to still work after filling up with sand, swamp water, and sludge, which would be decisive in wars like Vietnam. It had an effective range up to only 350 meters, but then most modern combat takes place under this. And it was a fully automatic machine gun.

While blindingly obvious to those who know guns, this last detail is confused by others, so it needs to be clear. "Fully automatic" means that when you put your finger on the trigger, the gun keeps firing until you release the pressure or it has unloaded all the ammunition in the magazine. It achieves this by channeling the gas released from the bullet to reload the next round into the chamber. The speed with which bullets are fired, not taking into account aiming or changing magazines, is known as the cyclic rate of fire.

An AK-47 has a cyclic rate of fire of six hundred rounds per minute. That means someone can unload thirty bullets in a standard clip in just three seconds, or they can attach a circular drum with a hundred bullets and unload them in ten seconds. The gun is also designed for the shooter to quickly detach the magazine and load another.

The revolution in automatic weapons changed the nature of warfare, as soldiers could no longer fight in the open or they would be mown down by bullets. If a half dozen troopers with Kalashnikovs traveled back in time, they could wipe out a battalion of those British redcoats.

The Soviet Union put the power of the AK-47 into the hands of fighters across the globe. In Vietnam, Nicaragua, Mozambique, and Ethiopia, the Kalashnikov was a potent factor for Soviet allies. As Chivers points out, the Soviet invention of the Kalashnikov was as important as its creation of a nuclear bomb.

> By the early 1960s, after the Cuban Missile Crisis had startled its participants . . . the Kremlin and White House comprehended that their mutual nuclear arsenals had made total war unwinnable.

Small wars and proxies would be the means through which the Cold War would be fought.

The Kalashnikov era had arrived.

We are living in it still.[8]

The American answer to the Kalashnikov was invented in, of all places, Hollywood. In the early 1950s, the workshop of upstart weapon company ArmaLite was a small building dubbed "George's Backyard Garage" (after owner George Sullivan) at 6567 Santa Monica Boulevard. Go there today and you'll find a pet hospital in its place, close to a marijuana dispensary and a gay bar. But on that very site in the 1950s, inventor Eugene Stoner was trying to figure out how America could build a better gun than the Soviets built. He came up with the AR-15.

Gun enthusiasts are fond of pointing out that "AR" stands for "ArmaLite," not "assault rifle." However, the rifle was developed with the military eyed as the main buyer, although it took some years to secure the deal. In 1959, ArmaLite sold the rights of the AR-15 to Colt, which took it on the road. In 1961, the U.S. government bought a thousand guns to supply South Vietnamese soldiers, and the following year, the U.S. Air Force bought 8,500 more.

Yet the Pentagon was still not convinced to take the AR-15 on as its main infantry rifle. First, it wanted to try the gun on some real flesh.

In 1962, researchers conducted ballistics tests for the U.S. Army to compare the AR-15 with the AK-47. Their report was dug up by Chivers. It's a surreal if sick story that brings home the power of these weapons.

They started by shooting live goats secured in tracks. In total, they blasted 166 of them from ranges of twenty-five to five hundred meters, pulverizing their hairy torsos.

Then they turned to human heads. It was hard to get American brain cases that they could blow apart, so they imported them from India. As the heads were no longer fresh after their trip, they added gelatin to give them the consistency of living ones.

In total, they shot up twenty-seven Indian cerebellums. When they shot at them with the AK-47s and AR-15s, the brain cases ruptured and fragmented. This is what the weapons are designed to do to humans.

The main discovery was that at longer ranges the AR-15 blew the heads apart into more fragments than the Kalashnikov did. It was a more powerful weapon, they concluded. The AR-15 was rebranded as the M16, and in December 1963 the Pentagon bought 104,000 of them, opening the door for millions over the years.

From 1963, Colt also manufactured a civilian version, which it called the AR-15 Sporter. "With Colt's new AR-15 Sporter you're ready for a new hunting adventure," says an early newspaper ad. The gun was almost identical to the M16, except that it was semiautomatic.

Again, while this is blaringly obvious to gun aficionados, some people get confused, so it needs to be clear. "Semiautomatic" means the gun fires once with each pull of the trigger. How fast people can do this varies, but top competitive shooters can fire three bullets a second pulling a trigger of an AR-15, compared with more than ten a second keeping their finger pressed down on a fully automatic M16. With this difference, the AR-15 is not considered a machine gun, but it's certainly a potent weapon.

In Vietnam, the fully automatic M16 had problems. Amid the humid jungles, it rusted and clogged, causing jams. The Kalashnikovs, meanwhile, resisted water and dirt and kept blasting. A few frustrated American soldiers said the M16s were good only to bludgeon the enemy and preferred to use captured Kalashnikovs. The early problems of the M16 are considered by historians as a factor in America losing the war.

Over the years, however, these issues were ironed out with better parts and cleaning kits. As the Cold War ticked on, America sold M16s to allies including Israel, the Philippines, Honduras, and Colombia, bolstering anti-Communist forces. The Soviet Union supplied Kalashnikovs to its own allies in even greater numbers, and thus automatic rifles spread to every major battlefield in the world.

To churn out millions of Kalashnikovs, the Soviet Union set up production in its client states, including Romania, in its Cugir factory. The fact that the guns seized from the Zetas would be traced there is unsurprising. The Romanian-made Kalashnikovs are a common weapon in the Mexican Drug War, with more than five hundred of them nabbed from criminals across Mexico in a four-year period.[9] The Cugir WASR-10s would also be used in other high-profile killings near the Mexican border, including the murder of agent Brian Terry and the massacre in El Paso.

Founded as a metallurgy works in 1799, when Transylvania was a green backwater of the Hapsburg empire, Cugir began making guns in the early twentieth century. When Romania sided with Nazi Germany in World War II, it sent hundreds of thousands of troops armed with Cugir guns into the invasion of the Soviet Union. This proved a fatal mistake. After the majority of the force perished in Stalingrad, the Soviet Union invaded Romania and established one of the most brutal Communist dictatorships of Eastern Europe, which allegedly killed hundreds of thousands of civilians. Initially, the Cugir factory was just reopened to make munitions, but in 1963 the Soviet Union gave the nod for it to craft Kalashnikovs.

Cugir built the AK-47s under license, which means Romania was given official permission to make the guns along with plans and instructions from Russian engineers. This contrasts with countries such as Yugoslavia, where engineers simply took apart AK-47s and made knockoffs. Over decades, the Cugir factory crafted millions of rifles, and almost thirty years after the Soviet Union fell, it's still banging them out.

In the bustling Romanian capital, Bucharest, I drink coffee with Aurel Cazacu, the ex-head of Romarm, the state company that sold its weapons across the world. Many in the Romanian gun industry are guarded and paranoid, the secretive habits of the dictatorship dying hard. But Cazacu is warm and charismatic, handing me cards from various private arms companies he works with now and rattling off an encyclopedic knowledge of the global gun business.

Cazacu describes how the Cugir factory hit its peak in the 1980s when it had twenty thousand workers, making it one of the biggest gun factories on the planet. Cazacu traveled to sign sales deals with armed forces the Soviet empire gave the nod to, which took him across much of Africa, the Middle East, Asia, and Latin America. Among the heads of state he met personally were the late Colonel Muammar Gaddafi and Saddam Hussein.

"The only places I didn't go were the North Pole and the South Pole." He smiles. "Everywhere in the world people want guns. Everywhere."

From Bucharest, it takes me six hours to drive to Cugir, in the heart of the Transylvanian hills. Like many of Europe's gun factories, it's in a remote place, away from major cities and too many prying eyes. In the small town, most families have a member who worked in the factory, and people are defensive of the hand that feeds them.

The factory is a huge complex, stretching from the town center into the knolls. It has high walls, like a prison, and military guard towers, although they are no longer armed. Sections of the factory have been shut down and are overgrown and deserted but the core still rumbles away.

Nearby, I visit the home of former factory worker Gheorghe Mureșan, a stocky sixty-seven-year-old with white hair and pale blue eyes. He started at Cugir Arms when he was sixteen and spent nigh on half a century there before recently retiring. We talk in his yard, sipping more coffee amid the pretty plants of Transylvania, his dogs barking in the back.

Gheorghe has fond memories of working in a Communist gun factory: a stable job, camaraderie with his workmates, satisfying physical labor. "There was much less stress then," he says. "Everything was taken care of."

While everybody knew there was a gun factory in Cugir, the government still tried to hide it from outsiders.

"People would be watching out who approached the town," Gheorghe says. "If any strange foreigners came by, then the alarm would be sounded. Access to this town was forbidden for foreign citizens." He narrows his eyes, myself a strange foreigner come prying.

He explains how the Kalashnikovs are made, how the life of the weapons used to shoot the ICE agents began. They use wood from Transylvania's forests and steel ore from its hills. Production has three stages: one line forges the component parts, another polishes them, another assembles them.

The biggest danger was explosions from gunpowder, which killed several of Gheorghe's fellow workers. But to minimize risks, they put distance between the parts of the factory making bullets and those making guns. He also fired the rifles to test them, which could provoke the odd accident.

I'd heard that a source of illegal guns was theft from the factories, the trick of making one for the line and one for the stash. But Gheorghe said this was hard in the Romanian police state, with checkpoints outside manned by soldiers, and the security has been maintained since.

Gheorghe carried on working after communism collapsed until his recent retirement, so he was at the factory when the guns that the Zetas used to shoot the ICE agents were produced. It strikes me how strange is our world when two men from thousands of miles away can be linked by a machine, one forging it, one dying from it. Globalized industry numbs our relationship to the goods around us, whether the meat we eat, clothes we wear, or drugs we take. Being a cog in a system removes our responsibility. And our guilt.

While Gheorghe made thousands of guns, he has little interest in shooting as a hobby. "Guns only serve for killing people." He shrugs. Sometimes, he watches TV and recognizes Cugir rifles in war zones. "They are used in conflict because that is their role," he says. "It's not my business where they end up." He has never been to Mexico, knows little of the drug war, has no idea who the Zetas are.

There are no guns in his home. I am more worried about the two dogs at the back. One of them is an expert at biting other dogs, his daughter explains, while the other is an expert at biting people.

––––––––––

When the revolutions of 1989 tore through Eastern Europe, the Communist dictatorships collapsed like paper tigers, most without bloodshed. In Romania, however, the old guard put up the most violent defense in the region, with police and soldiers shooting dead more than a thousand people, most after a firing squad executed the dictator Nicolae Ceaușescu and his wife on Christmas Day.

Those deaths marked the beginning of problems in the post-Communist era, with the Balkans struggling to transition into the global economy. Hundreds of factories were shuttered, the bland tinned food and no-frills frocks unwanted, the workers joining unemployment lines or heading to the West. But in Cugir, Romania did produce something that could be a valued consumer product. After the wall came down, there was a growing desire around the world for the legendary Soviet guns.

The upheaval that followed the collapse of communism is known in Eastern Europe as "the wild nineties." Amid the chaos, arsenals were looted throughout the region, with an infamous case in Albania of locals walking away with a hundred thousand Kalashnikovs from a factory.[10] The stolen rifles fed a black market of weapons flowing into Western Europe.

In other cases, governments themselves sold off the Cold War stockpiles, working with private brokers who flew them by the ton to gun-hungry countries, many in Africa. Viktor Bout reportedly made his fortune in this period hauling arms to Sierra Leone and Liberia as they were devoured by war. Later, the United States would work with private brokers to buy up the Eastern European surplus and sell it to allies in Afghanistan and Iraq.

When stockpiles were exhausted, the brokers worked with the factories to keep the rifles flowing.

In neighboring Bulgaria, I travel to Sofia to meet Todor Viktorov, one of a number of brokers in the region who sell Kalashnikovs, along with other Eastern Bloc hardware such as tanks. Thirty-two years old with a shaved head and sharp suit, Viktorov is hardworking and ambitious. Despite his youth, he has already been at his company for a decade and loves it.

"It's a very interesting business, the most interesting business in the world," he says, showing me a contract he has just won to sell hundreds of thousands of bullets.

The company he works for likes to buy its Kalashnikovs and ammo from Bulgarian factories, but as the demand is so high, they also go to Serbia and Romania. They sell to Iraq, where he has been five times; Saudi Arabia, the cash cow for the world's arms dealers; and across Africa, to nations such as Ghana, Nigeria, and Ivory Coast. Jet-setting across capitals, he makes an extraordinary amount of money for a young man from Bulgaria, where the average salary is six hundred euros a month.

"Basically, most of the people working in this business have a very good standard of living. In Bulgaria, I have two houses, I have four cars, a motorcycle, and I'm thirty-two years old. I'm not sure with another business how it would be possible to buy such things."

The gun industry certainly makes some wealthy, but relatively few. Only a couple of hundred people in the entire Balkans can likely make this kind of money from arms sales, and while the factories offer steady jobs, they employ only a few thousand people apiece. Cugir has only a third of the workforce it did at its height in the Cold War.

Viktorov works within the law, he says, selling only to countries approved by the Bulgarian Export Board, which means approved by the United Nations and the European Union. That counts out nations under embargo, such as Sudan, Libya, and Iran.[11] But even with the green-lighted governments, there are suspicions about where the guns end up. Reports show that weapons supplied to Saudi Arabia have materialized on the battlefields of Syria and Yemen.[12]

I ask Viktorov whether he is worried if guns he sold fell into the hands of the Islamic State.

"Basically not," he says. "Because we have official papers from Saudi Arabia. Also we have approval from Bulgarian authorities. So for us it is not an issue."

I try again. "Legally it's not an issue," I say. "But ethically does it ever worry you if something ends up in the wrong hands?"

He looks at me for a while and finally gives a one-word answer: "No."

I have to give credit for honesty. If you are legally safe, then why worry about what someone else does down the line? I find this across the industry.

Of course executives know that criminals and terrorists could end up with their products, but it's about sealing off your corner.

"My wish is to stay in this industry all my life," Viktorov finishes.

While Viktorov sells to armies in Africa and the Middle East, other companies shift the Kalashnikovs to the Americas. This means selling into the U.S. retail market, which requires turning a Soviet weapon of war into an American consumer product. Which gets into the labyrinth of American gun law.

Much of the world marvels (or revels in horror) at the liberalness of American gun laws and the constitutional right to bear arms. There is an impression that it is so much simpler than the lengthy lists of regulations governing firearms in other countries.

Anyone who has ventured into U.S. gun legislation, however, finds the opposite of simplicity is true. American rules are a complex and sometimes contradictory mosaic, mixing debate on the Constitution, Supreme Court rulings, federal laws, state laws, city regulations, ATF rules, and appeals against all of the above. This tangle gets ever more knotted by the constant tug of war between the so-called gun rights and gun control (or gun safety) sides, countering each other's changes.

The result is an uneven national patchwork that nobody is happy with. Attempted compromises are sometimes made that manage to annoy the gun rights side while not cutting to the heart of the measures desired by gun safety advocates. And there are gaping loopholes and bizarre restrictions on policing arms, making important parts of gun law unenforceable. Which the black market uses to maximum effect.

The legal arguments grapple through history all the way back to the Revolution. And not just to the American Revolution, but to the Glorious Revolution of King James II of England in 1689. In that year, an English Bill of Rights declared, "Subjects which are Protestants may have Arms for their Defence."[13] This is important because when scholars wrangle over the language of early American law, they go back to the old country for references.

When Americans finally booted out the British crown in the Revolutionary War, their Continental Army consisted of less than half regular soldiers and the rest militia. These ragged irregulars fought with a mix of weapons, beginning with any blades and blasters they could muster, but developing into a potent fighting force to be mythologized in the American imagination. They were crucial to the framing of the Constitution, and they inspire the modern gun rights movement.

Which gets to those few words that have such a massive impact on history, and not just that of the United States but of the world: the Second Amendment to the Constitution, written in 1791. On the entrance to its old headquarters in Washington, the NRA emblazoned the second half of it: "The right of the people to keep and bear Arms, shall not be infringed." This cut-down version sounds muscular and straightforward, or as Winkler says, the NRA's vision of "all right, with little room for regulation."[14] But the entire sentence written by the founders is painfully ambiguous: "A well regulated militia, being necessary to the security of a free State, the right of the people to keep and bear Arms, shall not be infringed."

This has led to the never-ending debate on meaning. On one side, jurists argue that the amendment means only those in a "regulated militia" have the right to be armed. But other jurists argue that "the right of the people" means everybody. For some hard-liners, this a "God-given" right that should extend to convicted felons. Surveys find most Americans are against repeal of the Second Amendment but do favor stricter gun laws.[15]

Another curious debate is whether the Second Amendment calls for people to be armed and ready to rise up against a tyrannical government. In other words, regular folks have to keep stashes of guns in their homes in case the United States becomes a dictatorship and they need to transform into guerrilla fighters.

I am not a pacifist and think there are occasions when armed resistance to tyranny is the only path. But the cliché is also true that violence begets more violence. In Syria, an armed rebellion led to a devastating civil war.

Meanwhile, nonviolent civilian uprisings have been markedly successful in bringing down dictatorships, such as the Communist regimes in Eastern Europe.

Either way, it is a hard stretch to allow a population to be constantly armed for insurrection. Few want regular Americans to own tanks and bazookas to take on the modern military.

Many Americans, including many gun owners, do not take this concept seriously. But for a significant number, it is a central tenet of their thinking and leads to the hard-line positions. There should be no national gun registry, they argue, because this would be a step for the government to take everyone's weapons. This becomes the underlying fear story of the gun movement, the driver of the modern militias.

For many decades, judges favored a more restrictive interpretation of the Second Amendment and upheld legal challenges to gun control laws. This was changed by the momentous 2008 Supreme Court ruling on *District of Columbia v. Heller*. The ruling favored a challenge by activists that the capital's handgun ban, which was designed to reduce firearm murders, was unconstitutional, as people have the right to bear arms. It opened the possibility of the gun lobby challenging any gun laws. However, that has not materialized (yet). And the popular argument is far from over, as the heated rhetoric after each mass shooting shows.

Over the past century, there have been a series of federal gun laws with major implications. And during this time, there has been intense debate over how to govern machine guns and assault rifles.

First came the National Firearms Act of 1934, and its follow-up Federal Firearms Act of 1938, which were in response to the trilby-clad outlaws firing tommy guns. Chivers suggests only a few hundred tommy guns reached the trigger fingers of American mobsters.[16] But either way, they made a loud-enough noise to be heard in the White House of Franklin Roosevelt.

It's notable that the government did not want to run into a Second Amendment argument, so the 1934 act didn't outright ban fully automatic weapons. Instead, it introduced a machine gun tax, which made them prohibitively expensive and required that those who did buy them be finger-printed and photographed, counting out most gangsters.

A more far-reaching law arrived in the turbulent sixties. The Gun Control Act (GCA) of 1968 is the most important piece of gun legislation after the Second Amendment, laying out the framework for how law enforcement has policed guns since. It led to the birth both of the ATF in its name and modern role, and of the gun rights movement.

Lawmakers drafted the GCA in response to the shootings of John F. Kennedy and Martin Luther King Jr., as well as the sight of Black Panthers marching into the Sacramento capitol building with shotguns and pistols. This big influence of the Black Panthers in shaping the law and the subsequent gun rights movement is another paradox in the American gun story. Gun crime, including murders and muggings, was also rising steadily through the sixties, leading to calls for a crackdown.

The act banned certain people from buying firearms, including felons, the mentally ill, and domestic violence offenders. It banned shipments across state lines and massively expanded a licensing system for gun stores.

To weed out offenders, the government created Form 4473, which gun buyers have to fill out at shops. The form has a series of questions asking if the buyer is a felon or a drug user, or has been in a mental institution.

At the time, buyers could simply lie on the form, and the shops had no way to check—or obligation. But to Second Amendment advocates, it was a slippery slope, a paper record of a gun sale that could be exploited by a tyrannical gun-grabbing government or foreign invader. It became the dreaded and hated Form 4473.

For a sense of this, check out a scene from *Red Dawn*, the 1984 film about Communists invading America. As resisters fight the invaders, a Cuban officer turns to a Russian trooper.

"Go to the sporting goods store," he says. "From the files, obtain Form 4473. These will contain descriptions of weapons and lists of private ownership."

The commie tyrants were using gun control measures to disarm Americans.

The gun lobby managed to shift the balance back with the 1986 Firearm Owners' Protection Act under Ronald Reagan. This hit the ATF with a range of restrictions, limiting its effectiveness—or to put it crudely, cutting its balls off. It also began a steady decrease in budgets and staffing for the ATF.

However, the law had one element that was a big slap to machine gun lovers. At the eleventh hour, New Jersey Democrat William Hughes introduced an amendment that banned all sales of new machine guns. Before opposition could muster, a Democratic Congress approved it, and Reagan signed it into law, a move that hard-line gun activists never forgave him for.

The law has been markedly successful in stopping new fully automatic weapons from being sold in the United States, which shows that some pieces of gun control can be effective. And while the machine guns made before this date are still in circulation, they have become scarcer, which keeps their prices rising. Look online, and you can find "pre-ban" machine guns for north of twenty-five thousand dollars.

A small number will still pay these amounts, get their fingerprints and photographs taken for their machine gun taxes, and join clubs where they spray automatic fire to their heart's content. Most gun enthusiasts, meanwhile, make do with semiautomatics.

The rules shifted again in 1989, when Patrick Purdy wielded a Chinese semiautomatic AK-47 to shoot dead five children and injure another thirty-two at Cleveland Elementary School in Stockton, California. The Bush administration responded by banning the imports of "assault weapons," especially AK-47s, citing its right to do so under the 1968 law.

Except it didn't. The law was made in a manner that importers could find a way around. One path was to adjust the design of AK-47s, changing the length or thickness of the barrel and getting rid of details such as folding stocks so that they could be reclassified as sporting rifles.

Furthermore, in the United States, companies could rebuild the guns with the assault rifle features, and as long as they had only a limited number of parts from the original, they could be classified as "Made in America." U.S. gun regulation had again found a way to confuse people, annoy those on the pro-gun side, and fail to solve the concerns for gun safety.

President Bill Clinton led a more vigorous attempt to take firepower away from murderers. In 1993, he signed the Brady Handgun Violence Prevention Act, known as the Brady Bill, requiring background checks to buy guns. It was named after James Brady, the White House press secretary under Reagan, who was shot and disabled.

While the 1968 law had banned felons and others, the dealers had no way of checking. The Brady law made the government build the National Instant Criminal Background Check System (NICS) to vet what the buyers write on the Form 4473. It has since stopped a huge number of gun sales to prohibited people—but also suffers from gaping loopholes.[17]

Clinton made the gun lobby even madder with the Federal Assault Weapons Ban in 1994. Pressure had been building from mass shootings, including those in Stockton in 1989; Luby's Cafeteria in Killeen, Texas, in 1991; and 101 California Street, San Francisco, in 1993. Still, it took years of hard campaigning to move on the issue.

To counter resistance, the ban included a sunset clause that would make it expire after ten years, and it was diluted from early drafts. It struggled to define "assault rifles," finally classifying them as having two or more of certain features such as pistols grips and folding stocks. Again, gun makers could get around these with modifications to make "sporting rifles."

Still, it significantly lowered the number of the most effective Kalashnikovs and AR-15s on the market for the decade it was enforced. It expired in 2004, right as cartel violence escalated in Mexico.

———

Back in Cugir, I talk to the factory's chief gun designer about how he made guns fit for American laws.

I found him by chance. Before going to Cugir, I submitted a request to go inside the factory and talk to the current director. The factory is still owned by the Romanian government, and the request was pushed right up to the economy minister, who sat on it as I wandered around and took photos of the guard towers.

Without his go-ahead, I couldn't get in the front door. But across the road, Cugir has a factory museum, so I went there and studied the exhibits carefully. A man in his sixties was arranging versions of Kalashnikovs on stands, including the Draco and WASR-10, the models used in the Zapata shooting. Chatting openly about them, he revealed he was the chief gun designer, the father of the Draco.

A lifelong factory worker, he was inspired by Kalashnikov to learn the art of gun design and was old-school, using paper and pencil rather than computers. He described how he worked closely with American importers to figure out the plans.

The WASR-10 was fairly simple, using the classic AK-47 but making it semi-automatic and adjusting the barrel length and other features for U.S. law. The Draco was a more unique design—what he claimed is the smallest Kalashnikov in the world. While it uses the same AK firing mechanism, it has a much shorter barrel and stock, so it is technically a pistol, making it easier to import. American buyers made up the name Draco as part of their marketing strategy; it's of course short for "Dracula," the favorite figure of Transylvania.

"I watch videos on YouTube of people in America using the Dracos and what they like about them," he said. "There is a video of one guy who says he fires with one in each hand."

In contrast to Gheorghe, the designer was a gun enthusiast and proud of the factory. "Until man is on this earth, he will want weapons," he said.

The American orders alongside those from regional brokers helped breathe life into Cugir and keep it afloat during the recession years. In 2010, our Draco and WASR-10 rolled off the production line. They were loaded on planes and flown to the East Coast of the United States, to be imported by the company Century Arms.

———

The SHOT Show held annually in Las Vegas is a multicolored, multifaceted, overwhelming, ballistic, gargantuan, flamboyant, and slightly surreal look at the U.S. firearms industry. The biggest gun trade show on the planet fills the sprawling Sands Expo and Convention Center, boasting more than 700,000 square feet of exhibition space. Closed to the public, it attracts over sixty thousand people from the industry, including gun makers, gun importers, gun dealers, gun repairers, gun specialist lawyers, gun trainers, gun lobbyists, and gun anything else you can think of. Representatives from armies and police forces around the world attend, sealing bulk orders in meetings in glass booths.

It takes days just to walk around the vast halls staring at the labyrinth of displays. It's not only guns. There are all the spillover products—anything you could imagine that has a connection to guns. These include gun polishers, gun store software, sights in all shapes and sizes, camouflage face paints, bulletproof jackets, full-on body armor that looks like Iron Man, vast displays of outdoor gear (including boots, tents, and entire cabins), contraptions to sweep up bullets, silencers, ear protection, night-vision gear, tactical headsets, and targets galore, from simple circles to pictures of turbaned "terrorists." Then there's the machinery to make guns and ammunition, from the industrial metal-cutters worth hundreds of thousands of dollars to the craft tools for local gun repairers and the many hobbyists who want to smith their own weapons.

In the heart of the expo, the NRA has a bulging display, and when I am there, I see Dana Loesch, then its spokesperson, signing autographs, taking photos with fans, and getting the present of an exotic rifle. There are various reflections of gun culture politics. One gun is engraved with the slogan IN TRUMP WE TRUST. The Black Rifle Coffee company vends a LIBERAL TEARS brew.

And there are the guns themselves. Gun after gun after gun. Guns small enough to fit in your shirt pocket to huge pods mounted on helicopters; exquisite long guns for competitive shooters to bargain bucket pistols; single-shot rifles to handguns with double drums of ammunition. The huge .50-caliber rifles grab attention, as magnets for attendees to stand behind and pose for photos; the grenade launchers are more discreet, weapons for sale only to military and law enforcement. And of course there are the Kalashnikovs and AR-15s, every variety you can imagine, including a bulging display of Century Arms, with the Dracos and WASR-10s that I saw in Cugir.

The SHOT Show straddles the two major markets of the weapons industry. The first is the market to sell guns to soldiers and police, both American and global, and for this the SHOT Show attracts the same people that do the circuits of the big arms fairs, where missiles and fighter jets are on display in Paris, Kiev, Cairo, Jakarta, and Karachi. The second is the market for civilians, or rather the dealers who sell to those civilians, and for this you see how guns are promoted as a consumer product, sometimes with bold action displays, sometimes with a lot of nerdy detail, sometimes with beautiful, scantily clad models posing with pistols. Back in the 1990s, Glock took a professional stripper to Vegas to promote its firepower.[18]

The marketing of guns as consumer products gets a huge boost from the endless gunfights in TV and movies. Gun publicists deliberately target prop managers, and a business has emerged of movie weapons specialists who link the studios to the gun companies.[19] This secured iconic gun-naming scenes, such as Clint Eastwood in *Dirty Harry* saying, "This is a .44 Magnum, the most powerful handgun in the world." Indeed, at the SHOT Show, there is a case with the very weapon from *Dirty Harry*, along with guns from *Die Hard* and *Lethal Weapon*, and even the old rifle from *Jaws*. But then moving pictures have also boosted cars, sunglasses, and cigarettes.

The American gun industry is like any other consumer business in various ways: it has an army of salespeople, product managers, and executives who grind numbers and get pressure on bottom lines. There is a specialized gun media, which lives on advertising from the gun companies and is omnipresent at the SHOT Show. Its language is super consumer focused, with product reviews, discussions of new features, and highlights of bargains.

It was in this consumer gun culture that importers brought the semiautomatic Kalashnikovs into the United States and made them a familiar feature in shops and shows. Kalashnikovs now sit alongside Colts and Remingtons, Glocks and Berettas, H&Ks and Smith & Wessons in the arsenal of American aficionados.

Century Arms, one of the biggest importers of Kalashnikovs, also straddles these worlds between military supplies and the U.S. consumer market. Providing guns such as the Draco and WASR-10, it has a solid following among American shooters. But, being a major dealer in military surplus since the sixties, it has been involved in controversy. The name of the company or its founders has shown up in reports on the Iran-Contra scandal, WikiLeaks cables about guns from Guatemala,[20] and the trace info on the guns from the ICE killing.

The company's main warehouse is in a small town in northern Vermont, where it keeps a low profile tucked away amid dairy farms. Vermont journalist Ken Picard visited to find an eighty-thousand-foot warehouse surrounded by a chain-link fence and barbed wire.

"The corrugated steel building sports no outdoor signage, except for a small listing on the industrial park's outdoor directory and a flag bearing Century's corporate logo: a world map in the crosshairs of a rifle scope," Picard wrote.

When Picard asked two local senators about it, a Democrat had never heard of it, while a Republican said, "I'm not 100 percent sure what they do."[21]

The exact details of Century Arms are opaque, the owners giving journalists a wide berth. When I sent them an email asking questions for this book, they didn't answer, as they also didn't answer questions from Picard or an investigation by the Center of Public Integrity.

However, bones of its story appear in various documents and news reports over the years.[22] Century Arms started business in the 1960s, after founder William Sucher was selling office equipment and a struggling customer paid for typewriters with some old carbines. Sucher teamed up with his brother-in-law Emmanuel Weigensberg to sell the weapons, and they made such a nice profit they moved into it full time. They began importing Italian guns by the pound and then moved farther east.

Weigensberg scored a fruitful deal in the 1980s as Reagan waged his covert war against the Sandinista government in Nicaragua, backing its enemies, the right-wing Contras. Amid the sprawling scandal of Iran-Contra, Weigensberg was a broker selling Chinese weapons to the Contras. He did this through another company of his empire in a deal described in the report into Iran-Contra by independent counsel Lawrence Walsh, which says Weigensberg made $240,000.[23]

After the Berlin Wall came down, Century Arms moved on to the stockpiles of Eastern Europe, and then to working with factories including Cugir to build Kalashnikovs. They are not breaking any laws by importing the weapons into the United States. But the reality is that many end up in Mexico, given that more than five hundred Romanian AK-47s were recovered from Mexican crime scenes in a four-year period. Among those were our WASR-10 and Draco.

Over the years I have looked at the economic logic of drug trafficking, how it functions as a business, and what makes it so extraordinarily violent. It's not that complicated. Take cocaine.

Cocaine is produced cheaply from the coca plants of the Andes, where peasant farmers get about eighty dollars for a heap of leaves. After gangsters (or guerrillas) put this through two chemical processes, it becomes a kilo brick of cocaine, worth about $1,500 to $2,000. This goes on a journey by plane, car, or submarine to reach the U.S.–Mexico border, where it is worth ten times that. And when it is divided into grams to be sold in a nightclub in New York City, it's worth more than a hundred thousand dollars, and two or three times that if it is cut up with crap.

The profit margins are so ridiculous that everyone wants a piece, and this leads to the most violent players taking over, and the creation of sociopaths like the Zetas. The United Nations estimates that the global drug trade is worth more than three hundred billion dollars a year, the biggest black market on the planet.

An important feature of the drug trade is that it is illegal along all the links in the chain. That kilo of cocaine is produced illegally in Colombia, trafficked illegally through Mexico, and sold illegally in America.

The black market in guns follows a distinct logic. The vast majority begin as legal products and at some point cross an invisible line and go into the black market.

There are other key differences. Illegal guns are a product that criminals sell, but they are also tools they use to control other rackets, such as drugs. The price of illegal guns can go up steeply, delivering traffickers a nice profit, if much less than that from drugs. But prices can also dip sharply from a host of strange factors.

In the case of our two guns from Cugir, they crossed this invisible line, from legal to illegal, in Texas in 2010.

JJ's Pawn Shop sits in a one-story brick building in the city of Beaumont, Texas, a big yellow sign saying, THE PLACE TO BUY GUNS & AMMO . . . WE TREAT YOU RIGHT. On August 20, 2010, Robert Riendfliesh, a twenty-five-year-old veteran wearing a camouflage hat, walked in the store. He bought ten brand-new WASR-10 rifles that had been preordered, registering the buy in his real name. Among them was the rifle with serial number 1981MF8477.

JJ's is a Federal Firearms Licensee (FFL) and so requires customers buying guns to fill out the dreaded Form 4473. It uses the information to do an instant background check online or by calling up a hotline. The FBI runs the person's name through three databases, particularly looking for felons and fugitives, but others red-lighted are those convicted of domestic violence misdemeanors and deportees.

Riendfliesh, who had fought in the Iraq War, was cleared to buy the Romanian rifles. It may seem surprising that somebody could walk into a shop and buy ten AK-47s without setting off alarm bells. But while gun dealers are encouraged to report suspicious activity to the ATF, at that time they were not obliged to—and the traffickers knew this.

Riendfliesh was not buying for himself but was what's known as a straw purchaser, someone with a clean record buying guns for criminals. Coming home from Iraq, he fell on hard times, and when he went to buy marijuana from a dealer he called Manny over in Baytown, he was told he could make extra cash buying guns. To walk in the shop and pick up ten Kalashnikovs in his real name, he was paid by Manny the stately sum of $650, or just $65 a gun.

This might strike you as a small amount for such a crime that could lead straight to your door. But the reason so many people can be recruited as straw buyers and paid small amounts is that the risk is not great. Most straw purchasers will get prosecuted only for lying on the form, as they say the guns are for themselves. While they can in theory do prison time, most won't, and indeed Riendfliesh would get only four years' probation in this high-profile case in which the gun was used to kill an American agent.

Manny was really Manuel Gomez Barba, a twenty-nine-year-old into drug selling and gun trafficking. A U.S. citizen, he hawked marijuana and crystal meth in Baytown, which was coming from the Zetas south of the border. In return, he supplied them with firearms, overseeing the buying and exporting of at least forty-four guns from Texas to northern Mexico between June 2010 and February 2011. (There were forty-four guns specifically traced to him, although he said in one statement that it was more like seventy.) The WASR-10 was among them, likely crossing the border in late August.

On October 20 at the Dallas–Fort Worth gun show, the stall of Off Duty Enterprises was offering a range of firearms. A stocky twenty-two-year-old man wandered through the crowd to ask for a Draco on the table. He showed his driver's license with the name Otilio Osorio, and the vendor put it through the instant check. Otilio was cleared and walked away with the AK pistol, serial number DC-2777-10.

He took the gun to his home in the Dallas suburb of Lancaster, which he shared with his brother Ranfieri, a marine veteran who had served in both Iraq and Afghanistan. Part of their home was converted into a workshop for repairing and customizing guns, with a vise, grinders, and spray-paint tools. They called themselves "Draco specialists."

But while they made spare change from repairs, their real profits were from running guns into Mexico. Along with a team of straw purchasers, they acquired at least 130 firearms between June and October. By the time of the attack on the ICE agents, they had gotten hold of over two hundred weapons.

The crew was delivering the guns to couriers, who would drive them to the border cities of Eagle Pass and Laredo, Texas, and then over the line to the Mexican cities of Piedras Negras and Nuevo Laredo, both Zeta strongholds.

Their modus operandi was simple. They would prepare the guns, pack them into duffel bags, and drive them in their Ford Explorer to a rendezvous point, sometimes in the parking lot of a nearby Walmart. Here they would hand them over to a contact, sometimes in a pickup truck, sometimes in a whole eighteen-wheeler, where the guns would be hidden among merchandise. The courier would drive the weapons to the border, where the Zetas would take them into Mexico.

By late 2010, the Zetas had become one of the most powerful cartels on the continent, with thousands of men at arms and a presence from northern Guatemala through big swathes of Mexico into Texas. They moved on a network of dirt roads that spiral across Mexico and intersect with the main highways. With such reach, the Draco and WASR-10 were transported through the Zetas' empire from the border to Tweety Bird's cell of operatives in San Luis Potosí. And there they were on the fateful day of February 15, 2011, when Jaime and Victor were shot on the highway.

The journey of the guns was complete. They began as plans on the paper of the Cugir designer, to be forged on the production line from wood and steel, shipped over the Atlantic into Vermont, sold retail at shops and shows in Texas, smuggled over the border into Mexico, wielded in the Zetas arsenal, used in the attack on Jaime and Victor, then seized by the ATF while their victim was buried in Brownsville.

After Victor was shot, he thought he might get a hero's welcome back home, major support from ICE, perhaps a promotion. But that didn't happen.

He obviously couldn't go back to Mexico, and his ICE bosses didn't want him in El Paso because they feared the Zetas could reach him there. So they sent him and his family to Washington. They checked them into a hotel. And left them there.

"That was when the real nightmare started," Victor said. Most of their possessions were left in Mexico City, and they hardly had any clothes, especially for a snowy Washington winter. "I needed everything. My wife and I needed everything. My kids needed everything."

His two children had been pulled out of school, but he couldn't enroll them in D.C., as he didn't have a fixed address and they needed vaccines after being abroad. He fought to get a house and establish himself, arguing with ICE to get basic expenses reimbursed, a fight that was still ongoing years later.

Meanwhile, Victor fought for justice. The Zeta leader Tweety Bird pleaded guilty in a U.S. court and was sentenced to life, but others in the attack remained at large for several years, gradually being arrested and extradited, and Victor had to testify in trials.

After the gun traces, those involved in delivering the weapons, the Osorios, Riendfliesh, and Barba, were also arrested. When they were convicted, they got a range of sentences: the straw buyer Riendfliesh was released on probation; the Osorios got seven and ten years; Barba got eight years for the guns, more for the drugs.

But disturbing information came out of their cases. It emerged that the Osorio brothers had been followed by federal agents long before the shooting, but they had not been arrested and carried on moving weapons to the Zetas. On November 9, three months before the hit, the Osorio brothers were even watched handing over forty guns to a courier in a battered tractor-trailer truck in a Walmart parking lot.

The courier was working as an informant for the ATF, whose agents surveyed the whole deal. The ATF let the truck travel two hours on the road to Laredo, then pulled it over and busted it. But they let the Osorio brothers carry on moving guns.

The investigation into Barba was also controversial. It emerged that he had been arrested back in May 2010 for selling thirty-one grams of crystal meth to a DEA informant. However, Barba was subsequently released on bail and went on selling drugs and trafficking guns, including the WASR-10 used in the attack on the ICE agents.

The U.S. Department of Justice Office of the Inspector General (which houses the ATF, DEA, and FBI) launched an inquiry and said that its "conclusions are highly critical of performance failures" in the case.

"There was adequate probable cause to arrest both Osorio brothers and Morrison [a cohort] following the transfer of forty firearms," it said. "All these errors had significant consequences. The firearms trafficking activities of the Osorios and Morrison went unabated until their arrests in February 2011, and the government missed an opportunity to curtail Barba's crimes."[24]

The blunders were not directly part of the Fast and Furious operation but they came out right as that scandal broke, and the media was reporting how the ATF watched two thousand guns be trafficked from Arizona to Mexico. The revelations shocked Victor, who felt betrayed by his government on all fronts.

"It's a very awkward feeling," Victor tells me. "Because you can always say, 'Would the Zetas have been armed the way they were if it weren't for these other weapons that came through the United States?' In other words, 'Would Jaime still be alive if those weapons that killed him were not in their possession?' Maybe. Maybe not. But the reality is that the United States didn't help the cause of the violence in Mexico by supplying them with more weapons."

Amid the bad feelings, Victor joined the parents of Zapata in various lawsuits against the U.S. government, the gun shops, and the traffickers for crimes including negligence. The names of the defendants included ATF agents and the very Department of Homeland Security itself.

ICE reacted by making Victor's life even more miserable. In August 2011, he had been relocated to Spain, where he hoped to get away from the whole situation and heal. Halfway through his assignment, they sent him what is called a "three r" letter: to resign, retire, or relocate.

Victor moved to the ICE bureau in Colorado, taking his children to yet another new town, another new school. There, the ICE bosses stripped him of his gun and equipment. They also tried to take his badge, but he refused to hand it over.

"I said, 'Okay, you can have your guns and you can have your equipment, but you are not taking my badge. I earned this badge and I worked for this badge and I paid in blood for this badge.' I had very severe PTSD. I was depressed. I had a lot of issues, physical, mental. I was just a mess."

Eventually, in 2015, he managed to get medically retired from ICE while one of his lawsuits was still in the courts. As an American agent who had survived the bullets of narcos, he was picked up by conservative news outlets, taking a hard line against the cartel problem and calling for being tough on border security, although he was still critical of the way ICE had treated him.

Meanwhile, Victor went on dealing with physical effects from the bullets. One cap was still embedded in his leg, becoming part of his body, and he was still having treatments for his back, still having therapy. Years after the shooting, it went on plaguing him.

"It ended my career. It was such a traumatic event, not only for me but the ripple effect, what happened to me, what happened to my wife, what happened to my kids . . . I almost went bankrupt. And when you think back, it's because I got shot."

It happens in a fraction of a second. But the effects can last a lifetime.

3

Gun Police

They think that because we are the gun police on the federal level that we are out to get everybody who's got guns, and it's not the case. We go after the hard-core violent criminals.

—DARRIN KOZLOWSKI, FORMER ATF SPECIAL AGENT

If I were to select a jackbooted group of fascists who are perhaps as large a danger to American society as I could pick today, I would pick ATF.

—REPRESENTATIVE JOHN DINGELL, IN THE NRA
DOCUMENTARY *IT CAN HAPPEN HERE*[1]

———

T he shots echoed across the parking lot of the bar, making revelers run for their lives, hit the ground, scream. It was at a drinking hole in the east of Greater Los Angeles, pushing into the San Gabriel Valley. On one side was a group of shaven-headed gangbangers from a local crew called the Bassett Grande. On the other were leather-jacketed bikers from the Mongols, one of the most notorious of the outlaw motorcycle clubs.

A leader of the Mongols, who held the biker rank "sergeant at arms," was angry at one of the Bassett Grande for looking at him funny and pulled a gun to threaten him. After he walked away, several of the Bassett Grande drew their pistols and fired, hitting the car of the Mongol sergeant, smashing the side mirror and rim.

Other Mongols ran from the bullets, among them a biker known in the gang as Dirty Dan. Brawny and bearded, Dan was what's called a "prospect," a recruit earning his way to be a "fully patched" member. He had carried the sergeant's gun in the vents of his truck and handed it to him before he made the threat.

Dan was also packing his own gun, but he didn't fire back when the bullets flew past him. He didn't want to kill anyone, even if they were shooting at his crew. Because he didn't have the Mongol mentality. He just pretended to.

His name wasn't even Dan. It was Darrin Kozlowski, and he was an undercover ATF agent infiltrating the Mongols. It was part of a sprawling case to bombard them with guns, drugs, and organized crime charges. And that meant him dodging bullets in a parking lot.

Kozlowski is one of a cadre of ATF agents who have gone undercover in biker gangs, participating in their rituals and uncovering their secrets. Others in this group include William "Billy" Queen and Jay Dobyns. Kozlowski is a bit of a legend within the ATF, infiltrating not just one but three different motorcycle clubs, immersing himself in the biker culture for decades. After hitting his fifties and retiring from the agency, he's finally able to tell his story, and he relays it to me as we plow through steaks at a BJ's restaurant in the Valley.

The row with the Bassett Grande was not the only time he'd been shot at. And he'd also had his head cracked open with a metal bar, faced off against the Armenian Power mob, which is linked to the Russian Mafia, and suffered death threats requiring a SWAT team to camp out at his home.

Considering he's had one of the most hard-core careers in American law enforcement, I'm struck by how down to earth and modest he is as he tells me the fine details of his undercover work between sips of iced tea. He risked his life again and again to take black market guns off the street and put gun-toting criminals in prison. His career illustrates how the ATF got so deep into infiltration and crafting conspiracy cases to go after gun crime—the espionage game of informants, undercovers, wiretaps, and cooperating witnesses that has grown to characterize federal law enforcement. It also spans the years of the ATF's biggest controversies and the most ferocious attacks on it, from Waco to the Oklahoma bombing to Fast and Furious.

Kozlowski is over six feet and two hundred pounds, with tattoos on his thick arms and an outlaw edge. I could see how the bikers believed he was one of them. He is better known as Koz.

To make sense of the fight against gun crime, and how Fast and Furious ever came to pass, we need to take a closer look at the U.S. gun police themselves in the ATF. It's a curious agency.

The ATF is one of the big federal law enforcement bodies, along with the DEA, FBI, and ICE, but stands as the poorest brother. In 2020, the FBI got an $8 billion budget, ICE got $6 billion, the DEA got $2.3 billion, and ATF got $1.3 billion.

All these agencies have their critics. But the ATF's detractors are the fiercest, calling it scathing names such as the "Bureau of Assholes, Twits, and Fascists." And they are the most powerful, including key elements of the gun lobby. This has led to legal straitjackets on the ATF, unlike those on any other government agency. Its job of going after gunrunners is challenged by low budgets and restrictions, and it's even banned from using databases to trace guns.

The ATF is less known than the DEA and FBI, and its agents don't enjoy the same place in popular culture. There are fewer portrayals of ATF agents in movies than there are of G-men and narcs. There isn't even a good nickname for the gun police.

Yet the ATF has played a major role in fighting firearms crime and, therefore, in reducing gun homicides in the United States. Despite its limitations, it has been effective in cracking down on certain gun-toting criminals.

It has also been the federal agency to claim the most personnel who have died in the line of duty. Former ATF officer James Moore wrote a fiery history of the bureau, *Very Special Agents*, in which he describes the dangers and bats back against the critics.

"This small federal agency has lost more agents to criminal gunfire than have all the other government investigative bureaus *combined*. But violent gun crimes drop when ATF agents are most active—and rise again when the agents' efforts decrease . . . Which makes one wonder: Who'd hold them back?"[2]

The ATF's successes make it another paradox in the gun story. While the United States boasts the most guns in civilian hands, it also has a federal agency that aggressively goes after certain gun crime. Many other countries don't have a specific gun police, even those that suffer horrendous levels of murder, such as Mexico, Honduras, and Brazil. Somehow, it hasn't dawned on them that having a specialized firearms squad is a good idea.

Then again, even the ATF is not 100 percent focused on guns. Officially called the Bureau of Alcohol, Tobacco, Firearms and Explosives, it still handles the odd cases of booze and cigarette smuggling, although the vast majority of its work now targets things that go bang.

The agency traces its roots all the way back to 1791, when the first tax laws were instituted on alcohol and tobacco and the first agents were hired to enforce them. It holds up the campaign against Al Capone and the bootleggers as a glorious chapter in its heritage, and on its website it calls Eliot Ness "a legacy ATF agent."

However, the unit only went after gun crime in a major way after the 1968 Gun Control Act, which provides the basis for its present mandate. At that point it was a division of the IRS, but as it mushroomed to take on the new work, it broke away to become an independent bureau in the

Department of the Treasury on July 1, 1972, the official birthdate of the modern ATF.

Koz was seven years old when the modern ATF was born, growing up in Chicago, where his working-class Polish parents fled the inner city for the suburbs. From a young age, he wanted a career in law enforcement, though he imagined being a regular cop, and never foresaw going undercover with bikers. He didn't even ride motorcycles as a teenager, although he had a few friends "on the other side of the fence," which would later help him blend in with the outlaws.

After getting a degree in law enforcement, he spent a year as a special agent in the Immigration and Naturalization Service (INS) and then laterally transferred to the ATF in Sacramento. He came into the agency just after the government put a muzzle on it with the 1986 Firearm Owners' Protection Act.

The ATF has been shaped by both the efforts at gun control and the movement for gun rights in America. That movement has no real comparison in the world. While there are scattered gun-rights groups in Europe, Asia, Australia, Africa, and Latin America, none has a fraction of the influence of the gun lobby and its biggest organization, the NRA.

However, the NRA was not always the hard-line group that people know and love (or hate) today. The story of its transformation reflects broader shifts in politics and America's unique take on gun culture.

When veterans of the Civil War founded the NRA in 1871, they didn't do it in the South but in New York. Colonel William Church and General George Wingate[3] had fought on the Yankee side, and Church had worked at the *New York Times*, of all places. On the battlefield, Church and Wingate were startled by how bad the aim of Yankee troops was; the National Rifle

Association sought to improve that in gentlemanly outings to practice marksmanship.

"An association should be organized in this city [New York] to promote and encourage rifle-shooting on a scientific basis," Church wrote in the August 1871 issue of the *Army and Navy Journal*.[4] He didn't even mention the Second Amendment.

When the National Firearms Act passed in 1934 to curtail the tommy gun slingers, the NRA vigorously supported it. "I have never believed in the general practice of carrying weapons," said then NRA president Karl T. Frederick, an Olympic gold medalist in sports shooting. "I think it should be sharply restricted and only under licenses."[5]

This position largely held through the upheaval of the sixties, when the NRA supported the 1968 GCA. The NRA's leader, retired general Franklin Orth, testified before the House on supporting the ban on mail-order guns, like the one used to kill Kennedy. "We do not think any sane American, who calls himself an American, can object to placing into this bill the instrument which killed the president of the United States."[6]

But after the new ATF was born, the more militant side of the gun rights movement shot to the forefront. Rising crime was a key factor in both the 1968 law and the radicalization of the NRA. Many Americans saw their firearms as key to their self-defense in the face of gangs, drugs, muggings, and murders. While the old leadership was out of touch with these sentiments, a new guard rose, led by a man who would embody the modern fight for gun rights and be dubbed "Mr. NRA," Harlon Bronson Carter.

A bronze bust of Carter sits dominantly in the NRA museum at its headquarters in Fairfax, Virginia, depicting him with a bald head and square jaw, a tough guy reminiscent of Yul Brynner as King Mongkut. His influence was indeed monumental, transforming a niche club of hobbyists into a mass politicized force, or as the NRA says, "shaping it into a political power-house that serves millions of members, protecting their rights as gun owners at every level of government."[7]

Carter has a personal story of gun homicide that provides a bloody genesis for the movement. For many years, the case was under wraps, and when he was asked about it, he said he was a different Harlon Carter. But after the *New York Times* uncovered the court transcripts in 1981,[8] Carter owned up: he'd shot dead a Mexican teenager in what he claimed was self-defense. He needn't have bothered hiding it, as his followers saw it as a badge of honor.

"In many ways, you couldn't script a better origin myth for the modern NRA," writes the author Laura Smith. "The scene had everything that would come to define the organization: home and family, a fervent sense of self-protection, vigilantism, and standing your ground. For the NRA's critics, it exemplifies the association's tacit approval of race-based violence and white impunity."[9]

The story goes back to 1931, when Carter was a seventeen-year-old high school student in Laredo, where his father worked in the Border Patrol. As the transcripts relate, Carter came home from school to find his mother distressed about three boys near their house. They were described as Mexicans, although it is unclear if they were actually Mexican nationals or Mexican Americans. His mother suspected they had stolen their family car three weeks before.

Carter said he would "see if [he] could not get the boys to come to the house and talk to her," and picked up his shotgun. He was already an experienced shooter and NRA member. Carter found the lads, who were between twelve and fifteen, returning from a swimming hole and ordered them to follow him.

The eldest boy, Ramón Casiano, retorted, "Hell, no, we won't go to your house and you can't make us." He then pulled out a knife, and said, "Do you want to fight me?"

Carter lifted the shotgun and pointed it at the chest of the fifteen-year-old Ramón.

"Ramón told him not to do it, and put aside the rifle with his hand," one of the boys told the court. "Then Ramón stood about half a pace backwards and laughed. Then the American asked him if he thought that he was not going to use the rifle, and fired at him."

Ramón died instantly.

The judge instructed the jury that Carter had acted without legal authority, and he was found guilty and given the modest sentence of three years. After serving two, the conviction was overturned on the grounds that the witnesses were arrested for other crimes and the judge had given incorrect instructions. With his record cleansed, Carter went into law enforcement.

Carter followed his father into the Border Patrol, rising to lead the whole force, and then to head the entire INS. In 1975, he became director of the NRA's lobbying arm and pursued a radical position of opposing all gun laws, at odds with the leadership. A House Judiciary Committee asked if he really wanted to overturn the 1968 GCA and allow felons, drug addicts, and the mentally ill to arm up. It was "a price we pay for freedom," he said.[10]

It was Carter who introduced the idea of the government wanting to "grab our guns" into the mainstream. In his testimony to Congress, he said that gun control was a dangerous incremental process, comparing it with eating a packet of potato chips.

"It is kind of like the old Bert Lahr commercial that used to be on television. He used to eat a potato chip and say, 'I'll bet you can't eat just one.' And I have no doubt at all that if it is a good thing to be in favor of a fourteen-day waiting period, next year ATF is going to be back and say we cannot do in fourteen days. We will have to take ninety. Frankly, I can see where that leads, knowing how bureaucracies work. It is a little nibble first and I'll bet you can't eat just one."[11]

The NRA old guard attempted to quell Carter in 1976, firing employees who shared his militant line.[12] Carter and his allies took revenge at the 1977 annual meeting, which is known in gun folklore as the "Cincinnati Revolt."

Coming in force of numbers, they took over the proceedings and passed motions to commit the NRA to fighting gun control, boosting funds for lobbying, and installing Carter as executive vice president. When Carter took to the stage he pronounced, "Beginning in this place and at this hour, this period in NRA history is finished."[13]

The NRA shifted to opposing all gun restrictions and became one of the most effective lobbies Washington has ever seen.

The first president the NRA endorsed was Ronald Reagan in his 1980 election. Reagan was a longtime NRA member who adhered to its old-school policy of supporting certain gun control. He signed a 1967 law in California to ban open carry, a response to the Black Panthers. But he moved firmly to the NRA's new radicalism.

Reagan's resolve was severely tested in 1981 when a failed songwriter, John Hinckley Jr., put a bullet "an inch from his heart."[14] The twenty-five-year-old Hinckley was obsessed with the movie *Taxi Driver*, about an unstable man who wants to shoot a politician, and even stalked the star Jodie Foster and sought to impress her. Captured on film, Hinckley's assassination attempt shocked the public that a gunman was able to beat the perimeter of Secret Service agents and sneak up on the president. As Reagan walked from the Washington Hilton to his limousine, Hinckley pulled out a revolver and unloaded six bullets into the presidential entourage.

The first bullet went directly into the head of White House Press Secretary James Brady, leaving him brain damaged and partially paralyzed. Bullets then hit a police officer and an agent before the final round ricocheted off the armored door of the limo and hit the president under his left armpit.

Just as the political shootings of the sixties were key to gun laws, activists in 1981 called for a handgun ban. Yet true to his support for the NRA, Reagan not only resisted more gun control but pushed for more rights for gun owners.

A curious chapter then followed. Buoyed on by the NRA, Reagan recommended abolishing the ATF altogether. It could have been a knockout blow.

However, the Treasury responded with a counterpunch, proposing that the ATF be merged with the U.S. Secret Service. This horrified the NRA, which feared this would give the gun police even sharper teeth. As former agent Moore writes, "Congressional committees debated the proposal until 1982 when the NRA, realizing that slaying the ATF beast would pit them against the competent executives of the government's most prestigious service, hastened to revive the crippled bureau. A compliant Senate supported the abrupt about-face."

Instead, the NRA switched tack to the Firearms Owners' Protection Act, which finally got approved in 1986. It's one of the NRA's biggest triumphs. Designed especially to protect gun sellers, the act reduced penalties for several of their offenses from felonies to misdemeanors. It made it tougher to go after unlicensed dealers and specified that collectors and hobbyists couldn't be prosecuted. It also said gun dealers could not have their businesses inspected twice in a year; so if they had been checked once, they had a free ride until the next January.

But perhaps the most far-reaching clause was to prohibit the government from keeping any database of gun owners or gun sales. For the NRA, a registry was the prelude to national gun confiscation. But for the ATF, it meant that they had to struggle to do basic searches on weapons from crime scenes.

It was after this act that Koz began his career. The ATF agents had been criticized and muzzled and had their budgets slashed. But this didn't stop them from pursuing a tactic that was growing in federal law enforcement—infiltration.

———

The most iconic illegal gun-buy scene in cinema is in the 1976 movie *Taxi Driver*. Robert De Niro as Travis walks into a cheap hotel room with the traveling salesman Easy Andy, who rolls out his wares. Travis spends about nine hundred dollars to buy a .44 Magnum ("They use that in Africa for killing elephants," says Easy Andy), a .38 snub-nose revolver ("That'll stop anything that moves," Andy says), a Colt .25 automatic ("That's a beautiful little gun"), and a .380 Walther ("Just given out to officers. Ain't that a little honey").

More recently, a gun buy features in the TV series *Sons of Anarchy*, about an outlaw motorcycle club. The scene depicts the bikers driving into the dusty countryside to join Irish mobsters selling fully automatic Kalashnikovs to Italian mafiosi. A car of Chinese gun sellers offering their own weapons shows up, so an Irishman guns down two of them and seals his deal.

The mechanics of the scene are of course complete fantasy. But the show is correct in portraying biker gangs as a central target of the ATF, especially of their undercover ops. In fact, Koz explains, the ATF has done so much work on bikers it has become the go-to agency on them; if other law enforcement needs intelligence on the clubs, they call up the ATF.

The probes into biker gangs highlight how the drug and gun rackets are so intertwined. Bikers certainly handle and traffic guns, and the ATF targets them for this. But the ATF will also seek drug trafficking charges against them. The gangs are deep into narcotics, and this is easier to prosecute, even for the gun police.

Outlaw bikers are a funny animal in the ecosystem of organized crime. On one side, they are an element of the counterculture, an icon of the rebellious outlaw spirit, a way for (mostly) men to ride bikes, get wasted, and have a good time. On the other, they are involved in drugs, prostitution, guns, and a spattering of murders.

Any biker will remind you of the difference between regular motorcycle clubs, who really do just ride bikes, and outlaw clubs, whose members are known as "one percenters." These include the Hells Angels, Bandidos, Vagos, Warlocks, and Mongols.

Still, there is debate as to how dangerous these gangs are and how much energy law enforcement should spend on them. In their defense, they claim that although they have a few thugs in their ranks, they are legitimate brotherhoods that give people a sense of belonging. Prosecutors argue they use this brotherhood to enforce their criminal activities, and if they hadn't been brought to account, then America would be a more dangerous place.

The most infamous outlaw biker is Ralph "Sonny" Barger, a founder of a chapter of the Hells Angels. He penned a defense of the club in a memoir, filled with plenty of bravado of conquering "old ladies" and "lighting people up."

"One at a time, we bullwhipped them and beat them with spiked dog collars, broke their fingers with ball peen hammers," he writes on hitting some rival bikers who stole his ride.[15]

Barger has some bad words for celebrities. He recounts the infamous night when the Hells Angels provided security at a rock festival with the Rolling Stones back in 1969. The Angels battered revelers with pool cues for messing with their bikes and then killed a young Black man who pulled a gun. Barger blames the Stones: "They agitated the crowd, had the stage built too low, and then used us to keep the whole thing boiling. They got exactly what they wanted—a dark scary environment to play 'Sympathy for the Devil' . . . Just because you sing well doesn't mean you can act like a bunch of assholes."[16]

He is equally scathing of Hunter S. Thompson, who hung with the Angels for his famous book, taking a beating from them. "When he tried to act tough with us, no matter what happened, Hunter Thompson got scared. I ended up not liking him at all, a tall, skinny, typical hillbilly from Kentucky. He was a total fake."[17]

Barger spent years in prison for drugs, guns, and assault. But he did manage to beat a landmark case when the Hells Angels were charged under the Racketeer Influenced and Corrupt Organizations Act (RICO). As Barger headlines his chapter on it: "RICO My Ass—the Law with the Funny Name."

Passed in 1970, RICO is the legal big gun for the federal government to target organized crime, from the Mafia to street gangs. Its essence is to prove there is a criminal enterprise with a name and hierarchical structure that is used to commit offenses such as drug trafficking, murder, and extortion. After bombs blamed on the Angels injured two California police officers, the feds hit them with RICO in 1979. The case highlights the ongoing argument about the nature of biker clubs.

Barger's defense was that while some Angels had sold drugs and murdered people, they did this as individuals and not as an organized crime syndicate. The prosecutors failed to provide enough evidence of the bikers conspiring to commit the crimes, and the jury acquitted Barger and his crew.

It was a major slap to federal prosecutors, who realized they would need stronger evidence to take down biker gangs—the kind of evidence you get only from the inside.

In Sacramento, Koz went after street gangs like the Bloods and the Crips, which made headlines in the crack era of the eighties. He made decent gun busts and took a few gangsters off the street. But he wanted to go deeper.

For many in the ATF, the job involves long hours of tedious work, driving around to inspect licensed gun dealers and wading through their paperwork. But Koz saw a few in the agency were going undercover with the gangsters. The bulky Polish American wouldn't get far joining the Crips, so he transferred to Milwaukee and developed his biker persona.

"I looked at it as a way for a guy like me, who didn't have an ethnic background to join an African American gang or grow up in a Hispanic neighborhood, to join a Hispanic gang."

Koz is blessed to naturally look like a biker, and he added to his commanding presence by sprouting stubble, growing his hair long, and sporting a leather jacket and boots. But he was missing an ingredient: he didn't know how to ride bikes. So he got lessons from an ATF colleague who had worked with bikers in Ohio and was soon racing around on two wheels to make gun deals.

Koz began doing "buy busts." This is a technique inherited from anti-drug work in which undercovers buy dope, and when the drugs are handed over, they badge the dealers and put on the cuffs. ATF agents do the same with gun sellers.

Koz scoured the streets for hustlers selling guns illegally. He found that looking like a biker didn't only help him get to white criminals but was also a good cover to approach Asian, Latino, and African American gangsters. Over the years, he would take many guns off the streets this way, including busting an Asian gang selling fully automatic Kalashnikovs and one hawker with a grenade launcher.

This is the kind of work many agents have done when they say they have gone undercover. But it is not deep undercover. To take the next step, Koz would need to assume a fake character so that he could build relationships with gangsters over years.

To understand the thugs that Koz was trying to infiltrate, it helps to look at the story of Billyjack Curtis. While Koz was taking illegal guns off the street, Billyjack was putting guns back onto them.

Billyjack wasn't a biker. But he has a similar profile, as a white working-class drug dealer who joined the Dirty White Boys prison gang. Billyjack's troubled life and attitudes reflect those of the roughnecks Koz was trying to blend in with. Billyjack even had a friend who bashed his own dad's brains out with a shotgun butt. His criminal career illustrates the modus operandi of running guns from small-town America. And it shows how the black markets of guns and drugs are inseparable.

Born in small-town Maine, he got his name from the *Billy Jack* movies of the sixties and seventies, about a half Navajo Vietnam vet who fights for justice. Billyjack's dad was also a Vietnam vet, and a gun lover who kept sixty firearms in their home. They lived in a poor corner of Maine, where his dad hunted in the forest for food, eventually making a living as a guide taking tourists bear hunting. When he was ten, Billyjack got his first gun as a birthday present, an 1886 Winchester that had been passed down. "It was one of the few guns I ever sold legally," he says.

Billyjack had a difficult childhood, from his poor and troubled family to being bullied at school for his ragged clothes—until he grew bigger and learned to fight and saw himself as a bully beater like his namesake in the movies. He found hope when he graduated from high school and made it into military intelligence training. But when he had dental work from a colonel, he was prescribed opioids; then he did caddying for the colonel, who gave him ziplocked bags of the pills. "Shit went downhill quick," Billyjack says. He developed an opioid addiction and got an honorable discharge.

With his separation pay, Billyjack headed to Lawrence, Massachusetts, where he had an army buddy linked to a Dominican gang. His military money went straight into a quarter pound of cocaine. He wanted to be a drug dealer like those in the films he was watching.

"You remember the movie *New Jack City*? There's all these big movies with these drug dealers and they are being glorified. And these gangsters all had guns. Believe me, that played a part in it too. We all think we're starring in our own movie. Really, we're just an extra in somebody else's movie. We're not the star of anything."

It wasn't hard for Billyjack to do the sums. Many of the white folks in rural Maine had access to guns. And they wanted drugs, with the opioid epidemic blowing up there in the nineties ahead of the rest of the country. On the flipside, the Dominican gangs had plenty of drugs and they wanted guns, as they faced stricter laws in Massachusetts. Billyjack could bounce from one to the other and keep trading up.

It was great money. Except Billyjack went from his pill habit into a hard-core heroin addiction. And he threw cocaine into the mix to keep high enough to be dealing.

"I was living off the speedball. I would mix coke and heroin," he says. "I would get my bulk package, I would take out an ounce of coke for myself, I would take out twenty grams of heroin for myself, mix it all together, and that was my sustenance for the week. I would use that around the clock."

The junkies in rural Maine would often steal guns, sometimes from their own families. Billyjack would pay them in cocaine and heroin and then trade the guns up in Lawrence for more dope.

It's wacky math. He could buy a pistol for what the user considered was $500 worth of cocaine, but he had gotten it for $200. Then he sold that pistol for what he considered $1,000 worth of cocaine, so he was multiplying his money. In turn, the Dominicans were paying less for the cocaine, bringing it from New York. It illustrates the elastic and connected prices in the drugs-to-guns black market.

The Dominicans liked handguns, which they could conceal on the street, and they liked badass-looking weapons to show off: submachine guns, firearms with bulging drum clips. Billyjack found better guns from junkies in the larger city of Portland, Maine, and began trading there, picking up a Heckler & Koch MP5, which scored him a lot of heroin.

One day, Billyjack was delivering a pistol and happened to have it in a bag full of bullets. He was pulling the pistol box out, and a Dominican was looking right past and finally asked what was in the duffel bag.

"That is ammunition," Billyjack said.

"Food?" the gangster asked.

"No, ammunition."

"Food, yeah. We call it 'food,'" he said. "How much for the food?"

"I don't know. Make me an offer."

"I'll give a dollar per shell."

"There's ten thousand rounds in there."

"I'll take them all."

Of course, the ten grand came in heroin, a bulging bag of forty "fingers" (heroin stuffed into the fingers of rubber gloves). Billyjack began driving around to Walmarts to buy thousands of rounds and then driving them up to the hoods.

While he was doing the circuit, there was a quadruple homicide in Lawrence involving Dominican gangsters. He didn't know if any of his guns were involved. But he knew he was supplying violent criminals.

The fact that guns can be bartered is a principal rule of gun-onomics. It's often for drugs, but there are other cases, as in Africa, of firearms being bartered for diamonds, ivory, or cows.

However, a problem with always bartering for Billyjack was that he could lack any real money. Drugs and guns become a currency that criminals trade other goods for: cars, TVs, sex. In some war zones, such as Yemen, guns are also used as a form of currency.

But you still need hard cash, and dealers fight over money. When one owed Billyjack, he broke into the dealer's house and got twelve thousand dollars from a safe. You figure that drug dealers won't call the cops. Except this one did, and Billyjack got four years in prison.

Behind bars, Billyjack got into vicious fights and took brutal beatings. And he joined the Dirty White Boys, a gang that spread through the federal system and leaked into state penitentiaries. With the protection of the DWB, he carried on dealing on the inside.

The issue of drugs and guns in prisons is telling. In Latin America, inmates will often have both. On a visit to a prison in Honduras, I even saw inmates with Uzis hanging off their chests. But American prisons are almost completely gun-free; the authorities manage to enforce gun control there. In contrast, American prisons are flooded with drugs. Billyjack describes how inmates got weed and heroin in by bribing a corrupt prison officer—until the guard got caught and ended up doing prison time himself.

When Billyjack got out, he found new places to score such as Florida, where crack cocaine was dirt cheap, and he could fly it back. "I did six trips from Tampa back to Maine with an ass full of crack," he says.

He discovered new tricks for smuggling the guns into Lawrence. One was to become a member of AAA, drive a car down the road from his home, and call for a tow truck. When the tow truck came, he would give an address in Lawrence. It worked like a charm, as police never search cars being towed.

But over the years he kept tripping up, breaking parole or getting into sticky situations that sent him back inside.

When Billyjack's father died, he skipped parole after the funeral and hid out at his parents' house in the woods. While he was there, a friend called Mike asked for a ride to his own father's house to pick up some clothes. He would pay twenty pills for the bother. It took Billyjack into a hellish situation.

When Mike went inside his dad's house, Billyjack waited by the car. He heard a bang followed by thuds. Mike had blasted his father in the head with a 20-gauge shotgun, then got a ten-inch knife and stabbed him fifteen times in the back. Finally, he took the butt of the shotgun and smashed his dad's head until it was largely separated from the body. It was revenge for years of child molesting, according to later court testimony.

Mike emerged from the house in bare feet covered with blood. He had brains on his pants. But he got back in the car as if nothing had happened.

"Is everything okay?" Billyjack asked him.

"Yeah, everything is fine," Mike replied.

Billyjack tried to remain calm but was freaking out inside. "In my head, I'm like, 'Oh my fucking God. Now he's going to fucking try and cap me.' So we are driving down the road, and I am looking for a telephone pole to drive the car into if he makes a move."

But Mike carried on nonchalantly, talking about a lumberyard where they had worked and wiping his hands on his brain-splattered pants. Billyjack dropped Mike at his girlfriend's house and made an anonymous call to 911. But police traced the call and brought him in.

In any case, Mike turned himself in at the county jail. He later pleaded insanity, and in a rare case got off. Billyjack was soon back in jail for jumping parole. And then out again and back dealing.

Billyjack's criminal career finally hit a wall when he hit his forties. The DEA got onto one of his associates, and Billyjack was caught up in the testimonies. He made a plea deal, part of which meant owning up to the gun trafficking. He bargained it down to a year, as he wasn't the main target, and the feds were more interested in the drugs. It again shows the stiffer sentences for drugs than for guns. When Billy finally got out of jail, he swore he was out of the game.

When I speak to him, he is struggling to make a living shoveling snow, barely able to feed his children.

"Honestly, I ruined my life, I'll tell you right now. I'm forty-six and I have nothing. I live paycheck to paycheck, below the poverty line. I don't know how I can make a future."

Being a gun trafficker is not as glamorous as it looks in the movies.

———

To blend in with such roughnecks, Koz had to build a convincing identity, which takes a lot of time and sacrifice. By then, Koz was in his thirties and married, with one baby and another on the way. He wanted to make a difference, but he was also attracted by the adventure.

"To me it was always the challenge, the adrenaline rush behind it, the ability to know that I can outsmart the criminals and get into these guys when people say you can't," he says.

In 1996 he moved to Los Angeles and began his first infiltration. Biker gangs are organized into chapters, which draw from a local area. This same territorial division is used in most mobs. Maras have cliques; drug cartels have plazas; the Mafia has families. Koz set his sights on the Hollywood chapter of the Vagos, which has a clubhouse just off Hollywood Boulevard.

*   *   *

It didn't take Koz long to find trouble. His way in was a street-hustler informant called Junior who had worked with local police. The ATF gave Junior a Harley-Davidson and sporadic payments of a few hundred dollars and encouraged him to hang with the Vagos.

Junior got close to a member who worked in a tattoo shop on the Sunset Strip. But the plan nosedived when Junior raced down Sunset Boulevard on his ATF-issued Harley and was hit by a car and killed.

Not giving up, Koz followed the lead himself. He dressed in his leathers and rode to the ink shop to explain that Junior had died. The Vagos tattooist looked Koz up and down and told him to take a trip. They got on their bikes and rode across Hollywood to the Vagos clubhouse. Koz thought this was a great opportunity, but he headed into the hornet's nest.

"We pull into a chain-link fence area where there were several other bikes parked. It's a white cinder-block building, no windows, and they went inside and had a meeting.

"I couldn't go in the meeting because I am not a member. And then after their meeting concluded after about an hour and a half, they walked me inside and shut the door. This is day one of me meeting these guys, and they patted me down for a wire. They discovered I was carrying a gun, and they started questioning me."

The gun was a Sig Sauer 9 mm, ATF issue. A dozen Vagos surrounded Koz, hardened criminals from their twenties up to their forties, the majority white, a few Hispanic.

Koz claimed he had just moved to L.A. and had the gun for protection. "It's not meant to be against you guys or anything like that," he said.

But they dropped the bomb. They knew Junior had been an ATF informant. They fired more questions, and one of the bikers pulled out a .357 revolver and pointed it straight at Koz, who was so nervous that he was visibly shaking. The bikers asked him what he was hiding.

"Yes, I am nervous," he blurted out. "Because I don't know you guys, and you are all of a sudden questioning me about someone I barely knew, telling me if he was an ATF informant, and I don't need this."

Koz sputtered whatever bullshit came into his head, fake jobs, fake addresses.

"I was just trying to talk myself out of a situation that I thought was going south really fast. In hindsight, I could have legitimately been killed in there, and nobody would have known. I wasn't wearing a body wire. So at the end of the questioning, I felt all I need to do is somehow get out."

The bikers finally opened the door, but they wanted Koz to come with them. He got on his bike and rode behind the pack. But when they turned one way on Hollywood Boulevard, he turned the other and slammed on the gas, heading to a meet spot with ATF agents. He was still shaking and dropped the motorcycle on the ground.

"I didn't put the kickstand down or nothing. I just let it go and told everybody I was done. I didn't want to do this anymore."

But Koz was just getting started.

A new break came a few weeks later. Koz's colleague was in Vegas making his own inroads into a Vagos chapter, and he said that Koz was a good guy who was given a rough treatment. Word spread to the Hollywood chapter, and they sent Koz a message on his pager (back in the days of those wonderful machines) inviting him to a party the following weekend.

They told Koz not to have a gun, as their rule was that only their members could take firearms into the clubhouse. This point grabs my attention. The Vagos wanted a monopoly of firepower in their turf, and I find similar rules in other gangs. They have their own forms of gun control.

Koz arrived to find a hundred Vagos had shut down the street and filled it with parked motorcycles. They were friendlier this time, and he talked casually over tankards of beer.

The clubs have a need to recruit to replace those who retire or are sent to prison, and the federal agents play on this. Koz portrayed himself as a guy doing odds and ends, which made him useful to work for them, and he was tough-looking. By the end of the night, Koz was invited to become what they call a "hang-around," an associate of the gang, on the first rung of the ladder. This meant he had to do shitwork, like hauling heavy stuff and running errands. But he was in the door.

After a few months as a hang-around, Koz moved up to the grade of a prospective member, or "prospect." For this, the Vagos made him fill out an application form with his name, address, jobs, and copies of his license and vehicle registration, and they gave it to a private investigator. But by this time, he had a whole fake identity created.

As a prospect, Koz would work security for after-hours parties that the Hollywood chapter hosted. They would charge entry, sell alcohol, and have strippers on a pair of poles while a DJ spun records. It was a good money-maker. And it was Hollywood, so a smattering of actors came to enjoy the grimy atmosphere.

One night, Koz was on security when an Armenian guy showed up and had too many drinks. "He was mouthy and disrespectful, and in the biker culture, disrespect is something they don't tolerate," Koz says. "We had to tune him up. I was there when that happened. I was part of it. If there was a patch [full] member that got involved into an altercation, then as a prospect member you would have to get engaged, or you could face being kicked out or getting your ass kicked by your own men."

As the bikers were punching the Armenian guy, Koz grabbed him and walked him into the parking lot. But the guy kept fighting, and other Vagos piled in, keen for blood. A biker rammed the Armenian guy's head into the side of a car and took off the mirror. "He was bleeding pretty bad. He was beat up pretty bad. But we didn't know who he was."

The incident highlights the hazards of deep undercover. Koz took part in the fight even if he was trying to limit the beating. Later he would handle the firearms of mobsters and watch them do drug deals. By such actions, federal agents can be accused of taking part in the crimes they are meant to stop. But they see the rewards of sending the criminals to prison as outweighing the risks.

It turned out the guy they beat was also a mobster, a member of Armenian Power, a gang that is strong in Los Angeles and has links to the Russian Mafia. Two weeks later, a mob of twenty Armenian Power thugs gathered in front of the clubhouse looking for retribution.

"The Vagos were getting nervous. They had access to weapons: ax handles, baseball bats, machetes, guns, knives, whatever. They thought something heavy was going to go down."

However, the chapter president went over to talk to the head of the Armenian Power mob. They came to an agreement not to beat the crap out of each other. And that agreement morphed into a loose alliance, making drug deals and respecting turf.

Amid the alliance, Koz went out with the Armenian Power, and one of them popped a trunk to show off twenty Kalashnikovs that he boasted were fully automatic. Koz was getting closer to the source of guns. In doing so, he was putting himself in the firing line.

Koz came closest to death when working security in the early hours. He was standing on the sidewalk in front of the clubhouse when a car drove past and a guy pulled a gun out and fired. It was a classic drive-by shooting.

"Somebody held out a hand with a pistol, turned their hand like out of a sunroof, and just went *boom, boom, boom*. I was probably ten feet from the shots. I couldn't even react. I just saw muzzle flashes and sounds and didn't even have time to duck or hit the ground. Luckily, maybe two or three shots fired and missed me."

Koz never found who pulled the trigger. A number of criminals angry with the Vagos could have been in the car. Koz just happened to be the one standing at the gate that night. But if the bullets had been a few feet over, he would have left two fatherless children.

As a prospect, Koz still wasn't allowed to carry his own gun when he was with the Vagos. But with bullets coming so close, he started packing anyway without telling them. Which got him into the freak situation of being arrested while undercover.

The arrest came as the Vagos were trying a curious shakedown. When a bar had refused to serve rowdy members, they sued it for discrimination and won. This gave them an idea for a new racket: they would provoke bars into refusing them service and then take them to court.

Koz joined the Vagos going mob-handed to a bar. But as the shouting got out of hand, the bar staff chickened out of ejecting them and called the cops. The officers spread the Vagos on the concrete and patted them down. Which was when they found Koz's piece.

"All the Vagos look at me like, 'What the fuck. You have a gun on you.' They put me in the squad car, and I can't break role. I can't say, 'Time out.' So I'm the only one to get arrested there, and I got taken to jail."

The LAPD station happened to have his next-door neighbor, a police officer, working there. Koz managed to speak to him one-on-one in the cell.

"Listen," Koz said. "You know me. Here is what is going on. We have got to make it look like it's legit. You can't tell anybody. But here, contact this guy."

He got him to call ATF, and they made the arrest look real. Koz got charged with an illegal gun, and it was even the Vagos who paid to bail him out. The mug shot shows him in a denim cutoff jacket over a checked shirt, a wild goatee and hard eyes, looking very convincing.

The agents talked to the judge and got him to convict Koz, while not giving him jail time. He is one of a tiny number of federal agents to have been convicted of a crime while undercover.

This had complications. While his conviction was in a phony name, his fingerprints were real, sent to an FBI database. To counter this, the ATF went to the FBI to stop it crossing into his true identity.

But in the end, the whole ruse turned out in Koz's favor. The Vagos believed he could never be a cop and gave him the green light to become a full member. He got to put a Vagos patch on his jacket: a red picture of Loki, the Viking deity of mischief.

Bikers take their patches very seriously. Losing the patch to another gang is a shameful act, and any civilian caught wearing a patch risks a beating. (So don't think it looks cool to put a Hells Angel skull on your jacket.)

Koz just had one last thing to do before he got to wear Loki—get rat-packed.

"They called me into a backyard of a residence, and there was a good amount of Vagos, maybe fifty, sixty. They had me pull my motorcycle in, and they immediately started punching me and knocking me off my bike. They were yelling and screaming at me, and I really didn't know what was happening. I couldn't fight back because there was too many of them . . .

"And then after, I don't know, thirty seconds, I get pushed in front of my president, who's holding up the full patch, and he hands it to me and tells me I got five minutes to sew it on. Then everybody gives you a hug and congratulates you. And then you're full patched. Everybody starts drinking, treating you like a member now. You've made it through."

The joy didn't last long. Within two weeks, the Vagos discovered that Koz was undercover.

The leak came from a dead man. Or rather, the dead man's girlfriend.

After the informant Junior perished in a bike accident, his girlfriend had rifled through his belongings and found Koz's business card. When she later ran into Vagos members, she told them about it.

"She spilled the beans that this is who he was working with, blah, blah, blah," Koz says. "And I got caught off guard again. It didn't take a rocket scientist to connect the dots that I was the ATF agent."

ATF got wind the cover was blown from another informant. It also picked up talk of the Vagos threatening to put Koz six feet under. "It was guys just getting pissed off, like, 'Fuck that dude. We're going to go kill him,' stuff like that."

The ATF wasn't taking the risk that it was just bluster. They sent a SWAT team to camp out in Koz's house, with his wife and two young children.

"My wife was very nervous at first, and it took me to calm her down, like say, 'Hey, listen. This is protocol.' The ATF SWAT team would rent a couple of minivans, and they would live in our house, so when I was coming home, I would have to radio to them."

The arrests came down soon after. On Koz's info, the ATF got a search warrant for a house that held the Vagos armory. They found over twenty-five guns including SKS rifles and sawed-off shotguns. They arrested over a dozen Vagos members in Los Angeles and other cities, charging them with firearm and drug offenses.

"In retrospect, it was a dent," Koz says. "But the impact is twofold. You get certain members criminally charged, but you also make the impact, because now they have got that reputation that they've been infiltrated, and they've been done from the inside."

The operation also served as a catalyst for the ATF to carry out more undercover stings. Koz joined thirty agents in launching an enhanced undercover program, pooling their experience to create procedures for long-term complex probes and building a cadre of agents who could pull them off. The tactic of big conspiracy cases, which got media splashes and which prosecutors made their names on, was getting sewn into the DNA of the gun police.

———

While the ATF was beefing up its undercover ops, it was still struggling with the restrictions from the 1986 act. To understand what that means in practice, you need to see the ATF National Tracing Center in Martinsburg, West Virginia. It's a graphic illustration of how the NRA has put such incredible clamps on a federal agency.

I visit on a rainy June morning, shown around by a program manager Neil Troppman, and Scott Curley, the ATF's deputy chief of public affairs. It's a vast gray federal building in the midst of rural West Virginia, with its rich greenery, spacious generic towns, and Civil War sites.

After a filter of security at the perimeter wall and a second filter of security in the building lobby, I'm in. Surrounded by boxes. Huge stacks of them. Boxes filling rooms and boxes lining corridors, boxes boxing people in at their desks, and, through a door into the back, pallets with . . . more boxes.

Each box is full of records from gun dealers who have gone out of business, a number that's topped seven hundred thousand, and more arrive every day. Some records are nice and neat, others with scrawling handwriting, and still others that have been soaked and dried, some in floods like the one in New Orleans. The high-tech tools in the center include trolleys to carry the boxes, guillotines to trim paper, and, only recently decommissioned, a room of microfilm.

The staff, a few dozen ATF employees and a bunch of contractors, work quietly around the boxes and trolleys and pallets, and sit in cubicles to make phone calls. At first, it looks like complete chaos, but as I watch and as Neil and Scott explain it to me, it starts to make sense. There is an order to the madness. In fact, there is organizational genius at work.

In this low-tech system with legal handicaps, the skeleton team traces guns. Huge amounts of them. It's in this one center that they trace every single request from police departments across the United States and every request from seventy-five to ninety countries each year where guns sold in the United States end up.

The Draco and WASR-10 used in the attack on the ICE agents were traced here. Rifles and handguns recovered at the San Bernardino attack were traced here. Guns used in the Las Vegas massacre, the Pittsburgh synagogue shooting, Parkland, Columbine, Virginia Tech, Sandy Hook—it's here all the traces took place.

And they are just the beginning. The bulk of the requests are from the many shootings that don't top cable news, that happen every day in Baltimore, St. Louis, Flint, Dodge City, Mexico City, Guatemala City, Bogotá. Then there are all the guns taken from criminals that haven't been used in shootings.

In 2018 alone, that was over 443,000 requests. And somehow they manage to try to trace them all. Without a searchable database.

This is the billion-dollar fact that many are unaware of. There is no searchable database for guns in the United States because the law won't allow it. If a car is in a hit and run, a police officer can type the license plate into a computer and, *bam*, they get the name of the owner. If they trace a crime to a house, they can check the tax records and, *bam*, there's the owner. Guns are a special case. The law actually stops the agency from using technology.

If you didn't know that, it's unsurprising. Many police officers don't know it.

"Even law enforcement sometimes calls up and says, 'Here's the serial number. Can you trace this gun real quick,'" Neil says. "'Well, no. We can do this whole process. But we're not entering the serial number into a database.'"

To make sense of the weirdness of the Tracing Center system, you have to go back to the most far-reaching tenet in the 1986 firearms act. The fear of a gun registry is the big collective paranoia of the gun movement, a dread that began in the sixties and was nurtured by the NRA. It's the idea that the American government, or the United Nations, or foreign invaders will use it to go house by house and take away people's weapons.

The efforts to stop a gun registry were written into 18 U.S. Code 926. This prohibits any records from active gun dealers being "transferred to a facility owned, managed, or controlled by the United States." In other words, none of the records of the 140,000 licensed gun dealers currently working can be stored here at the Tracing Center.

It's the records of the stores that go out of business that arrive, as otherwise they would disappear. But even with those, the code prohibits "any system of registration of firearms, firearms owners, or firearms transactions or dispositions be established."[18] So they can't put those records into a database.

But there is a caveat. The lawmakers did concede that tracing guns from crime scenes is useful. So the code still grants officials the "authority to inquire into the disposition of any firearm in the course of a criminal investigation."

It's at the Tracing Center where they have to deal with these contradictory instructions: don't keep records of guns but trace guns. So they constructed this archaic system. It wasn't so bad in 1986, when most of the government ran on paper. But as everything got computerized, it has become increasingly antiquated.

Except they do use some computers—but in creative ways. They have started taking photos of the paper records and putting the photos onto computers. This reduces the need for the tons of paper and could eventually allow them to get rid of all the boxes. But the information in the photos is not actually searchable; they still have go through them one by one. Again, it's a weird system created to deal with a law designed to make the job harder.

Exactly how they can use technology while respecting the law is a matter of fine legal debate. And the ATF's lawyers are keenly aware of the watchful gun lobby and the constant accusations that the government is secretly making a firearms registry anyway. An interesting example is when they receive records from a former gun dealer in a hard drive. As this is digital data, they have to print it out and then destroy the hard drive.

"They are digital, so by nature they are searchable," Neil says. "It's data, so we actually have a process that we audit, where we take that information and make it static and nonsearchable by name, so it's just like everything else. And then it's destroyed."

He still has a straight face.

Neil explains how the cranky system works when it comes to an actual search.

Police seize a smoking gun from a crime scene. They look at the serial number and call the Tracing Center. But the center wants more information that is etched on the gun: model and caliber, country of origin, name of manufacturer and importer, and any other markings. "We really need the full description of the gun to make sure we're chasing the right firearm," Neil says.

The problem is there is no single system for serial numbers. Every manufacturer has its own way, and some run duplicate numbers for different lines. Sometimes, the police officer may also confuse a patent number or something else for a serial number.

They finally get all the info over to the Tracing Center, and the team starts getting on the phone and sending emails. They get ahold of the manufacturer or importer, find out where they sent the gun. Then they go to the wholesaler, find out where they sent the gun. Then they go to the dealer, and if they are still in business, they call them, but if they are out of business, they go through the Himalayan mountains of boxes. Finally, they get the name of the buyer from the Form 4473. Although they may find out that the gun was stolen or sold privately, so they hit a brick wall.

Amazingly, they are successful in tracing many weapons. But it takes time. If there is a really urgent case, it can be done in twenty-four hours, but the average time is eleven days, which is a lot for a murder investigation.

I struggle to make sense of the muddle. If they are going to be searching through all the boxes anyway, how much would that really compromise gun owners if it were in a format that could be searched digitally? And if the name of the buyer is on a Form 4473 that can be checked anyway, is it such a big deal if it's held by the government?

For gun hard-liners, it is a big deal. It's the mantra that a gun registry is the first step to confiscation.

Scott, the ATF's deputy chief of public affairs, says there is also a logic to only going after the data of crime guns and ignoring the rest. "Just like with fingerprints. If I roll your fingerprints and I don't do anything with them, I can't link it to other dots. What good is it if I roll every fingerprint?" he says.

He hits back that the ATF still uses technology in other ways to tackle gun crime. Most traces now come through an electronic system called eTrace, even though they are searched for manually. The "ballistic profiles" of spent cartridges found at crime scenes are put into a database called the National Integrated Ballistic Information Network (NIBIN), where they can be linked to ammo from the same gun found at other crime scenes. All this info goes into what is called "Crime Gun Intelligence," a growing discipline within the ATF to use data from across the board to track down the shooters.

"You have to collect all the data from all the sources, put them together, and that helps you create those leads," Scott says. "It's connecting the dots. The more dots you have, the more connections you have, the quicker you can identify anomalies. And when you identify anomalies, that is where you can have the most impact."

They can also cross-reference the data with human intelligence gathered in the trenches by agents like Koz. Whose second undercover op took him to the very small towns of the Virginias that surround the Tracing Center.

———

Outlaw motorcycle clubs reach far, all the way to Europe and Australia and to many quiet corners of America. Whereas the bikers in Los Angeles operate in the multiethnic gang system, in rural Virginia they operate in mostly white small towns. Here, the Warlocks dominate.

According to their origin story, the Warlocks were founded by thirteen sailors on the USS *Shangri-La* aircraft carrier back in 1966. At home, they set up a mother chapter in Orlando, Florida, and spread through the South, especially recruiting veterans. Their patch: a blazing phoenix. One of their mottos: "Our business is none of your fucking business."

Like other bikers, the Warlocks got big into crystal meth as it spread wildly at the turn of the millennium. When the daughter of a Virginia police chief died of an overdose, a probe was launched. And when the local drug task force couldn't crack the Warlocks, they called in the biker specialists.

Koz and a fellow agent first moved to Woodstock, Virginia, population five thousand, before settling in nearby Winchester, population twenty-seven thousand. To see his family, Koz had to drive to Washington and take a five-hour flight to Los Angeles. But away from home, he could really live the biker lifestyle.

It was a tough start. In the small towns, everyone knows each other, and they are wary of the law. "Nobody wanted to talk about anything to do with the Warlocks, because they knew they would probably know somebody in their family," Koz says. "The Warlocks were kind of the big boys on the block. People either feared them or were in their corner."

They created a cover of working for a property management company, setting up a fictional office in downtown Winchester. When they zoomed around on their bikes and hung out at bars, the Warlocks finally accepted them as potential recruits, and they were back in the hang-around phase. If you were too keen, the gang could sniff you out as a fed. So Koz put in a whole nine months before he graduated to prospect. Over another seven months, he worked to get fully patched, and then he ran with them as a full member for another eight months, adding up to two years being a Warlock in the sticks.

As a patched member, Koz got to follow the drug operations down to Florida, where he met a ranking member with a fully automatic machine gun. He also saw the Warlocks make meth deals with their allies in the Hells Angels in Maryland. To build the case, he sewed a recorder under his patch and had a switch to turn it on and off inside his pocket. In biker culture, the patches are sacred, and nobody is allowed to touch them, so the recorder wasn't discovered. But it felt like it weighed a ton.

The Warlocks were looking hard for ATF infiltrators. Yet Koz was still carrying an ATF weapon, a Smith & Wesson five-shot revolver. This caused him a problem one night when a Warlock and his wife came into his cover house and spotted the gun in Koz's belt.

"He sees my weapon, and he wants to take a look at it," Koz says. "So I hand him my gun. You have to take care of little nuances, like how do you hand a gun in an undercover world to a criminal. Do you open the cylinder, unload it, and hand it to them like a cop? Or do you just hand them a gun? You know, we have to train ourselves to act like a criminal would. So I just take a loaded gun and hand it to them like a regular guy. And now he's got a loaded gun in his hand, and that's my gun, sitting in my house."

Winchester is very close to the ATF Tracing Center in Martinsburg. And that happened to be exactly where the wife of the Warlock worked.

"So when I handed them my gun, and his wife is sitting there, he looked at his wife and he tells us, 'Hey, my wife works for the ATF Tracing Center, and she can run this gun, and see whatever.'"

Koz was panicking, but after a few tense minutes the Warlock handed him back his weapon. After that, the agents would go into stores and buy guns in their false names, creating their own paper trails. They also had the issue of what to do with the woman infiltrating the gun police.

"ATF wanted to fire her immediately because of her being married to a member of the Warlocks, and we couldn't trust her. But I said, 'You can't fire her immediately because who is that going to point back to? And why are you going to tell her she got fired?' So they put her on ice for a little bit. And then they figured out a way to just dismiss her without her knowing it was because of her association to the gang."

The Warlocks were all white guys, but they cut across class lines. While many were workingmen or dirt poor, other members were wealthier, like a commercial airline pilot.

"There are people out there that want to be attracted to that lifestyle of bad-boy image, and they feel they can gain that through these gangs. Sometimes the gangs are taking advantage of them because they've got money, and they let them in because they pay a lot. But then they get the right to brag around and say, 'I'm part of this gang.'

"But then you've got to take the baggage that comes with it. So when criminal activity occurs, you've got a decent job like that, you can't just say, 'Time out, I didn't sign up for this . . .' You just as much run the risk of going to jail as anybody else."

They bonded in fights. When tough nuts challenged the Warlocks, they excelled in beating them down. And keeping true, Koz swung with the best of them. "Of course, you're defending yourself, but there are times, I will admit, that mentally you get to a point where your persona takes over."

Koz's friendships with the bikers also became genuine.

"We're not robots as human beings in law enforcement, so being under-cover in a role for that period of time, you do develop the friendships . . . You know deep down that they're a criminal. You know deep down that they shouldn't be in this gang. But somehow there is a commonality. These guys really go out of their way to like you, and you can't help but do that back. It's too complicated from a human-behavior standpoint to just turn that on and off like a light switch."

When a chapter member got killed in a bike accident, Koz and his partner were even pallbearers at the funeral.

Another issue was women. While most outlaw gangs don't allow female members, they like to hang around with them, especially strippers. To take the pressure off, Koz brought in a female ATF agent to pose as his girl-friend. They invented a cover story that she was living in California, and Koz used that as an excuse to disappear from time to time to see his real wife and children.

"It was very difficult for my wife because now she's almost like a single parent, because I'm gone so long. I missed a lot of things, things I'll see them talk about from time to time, and I'll have no recollection of it because I wasn't there. And it breaks my heart.

"But a lot of that family connection I have, and my kids, was also a lot of my driving internal force to do the right thing. And I had an ending to get back to. And not to fall too deep into the role where I want to be one of them."

*   *   *

The undercover work that Koz did, that the ATF, DEA, and FBI all do, raises deep ethical questions. Koz watched the Warlocks commit illegal activities for two years before the agents busted them. Bags of crystal meth don't have serial numbers, so you can't trace them the way you can guns. Federal agents have almost certainly watched bricks of heroin be trafficked that have ended up killing people who overdosed. But again, heroin can't be traced in the same way guns would be in Fast and Furious.

The feds see the risks as worth the result. Koz built a sprawling case stretching from Florida to Virginia to Maryland. When he finally broke cover in 2003, the feds arrested thirty-four bikers, including senior members of the Warlocks and Hells Angels, on federal firearms, drugs, and conspiracy charges. They hauled in 120 guns, along with cash, body armor, crystal meth, cocaine, and marijuana.

After two years of being deep undercover, Koz was looking forward to getting back to a normal life with his family. But the success only opened the door for the ATF to do bigger and bigger stings.

———

The relationship between gun rights advocates and the ATF is not black and white. Some agents are themselves gun enthusiasts. Some gun nuts are big supporters of law enforcement. But there is an edge of the gun rights movement that spews pure venom at the ATF and sees all its enforcement as illegitimate repression.

This hatred goes back to the first raids that followed the 1968 Gun Control Act. In 1971, federal agents stormed the home of veteran Ken Ballew looking for weapons and shot him, leaving him paralyzed. He would come to NRA events in a wheelchair holding a sign saying VICTIM OF THE GUN CONTROL ACT.[19]

"That disaster was the first of a long chain of Gestapo-like raids, sieges, and questionable arrests,"[20] Chris Knox, son of the longtime NRA lobbyist Neal Knox, wrote in a compilation of his father's articles. Such words are themselves part of a long chain of Nazi comparisons to the gun police.

The rhetoric made its way to Congress. In 1981, Representative John Dingell of Michigan infamously said in an NRA film, "If I were to select a jackbooted group of fascists who are perhaps as large a danger to American society as I could pick today, I would pick ATF." The fact he was a Democrat showed that the influence reached both sides of the aisle.

Events in the nineties increased the ire, starting with the 1992 Ruby Ridge siege. The case began when the ATF tried to infiltrate the Aryan Nations white-supremacist group in Idaho. Agents needed an informant and looked to Randy Weaver, a Vietnam vet and fundamentalist Christian living in the hills with his family and lots of guns. To put the screws on, the ATF set Weaver up to deliver two illegally sawed-off shotguns. But when he refused to cooperate, they charged him, and after he failed to attend a court appearance, an arrest warrant was issued.

U.S. marshals in camo descended on his ranch and got into a shootout that killed a marshal and Weaver's son and dog. This leads to a common insult you hear against ATF agents, of being "dog killers." The FBI joined in and shot dead Weaver's wife before an eleven-day siege ensued, and Weaver finally negotiated a surrender. Following court intrigues, Weaver was acquitted of most charges.

While it was a marginal event, Ruby Ridge galvanized public attention and dug deep into the American conscience. For urban liberals, it exposed the gun-toting crazies in the woods. For gun hard-liners, it confirmed the fears of a tyrannical federal government seizing their firearms, shooting their families, and killing their dogs.

The 1993 Waco siege was a much bigger flashpoint, and Koz went there with the ATF forces.

The gun police were concerned about the Texas compound of the Branch Davidians, fundamentalist Christians led by David Koresh, a thirty-three-year-old musician who claimed he was the messiah. They had evidence the sect was stockpiling illegal firearms, including machine guns. And there were reports filtering out of children being beaten and sexually abused. It would later emerge that in classic cult style, Koresh had banned his followers from having sex but slept with their wives and, according to a Texas children's hospital, raped their daughters as young as eleven.[21] The ATF got a search warrant and moved in.

The events are largely recognized as a debacle for the federal forces. Shooting broke out in which six sect members and four ATF agents were killed—the agency's worst day. The FBI took over what became a fifty-one-day siege, before a second shootout and ultimately a fire in which seventy-six of the Davidians, including Koresh, perished.

There is still debate as to who fired the first shots and who started the blaze. But for hard-liners, the fault is squarely on the federal agents, and it justifies their fear of a despotic government using force to take their guns, which in turn justifies the need for guns to defend against the government. The story fit perfectly into the talking points of the anti-government fringe: God-fearing Christians, gun-grabbing agents, and a massacre on an apocalyptic scale.

Amid the fires, the NRA mudslinging at the ATF intensified. In early 1995, it issued a heated fundraising letter: "It doesn't matter to them that the semi-auto ban gives jack-booted government thugs more power to take away our constitutional rights, break in our doors, seize our guns, destroy our property, and even injure or kill us . . . Not too long ago, it was unthinkable for federal agents wearing Nazi bucket helmets and black storm trooper uniforms to attack law-abiding citizens."[22]

The letter was criticized for inciting attacks on federal agents, especially as it came to light after the Oklahoma City bombing. On April 19, 1995, Timothy McVeigh drove a monstrous truck bomb into the federal building in downtown Oklahoma City, and 108 of the 168 victims worked for the federal government. The ATF had offices there and was a primary target, but its agents escaped the worst of the blast.

Gulf War veteran McVeigh said he was inspired by the novel *The Turner Diaries*, which depicts an uprising against a government taking away guns, and a genocidal race war.[23] He claimed the attack as vengeance for Ruby Ridge and Waco, which he had gone to protest. And it was carried out on Waco's second anniversary.

There was yet another ATF connection. It emerged that the ATF had an informant among the right-wing radicals in Oklahoma who had reported talk of a bombing. However, it had failed to act on the info.

The ATF in the nineties was thus whacked with criticism, accused of operational failures, and physically attacked. When the internet took off, the furor went online, where it continues today. On the Facebook page of the ATF, a story about the arrest of an armed drug dealer in Wisconsin has comments like this:

"The BATFE is an unconstitutional federal agency that must be abolished."

"Marshal law is in effect in all the United States of America."

"The Criminal Organization ATF and its Thugs with Badges."

I wonder how much the vitriol rattles the agents. Jonathan Lowy, chief counsel for the gun safety group Brady, says the NRA pressure has a significant effect.

"Either former ATF people or even current ones, off the record, will tell you that the ATF is terrified of offending the gun lobby," he says. "And they are terrified that if they step out of line with what the NRA wants, the NRA will get their budgets slashed." This makes the agency more cautious, especially on policing gun shops, he says.

However, various agents tell me that morale is good, with Koz saying the criticism never bothered him. "There is always going to be that opinion out there from those type of extremist groups, but throughout my career for thirty years, I don't think I've ever gone after anybody who didn't deserve to have what they had coming to them," he says. "A lot of the people I know that are on that side of the fence, gun enthusiasts and so forth, they know that we go after the hard-core criminals."

Koz would face the most fearsome of these in his last undercover role in the biggest-ever operation into a biker gang.

Their patch depicts Genghis Khan on a Harley. A video on their website has strippers pole-dancing while dollar bills "rain on them," and a biker in a baseball cap shouting, "Fuck Donald Trump. *Viva la Raza.*" Jesse Ventura, the thirty-eighth governor of Minnesota, calls them his "brothers." The federal government calls them a serious organized-crime threat and has even tried to take away their patch.

If outlaw bikers are a curious animal, the Mongols are an especially strange hybrid. They have tight links to street gangs, thanks to the recruitment of gangbangers in Los Angeles. Yet they are the only outlaw club to have claimed a governor in their ranks.

Jesse "the Body" Ventura spoke about his membership during an interview with Joe Rogan. He said the club helped him transition into civilian life when he came back from the Vietnam War in 1973.

"In my day, a lot of the outlaw bikers were former military," Ventura said. "You wanted your camaraderie. You wanted that brotherhood."

Ventura described the origins of the Mongols and how they were founded by Mexican Americans who weren't allowed in the Hells Angels. While white men joined, it remained a majority-Hispanic gang.

At the turn of the millennium, a street gang member called Ruben "Doc" Cavazos took over the Mongols and recruited gangbangers who sold drugs on corners. This drew the club onto the wrong side of L.A. gang politics. In Southern California, most Hispanic gangs have to pay "tax" to the Mexican Mafia, the prison mob. But when the gangbangers moved into the Mongols, they thought this made them exempt from the payment.

This set off a chain of violence as the Mongols faced off against the Mexican Mafia. A string of stabbings and shootings reached the attention of federal agents, who turned to the biker specialists. The ATF opened a probe into the Mongols that mushroomed into Operation Black Rain.

Koz and other agents initially planned to nurture informants and meet only sporadically with the Mongols. But as the operation sprawled, they got sucked in, and Koz ended up becoming a fully patched member of his third club.

"The more we went around these guys, the more we kept getting closer to them, the more they started to like us. The recruitment was strong to get us in. In their culture and in their mind, it's almost disrespectful to not want to join. It's like, 'Why don't you?' They believe in their patch so much that's like the highest level of achievement you can have."

While Koz was used to bikers, he was struck by the Mongols' propensity to fight. "The Mongols were the most criminal-mindset orientated that I've experienced and had more propensity for the violence. They had more of a gang mentality. Like, 'We are criminals who are now riding motorcycles,' versus motorcycle guys who became criminals.'"

Koz was in a bar when the Mongols broke into a fight with a local gang. He found himself rolling around a parking lot scrapping with an eager young gangbanger when a bouncer smashed him over the head with a steel baton. Koz was forty years old.

In the hospital getting six stitches, Koz asked his case agent if he really had to keep brawling with youths. "Why am I here in this case?" he said. "This is just getting ridiculous."

The agent asked him for a little more time to build the prosecution, which would be the most wide-ranging against any biker gang. Koz stayed on, risking the wrath of the Mongols and the Hells Angels, who thought he was a Mongol, as well as various street gangs. That's when the shooting with the Bassett Grande happened.

When they went to the bar for a typical drinking session, Koz, in his persona of Dirty Dan, was now a prospect carrying the pistol of the sergeant of arms in the vents of his truck. The sergeant was a convicted felon and didn't want to be cruising with the gun. He was also "a hothead" with "a short-fused personality" and soon got angry about members of the Bassett Grande "staring at him funny" and ordered Koz to get his piece.

This put Koz in a tough position. If the man shot and killed a gangbanger, then he would be an accessory to the crime. But to say no would jeopardize the whole operation.

"He was the sergeant at arms," Koz says. "I couldn't refuse any order."

The sergeant marched up to a Bassett Grande member in the parking lot and stuck the gun in his face. But the gangbanger held his ground.

"You ain't got the balls to shoot or pull the trigger," he said.

Other Bassett members ran to their vehicles for weapons. Seeing this, Koz pulled his own gun out and pointed, yelling at them not to shoot. The situation could easily have descended into a bloodbath.

"We don't know if he's going to pull the trigger or not," Koz says. "We are just hoping for the best, but we also can't break role in a setting like that and say, 'Put your gun away. We're ATF agents.' Then all of a sudden the cover is blown and we are going to get shot. It's almost going so quickly you kind of got to have to roll with it for the time being.

"Now everybody from the civilian side, they're seeing all this unfold, and they're screaming and yelling, and girls are panicking, and everybody is running."

When the police sirens wailed in the background, the Mongols sergeant lowered his gun and went back to a car with a girl. But it was when he was driving off that the Bassett Grande fired a rain of bullets. This led to the Mongols spitting blood for violent retaliation, which the ATF agents made sure they got on tape.

The risks paid off. Koz and his partners got wiretaps on the Mongols' phones and witnessed them moving large quantities of guns, drugs, and stolen goods and giving up info on murders. When they finally broke cover in 2008, the police arrested well over a hundred Mongols, charging them with firearms, drugs, and violence offenses, and many of them with RICO. Unlike the Angels back in 1980, Mongols' members pleaded guilty to rack-eteering and were given stiff sentences.

It was a big win for the government. But then prosecutors pushed the knife in further and launched a new case that dragged into 2019 to take away the trademarking of the Mongols' patch, with the argument that it was central to their conspiracy.

The case could create a precedent to use against other bikers, an attempt to smash the core of their identity. But the Mongols' lawyer argued it was a landmark test of freedom of speech, and on this count the government ultimately failed. While the jury found the Mongols guilty under RICO, the judge refused to take away their patch, saying the First Amendment protects "collective symbols."[24] Today, you can still see the Mongols cruising down the interstates with the picture of Genghis Khan on their jackets.

In the big scheme, Koz's undercover work took only a fraction of the guns off the street. But that is not the central point, I realize. The main logic of these ATF sweeps is not to shut down the circulation of firearms but to get the people who use them behind bars.

A key charge used was of "knowing possession of firearm by prohibited person," as many of the bikers were felons. Another was using firearms in connection with drug trafficking. When gang members are operating armed, they commit murders, the feds figure, and putting them in prison prevents that.

Koz himself looks back at his work as being a fight worth fighting.

"We don't do this job for the awards or accolades, at least the crew that I run with and hang around with. We do it because we truly believe in putting criminals that belong in jail, in jail. So for me to be able to accomplish what I have and infiltrate these different gangs that nobody has ever done before, I felt the sense of accomplishment . . .

"We know we're never going to eradicate these gangs. We know they're going to continue to exist. All the time, there is always going to be somebody to step up and take their place. But for us, it's always making a dent and making life miserable for them to want to do this type of lifestyle, knowing that feds are always going to be there to be on their ass."

I ask Koz if he feels in danger from the bikers. He could still run into them going to the movies or walking the dog. But he says that he lives in peace. Some of the bikers were actually relieved to get arrested, he claims, as it gave them a way out of the violent life, an excuse to step down. A partner even ran into a ranking Mongol in a store in Cypress Park.

"Nothing happened. There was just a hello thing. Some of them are obviously very bitter about the jail time and would love to take a run at us because of what we did. But they've got enough problems of their own from other rival gangs they're still under attack from. They don't have time to wonder about what we're doing. In my opinion, I don't really worry about it."

I meet a lot of people on both sides of the fence, criminals and cops, who are burned out and tormented. Koz isn't one of them. He seems like a happy guy. Which is an achievement itself in life.

The big focus of the ATF on bikers does leave me with questions though. I agree with the argument that they are organized crime outfits. Their reputation and structure give the members who commit criminal acts an advantage. If you owe drug money to a member of the Mongols, you are more pressured to pay it. Likewise, the organization allows that drug seller to use shared contacts to buy meth, MAC-10s, or whatever. Some members may not be part of that, like Jesse Ventura. But that gives cover to those racketeering.

Seeing the carnage that organized crime causes in Latin America, I feel that the way the United States has hammered its mobs since RICO was introduced in 1970 to be a generally good thing. If outlaw biker gangs had been allowed to grow in power unmolested, the country would likely be more violent today.

Still, I do wonder about the amount of focus on biker gangs and how so many ATF agents have got their crazy stories infiltrating them but not infiltrating the street gangs who leave more bodies on the concrete. One reason is that the agents simply can infiltrate motorcycle clubs. Many are white, and the bikers, despite their background checks, are not as tight as many gangs and cartels.

Going undercover in the MS-13 is more challenging. As is infiltrating the gangs in some of the most homicidal cities in the United States. Such as Baltimore, Maryland. Where we now turn.

4

Body More

It's the fixation with guns: the movies, the sound, the grip, the power. It's too easy to kill with a gun.

—TYREE "COLION" MOOREHEAD, CONVICTED MURDERER
TURNED ANTIVIOLENCE ACTIVIST

Ever since the first time I heard that boom, I knew I would rather be on the giving end than on the receiving end of that motherfucker.

—CHAIN, ACTIVE GUN TRAFFICKER

Chain sold many more guns than he can count on the streets of Baltimore. He sold them to drug dealers, to killers, and to people who just wanted protection. But he regrets selling only one gun: to a guy who used it to shoot dead one of Chain's best friends.

The guy came to Chain "beefing," meaning he was in a violent argument with someone and badly needed a weapon. As a seasoned gun seller, Chain could tell that the guy was desperate from a mile away and put the price up accordingly.

This is another rule of black market gun-onomics: if the customer is beefing, then the price shoots up. In mainstream economic terms, they are known as a "distressed buyer."

"If it's a beef, they don't give a fuck what it costs," Chain tells me. "'Cos when there is war, there is war. Fuck, you going to sit there and discriminate about the price when that price money save your motherfucking life?"

So Chain sold the gun for a big markup and was with his friends, relaxing and happy with the score, when five minutes later he heard the shots and they ran out. His best friend, his "brother," as he calls him, lay dead on the concrete. The guy he had sold the gun to was running away.

"I've still got dreams about that shit," Chain says. "I got more recurring dreams about that than the first time I had to do something to somebody."

Chain told me about how he traffics guns across state lines and spreads them around the corners as we sat on comfy sofas in a red-brick house in Baltimore, a giant TV playing a local Fox news affiliate with the sound turned down. It's a story that stretches through the decades of gun violence in the city and the repeated failed attempts by the authorities to stem it. And it shines light on the business of guns going from the legal market into the hands of gangsters in many cities in America.

I met Chain through Jelly Roll, a guy I worked with in Baltimore to learn about how illegal guns come into the city. Jelly Roll is a bouncer in nightclubs and does security for film and TV shoots, which is how I connected with him. He drove me around the corners, the projects, the clubs to talk to people who use illegal guns or are affected by them. Over days as we rode in his truck and we munched down vast plates of food, he explained how crime functions in the city, how it looks through his eyes. When he was younger, he had spent his own time on the corners selling drugs, had been shot, and had served time in prison. His own story was so compelling that when I went back to Baltimore, I sat down and taped hours of interviews with him too. It illustrates how entwined drugs and guns are in the inner cities.

A lot has been written about the violence in Baltimore, especially by David Simon in his groundbreaking books, which paved the way for his cult TV series *The Wire*. I concede that I am not only a fan of *The Wire*; I think it was a transcendent moment in television. A lot has also been written about race in Baltimore, including by the city's famous son Ta-Nehisi Coates. I won't try to give any broad understanding of the city that many resident writers have provided.

But I dig into three specific things in Baltimore that connect to our story of blood, guns, and money. The first is the mechanics of how illegal guns move through its streets, and how this links to the bigger black market in weapons in the United States and across the Americas. The second is the central relationship between drugs and guns, which really plays out in Baltimore The third is how the mechanics of gun violence in Baltimore compare with those in the other murder capitals on the continent. Because the ugly truth is that Baltimore, just forty miles from the nation's capital, suffers a homicide rate comparable to murderous cities in Mexico, Honduras, and Brazil.

The math of measuring murder rates is to count the number of bodies that turn up in a certain territory during a year and put this as a ratio against the number of residents. It's most common to count homicide victims per hundred thousand people.

It's not an exact figure. Some murder victims don't show up until years after they are killed. Some never show up at all. Sometimes police departments lie about the number of victims. Often a city morgue will come up with a different number of murder victims than the police department. But still, these ratios give a broad measure for comparing violence from city to city, country to country, year to year.

Many countries have murder rates of less than 2 per 100,000, including most of Europe, much of Asia, and a significant part of Africa. This shows that low levels of homicide can be achieved, and there is nothing natural or inevitable about sky-high levels of killings.

The United States overall had 5 murders per 100,000 in 2018. But certain cities were way above this. Baltimore had the highest rate for a city over half a million, with 50 per 100,000—and 88 percent of those killings were with guns.[1] The smaller city of St. Louis, Missouri, had an even worse homicide rate, of 60.

Latin America and the Caribbean suffer terrible murder rates. In a 2018 roundup of the world's fifty most murderous cities outside official war zones, the Americas were home to forty-seven of them.[2] Tijuana topped the list, with 138 murders per 100,000, followed by Acapulco and then Caracas, Venezuela. St. Louis came in at number fifteen and Baltimore at number twenty-three, with Detroit and New Orleans also featuring.

The overall murder rate in the United States has swung up and down over the last century. It increased into the 1930s, when it topped 9 per 100,000; went down in the 1950s, when it bottomed out at 4 per 100,000; increased steadily to a peak of 10 per 100,000 in 1980; went down to 4.5 in 2014; and edged up over the next few years, before sharply spiking in 2020, the year of pandemic and protest.

There are a bunch of theories as to why the murder rate has gone up and down. But there is no breakthrough proof for any of them, and advocates will often herald the theories that most suit their politics.

The most publicized arguments focus on the drop in murder from 1980 to the 2010s, which was felt especially in the biggest cities of New York and Los Angeles. The arguments tend to start with mass incarceration, with the national prison population shooting up in this period to its mammoth 2.1 million. There is a logic that if potential murderers are locked up, they physically can kill fewer people.

Yet there are holes in this theory. The prison population was already rising somewhat in the 1970s while murder rates were increasing. The mass incarceration didn't reduce homicides in Baltimore and St. Louis. And even if potential murderers were locked up, many nonviolent offenders were also doing lengthy sentences that destroyed families.

Either way, the idea of mass incarceration is out of vogue on both the left and the right. It was Trump who signed the First Step Act to reduce the federal prison population.

Gun laws and gun numbers also shoot their way into the debates on the murder rate. Gun safety advocates cite the stricter rules in New York and efforts to stop the flow of guns as factors in the decline in killings. Gun rights activists hit back with the large numbers of legal guns carried by civilians in states with low murder rates such as Vermont. They go on to claim that the more guns there are, the safer America is.

On investigation, the relationship between guns and murder rates is complex. Guns are almost certainly a factor in why the United States has always had a murder rate several times higher than that of European countries, and suffers from so many mass shootings. Yet the exact number of firearms doesn't have a clear correlation with the fluctuating murder levels. The total arsenal has increased steadily over the last century while murder rates have gone up and down. This increase has largely been in the fattening stashes of individual collectors. It may be that the sheer number of firearms in legal hands is less relevant but it is important how easily the most violent gangsters get weapons, and how many guns flood the streets.

Other ideas for why murders went down since 1980 include the burning out of the crack epidemic; the general rise in wealth, with gentrification in New York and Los Angeles; and more social work, with violence-prevention projects in key spots such as the South Bronx and L.A.'s Boyle Heights. There is also the controversial idea that legalized abortion reduced the number of unwanted children who would shoot people. Yet another theory is that lead in drinking water and gasoline causes brain changes that meant higher murder rates from the 1950s, and then cleaner water and unleaded gasoline made them decrease since the 1980s. There are cases to be made and lines of attack on all the hypotheses.

What is an undisputed fact, though, is that while the overall murder rates went down, the levels stagnated or went up in a smattering of places, including Baltimore, St. Louis, Detroit, and New Orleans. In 2017, Baltimore suffered its worst murder rate on record.

A tendency across the planet is that murders aren't spread equally around cities but bomb certain neighborhoods and especially hit poor young men. In Baltimore, 80 percent of murders were in a quarter of its neighborhoods, as reporter Justin George found in an investigation for the *Baltimore Sun*.[3] This means that in the murder-scarred neighborhoods, residents could really be living with ratios that are more like 150 per 100,000.

So what does this mean on the ground? Where violence is really bad, almost everyone will know a friend or an extended family member who has died from a gunshot. This causes trauma, and often bad financial implications, for the majority in these neighborhoods.

Some people on the front line have lost several family members from gun violence. Activist Erricka Bridgeford, who grew up in the Normount Court housing project in West Baltimore, lost a brother, a stepson, and a cousin to bullets.[4]

It is not only gang members who get shot. Stray bullets are an everyday worry, and not just in the middle of firefight. While pistols can accurately hit their targets only at close ranges, a 9 mm round fired at forty-five degrees can hurtle for a mile. This means you can be many blocks away from a shooting and a bullet can strike you. And many of the kids behind the triggers can't shoot straight.

On the afternoon of August 1, 2014, three-year-old McKenzie Elliott was playing on a porch on Old York Road in the Waverly neighborhood of North Baltimore. Her father was traveling back from work to pick her up and take her swimming. At four P.M., men on a nearby corner opened fire on a car. One bullet missed and traveled four houses down. It went straight through McKenzie's head, killing her where she played.

While McKenzie's death provoked outrage, she is only one of dozens of children and babies lost to stray bullets in recent years in Baltimore. Despite the United States having a twenty-trillion-dollar economy, infants still perish from such pointless bloodshed.

For those on the corners, the exposure to killing is off the chart. Jelly Roll has been seeing people die since he was a child. Now in his mid-forties, he has personally known more than a hundred murder victims and narrowly survived bullets himself.

"It's just a revolving door. Friends are killing friends," he says. "It's not the way it should be."

When I first connected with Jelly Roll, I talked to him on the phone to see if he could introduce me to people who were actively selling illegal guns. He said it was possible, but then they could always back out at the last minute, suspicious that I was involved with some police agency.

I flew to Baltimore on a red-eye flight, and we were meant to start work the following day after I had gotten some rest. But there was some confusion, and when I called Jelly Roll, he said he was coming to my hotel right away. He also said we were going to meet Mr. Barksdale.

I thought he was pulling my leg. Barksdale is the name of the drug-dealing family in *The Wire*. Did he really think I would believe this was a real person? Or, I wondered, was he using "Mr. Barksdale" as a code?

When Jelly Roll arrived, he explained that the Barksdales actually existed, that *The Wire* used the name of real drug dealers. We were going to meet the nephew, Dante Barksdale, who in *The Wire* is portrayed as the character D'Angelo.

We hit the street, and he got on the phone to Dante, who gave an address where he would meet us.

"What's he doing in that trailer-park trash?" Jelly Roll wondered aloud.

When we arrived, I thought we might see trailers, but it turned out to be government housing that was dominated by white people. For some in the city, white government housing is "trailer-park trash," and Black government housing is "projects." This stark segregation of the poor on race lines strikes me. Racism certainly exists in London and Rio de Janeiro, but the poor neighborhoods are still more mixed racially.

Dante was friendly and gave me his card. He had done prison time for heroin but was now coordinating a violence-reduction project called Safe Streets, backed by the city health department. We talked about *The Wire* and the portrayal of his uncle and himself.

"They killed me off in the second series," he said, shaking his head. Dante promised to ask around to help with potential interviews.

Jelly Roll said Dante was a good person to check in with, as he wielded a lot of influence in the city. If there were any problems, he could smooth things out.

As his name suggests, Jelly Roll has some fat and likes to eat. One day, we demolished a huge lunch of Southern food and two hours later went for nacho burritos. He is six feet two and 350 pounds. But Jelly Roll also has serious muscle. He played football in high school and has been bouncing people out of clubs for twenty years. Although now he says that bouncing wears him out.

"I beat someone and I'm tired," he said to a fellow bouncer when we were outside a club. "I don't know how many years I've got left doing this."

Yet Jelly Roll is polite and kind and doesn't give off a vibe of violence as we drive around town. When I ask him about this, he says that he makes an effort to do right after his past.

"I just feel like I'm trying to do more good than I did bad."

Jelly Roll was born on East Baltimore Street in 1973. When he was a baby, his parents gave him up, although he has never found out much about them. He was adopted by a couple who worked in schools and had two older children. They were good, hard workers, but he struggled to fit into the family.

As a child, he met Chain, who lived across the street. When they were twelve, Chain and Jelly Roll got into a fight over a video game. Jelly Roll's adopted mother saw them scrapping in the backyard and beat them both up with a broomstick.

"She definitely beat us with that broomstick, with the part you use on the floor—dust, dirt, everything." Jelly Roll laughs as he remembers it.

When Chain's mother discovered what was happening, she wasn't angry with Jelly Roll's mother. She joined in.

"Mothers worked together back then. If your kids messed up, it was an action."

Soon after, Jelly Roll exploded in size, his strength booming as he played linebacker in football. He fought in school to defend himself, but finding he was good at thumping people, he also bullied others, including a boy who went on to become a comedian in the city. "I was the butt of a lot of jokes for a while."

When he was a high school freshman, Jelly Roll's adoptive father passed away, a loss he felt deeply. The others in the family feared they couldn't control him and called an uncle to threaten him, which made him begrudge them more. He spent all his time on the street, and a friend introduced him to selling drugs on the corner of Bradford Street.

"I wanted some of the better things in life, and there was a whole bunch of glamor behind it. The money—you could buy anything. It was coming fast. And for someone who didn't have any, there was no reason to work. It was all enjoyment."

He joined a crew, which was just a handful of guys on the corner. To this day, most of the drug selling in Baltimore is by small block crews rather than sprawling organizations, Jelly Roll explains. Twenty-five guys is a big crew, and some are just half a dozen kids. While some may be loosely affiliated with gangs such as the Crips, or some members may have joined the Black Guerrilla Family in prison, they still operate in their neighborhood groups, dominating a territory of no more than a block or two.

There are bigger players who sell the drugs to dealers in whole chunks of the city. But they simply pass their product down the food chain and don't dictate how the crews operate. The neighborhood gangs fight it out for themselves.

Such decentralization is a recipe for violence. In cities where a crime group establishes a powerful monopoly, such as São Paulo, Brazil, the homicides can actually go down. When there is no control, any corner is a potential front line, anybody an enemy, boosting the body count.

Soon after Jelly Roll began selling, a friend gave him a firearm, a .32, and he kept it hidden near the corner.

Jelly Roll began selling weed, but by his final year of high school, he had graduated to heroin, cocaine, and crack. He missed most of his classes, but then he didn't see the point in going. On the corner, he was making $3,500 a week.

To get a sense of the history of drug selling in Baltimore, I go downtown to the office of lawyer William Purpura. He was on the defense team of El Chapo, and I had met him at the trial. (He was the guy who told the ATF to cool it with the grenade launcher.) Bald and trim in his sixties, Purpura has been defending gangsters since the 1970s, from Baltimore's most high-profile drug dealers to Latin American kingpins, culminating in El Chapo. Among the Baltimore traffickers he represented was Linwood "Rudy" Williams, convicted of conspiracy to distribute cocaine and heroin that he was bringing from Asia and sentenced to 130 years.

Since Purpura started working in the seventies, Baltimore has been a heroin town, he says, a place where people in the region come to buy.

"It's a marketplace for people to get the opiates from the nearby counties, from Pennsylvania, Virginia, West Virginia, as long as I've been here," he said. "It's the center for retail sales. Chicago is wholesale with all the cocaine flowing out, but here it is just retail. Street level."

Being a port helped establish it as a center for drugs, as did the connecting roads to Washington, Pittsburgh, and New York. Its reputation made the market self-fulfilling, and every junkie learned that if you want to score, you drive into Baltimore and head to Pennsylvania Avenue. A lot of addicts also stay in the city, creating a seething population of stationary users who can spend upwards of a hundred dollars a day each.

At the same time, Baltimore has a huge pool of recruits for the drug trade in impoverished neighborhoods. As Purpura explains, while New York is wealthy with pockets of poverty, Baltimore is poor with pockets of wealth.

"The people who are coming up and are uneducated and have nowhere else to go, they go into this trade because it's so much money to be made," Purpura says. "That's why there is much fighting on these individual corners for that type of trade. It's millions of dollars a day, no matter how you cut it, day in, day out."

Drug economies come in different shapes and sizes. In Honduras, the neighborhood gangs fight over scraps. In Mexico, the gangsters make huge money trafficking tons to the United States, spawning powerful cartels. In Baltimore, there is good money but distributed to many small crews, enough to keep them on the street, and enough to keep them fighting.

For Jelly Roll, making over three grand a week in high school was more money than he knew what to do with. But he found ways to spend it.

"After a good Friday night, what we call 'early Friday night,' around eight o'clock, we're done. The work and trade would be over, and we would finish up and close down, we would go to the mall, and we would pick weeks—say the first week, I would buy everybody clothes and shoes. And we would go right to the club. I remember washing up in the sink in a mall bathroom, putting our clothes on. We would go to a club called the Underground. We were underage, but we would pay a hundred dollars apiece to get in. We drank. We dated women that weren't our age. It was a huge turn in my life."

With good times came the bullets. The first attempt to kill Jelly Roll was around the time he should have been graduating from high school. It was on Bradford and Monument Streets as he was walking into a store to buy chicken.

"As soon as I hit the mouth of the alley, some guys started shooting at me out of a car. It was like they were sitting there waiting for me," he says. "Until this day I still don't know who they were, but I just know they couldn't shoot. 'Cos they shot everything but me."

He suspected the guys in his own crew. They had arguments because he used to stay out longer and make more money. Once he had earned his "re-up"—the cash to buy his next package of drugs—he would let product go cheap, accepting eight dollars for ten-dollar bags. He saw it all as profit, but his cohorts would complain that they didn't "take shorts."

One night, he was selling rocks of crack to a regular, and she warned that his friends were waiting in ambush.

"If you go out the end of the alley, your boys are waiting up there to kill you," she said.

He didn't want to believe it but wasn't taking chances, so he walked the long way around the block and came up behind his crew. Sure enough, they were waiting with their guns out. When he came up behind them, they pretended they were just chilling.

"There was no reason for them to have their guns out. We kept our guns in the gutter, or we kept our guns right on top of a tire," he says. "Until this day, I feel like I owe her my whole life."

Jelly Roll carried on selling on the corner, acting like nothing had happened, refusing to budge. But then he saw opportunities elsewhere and shifted to a part of town known as Chocolate City to set up his own crew. Drug selling in Baltimore operates a like a multilevel marketing scheme. You can start at the bottom of the pyramid and then rise up, creating your own pyramid beneath you. He would buy from a midlevel supplier and sell to his soldiers for a markup. He called his crew "the Carpenters" and they marked their clothes with Cs.

The second time that Jelly Roll got shot at was in a fight over a girl. He was casually seeing a woman who was gaining fame as a "Chocolate Model," posing on a semi-porn website. He didn't realize she had a boyfriend, until the guy went after him, firing at him from across the street—and missing.

Impervious to bullets, Jelly Roll gained a reputation. This got him body-guard work for aspiring rappers and security on movie sets and in clubs.

Working doors gave him a new outlet where he could sell his drugs. Which led to the third time he was shot at.

He was now twenty-two and on top of the world, making money, dating models, avoiding death. Working the door, he got the same Chocolate Model to help him pat people down. But when a guy groped her ass, a fight broke out, spreading from the club to the street. In the melee, Jelly Roll knocked out one guy, only for another to draw a gun and shoot him at close range. A .22-caliber bullet went straight through his chest, an inch and a half from his heart.

"The doctors made a funny joke. It was like, 'If you weren't so big, it probably would have killed you,'" he said. "Getting shot isn't the part that really hurts. It was when they took this long metal Q-tip and they pushed the bullet so it came out the other side. No pain medicine. No anything like that."

Fate had saved Jelly Roll's life again. But it wouldn't save him from prison. Police finally caught up with him when he was twenty-four. His partner got hit with drugs, weapons, and kidnapping charges and got eighteen years. Jelly Roll was lucky and got sentenced to five on pure drug charges, of which he served three, locked up in Maryland state prison in Hagerstown.

Arriving, he had to confront a prisoner who stole his biker shorts and tennis shoes; Jelly Roll battered him over the head with a weight in the gym. This largely warned others off, although he still got jumped a few times. But he said that overall, prison was more boring than terrifying.

"I mean how TV portrays it? It's not like a threatening situation. It depends on how you carry yourself," he says. "It's dreadfully boring. And after you've been institutionalized, once you pass like the fourth month, you've adapted. It's like you're in school and can't get out. It's like school twenty-four/seven. You're not in jail anymore. It's just a different type of housing. You find new ways to pass the time. New ways to eat. New foods are created."

Jelly Roll was already a father, so while he was incarcerated, his crew made regular payments to the mother. This is a deal respected by many on the Baltimore corners, a form of mutual insurance that helps them survive prison time, and thus keeps the whole drug game going.

When Jelly Roll came out, he went straight back onto the street to sell dope. And within six months he was arrested again and served another two years. Yet this still didn't stop him; he was addicted to the money and lifestyle.

Finally, when he was close to thirty, he was in a stash house when he spotted three police cruisers and two battering-ram trucks turning the corner. The militarization of police, exposed in the 2020 protests, was built up and tested in cities such as Baltimore, justified by the presence of so many guns. The only escape was jumping off a third-story balcony. He went for it. After hitting the ground, he lay still for a while until he managed to get up and walk to his car while the police charged past him and smashed the door in. Everybody else in the house got arrested.

The jump finally shook him. He was out of the drug game.

"I couldn't see another judge." He shakes his head. "I don't think it would have turned out well."

———

Jelly Roll takes me to a dope-selling spot on Laurens and Pennsylvania, what they call an "open-air drug market." I'm struck by how public it is. The dealers aren't in empty houses or back alleys but on a busy street in front of a store. There are two crews selling marijuana, one selling heroin. A steady stream of customers come and go. It's more open than in Amsterdam.

The situation is a paradox after covering the drug war in Mexico. I have flown with Mexican soldiers in helicopters, and watched them burn marijuana fields and raid stash houses of cocaine and heroin, operations bankrolled by U.S. aid. Yet here, forty miles from Washington, a crew openly sells heroin on a busy street.

Of course, the United States has locked up millions on drug charges over the years, including thousands from Baltimore. But after rumbling corner after corner and seeing the crews keep coming back, the senior police officers here realized it is largely pointless hitting the retail points. It doesn't stop either the flow of drugs or the body count. So they tried going after the guns.

Baltimore has few gun shops, and most of the guys on the corners are either underage or felons who aren't allowed to buy firearms. Instead, they go to dealers like Chain who sell illegally.

Jelly Roll calls Chain and explains I am a writer and I just want to talk to him for a book. But when we park outside the house, Chain calls Jelly Roll back and says he doesn't want to speak to me anymore.

"I'll just go in and say we can have a cup of coffee and a chat," I say.

"Don't say that," Jelly Roll hits back. "We aren't coffee people."

We finally manage to negotiate going into the house, and once I sit down and look Chain in the eye and make my pitch, he starts talking. Like Jelly Roll, he's tall and broad, played football and does security. But he has a harder edge and more threatening vibe than Jelly Roll. Still, he becomes animated as we get into the conversation, and we all laugh at the story of Jelly Roll's mother beating them both with a broom.

A friend of Chain's called Bam is also there. Bam sells illegal guns locally, while Chain both sells them and traffics them into the city.

I ask them when they first handled guns. Bam says he was ten years old when his big brother gave him an old .22. He took it to school in his book bag, and one day the football coach spotted it but turned a blind eye so he didn't get in trouble.

Chain says he was about the same age when his neighbors were firing off guns on New Year's Eve. His dad took him to the window and put a .44 in his hands.

"That was the heaviest handgun I ever felt in my life," Chain says. "I mean the barrel on that bitch—it was like that long. *Boom.* I shot back to the window, and my father grabbed me. My father grabbed me because I was looking down the barrel. He said, 'Don't you ever look down the barrel of a fucking gun with your hand on the trigger.' He took it from me. And ever since the first time I heard that boom, I knew I would rather be on the giving end than on the receiving end of that motherfucker."

Chain got into drug selling like Jelly Roll did, rising up the pyramid, getting shot at and shooting at people. But he discovered that while everybody was selling drugs, only a few sold guns. He got a start in the business when junkies from out of town offered guns for drugs. Some would take the weapons from family gun stores or their family collections.

"You on the corner, you got motherfuckers coming from West Virginia, Pennsylvania, way the fuck out somewhere. Yo, they want drugs, we sell drugs. They say, 'Yo, I ain't got no money, but I got these brand-new handguns.' 'Let me see what you got. Yo, keep bringing that shit through here.'"

This is the same rule of gun-onomics described by Billyjack: bartering guns for drugs because of their elastic prices. Chain was closer to the source of drugs, buying from the big Baltimore distributors, and he saw it as a game of getting the better of the white guys from the sticks.

"We ain't losing. We winning. Let me tell you something. You bring me a gun from Virginia, and I got some dope. You going to say, 'I want six hundred dollars for it.' I'll be like, 'Six hundred dollars? Come on.' So I'm going to break you off a nice piece, and that piece will be the biggest piece that you seen. But that piece that I gave you, in my eyes, ain't worth no more than two hundred dollars, so I won.

"You thinking you won, 'cos you are going to take that piece I gave you back to your little town, and you might make twelve hundred dollars off of it. I don't give a fuck. I'm getting a twelve-hundred-dollar pistol for two hundred dollars' worth of heroin. Thank you, my friend. That is the good American bartering system."

One thing Chain has to watch out for is guns that have been used in a crime, especially a murder. A crime gun can still be sold but for dirt cheap, only a fraction of its store price—sometimes under a hundred bucks. This is another law of gun-onomics: once used in a crime, a gun drastically loses worth. In business terms, it becomes "a devalued product."

While Chain was marking up, he saw a way to make even more money: by trafficking the guns into Baltimore himself. He pumped the iron pipeline.

Back in the 1960s, many of the guns used in shootings in American inner cities were cheap handguns, often made in Italy and Germany. They became known as Saturday night specials.

It's not certain where the term came from, but one version is that it was from hospital emergency rooms in Detroit, which had a lot of gunshot victims on Saturday nights. Some claim it's a racist term. But then some of those claiming it's a racist term are white gun rights hard-liners keen to attack gun control.

One of the first reported uses of the term was on a *New York Times* front page in 1968, which said the "Saturday night specials" were "a favorite of holdup men."[5] Following the Gun Control Act, the government attempted to stop the flow of the cheap handguns by withdrawing hundreds of thousands of import licenses. But the restrictions just boosted American makers selling their own versions of them. This is like the balloon effect in the war on drugs. You grab the balloon on one side and the air travels to another part.

Politicians reacted again. Certain states had been passing their own more-restrictive gun laws since the late nineteenth century, and with the rise of urban violence from the 1960s, they went up a gear. In 1972 Maryland required that police issue permits to those who wanted to carry handguns, and in 1988 it passed a law banning the sale of certain handguns altogether, buoyed by a group called Citizens for Eliminating Saturday Night Specials.[6]

Unfortunately, the laws opened up business opportunities for enterprising criminals. They could buy guns in states with lax laws and traffic them to more restrictive states for a markup. The iron pipeline was born, moving tons of gunmetal up I-95 to cities such as Baltimore, Washington, and New York. There are also pipelines shifting guns from Midwestern states into Chicago and Western states into Los Angeles.

The effects of the pipeline can be seen in ATF trace data, gathered by the team in Martinsburg. In 2017, the majority of the guns (53 percent) seized from criminals in Maryland and traced were originally sold in other states. The biggest providers were Virginia, West Virginia, Pennsylvania, and Georgia.

That still meant 47 percent had been sold in Maryland. However, this included guns that had been bought before the ban and had been kicking around for years until they were used in crimes, some after being stolen. Guns are durable goods.

Chain traveled to Georgia, where he made contact with a white guy living in the countryside near Atlanta. The guy had steady sources that could get him new guns and a workshop where he could tear them apart and reassemble them with different components, making them harder to trace.

"It's nice because down there it is so free," Chain says. "Police don't come to these people's property unless they call. So you've got a house that's here, but you've got a shed that might sit two miles back in your yard that's nothing but your devil's playground. You've got every fucking thing that you can imagine. For me, it's like walking into a weed store, or a fucking porn store. A porn store with chicks in there and shit."

The source could provide Chain with anything he wanted, including guns converted to fully automatic. Chain likes AK-47s with the twin fifty-bullet drums, which he refers to as "gorilla nuts," and which fetch a high price in Baltimore.

As he got experienced in the business, Chain connected with his own straw purchasers, the people with clean records who buy the guns for a fee. Chain added another twist. He would agree with the straws that they would fake a robbery afterward. That way they could make money from the insurance company, plus the buyer had reported a theft, which protected them from being charged. It is an effective scam.

"I'm going to give you five thousand dollars, and you are going to buy all this shit. And then next weekend you go on vacation. Damn—somebody broke into your house and took all your shit. Man, you just got five thousand dollars back from the insurance company. The guns are gone, reported stolen. Like I said, what we look for is the unicorn."

Stolen guns are another big source for the black market. Criminals burgle houses and rob cars across the United States, often finding firearms left in insecure places like glove compartments or on tables, rather than locked in safes. In other cases, gangsters go into gun stores and often find lax security. This is another rule of gun-onomics: it's cheaper to steal a gun than to buy a gun.

A report by the *Trace* and the *New Yorker* followed a crew who were burgling gun stores in North Carolina.[7] Security footage shows the robbers crawling through a ventilation system and crashing down into the store. They pull the guns off the wall and stash them in bags, grabbing twenty-one weapons in sixty seconds. In another robbery, they can be seen finding cases unlocked and easily sliding them open to get the weapons.

Gun stores are not penalized for such slack security unless there is a specific state law about it. It's another NRA victory that national laws do not mandate this while they dictate security rules for pharmacies, explosive makers, and banks.

The robberies add up. Between 2012 and 2017, burglars stole more than thirty-two thousand firearms from U.S. gun dealers, the report found. They traced one gun stolen in North Carolina and trafficked on the pipeline to Baltimore. On May 10, 2015, it was used to shoot dead Harry Davis Jr., a thirty-six-year-old builder, as he prepared for Mother's Day celebrations with his wife.

Chain runs the guns back up I-95 hidden in cars, using rentals and dressing up smart. It's rare for police to flag down cars on major freeways anyway. In

Baltimore, though, there is more risk of being stopped, so Bam hides guns in the car speakers as he drives them around the city.

They have endless customers for their wares. Most of the corner dealers in Baltimore rarely leave their side of town, let alone drive across several states to buy guns. So Chain can get double or triple what they cost in the stores.

"There's big money in it," Chain says. "Big. You'll make more money selling guns than you will selling drugs. Because every motherfucker that's on the corner trying to sell drugs needs a gun. So guess what? You've got nine hundred and seventy-five motherfuckers on the corner, nine hundred and seventy-five that need at least two guns. One that they can keep outside with them and one in the crib just in case the one outside gets stolen or the police round it up. So you know right there that's one thousand nine hundred and fifty motherfucking gun sales that you got. You're goddamn right I sell guns. You fucking right. I'll take my chances. Fuck it. It's Baltimore."

While Chain sells some rifles, the big demand in Baltimore is for pistols. The corner crews want guns they can hide easily and quickly pull out; you can't stash a rifle on top of a car tire. The vast majority of the murders in Baltimore are committed with handguns rather than rifles. Popular guns include Glock 40s; Sturm, Ruger & Co. 9 mms; and Smith & Wesson .38s.

This fact is used in the argument over assault rifle bans. Those against them point out that most murders in the United States are carried out with handguns so a rifle ban wouldn't stop them. They are right. But this doesn't lessen the destructive power of AK-47s and AR-15s, especially to massacre people in crowded places. It just means that handguns also lead to a lot of murder, which politicians in inner cities have been wrestling with for decades.

I ask Chain about any regrets he has, and he tells me about the gun that killed his friend. I wonder how many guns he sold that were used in murders. He probably doesn't know himself. When I push him on whether he feels guilty, he retorts that the system is rotten to the core and he can't see anything changing.

"My problem with society is this: you give me every fucking thing in this world to condemn myself, and then when I make it, you got a problem with it.

"I'm not supposed to make and burn DVDs. But you sell DVD burners at fucking Walmart. I'm not supposed to sell dope or coke or guns. But you sell that shit all day long. I can go to any gas station nearby and get baggies and tie-ups for the drugs. Come on, man. You want to find a solution to it, you got to start with the motherfuckers that making money. It's easy as shit. Nobody going to want to stop guns. Nobody want to stop drugs.

"Before it was . . . white people fucking killing Indians, and then it was whoever the fuck else. What is, has always been. Killing no matter how nobody want to look at it is the cycle of life. Unless you a fucking vegan, everything you eat has to get killed. Nobody eat no cow that died of natural causes. I would love for it to change. But it ain't."

His words echo others I have heard from successful criminals living on the front lines of violence from Brazil to Mexico. As a journalist, I like to seek solutions, to imagine a future in which there aren't cities with sky-high murder rates, where there aren't three-year-old girls being shot in the head with stray bullets as they play on their porches. But for some tough and enterprising men growing up in the thick of it, they accept the reality. This is the way it is. And they look at how to make the best of the situation.

Chain has a lot of blood on his hands. But then so does the system.

———

While there are thousands of people selling drugs in Baltimore, it is only a fraction of the gang members who are actual killers. This is true of much of the gang violence in the United States and across the world. A small hard-core group is behind most of the bloodshed. Among the crews, certain members have the nerve to take lives.

Across Baltimore, Jelly Roll introduces me to Tyree Moorehead, known as Colion. Now in his forties, he is working as an activist against violence with a project to create "No Shoot Zones." But Colion was a stone-cold killer on the run for murder when he was just fifteen and did close to two decades in prison.

While there is a lot of poverty in Baltimore, Colion came from an especially difficult environment. When he was two weeks old, his father was arrested for murder, and Colion met him only when he himself was imprisoned at fifteen. His mother was a heroin addict, so Colion says it was like he was born with the drug in his system. When he was eleven, he told the dealer that it was embarrassing that his mother was on the street buying dope. The dealer said Colion could take the drugs to her himself and recruited him into the crew.

"It was all I knew. I didn't get a chance to compare it to a better life," Colion tells me. "I didn't get a chance to see it on a movie first. I lived it first. When I see it on a movie, I was like, 'That's fake.'"

Colion first stole a gun and tried to shoot someone when he was eleven, before he realized it had no bullets and older gangsters took it from him. By thirteen, he bought a .38 and began shooting for real, and by fifteen he was a hired gun, the youngest in an area known as the Boulevard, which, he said, meant "blood, love, violence, and death."

"Even though they was all older than me—they all in their twenties, I'm fifteen—they know I'm the one to go to," he says. "I really was taking life for money, it's sad to say, of my own people."

That year, he volunteered to hit a guy who had stolen from the crew. But the target was misidentified, and he shot an innocent man, a civilian, as he came out of an elevator. He was featured on "Maryland's Most Wanted," going on the run and exchanging fire with the police before he was arrested the day the movie *Juice* came out and he was taking his young cousins to the cinema. As it was a murder rap, he was locked up in an adult prison at fifteen.

Colion's background is eerily similar to those of hit men I have interviewed in Latin America. Many, too, come from deprived urban areas and suffer abandonment. And guns make it easy to convert the capacity to murder into big body counts.

This gets back to a core argument about guns: that they are only tools, and that it is the murderous intent that matters. If Baltimore drug dealers weren't all shooting each other, the argument goes, they would be stabbing each other. As they are in London.

London, where I lived for several years, does indeed have a problem with knife violence. And President Trump famously picked up on it in a speech at the 2018 NRA convention.

"In London, which has unbelievably tough gun laws, a once very prestigious hospital right in the middle is like a war zone for horrible stabbing wounds," Trump said. "Yes, that's right. They don't have guns. They have knives. And instead there's blood all over the floors of this hospital. They say it's as bad as a military war zone hospital. Knives. Knives. Knives." (To the end chant of knives, Trump made a rather comical stabbing gesture.)[8]

One thing I was surprised to find is that the projects of Baltimore are physically no worse than the government housing of London, which we call council estates. In fact, they look similar. The gangs of London estates, like the crews of Baltimore, are also small groups.

But the evidence does not bear out that knife violence is as bad as gun violence. The year 2018 was a thirteen-year high for murders in London, the majority stabbings. But this brought the homicide rate to only 1.5 per 100,000. Meanwhile, Baltimore had a rate of 50 per 100,000—or thirty-three times higher. No European city has a level of murder remotely close to this.

There are other factors pushing the murder rate in Baltimore. The poverty is so widespread, the drug market booming, the alienation more profound. But it's a hard fact that in every one of the fifty most violent cities in the world in 2018, the vast majority of the killings were with guns.

It is also telling that the violence levels in the modern hot spots don't even compare well with the murder rates in medieval Europe. A study of London killings in the 1300s by the University of Cambridge found a homicide rate of about 20 per 100,000[9]—less than half that in Baltimore and one-seventh that in Tijuana in 2018. Knives were also the most popular murder weapon in London back then, followed by staffs (clubbing people with Gandalf-esque sticks) and then swords.

The enormous flow of illegal guns in the Americas today is surely a factor driving levels much higher than they were in the bloody Middle Ages.

C. T. Mexica, known as Cuate, is both a veteran of gang violence and a scholar of it. He grew up in Texas and Washington State in Hispanic street gangs and was incarcerated for most of his teenage years after he shot another teenager, who fortunately survived. Inside youth prisons, he was exposed to brutal knife violence. Reading and studying behind bars, however, he went on to get his doctorate, and a university career.

I met Cuate when I presented a book at the University of Arizona and we broke off to a bar to have an epic conversation about crime, violence, and Mexico, a conversation that we've been carrying on over tacos, mescal, and blackjack in various cities.

Cuate says there is a big psychological difference between knife and gun violence. Stabbing someone means getting up close and dirty, while pulling a trigger is too easy, he says.

"Knives scare the shit out of people, Ioan," he said to me. "When people see you with a knife, especially when you are incarcerated, and you stab someone, they fucking flip out. Other than rape, it is the most brutally intimate form of violence that I know of. You can hear the knife entering them, you can hear them grunt, you can hear them squeal and scream. And you get the blood on you. You never forget that smell.

"Guns are very impersonal. You can shoot at people and run off. You can even do it from afar. It is so easy for someone to just pick up a gun. And you see this with the school shooters. A lot of those guys don't have straight-up training and marksmanship and proper weapons handling. Anyone who is the biggest coward can pick up a gun and commit acts of atrocity. But if you put that dude in a jail facility and give them a shank and say, 'Go out there and use it,' most won't. They will check in. You have to be a true believer."

It strikes me that even the language describing knife violence is more visceral than that of guns. You will probably be shuddering more from Cuate's talk of stabbing than from the descriptions of shootings.

This affects media coverage. A single gang decapitation garners more coverage than many gang shootings. Yet guns are used in most murders. Gangsters easily fire them from cars; assassins use them to dispatch victims without getting dirty; skinny fifteen-year-old kids shoot dead well-built grown men.

As Samuel Colt said to promote his pistols in the nineteenth century, handguns are equalizers, which even the weakest can use. That can be a bad thing.

During Colion's final years in prison, he became recognized as someone who could "squash beefs," or talk people down from killing each other, and he began to see himself as a peacemaker. When he was released in 2015, he moved back to Baltimore, and in the first two months there were five homicides within blocks of his home. He was shocked to see old people terrified, citing one woman who saw three killings.

"On the third one, they shot a kid right in front of her door," Colion says. "I'm thinking the woman is so traumatized, seeing three young men she watched as kids grow up, their heads blown off in broad daylight. It took a toll on her, and she passed away."

Colion looked back at his younger self and realized the terror he had caused, how it was traumatic for the whole community. He decided to take action and talked to local gang leaders. Because he'd served much of his life behind bars, they knew he was no informant.

"I walk up to these dudes. I say, 'Man, what did this grandmother do in the sixties and seventies to deserve to see y'all slaughtering these young men she watched as kids?' Nobody can answer me."

He negotiated with gangs in his neighborhood to create a No Shoot Zone of four blocks, where residents knew they would be safe, where children could play without fear, where old people could sit on their porches and not be witnesses to murder. To be clear where the territory was, he sprayed the words NO SHOOT ZONE on the sidewalks.

As the months passed without bullets on those blocks, Colion took the message to other neighborhoods. If a civilian was shot, especially a child or woman, or residents came to him and asked for help, he would paint NO SHOOT ZONE. After three years, he had painted eighty-six zones covering three hundred blocks of Baltimore. They were violated by shootings on only four occasions, he claims.

Colion's efforts are part of a broader movement from communities themselves, including ex–gang members, to stop the violence across the United States and more widely across Latin America and the Caribbean. In Los Angeles, where gang violence has been drastically reduced, groups such as Homeboy Enterprises and Homies Unidos have had a significant effect. They are a surely an important part of any solution to the murder epidemic in the Americas.

Colion agrees that guns make it too easy for gangbangers (including his former self) to take lives.

"It's the fixation with guns, the movies, the sound, the grip, the power," he says. "It's too easy to kill with a gun. And it's too gangster. You ain't got too many movies with knife killings. You know they didn't make it look too good."

These weapons are flooding into Baltimore, Colion believes, with the hand of the authorities themselves. "I know exactly where they are coming from. They are coming from the government."

When I ask him why on earth the U.S. government would want poor men and boys to be blasting each other, he replies that it is to exterminate African Americans, whose labor is no longer necessary to drive the U.S. economy.

"I think that our race isn't needed anymore. I think that Black people are beyond extinct. There is too much violence, too much to deal with," he says. "So let's dump guns and drugs in that hood. Let them finish each other off. You don't even have to drop a bomb on us and shit."

His feelings echo long-held theories about deliberately flooding guns and dope into African American communities to destroy them. Unless the situation stops being so dire, those ideas will keep being vocalized.

Later that night, I go with Colion to paint a No Shoot Zone on the corner of North Patterson Park and McElderry Street.[10] It follows a drive-by shooting a day earlier of a fifteen-year-old who is fighting for his life in the hospital.

Colion meets up with two women from the neighborhood, and he paints his letters on the sidewalk. It's late and nobody is about, but they stream on Facebook to get the message out.

It seems a hard call that these words on the concrete can stop bullets and save lives. But then a desperate situation requires desperate solutions. And as I watch them, a question rings out loudly in my mind.

Where is the government?

———

The long-running battle against black market guns is fought at many levels of U.S. policing. It is waged by the ATF in their stings with agents like Koz. State troopers add to the seized firearms in sweeps and searches. But a huge front is fought by city police, from specialized anti-gun units to cops on the beat.

New York was one of the most successful cities in reducing violence in the United States. In 1990, the Big Apple suffered 2,262 murders, winning it bloody infamy the world over.[11] In 2018, it recorded 295 killings—a drop of 87 percent.

Again, many factors are at work. But the NYPD had one of the best-funded and most aggressive gun squads, called the Firearms Investigations Unit. In March 2017, the NYPD joined prosecutors in what they claimed was the biggest gunrunning case in Brooklyn.

"We charged more defendants and recovered more firearms than in any other case in Brooklyn's history," Acting District Attorney Eric Gonzalez said at a press conference.

In total, the police got 217 guns, including MAC-10s, Glocks, AR-15s, AK-47s, and a Desert Eagle, and charged twenty-four people on a gargantuan 627-count indictment. A crew linked to the Bloods was buying the arms in Virginia gun shops and shipping them into Brooklyn neighborhoods including Bedford-Stuyvesant, Fort Greene, Sunset Park, and Boerum Hill. Sometimes, they would come on the bus, stashing the guns in bags in the luggage compartment.

The case confirms the markup on iron-pipeline guns. They were selling hand guns for $800 to $1,200 apiece and rifles for $1,800 to $2,200, proceeds used to buy "drugs, jewelry, clothing, and sneakers, in addition to sending money to jailed associates," the NYPD said.

The crew stumbled into trouble when they sold to an undercover officer in the gun unit, leading to the police putting wires on their phones. Excerpts from their taped calls reveal them bragging openly about trafficking weapons.

"It's a handheld chopper. It's an AR type . . . Yeah, yeah, it pierce armor," one of them said on a call.

"The Glock 26 and the motherfucking, uh, the Hi-Point. I'm a try to get the both of them," another said.

Other words they used for guns were "straps," "glizzies," "glicks," "jawns," and "joints."

Overall, the modus operandi of the group makes them look amateur and just waiting to go to jail. But then you don't need to be a criminal mastermind to run guns in the United States. After all, you are just buying something in a shop, shipping it over a state line, and selling it for triple the price.

"When twenty-four individuals can readily engage in interstate trafficking of 217 handguns, rifles, and assault-type weapons, this nation has a serious gun-control problem," New York City police commissioner James P. O'Neill said at the press conference.

Still, the police in New York can at least boast that their efforts at seizing illegal guns have paid off. In Baltimore, it's a different story.

*   *   *

Mike Wood served in the marines before working in the Baltimore Police Department from 2003 to 2014, going from the street beat to the narcotics unit. On leaving the force, he become a vocal critic of the city's policing (including on *The Joe Rogan Experience*) and an interesting voice on American crime.

Now doing academic investigations into policing, he recounts his experiences to me in colorful detail. The Baltimore police force felt disorganized and chaotic after the military, he says, but when he started running after drug dealers through the projects, he soon learned to enjoy the action.

"People are explaining it as scary. I didn't find it scary. I found it fucking fun," he said. "I felt like a cheetah chasing gazelles. I was excited. I also started to feel when I knew those people, I started to see them not as gazelles . . . It was like, this is not like the right perspective to have."

When I ask him how the strategy of policing guns changed in his years on the Baltimore force, he laughs.

"Nothing has ever changed in Baltimore. It's an absolute joke. There's not a crime plan at all," he says. "Baltimore has been doing the exact same plan with the exact same responses since the seventies. The exact same areas. And they are literally doing it now . . . It's the ultimate investment fallacy in American policing. It's hilarious."

The policing consists of hitting low-level drug dealers and charging them with drugs and gun crimes while not stopping the flow of firearms into the city, he said. While guns are taken off the street, people can always find a new dealer like Chain to buy another piece.

"You have a supply-and-demand issue. So if you are just taking away the end of the supply chain, and they are making guns every place at a greater rate than you are taking them off, it's an absolutely fruitless endeavor . . . It's like trying to get water off the planet."

Still, officers were given big incentives to put sheer numbers of guns on the tables, he says, which led to suspect practices. It is widely said in Baltimore that if you give police a firearm, they will overlook other crimes.

And all the pressure helped lead to a stinking scandal of the city's Gun Trace Task Force (GTTF).

The horror story of Baltimore's GTTF case was well covered, especially in the *Baltimore Sun*. There is also a book on it by the journalists Baynard Woods and Brandon Soderberg, aptly subtitled *The Rise and Fall of America's Most Corrupt Police Squad*.

The tale first got told in the 2018 trial, which described how seven active officers on the GTTF, along with a former officer, were running as a rogue unit. They were plainclothes, meaning they were not undercover like Koz but rolling in unmarked cars to run up on criminals. In Baltimore these are known as "knockers."

The squad of knockers was planting evidence, working as security for drug dealers, robbing other drug dealers, and putting seized dope back on the street. They also committed massive overtime fraud. While they were already making more than eighty thousand dollars a year, they would increase this by clocking hours when they were on the beach or working a barstool.

Their corruption was so blatant, they look like caricatures of rotten cops in a crime noir novel. When I sent a message to Jelly Roll saying I could see them making a movie about this, he replied, "There was a similar movie. *Training Day*."

Yet the crew took guns off the street. In a ten-month period, they confiscated 132 illegal firearms and made 110 arrests.[12]

Defending a member of the GTTF called Daniel Hersl was William Purpura, the Baltimore lawyer who defended El Chapo. Purpura described to me how there had been an institutional failure in letting them run wild precisely because they were bringing in guns.

"They were given too much leeway. There was no supervision. And they just took off," Purpura said. "They were given free rein, and that is what really enabled them to continue. As long as they were taking guns off the street, everyone was happy, and they were recording two, three, four guns a night. In essence, there was a blind eye cast to whatever they were doing."

Tragically, a good idea—of taking weapons off the streets to reduce murders—led to more abuse. The road to hell is paved with good intentions.

The task force seized firearms with suspect methods. A favorite was to drive fast into a corner crew in an unmarked car and beat down everyone who ran. Their main spree of seizing guns and robbing drug dealers was during a spike in violence after the Freddie Gray killing that made the police department desperate for results. But their crimes date to before the murder and are entwined in that tragedy.

I talk to the journalist Baynard Woods about his years covering Baltimore and his work on the GTTF story. Baynard is from a rare breed of long-form journalists, working at the alternative weeklies, reporting deeply from the street and reflecting it in well-crafted pieces.

He first got wind of the rough tactics of Officer Hersl back in 2014 when he got to know an up-and-coming Baltimore rapper called Young Moose. Hersl had watched a video of Young Moose that appeared to have real drugs and guns in it and used it as probable cause to raid his house. In return, Young Moose incorporated the detective into his lyrics. As he raps on the song "Tired,"

> Detective Hersl, he a bitch, I swear to God he ain't right
> Heard about my rap career, he trying to fuck up my life.

Baynard found that Hersl had a reputation, both on the streets and the force. "Other cops would use 'Hersl' as a verb, like, 'Is this legit or did you Hersl him.' It's like everyone knew about this guy," he says.

For protesters, Hersl became a symbol of police brutality, with chants of "Fuck the police" morphing into "Fuck Hersl." When the unrest broke out in 2015, Baynard says, angry youths were looking to get their revenge on knockers, and looking for Hersl himself.

Amid the many African Americans tragically killed by police, Freddie Gray died in police custody in 2015, sparking the protests in Baltimore and leading up to the protests across the United States in 2020. The twenty-five-year-old Gray was detained for carrying a knife on the morning of April 12, 2015. Video shows him screaming as he was piled into a police van and shackled. He sustained a spinal cord injury in the van, according to a medical examiner, and was taken to the hospital in a coma.[13]

When he passed away a week later, the city exploded. Many protesters were peaceful. But in the unrest, broadcast live on cable, people also fought with cops, set vehicles on fire, and looted stores. A state of emergency was declared, and the National Guard came in.

Baynard, who covered the unrest, joins many in Baltimore in calling it an uprising—a word later used for the movement in 2020. "The feeling that it was an occupying army, and the long-term feeling that you were being waged war on, boiled over, and people were ready to fight back," he says. "It really was almost a revolution. And the police responded to it like a counterinsurgency."

I ask Baynard what he thinks about the counterargument: that police killings pale in comparison to the murders by gangsters.

"Those things are tied together," he replies. "In East and West Baltimore, you don't get a response to calls for patrol, murders are unlikely to be solved, and yet you have these officers who are jumping out and searching you and strip-searching you, abusing you, and beating you up . . . When the police don't care about your community members who are murdered and then they murder people, that's a problem."

Following the unrest, homicides spiked even more, reaching a record number in 2017. There are numerous theories about why this happened.

The first is an argument that officers held back, scared that any policing could get them in trouble, a phenomenon known as the "Ferguson effect." (When violence surged nationally following protests in 2020, the Ferguson effect was alleged to be happening nationwide). A second theory is that Baltimore residents lost faith in the police and took justice into their own hands. The "anti-snitch" culture is effective when the police are seen as the enemy. Another theory is that gangs fought over the profits from the drugs looted. And yet another is that corrupt cops stirred up violence. Especially the GTTF.

In the trial, a witness testified that the head of the unit, Sergeant Wayne Jenkins, would come to his house to drop off drugs to sell back on the streets. On the night of the riots, Jenkins turned up with two trash bags full of prescription drugs that came from looting.[14] Other times he took the dope straight off dealers, who couldn't exactly go to the police to complain.

The robbing of dealers by police can provoke violence. If a dealer has lost his drugs and has no arrest sheet to show for it, he is suspected of stealing them himself, which can lead to retribution. In one case, the GTTF ripped ten thousand dollars off a dealer, who was later shot dead.

Retired officer Mike Wood says such corruption went beyond the GTTF. "The police themselves are the fourth cause of violence. Baltimore would literally be less violent if you just made them detectives and stopped doing enforcement."

This sense that policing has been an utter failure in Baltimore runs deep. It is common to hear people say there is no law in the city.

Personally, I think there are degrees of lawlessness—or to be more precise, in the deterioration of the rule of law. Compared with cities I have covered in Latin America, Baltimore still has a way to fall. The drug dealers do not openly carry rifles and grenade launchers, like those in the favelas of Brazil. The gangs don't carry out widespread kidnappings for ransom like they do in Mexico. And the murder rate is still less than half of Tijuana's and a seventh of that of Medellín at its worst. As the poet Dante wrote, there are many levels of hell.

Yet it still stuns me that a nation as powerful as the United States cannot reduce the rampant murder levels in certain cities. I ask Baynard if he thinks these are simply blips that will be smoothed out eventually. Surely, one day Baltimore will have falling crime, like New York. He points out that the opposite could happen.

"We've seen inequality grow and grow, and that's what this is, a result of inequality," he says. "I believe in many ways Baltimore is the future for

America rather than New York." When the unrest broke out in 2020, he tweeted that his claim was coming true.

The failure of the campaign to take illegal guns off the streets of Baltimore is disconcerting. For Baynard, it raises deeper questions about the politics of gun control. If the police don't protect people in these environments, he asks, do they need weapons to protect themselves? And is kicking down people's doors and putting them in prison for those guns only causing more harm?

"My opinions about gun control changed," he tells me. "I realized that while, to me, the fears of the Second Amendment guys, of jackbooted thugs coming and kicking in your door and taking your arms because Barack Obama sends them or whatever, is laughable. It's much less laughable when someone in West Baltimore says that, because that is what the Gun Trace Task Force guys are doing."

His idea reflects a notion that has gained some steam on the left: that the Second Amendment has never been respected for African Americans. When the Black Panthers took their shotguns to Sacramento, this helped bring about the Gun Control Act.

There is veracity to this. But still, there is unlikely to be much support for convicted felons in Baltimore or anywhere else to be allowed to win back their right to carry guns. And I don't think there should be. For many people in these violent areas, the solution is fewer guns, rather than more. But as Mike Wood says, the government needs to go after the supply chain and not just the guys on the corners.

Jelly Roll is a convicted felon but still carries a gun sometimes for protection. I ask him why he takes this risk.

"It's better to have it and not need it than to not have it and need it," he replies. "I've lived in the projects all my life. That's all my kids know. I have to protect and provide for them. It's not going to be safe. I walk outside my door, and they're selling coke and weed twenty-four hours a day. There are no police for me."

Jelly Roll's point of view raises questions for me. He is a caring father who supports his family, and has recently become a grandfather. For him to do years in prison for carrying a gun to protect himself would be terrible. Yet it is felons who commit much of the gun crime.

Jelly Roll himself has mixed feelings on gun control. He says the buyback programs—when people can exchange the guns for money, no questions asked—are good. He also likes the No Shoot Zones. But he says that if everyone could legally carry guns in Baltimore, including "elders" like himself, it could create a deterrent to stop others from drawing and shooting.

Several months after my second visit with Jelly Roll in Baltimore, he puts disturbing pictures on his Facebook. His two-year-old grandson is in the hospital with a bullet wound. His daughter was driving, and a man got out of a car with road rage and shot wildly. A few days later, the alleged shooter is arrested, a thirty-three-year-old felon. Jelly Roll writes to thank the Baltimore police for the arrest and to thank God that his grandson should make a full recovery.

Since Jelly Roll retired from selling dope, he has been earning his living doing security. His best gigs are clubs where he gets payoffs from underage kids, many of them drug dealers. He makes $1,500 a night doing this, which keeps his head above water for a couple of weeks.

I ask him how he sees his life. He survived bullets and prison and lived to enjoy grandchildren playing on his lap, to celebrate his daughter recently graduating from high school. Does he value this as an achievement in itself or live with regrets? His answer surprises me.

"The biggest thing that haunts me, that I've never even talked about, is that when you start selling drugs, you actually kill people," he says. "If you talk to any drug dealer that is retired from the game, he'll let you know that he's a murderer. You never know how many people you actually killed from the poison that you put into their hands. That is the burden that I carry to this day. There is no amount of right that I can do. And I feel that I am just going to pay for it some way ultimately."

I have seen drugs around me since I was a barely a teenager, and covered drug trafficking as a journalist for two decades. But while I often thought about how paid killers process their guilt, I didn't think about drug dealers doing it. Pulling the trigger on someone is one thing. Selling a product, which people choose to use, is different.

Yet heroin is perilous. In 2017, there were more than seventy thousand overdose deaths in the United States, including fifteen thousand from heroin. Jelly Roll knew that his drugs were used by people in his own community.

When you add up the numbers of drug deaths over the years, the figures are stunning. From 1999 to 2017, more than 702,000 Americans died from drug overdoses.[15] Many were from abuse of legal pharmaceuticals, but heroin, cocaine, and crystal meth all contributed heavily to the body count. That is more deaths than in the American Civil War.

El Chapo sold infinitely more drugs than Jelly Roll, and I wonder if he feels any guilt as he spends long days in solitary in the supermax in Colorado. Or did the fact that his drugs went to gringos in a foreign country lessen that. Or does he just not give a damn.

Likewise, I wonder about the guilt felt by gun sellers. I don't want to compare them directly to drug traffickers who are breaking the law; gun sellers are doing something the government sanctions. Yet I wonder if there is a difference in the feeling of guilt the further away they are from the deaths. Does it change things if they hear a gun they sell is used to kill Americans, whether at a school shooting or on the streets of Baltimore, or when the guns go to a foreign country and are used to murder people thousands of miles from their loved ones?

5

The Border

The border between Mexico and the United States is not just a line on a map . . . In the American imagination, it has become a symbolic boundary between the United States and a threatening world.

—Douglas Massey, sociologist

If someone is a sicario, people better respect him. If he belongs to organized crime, they respect him more than someone who finished college.

—Irving "Axer" Rodriguez, Ciudad Juárez rapper

———

It takes us ten hours to drive from the border at El Paso to the Dallas gun show. East of El Paso, I am struck by the nothingness for miles, the wide-open sprawl of cacti, dirt, and stones; the far-off hills with their lunar landscape. I have been to El Paso many times, but always crossing in from Ciudad Juárez or arriving by plane, and this is the first time I have driven east in a car. It makes me think how El Paso would have been before the days of planes, how cut off from other American cities.

I am with a radio producer, Sean Glynn, and two brothers, a photographer and newspaper editor from Ciudad Juárez. We are tracing the steps of Jorge, a twenty-three-year-old gun trafficker Sean and I interviewed the day before in the Juárez prison. Jorge used to drive every weekend from Mexico to gun shows in Dallas to buy firearms and smuggle them south. We are going to check out details of his story.

The elder brother, Joel, puts Queen on the car stereo, and we sing along jokily to "Don't Stop Me Now." "Two hundred degrees, that's why they call me Mr. Fahrenheit," Freddie Mercury croons.

The wide-open landscape stares back. It gives me a sense of how big and eerie this terrain is, flowing from the Chihuahuan Desert into semidesert into the Sonoran Desert. This is the land the border slices through, a line that Mexico and the United States have struggled to police for 170 years. It has long been crossed by smugglers with alcohol, looted pre-Hispanic artifacts, endangered animals, opium, marijuana, cocaine, heroin, crystal meth, and, of course, guns.

The geography of the U.S.–Mexico border makes it treacherous to police. At almost two thousand miles, it is among the longest borders on the planet. It begins in the Pacific Ocean (another smuggling corridor) at Tijuana–San Diego and crosses patches of soft earth, which are easy to tunnel through. The Sonoran and Chihuahuan Deserts are sparsely populated, mountainous, and filled with jagged rocks, spiky plants, and coyotes. The Rio Grande opens into a broad estuary that floods its banks, making fencing difficult.

Trump's idea of a border wall is not new. As far back as 1909, the government built a fence on the California border to stop cows getting ticks that were prevalent in the south. In 1918, a cross-border gun battle in Nogales killed twelve people, including the Mexican mayor. Following that, the

United States erected a six-foot fence through the middle of the border town.[1]

The fences spread and grew higher and thicker over the decades, joined by other defenses such as anti-car spikes. There were periodic surges to extend and reinforce sections, such as in 1990 and following the Secure Fence Act of 2006 (which sixty-four Democrats voted for).[2] When Trump finally secured funding, he added more fencing to the mix of barriers, spikes, and radars, while he was unable to fill all the gaps in the mountains and estuary.

But Trump's chants of "Build the Wall" at rallies put border issues on the front pages. He played on a vision of the border as a frontier to a dangerous world that had been growing in people's minds, as sociologist Douglas Massey wrote in an essay during the 2016 election campaign.

"The border between Mexico and the United States is not just a line on a map. Nor is it merely a neutral demarcation of territory between two friendly neighboring states. Rather, in the American imagination, it has become a symbolic boundary between the United States and a threatening world. It is not just a border but the border."[3]

There are real concerns about the growth of the cartels. However, the paradox is that while some of Mexico's cities on the Rio Grande are among the most murderous on the planet, the U.S. cities such as El Paso are among the safest. And there is a real and complex debate about immigration. But perhaps a more important front line is in the farms and factories that have enjoyed paying lower wages to undocumented workers. During the coronavirus crisis, these workers suddenly became *essential*, while they were still *illegal*.

From the south, the border takes a different light. It is the path to opportunity that has been celebrated by millions of Mexicans for a century. It is a source of huge business, with cross-border trade topping half a trillion dollars in 2019. Yet it symbolizes the barrier to a more powerful and sometimes aggressive neighbor, an image reinforced in Border Patrol shootings, imposing fences, and bright searchlights illuminating buffer zones that you can see at night from Mexico.

For organized crime, which straddles both countries, the border represents something else still: a way to make mountains of dirty money. And guns and drugs are intertwined here but inverted: the drugs go north and the guns go south.

Guns have flowed south from the United States since the country was founded. In Mexico's own War of Independence, which began in 1810, the warrior priest José María Morelos was supplied with U.S. arms, including six boats bulging with American guns that anchored in the port of Zihuatanejo.[4]

After the United States defeated Mexico in the 1846 to 1848 war and made the Gadsden Purchase in 1853, the demarcation of the current border was set. Gunmetal kept oozing over the new line that ran along the Rio Grande.

When the Mexican Revolution erupted in 1910, American guns armed both rebels and government troops. Writer J. David Truby documents how a wagon loaded with hay rolled into the village of Emiliano Zapata, in southern Mexico. Hidden underneath were sixty Winchester rifles, thirty Colt revolvers, and 2,800 rounds of ammunition. "The Zapata peasants had their start-up arsenal of vintage American frontier weapons to fight the federal troops," Truby writes.[5]

Truby points to gunrunners in Texas supplying weapons throughout that revolutionary war, in which a million people perished. U.S. mercenaries also fought with the rebels, including machine gunner Sam Drebin, known in his time by the politically incorrect name "the Fighting Jew." The U.S. government would sell guns only to the conservative Mexican government forces, who also wielded Mauser rifles from Germany.

Throughout the twentieth century, a southward dribble of guns continued. After an assassin shot dead presidential candidate Luis Donaldo Colosio in 1994, the murder weapon was traced to a San Francisco gun store.[6] When Mexico's next great battle, the Mexican Drug War, erupted in the early twenty-first century, the stream turned into a river.

* * *

The nature of this "drug war" is hotly debated. The Mexican government mobilized most of its active military into the fight from late 2006, and has yet to send the soldiers back to the barracks. Cartels formed increasingly sophisticated paramilitary wings, with gunmen wielding rifles and grenade launchers, dressed in camo and moving in armored vehicles with distinct insignia. The body count shot up from 2008 and has remained sky high since, hitting a new record in 2019. Single battles have involved hundreds of gunmen against thousands of police, with seventy-two people slain in a single massacre.

However, the fighting is not only over drugs but a range of rackets. Cartels have moved into a portfolio of crimes including human smuggling, oil theft, product piracy, sex trafficking, wildcat mining, extortion, kidnapping, and, of course, gunrunning. While "drug cartel" may be the established shorthand, it would be more accurate to call them "crime cartels."

The sides are constantly shifting. Some cartels have fragmented into smaller *cartelitos* that control chunks of states under the command of young and bloodthirsty lieutenants. Soldiers, police, and politicians are constantly being arrested for working with the gangsters they are supposed to be fighting. The victims include a huge number of "civilians"—journalists, priests, students, or anybody who upsets the wrong people, or is hit by a stray bullet. And with widespread impunity, it is hard to know when the dead were victims of cartels, of security forces, or of unrelated murders.

Unlike in a traditional insurgency or civil war, there are no clear political or ideological divisions between the combatants. Few in power want to call it a legal armed conflict; in Mexico that would mean recognizing cartel gunmen as formal belligerents, while in the United States it would mean taking more refugees.

Overall, I believe it is best understood as a new type of hybrid conflict, a mix of crime and war, which you can see plaguing various countries in the twenty-first century. The Mexican Drug War is driven by the fighting among cartels and rotten security forces, but it encompasses a broader range of violence and terror, including the rise of vigilantes, mass disappearances, and widespread kidnapping. It is a *period* of bloodshed and instability, like the three decades of "The Troubles" in Northern Ireland, but much more lethal.

Frustratingly, it is a conflict that is impossible to win but hard to get out of. Mexican president Andrés Manuel López Obrador took power in 2018 and repeatedly declared, "the war has finished." But after a spike of murders and massacres, he ordered the army to stay on the streets for the rest of his term.

However, the legal frameworks developed to address the wars of the twentieth century cannot easily be applied this new type of conflict. We need to create novel mechanisms to de-escalate the crime wars of the twenty-first century. And a starting point is to stop the guns flooding in.

When I was a green journalist covering Mexico for the Associated Press, I got reprimanded by one of my bosses, the legendary border reporter Eloy Aguilar, for trying to sneak the phrase "dusty border town" into my copy. He rightly pointed out it was beyond cliché. However, when you visit Nogales, Sonora, surrounded by desert, it is indisputably dusty, and its downtown cantinas with swing doors and latrines where you pee on lemons are undeniably folkloric.

On a trip there, I walk along the Mexican side of the fence with local journalist Milton Martinez and a friend he has known since childhood, nicknamed Flaco, or Skinny. As his name suggests, Flaco is slim, if not wiry, wearing fat Ray-Bans over his sunburned face and graying hair.

Flaco describes how he has taken people and drugs over the border for three decades. His story illustrates the evolution in the economics of smuggling and how cartels took over the whole business. He also describes how permeable the border still is going northward, with all the defenses of the United States, let alone how wide open it is going south into Mexico.

Flaco grew up in a ramshackle neighborhood called Buenos Aires that runs up to the border. Back in the eighties, Flaco would pop into the United States freely through holes in a wire fence, go to the store, and pop back into Mexico.

The first time Flaco guided people over the line was in 1984, when he was a fifteen-year-old schoolboy. Some migrants from southern Mexico came asking how to get into America, and he showed them a popular hole in the fence for a tip of fifty cents. Today, with the beefed-up border patrol, radars, and steel fences, smugglers offer a sophisticated operation, leading people on treks for days through the Sonoran Desert, and then in trucks to cities all over the United States. They charge as much as five thousand dollars for the service.

"From fifty cents to five thousand dollars," Flaco says. "As the prices went up, the mafia, which is the Sinaloa Cartel, took over everything here, drugs and people smuggling."

Known as coyotes, the human smugglers used to work independently or in small groups. But as the cartels became bigger and more violent, they made the coyotes work for them, and took the lion's share of profits. Today if migrants try to cross the border without paying, they risk getting beaten or murdered by cartel goons. The Sinaloa Cartel of El Chapo dominates Sonora and much of Baja California.

As the United States erects new barriers, it keeps pushing the traffic farther into the desert, deeper into the ground and deeper into the cartels' hands. This underlines a problem that has frustrated successive American administrations. Strengthening defenses does not stop smuggling. It only makes it more expensive, which inadvertently gives more money to criminal networks. The cartels have taken advantage of this to build a multibillion-dollar industry, which they protect with brutal violence, in turn destabilizing Mexico and providing more arguments to strengthen border security.

Flaco's career illustrates the endless enterprise of traffickers in getting their products (and people) over. In the 1980s, while pilots like Fernando Blengio were flying loads of cocaine, Flaco was on the ground lugging backpacks of marijuana. Buenos Aires has produced generations of smugglers, and its residents refer to those who carry drugs as burros, or donkeys.

"When I first heard about this, I thought they used real donkeys to carry the marijuana," Flaco says. "Then I realized, we were the donkeys."

He got paid five hundred dollars for his first donkey trip when he was in high school, which encouraged him to drop out for easy money. The fences haven't stopped the burros, who scale them with ropes or their bare hands. This was captured in spectacular TV footage showing smugglers zipping over the fence into Nogales, Arizona, seeing the cameraman, and then zipping back into Mexico. Trump apparently saw it, saying on a visit to the border that they are like "professional mountain climbers."[7] But solid walls are also problematic. They, too, can be scaled, and they make it harder for the Border Patrol to spot what smugglers are up to on the Mexican side.

Flaco graduated to building secret compartments in cars, which he calls *clavos*, fixing them into gas tanks, into the chassis, and in the wheel hubs. The smugglers drive these "trap cars" right through the "ports of entry," the customs term for the fifty official crossings over the land border.

Trap cars are the top way to traffic high-value drugs, such as cocaine, heroin, and crystal meth. As seizures show, customs agents nab far more value in vehicles at official crossing points than the Border Patrol does stopping burros in the desert with their packs of weed.[8] And this is the main reason that a wall won't stop drugs.

Meanwhile, shutting down the drug flow in cars has long proved impossible. The problem is the sheer number of vehicles heading north. When you have ten thousand cars a day at one port of entry, you can't search them all. And smugglers deliberately allow a vehicle with a smaller load to get caught, while other cars with more drugs ride through.

It's also hard to find the compartments. When customs agents learned to look for switches, smugglers figured out how to do without them. New trap cars can be opened only with complex procedures, such as when the driver is in the seat, all doors are closed, the defroster is turned on, and a special card is swiped. And any compartment that can hide kilo bricks of cocaine can hide guns and gun parts.

*   *   *

Sophisticated engineering also goes into the tunnels that turn the border into a block of Swiss cheese. Between 1990 and 2016, there were 224 tunnels discovered, some with air vents, rails, and electric lights. While El Chapo became infamous for them, it's a myth that he invented them. Flaco says they are as old as the border itself, beginning as natural underground rivers.

Back aboveground, catapults are a spectacular smuggling method. "We call them trampolines," Flaco says. "They have a spring that is like a tripod, and two or three people operate them." Border patrol agents captured one on the fence near Douglas, Arizona. It looked like a medieval siege weapon.

Freight trains also cross the border on their way from southern Mexico up to Canada. While agents inspect them, it's impossible to search all the carriages, which are packed with cargo from cars to canned chilies. The smugglers often pay the train workers to let them ride on board, Flaco says. He was once caught with a load of marijuana on a train in Arizona, but he managed to persuade police that he was an engine driver and only did a month in jail.

Flaco was later caught by Mexican police and served a five-year prison sentence from 2004 to 2009. When he was free again, he went back to smuggling, seeing no other way to earn a living.

The range of smuggling methods go on. Some Colombians solidified cocaine and made it into a fake soccer World Cup trophy. Surfers sped around the fence in Tijuana–San Diego with dope on their boards. A man arrived at Mexico City airport with heroin packed into false buttocks. (It exploded, causing his death.)

To come back south with guns and suitcases of dollar bills is even easier. But traffickers still benefit from corruption on both sides of the border, as gun smugglers explained.

———

Mexico has one gun shop.

Or to be precise, there is only one store in the whole of Mexico that is legally allowed to sell new firearms.

Mexican gun laws themselves are not as draconian as you may think. There is actually a right to bear arms in the Mexican Constitution of 1917, the document that aimed to end the grueling Mexican Revolution. Article 10 states, "The habitants of the Mexican United States [that is what Mexico is officially called] have the right to possess arms in their home, for their security and legitimate defense, except for those prohibited by Federal Law and those reserved exclusively for the Army, Navy, Air Force and National Guard."

Therefore, in contrast to what it says in the U.S. Second Amendment, the Mexican Constitution specifies that firearms can be used for self-defense but adds that the government should have the biggest guns. It looks good on paper.

You can get these guns only in the one shop, which is run by the Mexican army and sits in a defense department building in the west of Mexico City. With the snappy name of Directorate of Arms and Munitions Sales, it has layers of reinforced walls so gangsters can't rob it like they do U.S. shops. When you go in the lobby, you have to line up and hand in your identification plus your cell phone and walk through metal detectors. It reminds me of checking into prisons.

Quite a few guns are on offer, similar to what you can find in a store in Texas, including AR-15s and German and Italian semiautomatic handguns. Except the price would make American gun aficionados choke, with ARs at two thousand dollars.

It's not so much the cost putting people off, though, as the red tape. A gun buyer has to hand in seven pieces of paperwork, including a letter from their work and proof they have no criminal record. After filing everything correctly, they have to wait for the government to approve their request, which can take months. And when they finally walk away with their gun, the government has all their details filed into a gun owner's registry.

The shop still sells about nine thousand guns a year to the public and another seven thousand to private security companies, which include a lot of former police and soldiers. If you hire an armed guard in Mexico, you are likely to get an ex-cop with a gun from this shop.[9]

But the restrictions make straw buying difficult, so Mexican criminals don't generally use the store as a source. Especially considering how easily they can get guns from El Norte.

If you try driving from the United States into Mexico, you may be surprised how easy it is. Chances are that you won't get stopped and that you can cross an international border without so much as flashing a passport.

But gun smugglers don't leave it to chance. Their problems can start on the U.S. side, where the Border Patrol operates about seventy inland checkpoints on roads toward the line. And once they cross over, agents from Mexico's customs and immigration, police, and soldiers are lurking. Still, corruption helps the gunrunners.

Tony, an electrical engineer from California, told me his story of using a government credential to smuggle firearms over the river from the nineties to the noughties. He is not a career criminal but a professional American who strayed into organized crime for a phase.

Tony grew up in the Northern Californian city of Napa, the son of a single mom from Michoacán, Mexico. While some of his cousins got into gangs, he was a nerd, loving to play with amateur radio. After getting his associate degree, Tony went to work for a company running infrastructure for cell phones, pagers, and air-control signals. The company vetted him, even interviewing his mother, and found a clean sheet.

A couple of years on, he was sent to the southern border as a route patroller, maintaining towers and cable lines from El Paso to near Tucson, driving long hours in his company truck to rural sites. He also went into Mexico to maintain installations, and as they were bouncing signals for the Federal Aviation Administration, he had official cover to cross the border.

Various police officers and Border Patrol agents from the American side have been caught working for cartels. In 2011, prosecutors charged the mayor and police chief of Columbus, New Mexico, with trafficking guns to the Juárez Cartel. The police chief even obeyed a cartel request to do a traffic stop on ATF agents.[10] Smugglers will also corrupt the private sector. Air stewards, ship crew, and train workers can all lend a hand in moving merchandise.

Tony began dating a girl called Esmeralda who was from Juárez but lived in Las Cruces, New Mexico. She introduced him to her brother Octavio, who was older, with a pockmarked face and handmade tattoos, and they became friends, going to a bar run by the Bandidos Motorcycle Club, a force in the area. Tony learned that some of the Bandidos worked with cartels in Mexico, providing muscle for them north of the border.[11]

One night, Octavio asked what was the craziest thing Tony ever did. He replied that when he was working for Kmart as a student, he had a scam for stealing box loads of inventory. Octavio asked if he would take some boxes of something else over the border in his company truck.

"I don't run drugs," Tony said.

"No, no, no. It's nothing with drugs," Octavio replied. "It's just hardware."

Tony knew that "hardware" meant guns because he had heard Bandidos use the term. He puts his choice down to youth. "I'm young. I'm dumb. My moral compass was not there. I didn't have any kids."

He also said he was angry at the world for a rather bizarre reason: rapper Tupac being shot dead. "I was a big Tupac fan. His whole thing was pretty much 'Fuck the world. I'm a gangster. Live by the gun, die by the gun.' I was pissed off they killed him."

Octavio went to the cable company's storage facility in Las Cruces and gave Tony three large crates, the type used by rock bands on tour. They loaded them in among the radio gear. Octavio offered Tony muscle relaxants to look calm in front of cops, but Tony said he wouldn't need them. He drove over the border using a quiet crossing at Santa Teresa and then east to Juárez. Both the Border Patrol and the Mexican officers knew him from his work, so they waved him through. Arriving in Juárez, he went to the company's site and used it to hand over the crates to Octavio's cohorts.

Tony didn't look in the crates on the first two runs. But on the third, Octavio popped one and he saw it bulging with disassembled rifles.

"These right here are just partial of what we have other people running down there," Octavio said. "Once it gets over there, they assemble them."

"You just load them on," Tony said. "If I don't know nothing, then they can't get nothing."

After four runs, Octavio gave Tony a stack of bills totaling $6,500. But Tony said he wasn't doing it for the money.

"I had a chip on my shoulder, and I got a thrill out of this. It got my blood going. It got me like, 'Ooh, I'm going to do this and I'm going to get away with it.'"

He carried on running guns and sometimes crates of cash south, making twelve hundred to fifteen hundred dollars a trip. Octavio appeared to work for a branch of the Juárez Cartel, which controls that section of border. But Tony didn't ask Octavio, as he thought it smarter to keep his mouth shut. They would talk on the phone using codes. Tony would say, "The store is open," to signal he was making a work run to Mexico.

One time, Tony had a scare on the Mexican side. He had just crossed from the town of Santa Teresa when a Mexican police officer pulled him over and said he was going to search his truck.

"This is a government vehicle," Tony protested. "In order for me to authorize you to search this vehicle, you are going to have to call my boss. This is FAA equipment."

It was a lie, but Tony was rolling and he upped the bluff.

"As I am sitting here talking to you," Tony told the cop, "there is a vast amount of time that is being wasted. And there is an outage in Mexico that I have to go to."

"What are you talking about, an outage?" the cop replied.

"I am a field technician, and I have been sent to come down and repair some microwave equipment, because the FAA has grounded the airplanes because of equipment failure."

Tony flashed his U.S. government identification, and the officer backed down and let him through.

He soon learned that Esmeralda was pregnant and decided it was time to quit. He didn't want to be a father in a Mexican jail.

Tony invested his earnings in a trailer and piece of land. He did one last run and told Octavio he was done. But to smooth over his exit, he invited in a coworker, Freddy, who had two kids and was desperate for cash. Freddy took over the gun trafficking with fervor. While Tony had spread trips out, Freddy went all the time.

For a year, it was going great for Freddy, who was making tens of thousands of dollars on top of his salary. Until there was a quarterly meeting for the route patrollers and he didn't show up. Tony went to his house, and his wife hadn't heard from him for a week, so he informed their boss that Freddy was AWOL.

Tony would never see Freddy again, and never asked Octavio what happened.

"If you start asking questions, it always leads to 'Why are you asking?'" Tony said. "In some respects, I do feel bad if he did end up getting killed. But then again, I didn't hold the gun up to his head to tell him to do it."

Soon after Esmeralda had a daughter, she and Tony broke up. Tony got a job with a new cable company and got back in touch with Octavio, who was serving a stretch in federal prison. Octavio said they didn't need gunrunners but wanted scouts to spy on the Border Patrol.

Tony saw it as low risk, as he didn't have to smuggle anything. He bought a device called a spectrum analyzer that allowed him to see when the Border Patrol were talking on their radios and used a programmable scanner to listen in.

"I could hear them positioning their agents, and I could hear pretty much where they are going," he said. "And they didn't necessarily talk in codes, not like police do. They would actually just talk to each other. 'Hey,

I'm over here at this point?' And what they would do is use checkpoints and give them names with mile markers. I was able to connect the dots.

"And another thing they did a lot that was really stupid is they would give away their longitude-latitude coordinates. That's pretty much a universal language there."

Tony zapped the info to the cartel in Mexico, who would use it to move drugs and people. The cartel paid Tony five hundred dollars a week for his surveillance. By then, he was doing it purely for the money, and he bought a pickup and a '49 Chevy Fleetline.

The September 11 attacks complicated the racket, leading the U.S. government to beef up security. "That changed the game," Tony said. "That put the military on the border. It brought a lot of attention."

Then Tony was hit by heartbreak. Esmeralda sat him down and revealed his daughter wasn't really his daughter but was fathered by her ex. He went to child support, and they confirmed it. Tony asked Esmeralda why she hadn't told the truth. She said that she was scared he would have gotten angry and informed on her brother, giving up the gunrunning operation.

" 'You don't know me that well. I would never have done that,' " Tony told her. " 'I would never have turned on your brother. I would never have turned on anybody.' "

His adventure of romance and smuggling on the border seemed a farce. Tony left it all and headed back to California with two duffel bags. He gave Esmeralda the trailer, the deed to the property, and his two cars.

"I gave it all to her and told her to give it to my daughter. Even though she wasn't mine," he said. "I chose to leave to start my life over back in California."

He never heard from the cartel again.

After the hurt, Tony told himself he would never get married. But that didn't last long, and that same year, he met a woman and fell in love; they would tie the knot and have two kids.

He got a job in the maintenance department at a university and became a regular middle-aged guy, playing with his children, surfing the net, messing with drones. His foray into the cartel world was like a dream from a former life, and he was one of the few who never went to prison. I asked him if he carried guilt, as those guns were likely used to murder.

"I do, I really do," he said. "What made it even worse was when this whole Fast and Furious operation came about during the Obama administration. It pissed me off. Because this had been going on for a long time. And there hadn't been a stop to it. Nor do I see in the future any stop to it. I did it. Then the government got caught out doing it . . . No matter what, a gun is a gun. It is used for one purpose only. And that is to kill somebody or to hurt somebody."

Tony's story gives a glimpse into one of many trafficking operations that move guns over the southern border. They take different shapes and sizes. Individuals do it, families do it, cartels do it, small gangs with only loose relations to cartels do it.

Sometimes the firearms are piled high in trucks. The Zetas tried to move one with 147 Kalashnikovs from Phoenix over the border at Laredo.[12] The ATF caught onto it and seized the guns before they went over the line. But often, smugglers are moving just handfuls of guns at a time.

Tony was only on the fringes of this gun trafficking. But in Juárez prison, I found someone at the heart of it.

For many years, I have been going into prisons in Mexico to interview inmates about their lives and crimes. The penitentiaries vary. Some are crowded and chaotic, with people rotating sleeping hours to share crammed floor space and inmates selling each other merchandise like it's an indoor market. Others are divided by rival cartels controlling different wings. Many have erupted in bloody riots.

When police storm prisons and search cells, they often find firearms stashed, including fully automatic Kalashnikovs and grenades. Gangs pay and intimidate guards to smuggle the hardware in. When prisons are head-quarters of gangs and full of guns, it's a crazy, inverted state of affairs.

In U.S. penitentiaries, as Billyjack related, inmates are rarely able to smuggle guns inside, although they get drugs in. This is an interesting point in gun control: there are some places, such as prisons and airplanes, that even hard-core gun rights activists believe should be firearm-free. And keeping those guns out is not something that happens naturally but that comes from a concerted effort.

The state prison in Juárez has suffered from the guns inside, with a 2011 riot in which inmates shot seventeen other prisoners dead. I go in through the lines of security with veteran Juárez photographer Miguel Perea and the producer Sean. The warden has agreed to bring us an inmate convicted on Mexican federal firearms charges, and he allows us to meet him in a patio away from the other prisoners. The privacy helps, as prying eyes can be dangerous, the cartel seeing an inmate talking to us as akin to snitching. In a tragic case, some gang members in a nearby prison gave a TV interview from a cell and were murdered within hours of the broadcast.

Jorge arrives and sits down. He's a slight twenty-three-year-old with a goatee, and is unthreatening in contrast to the tough assassins with their thousand-yard stares. He looks nervous but relaxes as we get into the conversation, which probably breaks the boredom of long days locked up. He tells the story of growing up in a small Chihuahuan town, six hours south of the border, and his foray into gunrunning.

It wasn't a tough choice moneywise. Toiling as a laborer for the city paid Jorge three hundred dollars a month; running guns over the Rio Grande could score him ten thousand bucks on a single trip.

Jorge was almost nineteen and hungry to make something of himself in his small town. His dad had brought him up comfortably by buying cattle from local ranchers and selling them to American meatpacking factories. Jorge also had hopes of going into business and wanted to get some education. But when he got his girlfriend pregnant, he dropped out of high school, desperate for funds; for his own place, a car, powdered milk.

Enterprising friends got into the drug trade, growing weed and opium in the nearby hills and selling it to the cartel, or smuggling bricks of cocaine and heroin over the border in trap cars. Some turned to the dark craft of *sicariato*, or hired killing. But Jorge didn't want to be another mutilated corpse on the crime pages of the local tabloid. Instead, he sweated in the scorching Chihuahua sun, mixing concrete and laying bricks, and at the end of the day he collected his two hundred pesos, about ten dollars, barely enough for a pack of diapers.

He bought the first gun as a favor. Thanks to his dad's cattle business, he had a visa to cross into Texas, and he had a friend who worked in construction in Dallas. On free days, he would ride the bus up to buy cheap clothes, sunglasses, and boom boxes, and then take them back to his pueblo to sell for a small markup. A friend heard about the trips and asked him to get a popular American consumer product—an AR-15.

The friend was connected to the cartel, so it was hard for Jorge to refuse. He asked around and found the trick was to buy at a gun show, making sure he didn't leave any ID to trace the sale. He found one in Dallas and went there, finally finding someone who would sell to him with no identification.

Back in Jorge's pueblo, his friend was delighted and gave him three hundred dollars for the effort, doubling his month's wages. A day later, the friend came back to say he knew other people who wanted rifles, and they would pay $2,300 apiece, or more than triple what they cost in Dallas.

Jorge knew his friend ran with mobsters, but the money seemed too good to refuse. He decided he would do a few runs to make some capital and invest in a legitimate business. He recruited his buddy in Dallas to help him buy the guns and bought a truck to carry them.

Each weekend, Jorge would drive from his town in Chihuahua to a Dallas gun show. He would buy a batch of weapons, seven, ten, twelve, sometimes up to fourteen. They included a mix of rifles and pistols but always several AR-15s, the most popular sell in his pueblo.

Jorge's trafficking coincided with a boom for AR-15s in the United States. Back in the seventies, AR-15s sold only sparsely, and Clinton's Federal Assault Weapons Ban in 1994 took many off the shelves. But in the years after Bush lifted the ban in 2004, the cult of the AR-15 really took off. With the patents on the basic AR-15 design expired, competing gun makers aggressively marketed their own variations of the rifle, giving them different names. Gun enthusiasts began claiming the AR-15 as a lifestyle, a symbol of both America's military prowess and the right to bear arms. They said that "AR" stood for "America's rifle."

During the 2010s, AR-15 sales surged. Threats to ban the guns under Obama, especially after Adam Lanza used one to massacre schoolchildren at Sandy Hook Elementary School in Connecticut, drove people to stock up. In 2012 alone, U.S. factories made more than a million guns for the domestic market that were AR-15–style or were "modern sporting rifles" with similar features.[13] More than a million more such guns were sold in various years, including 2013, 2015, and 2016. Thousands of those headed south to Mexico.

Jorge also smuggled several .50-caliber rifles. These supersize weapons fire bullets the size of small knives, and army snipers use them to shoot long distance and blow through armor. Despite their military potential, customers can buy them in stores in Texas and Arizona as easily as buying a pistol.

Jorge would buy used .50 calibers for five thousand to seven thousand dollars apiece and sell them for triple. New .50 calibers usually cost over ten thousand dollars.

The cartels love them. They take skill to fire, but the Mexican mob hires vets, from the Mexican, U.S., Colombian, and Guatemalan armies. They use the .50 calibers to blow through vehicle armor (as the military says, "anti-matériel"), sitting on the hillsides and firing at police and military convoys. The dozens of examples include the Familia cartel using a .50 caliber to hit a Mexican army M-17 helicopter in 2011, injuring two officers and forcing it to land, and the Beltrán Leyva cartel using a .50 caliber as part of an attack on police vehicles in 2009 that killed eight officers. In 2019, Sinaloa Cartel gunmen used .50 calibers when hundreds of gunmen took over the city of Culiacán in response to the arrest of El Chapo's son. Military video shows a bullet from one blowing off a chunk of a soldier's leg.

The fact that .50 calibers are so obviously military-grade weapons, and seeing them used effectively by cartel gunmen, sits uneasily with the gun lobby. So advocates shift to deny they come from the United States, although there is plenty of documented evidence they do.

However, attention to them has been limited, because they are not used much by American gangsters. If criminals in the United States did start ambushing police cars with .50 calibers, the reaction could be thunderous.

Jorge would buy without any identification, which he described in an interesting way, not fully understanding the U.S. law.

"There's a black market right there at the gun show. You buy from the person who doesn't ask for any paperwork. If you go over to a person, ask for the price, and then they say, 'I need your license,' then you say, 'I don't want it,' and go with someone else. The seller who tells you they don't need anything, that's where I used to buy."

Jorge would also buy through Facebook, using specialist pages where guns were bought and sold. When the issue of guns being traded on Facebook and Instagram gained attention in 2016, Facebook announced it was banning their sales. However, a report in the *Wall Street Journal* in 2019 found that people were still buying guns there using codes, such as pretending to sell gun cases but showing off the firearm that was really for sale.[14]

Moreover, various websites now specialize in one-to-one gun sales, including GunBroker and Gunbuyer. They have created a sprawling alternate market for guns on the web.

Jorge bought fridges and cookers and stashed the guns inside them. To be extra careful, he went to the effort of declaring the kitchen goods and paying import duties on them. Back in his pueblo, his friend would sell the guns quickly. "Clients will always be there," he says. The guns in his pueblo came almost exclusively from the United States, he claims.

Jorge demonstrates a certain model of gun trafficking. He was part of a three-man team with the guy in Dallas and the guy in the pueblo. Jorge didn't pay bribes to officials to get the guns through. But he did pay off the cartel, the real power. Jorge handed over one quota to gangsters for the right to smuggle guns over the border at Ciudad Juárez, and another for the right to sell those guns in his pueblo. This payment system illustrates how the cartel operates like a shadow government that oversees criminals and many other aspects of life in its strongholds.

The cartel payments could add up to ten thousand dollars a month. But paying the mob stopped Jorge from finding himself tied to a chair getting his head cut off. And he was making so much cash it didn't matter. On a single sale, he could make $1,700, and in some months he moved over fifty weapons.

He forgot about his plan to retire as he earned more money than he could have imagined. As he turned twenty, he was able to buy a house outright, a brand-new truck, look after his wife, keep mistresses on the side, and take drugs and party. To explain how his lifestyle had changed from broke to ostentatious, he told friends that he was working construction in the United States.

"At the beginning I felt bad, but I got used to it. In the end I didn't care," he says. "It's the way you can have a good time. You sell weapons, you earn money, and you have fun. I bought a brand-new truck, a motorbike, women, drugs. I had everything."

Business finally went bad because of a dispute with his cousin. When they had an argument, his cousin "put the finger," or informed, on him, giving soldiers the license plates and time he was crossing, and describing where the guns were hidden. The soldiers searched and found the pistols and rifles. "If I hadn't gotten snitched on, I would maybe still be working on the same thing," he says.

Jorge was busted with a relatively small stash of four AR-15s and two 9 mms. But it was still enough to get him eight years and eight months in prison. When Mexico does convict on firearms charges, it can give harsher sentences than the United States does. Although that is a big "when."

When we talk to Jorge, he still has six years and five months to go and is counting every day. He says that when he gets out, he will go clean, look for a decent job, a business, provide for his daughter. But when we ask him about the violence ending, he shrugs his shoulders. "This will never end," he says.

Optimism of a better world around the corner is often for those who don't live in the war zones.

———

It was following this interview that we were driving on the road from El Paso to Dallas, looking at the wide-open terrain—and going to a gun show to see how easy it is to buy AR-15s with no ID. Texas is big for gun shows, with most weekends counting at least two events in different parts of the state. The town with the most is Mesquite, on the east of the Dallas urban sprawl. The Visit Dallas website describes it as the "rodeo capital of Texas." Breitbart News calls it "the Gun Show Capital of America."[15]

Arriving in Mesquite, we walk into a sprawling fair with seven hundred tables. The SHOT Show in Vegas is trade only, but this is open to the public for a nine-dollar fee. Besides that, it looks similar, with loads of tables and loads of guns, sellers hawking everything from antique firearms to the latest pistols and rifles, plenty of Kalashnikovs and plenty of AR-15s.

We try a couple of sellers to ask if they will give us a rifle without a paper trail. But they say they are licensed sellers, FFLs, and need Texas ID. But then we crack it. We find private sellers who say they can sell guns with no paperwork, and we record it, as is legal under Texas law. As one conversation goes:

SEAN: Hi, how are you? Is that the cash price for the AR-15?
SELLER: Yep, no tax or paperwork.
SEAN: So cash is all I need?
SELLER: Yep.

SEAN: So what about ID?

SELLER: You don't have to have ID on private sales.

And that was it. It really was possible to walk into a gun show and buy an AR-15 with no paperwork. Jorge had described it as a black market, the gunrunner himself thinking that the sellers must be breaking a law. The crazy thing is that they aren't.

It gets back to the infamous private-sale loophole at the heart of the gun debate. Many call it the "gun show loophole," although that is a bit misleading because it is not a question of whether it is at a gun show or not, but whether it is from a private sale or a licensed dealer.

When the GCA and then the Brady Bill were approved, they did not apply to private sales, a measure strengthened by the 1986 act. The argument was that if someone is selling an old gun, often to a friend or family member, then that is a private transaction that shouldn't be subject to trade regulations. No paperwork necessary.

But here in the gun show, it wasn't selling to friends and family. And it wasn't just the odd weapon that collectors were offering. On various tables, so-called private sellers had dozens of weapons, including many AR-15s and Kalashnikovs. Many looked brand-new, with some boxed up. As another conversation went,

SEAN: Is that a cash price?

SELLER: Yeah. No tax, no paperwork, out the door. That one's unfired. We got one magazine with it.

SEAN: Unfired?

SELLER: Unfired. Brand-new.

People shouldn't use the private-sale loophole to do business, but this is a classic way to abuse the law. You buy from a gun shop and sell at a markup with no paperwork. There are various documented cases of people doing this, including one in Florida, which I detail in chapter 9.

If people are actively "engaged in the business of selling firearms" without a license, they can be charged, and the ATF agents go undercover into gun shows. But these are hard cases to make, so the ATF will normally warn sellers first. And with a shortage of agents, a lot goes under the radar.

Jorge used the private-sale loophole to take guns to the cartels in Mexico. Others take guns to gangs in the inner cities. Even an MS-13 member, in the country without papers, could be buying them. This gets to the clash between law and order and gun rights.

Even under the loophole, collectors should not sell a gun if they have knowledge or suspicion the buyer is a criminal. But many ignore this, as I watched happen in front of me. A tattooed woman with her boyfriend was looking at a pistol offered by a private seller. She asked him about another model, and he said a friend had it but that friend was a licensed dealer, so she would need ID. She shook her head, insinuating she had a record. The private seller went ahead and sold her a gun, taking a credit card payment. The case in chapter 9 shows examples of this practice that the ATF have on tape.

This loophole is what the battle about universal background checks is all about, a battle that gets into heated arguments and a barrage of statistics.

For gun safety advocates, the idea of a loophole is stupefying. The whole point of a law is that it should be applied universally, or else why have it? It's as if people were allowed to privately sell pharmaceuticals to whomever they wanted with no prescriptions, or brewers could privately sell alcohol to minors. A loophole undermines all enforcement.

It's not just a handful of people at the odd gun show buying weapons under the loophole. Far more use it to buy through contacts or online.

In a survey by researchers from Northeastern University and the Harvard School of Public Health in 2015, researchers interviewed gun owners who had bought a weapon in the previous two years. It found that 22 percent acquired their last firearm through a private sale.[16] This leads to an oft-cited figure that about one in five guns in the United States are bought without the background check.

Nobody knows how many of these guns are used in crimes. Following them is difficult, as once a gun has gone through the hole, there is no record. A gun can pass through multiple hands: a criminal can acquire it directly, or a black market seller like Jorge can sell it on.

The U.S. Justice Department conducted a survey of inmates in state and federal penitentiaries to shine some light into the black hole.[17] It interviewed convicts who possessed a gun when they committed the offense for which they were doing time. They included murderers, armed robbers, and many drug dealers.

The survey found that 43 percent of these criminals had gotten the guns off the black market, from dealers like Chain hawking weapons to the corner boys. These dealers themselves can obtain guns through the loophole, as well as other methods like straw buying.

The fact that the black market was the biggest means for criminals buying guns is notable. As Chain said, most corner dealers won't go to great efforts, traveling far or recruiting their own straw buyers. They just go to a black market dealer, even if they are paying triple the price.

Only 6.4 percent of the criminals had personally stolen their guns, which goes against an argument some make that this is the main source. However, the gun traffickers may have sold them stolen weapons.

The survey found another 8 percent of the prisoners had purchased the guns from a friend or family member. That means they were bought using that private-sale loophole. Another 10.8 percent of the inmates were given the guns or had someone else buy them, meaning straw buyers.

Only 1.2 percent said they had personally bought the gun at a show. This is of course a tiny percentage, a point raised by gun rights advocates. However, it would still account for several thousand jailed gunslingers. And the survey found that another 5.9 percent had gotten guns from "other sources," including the internet, which can go back to the private-sale loophole.

The data shows that a huge number of felons and other prohibited people are trying to buy weapons. In the single year of 2017, for example, 181,000 people attempted to buy guns and were denied in the check. Between 1994 and 2019, the system denied 3.5 million buys. Time and time again, felons, wife beaters, even fugitives give buying guns a shot and are knocked back by the checks.

Meanwhile, shooters have used the private-sale loophole to carry out various high-profile crimes. Among them, Seth Aaron Ator wielded an AR-15 to kill seven and injure twenty-two outside a movie theater in Odessa, Texas, in August 2019.[18]

Understanding why there is a loophole gets to the fervent politics of gun control in the run-up to the Brady Bill. As the activist Richard Aborn, who helped shape the law, wrote: "The battle over the Brady Bill was a long and torturous struggle from its introduction in 1987 to its final passage on November 24, 1993."[19]

The gun lobby opposed any background checks at all, successfully blocking the bill at various stages for six years. The bill's advocates were struggling to get even licensed dealers to do checks, let alone collectors. But support grew amid the urban violence of the period. After Clinton took the presidency in 1992, he said in his State of the Union address, to big applause, "If you'll pass the Brady Bill, I'll sure sign it."

The gun lobby switched focus to making sure the act was watered down. One victory was the private-sale loophole. They were also concerned about the length of time that checks would take, as buying guns, like any other consumer product, is often done on impulse. They pushed for creating the National Instant Criminal Background Check System, getting another loophole that limited extended checks to three days, even if there was information pending.

"The group had triumphed," writes Jennifer Mascia for the *Trace*. "It managed to maintain political cover with supporters by fighting an unflinching war against the bill in the public arena while simultaneously watering it down from within."[20]

Gun safety advocates saw the problems right away, but as the years went on, it became apparent it was a bigger and bigger issue. Various states went ahead and legislated themselves. Twelve now require universal background checks at the point of sale. They do this by making private sales go through a licensed dealer. The dealer takes the Form 4473 and does the check, usually for a small fee. But the majority of states still have the gaping loophole, including two of the four border states with Mexico.

The drive for universal background checks is the gun safety measure that garners the most support. A compilation of Gallup surveys showed 86 percent supporting them, even while only 63 percent favored stricter gun laws.[21]

The gun lobby struggles to argue why a law shouldn't apply to everyone. Advocates tend to stress that universal checks won't stop crime. They point out that criminals can buy guns from various sources or that some criminals and terrorists can pass background checks.

Yet this is wobbly ground. Saying a measure won't completely stop a crime applies to anything in law enforcement. The point is to take various measures to reduce a problem as much as possible. Security cameras won't stop all theft, but that doesn't persuade stores they shouldn't be used.

Another argument is the old fear of the tyrannical government taking away guns. As the *National Review* said in an editorial after the shootings in El Paso and Ohio: "Universal background checks require the creation of a national gun registry that can be used to check compliance . . . A government that knows where all the guns are is a government that can stage a confiscation drive—or, in the Orwellian parlance of modern gun-controllers, a 'mandatory buyback' drive."[22]

This idea that checks would automatically lead to a gun registry is not actually a given. The ATF's National Tracing Center at Martinsburg does the dance of not having a gun registry while still hunting down the Form 4473s on sales from licensed dealers. But it gets back to the core notion that the

American people need guns to rise against an oppressive government. Advocates want people to stockpile in case of a future insurrection, and deliberately want many of those guns to be in mysterious places where the "gestapo" gun police can't find them. In other words, they want the law to fail.

This extreme interpretation of the Second Amendment makes it hard to reach a consensus on gun policy. If you really believe people should be armed for an insurrection, and the government shouldn't know where the guns are, it's challenging to keep weapons away from gangs, narcos, and terrorists. As Harlon Carter said, this is "a price we pay for freedom."

———

How many guns exactly are sold in the United States and smuggled to Mexico?

The true answer is that nobody knows. Not the ATF. Not the NRA. Not the Mexican government. Not even the cartels.

Black markets are exactly that. We can't pick up spreadsheets of gun sales to gangsters, just as we can't pick up spreadsheets of heroin sales to junkies. If anyone offers exact numbers for black market sales, then be very suspicious.

The problem is that the majority of guns are likely never captured, just as the majority of drugs are never seized. I spoke to the pilot Fernando about this from his years in the business. I asked what percentage of cocaine got busted. I thought he might say 40 or 50 percent. The traffickers are making so much money, they could swallow this. But he said about 20 percent. Which means that for every ton of cocaine that law enforcement seizes, another four tons are sold and snorted.

Nevertheless, we can look at certain hard data and studies that use that data to make wider estimates. The first is the data given out by the crew from Martinsburg. Every year, the Mexican government sends serial numbers of thousands of seized firearms to the trace center, which goes through them in the usual sequence of phone calls, emails, and sifting through papers.

In 2018, the Mexican government sent the records of 16,343 guns. Of these, the ATF traced 11,506, or 70 percent, to the United States; these included 8,326 that were made in America and 3,180 that were imported from other countries but then sold in America, like the Kalashnikovs from Cugir. The other 4,926 were classified as "undetermined source country for firearms."[23]

This was a typical year. As I have said, in the twelve-year period from 2007 to 2018, over 150,000 guns were definitively traced from Mexican criminals to the United States. This is the most important figure, and it's a huge deal. It is irrefutable proof there is major gun trafficking over the southern border to one of the world's cruelest conflicts.

But you also have to read the ATF data carefully. In the case of 2018, it doesn't say that the guns not traced to the United States were confirmed to be from elsewhere. It says that they were from an "undetermined source country." In some of these, the ATF explains, "the trace request was unclear as to the manufacturer, country of origin and the importer." This could mean that a serial number was given incorrectly, which Neil Troppman in Martinsburg says happens a lot, or that amid the chaotic system of gun records in America, the files were lost. In other words, more of the guns could potentially be from the United States, but effective traces were not made.

Then comes the data from Mexico. The Mexican government seizes more guns than it gives serial numbers to the ATF. Some use this to argue that it is really holding back many more weapons that are not American.

It is likely that Mexican authorities do not give the serial numbers of guns they know have been pilfered from their own armed forces. But there is no way that covers all the other guns. Some seized guns have the serial numbers filed off. In many other cases, the guns are simply lying around police stations in far-off parts of the country where the officers have no access to the ATF eTrace system. There is no evidence the percentage of these that are American would be drastically lower than the percentage of the ones that are traced.

Some gun advocates make the wild claim that the majority of cartel guns are really stolen from the Mexican army. I look at this important issue of "leakage" in the following chapter. But there is absolutely no proof this accounts for the majority, and the raw numbers point massively against this. Reported losses from the Mexican security forces are less than two thousand guns a year, compared with hundreds of thousands of guns estimated to cross the border. The Mexican army has 206,000 soldiers in total, and it keeps enough guns to arm its personnel.[24] This is compared with the 393 million guns in civilian hands in the United States.

Still, I think to argue too much about the percentage is to miss the point. We have the hard fact of the 150,000 guns traced from extremely violent criminals to the United States. Whatever the exact percentage, this is a massive amount of guns to a brutal battleground—and one that affects the United States in a bad way. Another hard fact is the quantity of gun stores in border states.

America has a hell of a lot of gun sellers. The ATF website lists the Federal Firearms Licensees across the nation; at the end of 2017, there were a total of 134,854. To put that in perspective, the ratio of firearms licensees to McDonald's is almost ten to one.

Not every FFL is a gun store that you can see from the street. The number includes importers and manufacturers. But the gun stores, pawnbrokers, and collectors selling to the public total 118,850, still a colossal number.

These FFLs are disproportionately in border states. Texas was at the top, with 10,810. California, despite more restrictive laws, was second, with 7,530. Florida came third, with 7,201—and is a big source of trafficking over the Caribbean. In total, the four states bordering Mexico had almost 23,000 FFLs.

It was by using data on these shops that investigators made the only serious report to estimate the total number of guns flowing over the southern border. Titled *The Way of the Gun*, the report was published in

2013 by the Igarapé Institute and the Trans-Border Institute of the University of San Diego. The investigators looked at the volume of gun sales in border states and used a geographical information system, with correlating data, to estimate how much of these gun sales was feeding the domestic market and how much was going to Mexico.

Their conclusion was that trafficking was even worse than we previously thought. They calculated that 253,000 guns could have been trafficked over the U.S. southern border each year between 2010 and 2012. This was triple the amount they estimated for the 1997 to 1999 period, before the Mexican Drug War erupted and the Federal Assault Weapons Ban expired.

They also examined what this meant in money terms. Looking at the type of guns smuggled and prices, they estimated the sales to Mexican gangsters made $127 million a year for the U.S. firearms industry. So the last two decades of Mexico's drug war could have meant well over a billion dollars in revenue.

This is still a relatively small amount of the total U.S. gun industry, at about 2.18 percent, the report estimates. But it is significant for individual dealers.

The report was ambitious to try to find concrete numbers within the murky world of organized crime and the jumble of American gun regulation. It is an estimate. Still, their result is staggering, and no one has picked the report apart. But it was depressing it didn't have more impact. Even if a quarter of the amount of guns was feeding the Mexican conflict, it should be a serious issue on the agenda. Perhaps after Fast and Furious, the Obama administration was loath to touch anything on guns and Mexico.

The report's work on the revenue to the gun industry is notable. Owners of the big gun makers are rich, with Gaston Glock a billionaire. But from talking to U.S. gun dealers, I realize their markup on each weapon is small, sometimes less than 10 percent, or under a hundred dollars a gun. "It's not easy, and it's not a lot of great money," says Mike Detty, who was a gun seller in Arizona. Some sellers are veterans who rely on their military pensions and trade in guns for a bit of extra money on the side. It is a business driven by hobbyists.

When sellers are struggling, it means criminals are important customers. But it's infuriating to see the small profits versus the huge cost to life.

A gun dealer makes a hundred dollars selling a Kalashnikov. A straw buyer gets paid a hundred dollars to buy it. And that single Kalashnikov could be used in Mexico to slay dozens of victims. Back in Ciudad Juárez, I talked to a man carrying out this wanton murder.

In my reporting over the last two decades, I have talked to a tragically large number of gangsters who are serial murderers. All have been men except for one serial hit woman (whom I interviewed in the Philippines). I have found three broad psychological profiles.

There are those who have regrets and feel bad about what they have done. There are psychopaths who have no empathy for their victims or actually enjoy it (they are the scariest). And there are those so high on drugs and adrenaline, they don't seem to have any feelings for what they are doing. At least not at the time. Carlos, a veteran killer for the Barrio Azteca, was in this third category.

The Barrio Azteca is a curious hybrid between a U.S. prison gang and a Mexican cartel. Founded in Texas penitentiaries by inmates from El Paso and Juárez, it grew as members were released and deported, sprawling into a cross-border organization that joined forces with the Juárez Cartel.

Ciudad Juárez is the second-biggest city on the Mexican side of the border, and is a lucrative route, with billions of dollars of cocaine, crystal meth, heroin, and marijuana moving into Texas and then across the United States. When El Chapo tried to take the city in 2008, the Barrio Azteca became a force on the streets fighting to stop him. They drowned the avenues in blood, carrying out atrocities such as the massacre of fifteen high school kids in the Salvárcar neighborhood in 2010.

In all the fronts of the Mexican Drug War, the battle for Juárez has been the most homicidal, with the city suffering nine thousand murders in four years. It ended only when the Juárez and Sinaloa Cartels made a truce, which allowed the Juárez mob and its Barrio Azteca legions to keep the heart of the city, controlling local drug selling, prostitution, and two international bridges, and the Sinaloans to control the valley to the east of the city, where they move high volumes of drugs over the rugged borderland. As Carlos explains, this deal is fragile.

Sean and I find Carlos through the photographer Miguel, who knows a recovering heroin addict who is friends with the Aztecas. Carlos first says he will meet us in El Paso, which is safer for us, but then changes his mind and says it has to be in Juárez. We are told to go to a supermarket parking lot in the evening, and from there we follow a car into a sketchy barrio, where we finally pull up and are ushered down a dirt path, past a young girl, into a safe house. Carlos is sitting in a bare room along with a cohort who has a rifle over his lap.

Carlos is in his forties, with a shaved head, handlebar mustache, and scars over his face and body, and he dominates the conversation. The younger cohort is in his twenties, slicker, with a goatee. He speaks less and fiddles with the rifle. They both look high as kites, and Carlos talks rapidly about cocaine and pills.

Carlos has served time in two prisons in Texas, been deported, and served time in Mexico. He speaks Spanish with a lot of border slang and mashed-up English words. He talks about "gangas," "homies," and "clickas." He calls Juárez "Juáritos," and El Paso "El Chuco." (This is because it was home of the Pachuco subculture.) He refers to guns as *juguetes*, or toys.

When I ask Carlos about his own brushes with violence, he reveals that he has been shot four times, pulling up his T-shirt to show the fleshy bullet wounds on his belly. But he has shot many more people, he says, going on what he calls "missions" to take out anyone the gang commands.

"It depends on our orders," he says. "For example, we go after someone that didn't pay or belongs to another gang. We have to study him first, but

"Guns and freedom." Members of a right-wing militia training in Georgia. ANADOLU AGENCY/GETTY IMAGES

Golden guns. Weapons seized from drug traffickers in Mexico's "Narco Museum." IOAN GRILLO

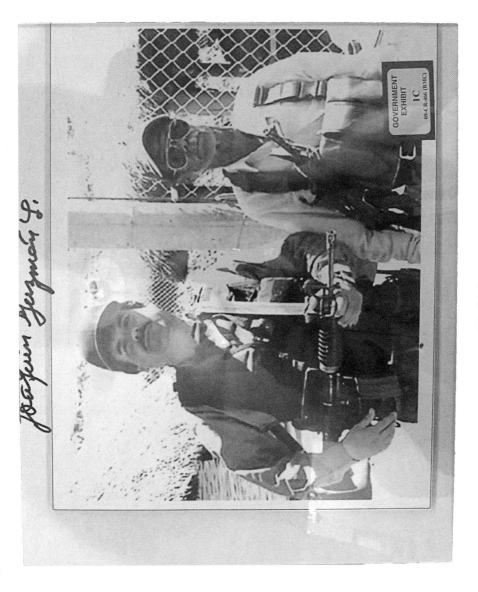

An evidence photo of Joaquín "El Chapo" Guzmán, signed for his lawyer. IOAN GRILLO

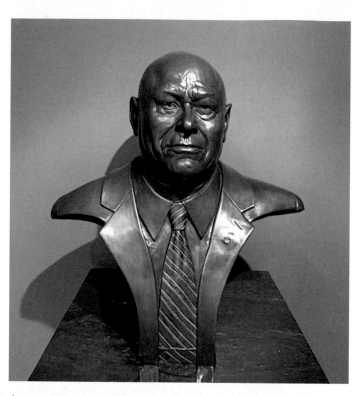

The NRA that Harlon Carter built. A bust of Carter and the NRA stand at the CPAC.

IOAN GRILLO

The biggest firearms trade show in the world: The SHOT Show in Las Vegas.

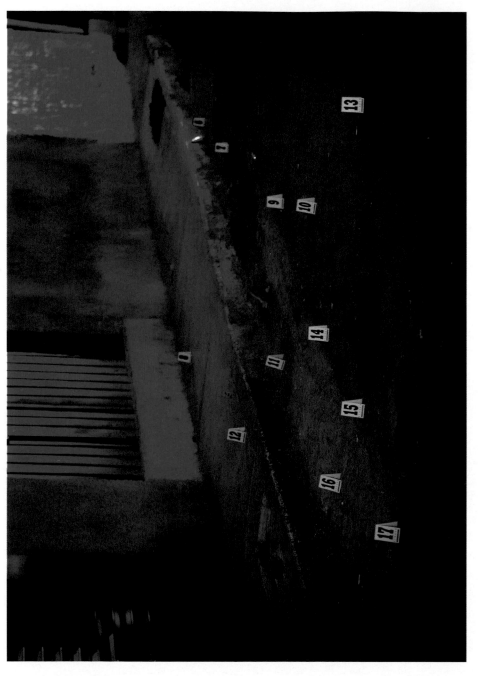

Another day, another shooting. Bullet markers at a crime scene in Mexico City. ROSS McDONNELL

"No Shoot Zone." Tyree "Colion" Moorehead after he has painted up a corner in Baltimore, Maryland. IOAN GRILLO

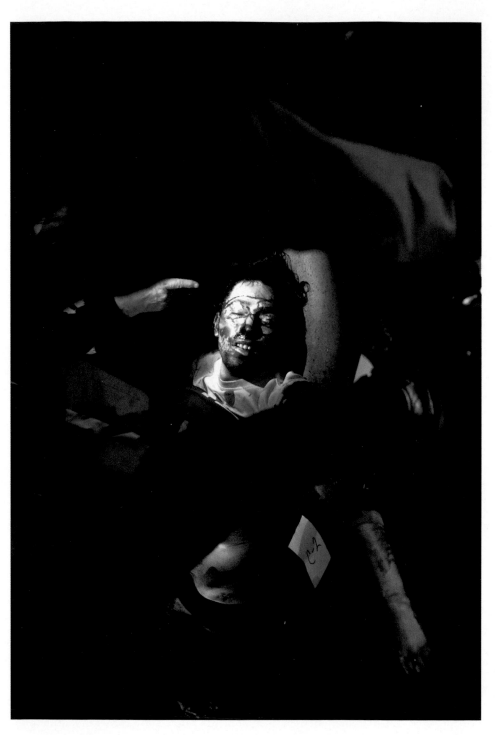

The horror. A gunshot victim in Mexico City. ROSS McDONNELL

The terror. The outline of a gunshot victim in Mexico City. ROSS McDONNELL

"The world's longest war." A fighter of the Revolutionary Armed Forces of Colombia before the peace process. OLIVER SCHMIEG

A hybrid crime war? A self-defense squad in Guerrero, Mexico. ROSS McDONNELL

"I don't know if there is forgiveness for the things I have done." The *sicario* Fresa poses with guns in San Pedro Sula, Honduras. PATRICK TOMBOLA

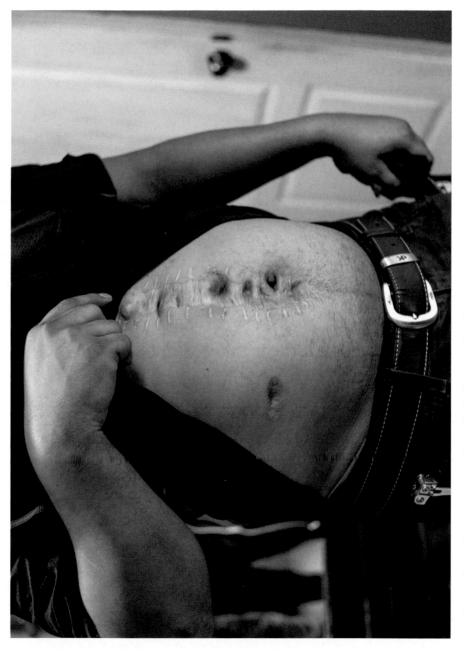

"We have to be ready to die." Fresa shows the bullet wounds in his stomach. PATRICK TOMBOLA

The wounded innocent. Katery Ramos, in wheelchair, and her mother talk to journalist Orlin Castro in San Pedro Sula, Honduras.

PATRICK TOMBOLA

Exodus. Refugees and migrants from Central America cross the Suchiate River into Mexico. IOAN GRILLO

A game changer? The March for Our Lives in Washington, D.C. WIN McNAMEE/GETTY IMAGES

that's the job of the hawk. A hawk is someone who is watching over people—the time this person comes and goes, all of that. The hawk notifies us. We have the order, and when the hawk tells us that that person will be somewhere, we are ready."

He has been using guns since he was a teenager and received training from corrupt police officers working for the cartel. They use pistols for a discreet job, he says, but they prefer Kalashnikovs and AR-15s. Different members of the gang have their own favorites, but he is an AR-15 man.

I ask where the guns come from.

"They come from El Paso, from El Chuco," he says. "We get them on demand, and anything we want comes from there. We call a homie, or someone high up, and we tell them we need a toy or two, and they hook us up. They make some calls, and we wait for them across the bridge. Or we send somebody to pick them up. If we want a .9, a .45, a .380, or a .32, anything we want, they bring it here."

Carlos explains that the people who buy the guns are members of the Barrio Azteca, so they are not allowed to make any profit on them. But they are given money on other jobs and taken care of when they are in prison. This teaches another lesson in black market gun-onomics: a big criminal organization can utilize its manpower to get weapons cheaper.

I ask him where exactly they are buying the guns.

"There are some places in the United States where they sell weapons and they don't ask for a license," he says. "No identification. They are corrupt there too. There are places where they should only sell one weapon to someone who is registered but they sell several weapons. It's at the same gun shops they sell weapons under the radar."

Carlos was not only referring to the private-sale loophole but also talking about gun shops selling weapons illegally. Most gun sellers work hard and respect the law. But there are documented cases of those who don't. The ATF finds gun shops that commit crimes such as selling weapons without conducting background checks or mysteriously "losing" guns from their inventory. A *New York Times* investigation found that corrupt dealers rarely lose their licenses.[25]

In some cases, gun shops have sold huge amounts of inventory to criminals. Back in 2000, a firearms dealer in Ohio sold 182 guns to a man, including 85 in a single purchase. The buyer was selling them on to criminals in Buffalo, New York.[26]

Some hope that the cartel wars will burn out because the gangsters will just kill each other off in the end. Considering there have been 277,000 murders in Mexico over a decade, this has wiped out a lot of hit men.

The problem is the cartels keep finding people to take their place. There are cases of those forced to work, but there are also many recruits who want to do it. The economic factors are, of course, key. Mexico has a minimum wage of five dollars a day, while people want the consumer goods in the stores and on TV. There are also many neglected teenagers in the barrios of Juárez, sometimes the orphans of other hit men, sometimes left by single mothers who have to work in the assembly plants or the sex industry to get by. Carlos describes how they look for those who have difficult childhoods to turn into a new generation of gunslingers.

"First, it's the attitude, and you can see from an early age if people are bad," he says. "You can see in some children that they are sweet, and they follow good social norms coming from their parents. But the kids who have been mistreated by their parents, they have a cold look, and those are the people that are useful for the job. They make for good bad guys, good sicarios."

I have encountered this point before. Many of the coldest killers come from broken families. Loving parents are extremely important for our societies. Abandonment, it seems, breeds people who are more vulnerable and can be turned to cruelty.

When I ask Carlos about Trump beefing up border security, he laughs and says it will help the gang. Deportees mean more potential manpower. "They will send us all the bad guys, and we'll get bigger and bigger," he says. "The more and more we are, the more powerful the gang will become."

Carlos's talk of recruiting teenagers underlines the worrying trend of child soldiers in Mexico. This has exacerbated the conflict, as the teenage killers are out of control, and other teenagers become targets of their massacres.

The problem has been building up over two decades. When I first traveled to Juárez in 2005, I went into a youth prison to interview a fourteen-year-old convicted of double murder. I was shocked by the piercing thousand-yard stare on one so young. The prison social worker told me the cartel was recruiting the teenagers, as it knew they would get maximum sentences in Mexico of five years, or in some states only three.

In 2010, Mexican marines captured a fourteen-year-old hit "man" known as El Ponchis, or Stocky, in the state of Morelos, and he confessed in front of TV cameras to decapitating four victims. After three years, he was released and apparently went to San Diego, the city where he was born.

In August 2019, police in the border city of Nuevo Laredo shot dead a sixteen-year-old hit man known as Juanito Pistolas, their bullets tearing his head from his body. Juanito had been in the ranks of the mob since he was thirteen, joining a cartel death squad called La Tropa del Infierno, or the Squad from Hell. Several rappers wrote ballads about him, and how his very nickname is related to guns. As one goes (in Spanish):

> *He's called Juanito Pistolas, because he like guns*
> *It's not what he wanted, but he is good at firing them.*

I made a documentary about a crew of rappers in Juárez during the height of the city's war and have stayed in touch with them since, especially Irving Rodriguez, who raps as Axer Kamikaze. Axer went through a phase of gangbanging but backed off after he saw friends shot dead and discovered music. He puts on shows, trying to encourage youths away from violence, but often finds himself stuck in the middle, with soldiers storming his barrio on one side, and cartels recruiting kids on the other.

After meeting the Barrio Azteca, I caught up with Axer and asked why teenagers on the border are so enticed by guns. He says a problem is the normalization of violence, the way it is so common that you don't get shocked by it. He recounted a harrowing episode when a friend was murdered just after he'd hung up the phone with him.

"It hurt. But we learn to grow, to live with this," Axer says. "Now it's even something that goes unnoticed. It doesn't even stick in our minds. The only thing that happens is that you grow tough, you become rude, you grow strong. That's it, I don't know what else to explain to you. But to be honest, I'm no longer shocked by the violence in Juárez."

Another problem is the abundance of guns. Because the cartel can buy new weapons so easily, they unload old firearms onto the street, sometimes guns that have been used in too many murders. In Juárez, these firearms are called *quemado*, or "burned," and can be sold for as little as a hundred dollars, Axer says. This is the same rule of gun-onomics that Chain described of the devalued product.

"People take whatever money they can get," Axer says. "But if you get caught with it, you don't know how many crimes the gun has been used in."

This abundance of guns creates a market among teenagers in schools. Axer describes how a classmate's mother was killed, and the kid found her gun and sold it for forty dollars. In another case, Axer said that a kid was showing off a .38, so they jumped him and stole the gun.

This goes to a key point in the gun debate. An argument made by gun rights activists is that the Mexican gangsters are going to buy the weapons from somewhere. If they don't get American guns, they will get German guns, and if they don't get German guns, they will get Chinese guns. Where there is demand, there is supply. The traffic cannot be abolished.

But the quantity matters. And the fact that Juárez sits right next to Texas and its ten thousand FFLs means that supply is tremendous. There are so many guns that schoolchildren get ahold of them; any teenage drug dealer in Mexico can have an AK; killers fire five hundred rounds at a victim and murder innocent bystanders. If the number of guns were just reduced in Mexico, it might reduce the blood.

The ones who have the guns are the people the youths look up to. "If someone is a sicario, people better respect him," Axer says. "If he belongs to organized crime, they respect him more than someone who finished college. We're wrong culturally."

This culture makes it easier for veteran gangsters like Carlos to recruit abandoned youngsters. Axer says he has seen how they entice children, and it is evil.

"I've known people who are thirty or forty years old that are very, very bad," he says. "They're demons. They go with a youngster to talk him over, tell him how the business works, and how much he'll earn, and how he'll have power, and how the police will not stop him but let him go. And a young person, who lacks conscience and has very little experience, says, 'Yeah, I'll do it.' It's the easiest thing to go to someone younger to brainwash him into killing someone."

This reflects a broader societal failure in Mexico, Axer says. He reflects that they can curse the U.S. gun trafficking and curse Trump. But they also have to look at themselves.

"As a society, we've failed to educate our children," he says. "It's unnerving, but we're part of the problem. If we're going to blame someone, it can't be the president. It's also us as a society. Here."

To understand the impact of gun trafficking into Mexico, we need to look at the human cost of the violence. The guns contribute to a cycle of conflict that includes not only the gunshot victims but also mass kidnapping and disappearances. But the scale of carnage in Mexico is so overwhelming that it can be hard to make sense of in a human way. The raw numbers are jaw-dropping, but hearing about hundreds of thousands of murders means little to us emotionally. As Stalin is purported to have said, a single murder is a tragedy, a million is a statistic.

There are thousands of photos of dead bodies, shot, tortured, dumped. But after a while, they look alike, corpses sprawling on the grass, on the concrete, in cars, in bars, in homes. Fernando Brito, a photographer in Sinaloa, tells me he has taken pictures of more than two thousand bodies. Another day, another corpse, another photo feeding the newswires.

The mutilations make bigger headlines than the gun battles. Five human heads rolled onto a disco dance floor. Twelve headless corpses dumped in a town plaza. Forty-nine bodies with their heads, hands, and feet cut off thrown onto a road. When someone is decapitated, they are no more dead than when they are shot, but the idea is somehow more terrifying. It's perhaps that the visceral image of a mutilation echoes with us more than the image of being killed by a bullet that we can't see as it rushes through the air.

Little details stay with me. The expressions on the faces of the corpses. Sometimes they look eerily calm, sometimes they look baffled in their death. It's the indignity of the victims. When I see them with their clothes torn off, their bellies sticking out, there is something humiliating that jars me, and comes back to me in my dreams.

One thing that has stuck is the stench of rotting human flesh. I smelled it at a crime scene near Culiacán, Sinaloa, from a body that was in a canal for several days, putrefied. I smelled it in the morgue in Monterrey, when they trucked in the forty-nine severed corpses. It's a scent as distinct as that of marijuana, of feces, of sweat. A smell that tells us we are all just flesh and blood and we can rot like meat in a butcher's shop.

This stench of flesh was unleashed when police dug up bodies in a mass grave on the outskirts of Veracruz, a port city on the Gulf of Mexico. It was next to a housing development called Colinas de Santa Fe, a middle-class neighborhood of identical brick houses, painted in pink, blue, and green, with basketball hoops and kiddie bikes with bells in the yards. As more bodies were unearthed, the neighbors filed a complaint that the smell was seeping into their homes.

By mid-2017, police had found thousands of decaying body parts in the field, including more than 250 skulls. It is, to date, the largest mass grave discovered in the Mexican Drug War.

These mass graves are another illustration of the depths of the conflict. In August 2019, the Mexican government revealed that almost five thousand bodies had been dug up in more than three thousand unmarked graves since 2006.

But it was not police who discovered the mass grave in Colinas de Santa Fe. It was mothers searching for their disappeared children.

One of those mothers was María de Lourdes Rosales, whom I visit in the port city of Veracruz. As I go into her home, the warm fifty-nine-year-old describes her tragedy and weeps over the photograph of her missing son, Jonathan Celma.

María had a good life, working as an executive secretary, enjoying time with her grown-up children, looking forward to retirement. But tragedy struck in 2013. Four men bearing pistols stormed a house and dragged away Jonathan, then twenty-four, and his girlfriend, right in front of the girl-friend's family.

Guns are not only used to shoot people. The threat of shooting allows gunmen to carry out other crimes like these abductions. Guns give power to those who hold them and make powerless those facing them.

As with so many cases in Mexico, it's unclear why Jonathan was targeted. He worked in customs, which means he could have crossed a cartel importing drugs. But then cartels target victims for just looking at someone.

Several days later, María received a call demanding a ransom. First, they wanted fifty thousand pesos (about two and a half thousand dollars) so that she could talk to him on the phone. But when she went with the money, she only heard one word, a voice crying, "Ma," which might not even have been him. Then they stopped calling. The cartel will often kill victims and then get money from a family pretending they are alive.

María went to the police, but when there were no advances, she desper-ately went around town, asking anyone for information. She found other mothers doing the same, and they banded together, creating a collective, helping one another with the pain. Similar groups formed all over Mexico, with the government revealing in 2020 that there were over sixty thousand disappeared.

The threats came. A man called, telling her to stop looking or he would fuck with her other children. But she carried on. "The fact is that you have to be brave," she says. "Because they are our children. It's not a car that went missing."

One night, men followed María's other son from a bar. They beat him and robbed him and told him she had to stop her search. María helped him leave Mexico, and she carried on searching

On a march on Mother's Day, an old man got out of a car and handed out flyers to them. María saw it was a map of Colinas de Santa Fe with the fields marked. They told the police, but the officers still failed to act. So the mothers went themselves and began digging. When they unearthed human remains, the state prosecutors were forced to send forensic specialists. They exhumed the biggest mass grave in Mexico.

Still, María was unable to identify if her son was among the victims. Many of the body parts were heavily decomposed after years underground. And there were other mass graves around Veracruz. In 2018, María helped uncover one with the remains of another 166 victims.

Not being able to find her son meant no closure. It is even worse than just having your child killed. The grief was too much for some. Her friend, who had been searching for her daughter since 2013, died of a heart attack at fifty-four.

"For us there is no longer happiness," María says. "I just had a grandson, and you enjoy it, but it's not the same. Everything has changed. Something in your life is missing—your heart, your soul. The only goal that one has is to find them, alive or dead."

Finally in September 2019, Jonathan's body was identified among the dead of Colinas de Santa Fe. María had been searching for him for more than six years.

To put the tragedy of the Mexican Drug War into any human terms is to look at the struggles of victims like María.

6

Leakage

Nobody resists a cannonball of fifty thousand pesos.

—ÁLVARO OBREGÓN, REVOLUTIONARY GENERAL
AND PRESIDENT OF MEXICO

O n a Sunday morning in autumn, I sit in a room full of books on a quiet street in Freiburg, Germany, eating delicious apple pie and talking to a schoolteacher in his sixties, Jürgen Grässlin. The building is an anti-armaments center, with white doves painted in the window, and Jürgen, its key activist, has come amid celebrating his granddaughter's birthday and going to see Freiburg play soccer. Despite his schedule, he likes to talk and serve coffee and apple pie, and I keep him chatting for several hours, while his wife keeps calling to say he has to get a move on.

This tranquil scene seems a million miles from the mass graves of Mexico. Yet there is a direct link: German guns.

When he is not teaching, Jürgen tirelessly researches the firearms trade, especially Germany's biggest gun maker, Heckler & Koch. For years, he knew its guns were reaching the hands of killers but struggled to find evidence of wrongdoing that would stand up in a court. He finally discovered his case in Mexico, where H&K rifles were used by police who worked with a drug cartel to disappear forty-three student teachers in the town of Iguala, Guerrero, one of the most painful episodes in the Mexican Drug War. Paintings of the victims, and the words "We are missing forty-three," adorn walls across Mexico.

Thanks to a whistleblower, Jürgen discovered the sales to the Guerrero police that violated German law. So in a David and Goliath case, Jürgen, the soccer-and-apple-pie-loving schoolteacher, took H&K, the global gun company, to court. And won.

In February 2019, a court in Stuttgart fined Heckler 3.7 million euros and gave two former employees suspended prison sentences.[1] Perhaps the ruling was lenient; Mexican families are crying for their lost children, and men who supplied guns stayed free. But it still dealt a square blow to the company and sent ripples across the global gun business.

The case illustrates the other major source of arms for Mexican cartels: the nation's own security forces. Up to this point, I have focused on the traffic from the United States. Now it's time to look at the corruption from Latin American armies and the companies who supply them. It's a grim story. But Jürgen's slingshot win provides some hope.

The gun maker Heckler & Koch sits in the quaint town of Oberndorf in the hills of the Black Forest. I walk there with another peace activist, a reverend called Ulrich Pfaff, who is sprightly in his seventies, marching up the steep green paths that surround the H&K factory. He points out where I have to avoid stepping or I could be arrested for trespassing.

It's a smaller factory than Cugir's in Romania and higher tech. With sophisticated machinery, it has only about 750 workers to churn out millions of guns.

Perched in the beautiful Neckar Valley, the town of fourteen thousand boasts a dynamic history of gun making. In 1874, smiths here founded Mauser and built the most popular infantry firearms of the era, which they sold to governments from Turkey to China. Latin American generals were fans of Mausers, and soldiers wielded them in Argentina, Bolivia, Chile, Brazil, Colombia, Ecuador, Peru, and, of course, Mexico.

When Hitler rose to power, Mauser became gun maker for the Reich and used prisoners from labor camps for shitty jobs outside the factory walls. When the Allies won, they took machines from the factory, and Mauser was shuttered. However, three of Mauser's former workers founded their own company, H&K, in 1949, which was ready when Germany was allowed to restart its weapons industry a few years later.

In the mid-1950s, H&K developed the Gewehr 3, or G3, an infantry rifle that was embraced by NATO along with dozens of armies, competing with the Kalashnikov and the M16. The weapons spread, supported by what Jürgen describes as a "military-industrial-political" complex that developed in Germany. There are now an estimated fifteen million G3 rifles in eighty countries, arguably making it the second most popular gun after the Kalashnikov. The quaint town in the Black Forest supplied the wars of the world.

Jürgen's relationship with Heckler & Koch goes back four decades to when he served in the German army and was trained to use a G3. It was the Cold War, and Jürgen was sent to shoot metal targets with the image of Chinese faces. He refused.

"I said, 'I don't want to kill Chinese people. I don't know any Chinese people, but maybe they are nice men, like the Germans, or the English, or the Mexicans.' Because people usually are friendly and are peaceful."

The officers locked Jürgen in a cell and tried to get him to shoot the next day. He refused again, and was sent back to the cell.

Refusing to shoot metal may sound ridiculous to some. But Jürgen's pacifism came from a generation of Germans in the shadow of Hitler, disgusted their country had started two world wars and committed genocide. His own father had been a boy soldier of sixteen, surviving the western front with scars and trauma.

Finally released from the army, Jürgen became a pacifist organizer as he began teaching. In the 1980s, the German peace movement mushroomed, sprouting groups in every town. While most activists were concerned about nuclear bombs, Jürgen focused on nearby Oberndorf. Guns from H&K, he claims, would be used to kill two million people and injure seven million, making it the deadliest arms company in Europe. "The most devastating weapon all around is the rifle," he says. The villains who used G3s included Idi Amin in Uganda, Turkey repressing the Kurds, and apartheid South Africa.

Jürgen marched with thousands on the gun factory and blockaded the entrance, leading to his arrest and court cases, which he beat. But he realized it was not enough. He started investigating everything he could about the company, traveling to countries where the G3 left corpses and cripples.

As he gathered evidence, H&K's fortunes went up and down. It boomed throughout the eighties, but the end of the Cold War caused it to slump and get into debt with banks before new shareholders stepped in.

This is common in the economics of the gun trade, with many companies going through periods when they fight for survival. In 1997, Belgium gun maker FN Herstal was bailed out and bought by the Walloon region government, which still owns it. In 2015, Herstal, in turn, won a U.S. government contract instead of Colt, which then filed for bankruptcy protection.[2]

The challenge is that firearms are durable goods, and people don't need a new one every couple of years, like they do cell phones or blue jeans. They depend on coveted government contracts and on seeking new markets. H&K's break was September 11.

"I think Heckler & Koch would not exist without 9/11, because at that time there was no money anywhere, there were not enough orders, the technology was old," Jürgen says.

The War on Terror reactivated arms spending as the Middle East went up in flames. Still, H&K struggled to sell the thousands of rifles the factory could churn out. Which led, Jürgen says, to a wave of corruption, including the Mexico case.

*   *   *

Under pressure from the peace movement, the German government tried to institute an "ethical" arms policy. Even beyond the United Nations embargoes, it stopped sales to countries with serious human rights violations. It would give guns only to the good guys.

This was a problem in selling to India and Mexico, both big customers with shady human rights records. So in 2003, the German government released guidelines that the companies could not sell to certain areas in those countries. In Mexico, four of thirty-two states were prohibited: Chiapas, Guerrero, Jalisco, and Chihuahua.

This ruling was made before the Mexican Drug War kicked off and reflected concerns about repression of left-wing rebels such as the Zapatistas. In the turbulence that followed, corrupt police working with narcos emerged in many states like Veracruz, Tamaulipas, and Coahuila, all where police had German guns. Even so, H&K still managed to break the limited selling ban.

When a whistleblower contacted Jürgen, he was cautious and went through security protocols, changing cars and meeting in the forest. The source was an ex-employee of H&K who had trained police to use G-36 rifles, a newer, lighter weapon. He even showed emails from Guerrero police thanking the company for the course. In total, more than four thousand guns had gone to the banned states. Fully automatic, the G-36 has a cyclic rate of fire of six hundred rounds a minute.

"If you are a drug baron, the G-36 is a perfect weapon to kill a lot of people in a short time," Jürgen says, spraying his lips to make the sound of automatic fire.

Jürgen went to court in 2010, but the case took years to resolve. During this time, in 2014, police in the town of Iguala, Guerrero, attacked the student teachers. First, they fired on them, killing two. Another would be found on the street with his eyes gouged out and skin flayed. The police then detained the forty-three students, before they disappeared from the face of the earth. Mexican prosecutors claimed the police handed the students to cohorts in the cartel, who burned them on a bonfire, but the case is unresolved, tangled up by spoiled evidence and a botched investigation.

Following the disappearance, Mexican federal forces descended on the Iguala police base. Among the arms they seized were the neat sum of thirty-six G-36s, most of which had been fired.

The case dragged on, but the teacher persevered, pouring in his savings, and a German court finally delivered the blow in 2019. It was a lukewarm victory for Jürgen. Some of the accused were found not guilty on the grounds that they didn't know what was going on. Nobody was sent to prison. But H&K reeled, underlining in a statement that it had now changed its policy. "As a result of the regrettable incidents, the company has made drastic and extensive changes to effectively eliminate such events in the future," it said.[3]

I ask Jürgen about his deeper beliefs, what kind of rules on guns should exist. He says he dreams of a world with no armies, but knows we won't see this in our lifetimes, so we can take small steps, write, investigate, inform, and in some cases strike.

I personally have a more pragmatic view. Seeing so much bloodshed in Mexico, I feel we need soldiers and police with guns but can just hope to make them better. But even this can seem like a utopian wish, as Mexico's problems of gun corruption go deeper still.

———

If you ask in Mexico City where to buy an illegal gun, many people will tell you Tepito. Known as the Barrio Bravo, the legendary neighborhood is packed with market stalls and famed for selling anything you desire. Vendors line its crowded streets hawking gleaming white tennis shoes, flat-screen TVs, and rare-breed puppies, along with statues of the Santa Muerte. In back alleys, dealers offer cocaine and crack, marijuana and meth, although they are more discreet than those on Pennsylvania Avenue, Baltimore.

Buying illegal guns is rarely as easy as buying drugs, and in few places are they hawked openly. If you were to walk into Tepito and ask for a firearm, you likely wouldn't get far. Even in these bad areas, guns are mostly sold through contacts.

I find mine through Jorge, a former boxer who trains youngsters in the barrio. Tepito has a tradition of producing champs, especially in the mid-twentieth century, with thumpers like Luis "Kid Azteca" Villanueva. In Jorge's gym, the ring is surrounded by beautiful photos of young men and women posing in gloves and holding up belts, from the 1930s to the present day.

Jorge seems to know everyone in Tepito, and he stops at each stall to ask people how they are doing. We walk over to his house on the edge of the barrio to meet a neighbor who sells guns. Jorge lives in a traditional *vecindad*, an old building with homes surrounding a courtyard. His house is decorated with photos of him boxing and photos of his wedding day, and has curtains in place of doors and smells of meat and corn emanating from the kitchen.

The neighbor Valentino, or Val, arrives. A short man shy of fifty, with sunburned, scarred skin, a limp, and a surprisingly soft voice, Val sits on the sofa and we start talking. Before long, he digs into his pants to pull out a pistol, a Smith & Wesson 9 mm, with a fourteen-round magazine, made in Springfield, Massachusetts, USA. He takes the bullets out to show how clean it is and says he's going to deliver it to a customer for 25,000 pesos, or about $1,300. It's several times the price of U.S. shops, and more expensive than it would be in Juárez or Baltimore, but this is Mexico City, a thousand kilometers south of the border.

The price of illegal guns varies in weird ways, affected by factors including how far they travel and the demand. When vigilantes rose against a cartel in Michoacán state in 2014 and everybody wanted guns right away, the price of AK-47s shot up, with people telling me they were selling for up to $5,000, or more than six times what they cost in U.S. stores. War turns everyone into distressed buyers.

I ask Val where he started selling guns. The answer is unsurprising if depressing. He began when he joined the Mexican army.

*   *   *

Val was born into a family of ten brothers and sisters in the center of Mexico City, their father away from home working in the Volkswagen factory in nearby Puebla. There were fewer guns when he grew up in the seventies, with people instead fighting with knives and fists. Val wanted to make something of himself, so he signed up for the army.

Wielding a Heckler & Koch G3, he was sent to different states around Mexico. One night, his commander asked for six volunteers, and he stood up, keen for action. They drove into the town of Cuernavaca and were told to go into a house, shoot dead two people, and make it look like a mugging. They turned their army shirts inside out, cocked their G3s, and sent their victims to hell. He didn't know who the targets were and didn't ask. But he got paid, and went on to carry out eighteen hits while in the army. He was never shot at once. "I was just following orders." He shrugs. "I was a teenager."

The officer started handing him guns to sell. They were not army-issue but seized weapons from gangsters put back on the street for a profit. Sometimes, he would be in the mountains, and they would rumble heroin producers with guns, drugs, and piles of cash. They could let them go and take their wares, or arrest them and take half. It was the Baltimore gun task force on a bigger scale.

They would also get guns through fake buyback programs, turning up in villages to see who had weapons, pretending they were "de-pistolizing" the country. The army was an ideal place to sell firearms, he says, because you had people from many different states with their own networks.

"There's a big building with a thousand of us living in it, some from Michoacán, some from Guerrero, from all over the country—you know loads of people," he says. "One says, 'I need a pistol,' so you show him the gun, and he says, 'How much do you want?' and the business starts."

The corrupt soldiers also sold to criminal groups en masse. One time, Val delivered seventy guns to a buyer in the town of Copala, Guerrero. He wasn't sure who the buyer was, but the area is both important for drug trafficking and has landowners with a history of violence against rebellious *campesinos*.

When I ask about how high up the corruption in the army goes, he laughs. "We had a saying," he says. " 'There is no general who can withstand a cannonball of a hundred million pesos.' " (I find out later this is a variation on a saying by Álvaro Obregón, a Mexican revolutionary general and president.)

Leaving the army, Val became a carpenter but continued selling guns on the side. He kept on getting weapons from his contacts in the military, as well from the police.

Val describes the same gun-onomics factors as the other dealers. If a gun is "burned," or used in crimes, he will lower the price. If someone is "beefing" or in trouble, he will raise the price. He can tell how desperate people are because they will frantically say they want the gun right away, and pester to see if he has it.

He hides pistols in the airbags of his car, one in the steering wheel, the other in the passenger bag. Sometimes, customers will want to check the guns, so he lets them take a shot in the labyrinth of backstreets in Tepito. "One single shot is fine."

He went to prison only once. He was desperate for money and held someone up, got caught with a Colt .380 pistol, and was sent to Mexico City's northern prison from 2008 to 2012. "Three and a half years for just one gun!" He sighs.

He works independently and doesn't pay a quota to a cartel. The major cartels don't dominate Mexico City like they do the border, although there has been a growth of a *cartelito* that sells drugs and does shakedowns in Tepito. Val will supply its members with guns if they need, or help do a hit.

He also does occasional private murders for money. These are not so much gang hits as personal acts of revenge, over affairs, rapes, or money. For these private jobs, he says, he works for "pure people who are recommended" and he can get 50,000 pesos, or about $2,500.

Val supplies it all. You can hire him to build you a bookshelf, sell you a gun, and shoot the person annoying you.

This adds to the tragedy engulfing Mexico. The way that murder for hire has filtered down to neighborhood operators is a perilous trend that keeps pushing up the body count. *Sicarios* don't just kill over drug deals. They can kill because somebody feels like it.

———

The corruption described by Val may shock some. But for many in Mexico, it is what they expect. When I first moved to Mexico, I used to think people were too conspiratorial in not trusting the government at all, in thinking everything was a lie. Until I realized the government really could be that bad, and I was naive.

It was like with the case of El Chapo. He was first caught in 1993. He escaped in 2001. This was allegedly in a laundry cart, but some people think that the government was lying, and he really walked out the front door. Marines caught him again in 2014. When a TV presenter asked me if he could escape again, I said no chance. He was too high-profile, and there was too much at stake for the president. And then El Chapo escaped again. The official story was that he escaped in a tunnel, but a lot of people believed he walked out the front door. Again. By this point, I didn't know what to believe. So when a news anchor asked me if he could escape a third time from a Mexican prison, I said, "Nothing's impossible here."

The rest of the world is grappling with a post-truth society. Mexico has been living in one for decades already.

So it goes with police corruption. A police commander in the state of Michoacán known as El Tyson used to be friendly with the press, the image of a stocky crime-fighting cop. Yet it wasn't only discovered he was working for a drug cartel. And it wasn't only discovered he was decapitating victims. He confessed that he would get young recruits to hack up bodies to make them lose their fear.

And it's not only Mexico. Tragically, corruption is a problem in many countries in Latin America, although there is a rising fight against it. Since 2000, former presidents have been convicted and jailed from Brazil, Peru, El Salvador, and Honduras, and charged with a crime in Argentina, Guatemala (two presidents), Peru (another president), Bolivia, and El Salvador (another president).[4] Yet more are being investigated, and many others have been accused in journalistic investigations. And that is before you get down to cabinet members, governors, and, of course, generals.

Back in 1973, President Richard Nixon gave a plaque with piece of moon rock picked up by Apollo 17 astronauts to the Honduran people. In the 1990s, it disappeared from the Honduran presidential palace. A general reportedly sold it for fifty thousand dollars. Police recovered it in a sting operation in Miami, where a dealer was trying to sell it for five million dollars, and it was given back to Honduras.[5] If a general can steal a chunk of moon rock, he can definitely steal a bunch of firearms.

There are prominent cases of government guns turning up in the hands of criminals. When federal forces took over the police base in Acapulco in 2018, they discovered that 342 guns, or 19 percent of their armory, were missing. Other towns have suffered the same fate. Between 2006 and 2018, there were officially 15,592 guns that went missing from Mexican police or soldiers, Mexico's defense department reported.[6]

In May 2019, streets vendors were protesting in the central plaza of Cuernavaca while news cameras filmed. A young man walked out of the crowd with a Glock 9 mm and shot two of the protesters dead. The murder was captured in full on camera. As the killer walked away, journalists pursued him, asking him why he did it, until he was wrestled to the ground. Which bought attention to the Glock. It turned out it had been seized by criminals in 2017 and checked into the evidence room of the Cuernavaca police station—from where it disappeared back onto the street.[7]

Heading south, you find the story repeated. In 2010, thieves stole twenty-two RPG-7 grenade launchers from a military armory in Honduras. Over the following years, various Mexican cartels showed up with RPG-7s. One was used to shoot down a Mexican army helicopter, killing five soldiers and a police officer.

This gets back to the problem that weapons cross borders. RPGs are built in Russia, stolen in Honduras, and used to kill in Mexico.

There has to be a limit on how many guns the police and soldiers in Latin America can be losing. If they were selling all their guns to criminals, they would be on the street disarmed, but they still manage to have enough for their own personnel. As stated, Mexican police and soldiers are officially losing less than two thousand guns a year. Meanwhile, there are hundreds of thousands of cartel affiliates in Mexico. So the theft from Mexican security forces provides a few of their weapons, while the trafficking from the United States provides far more.

It is not just corruption; violent thieves also genuinely rob guns from police and soldiers. In the first three months of 2019, an average of one police officer was murdered a day in Mexico.[8] Taking into account population, this means that police in Mexico were killed at a rate that is sixteen times higher than in the United States.

Under such circumstances, police often prefer to surrender their weapons. In the state of Puebla in 2019, gangsters took eleven police officers hostage, beat them, and stole their guns before they released them. A security camera shows a thug standing above a cowering officer and removing his rifle.

This creates a vicious circle. The gangsters outgun the police, which means law and order breaks down, which allows the gangsters to steal more guns. The question is how to break the circle. And this is especially hard when the iron river flows from the north.

The corruption in Latin American security forces raises other questions. Should companies even be selling them guns if so many are pilfered by criminals? Heckler & Koch is just one of the gun sellers. Many others are American.

Between 2008 and 2018, U.S. arms companies legally exported $899 million worth of arms to Mexico, according to the Stockholm International Peace Research Institute.[9] These include mountains of AR-15s, which are a standard weapon for many Mexican police forces.

The leakage from security forces is not only of weapons supplied recently. Back in the 1980s, the United States supplied the government of El Salvador as it fought a brutal civil war. It was the biggest investment by Washington in the Cold War in Latin America, with $4 billion worth of military aid, including over thirty thousand M16s and a whopping 266,000 M-67 grenades.

While the war ended in 1992, many of the grenades are still being thrown. In 2006, Salvadoran prison guards searched a woman visiting a penitentiary and discovered an M-67 grenade hidden in her vagina. She was trying to bring it in for her boyfriend to blow his way out of jail. The following year, guards at another prison caught an inmate with a grenade in his rectum.[10]

The grenades grab the attention of cartels. In 2013, Salvadoran police found a stash of 213 grenades hidden in the patio of a warehouse. They said the Zetas had bought them to take home to Mexico.[11]

Many grenades have indeed made it to the Mexican battlefields, where the majority of explosives appear to come from Central America, the M-67 being the most common seized.[12] While they claim fewer bodies than bullets, they add another layer of terror. Assailants throw grenades at police convoys and TV stations, into bars and brothels, and, in 2018, lobbed them at the U.S. consulate in Guadalajara. In one raging battle in Matamoros in 2010, cartel thugs threw more than three hundred grenades.

After a war ends, the arms-reduction sages say there needs to be a strenuous effort to clean up guns and bombs. Tragically, that didn't happen in El Salvador. If it doesn't happen in Syria, Ukraine, Libya, and Afghanistan, whenever those wars end, then more war guns will become crime guns.

Critics of the U.S. exports to Mexico's security forces point to the human rights abuses committed by soldiers. Even when they are not giving their guns to gangsters, soldiers are accused of massacres. The most high-profile cases include shooting dead twenty-two suspects in the town of Tlatlaya in

2014 and shooting dead forty-two in the town of Tanhuato in 2015. President Andrés Manuel López Obrador claims such massacres have ceased. But that is far from clear.

The cases of wrongdoing are very real. But should this stop all arms exports to Mexico and make it suffer a UN embargo like Somalia's?

I personally would have a problem with that too. If the Mexican government was banned from buying guns, but cartels could arm up from the iron river, the situation could get even more catastrophic. Nevertheless, more pressure is certainly needed to stop guns from falling into the hands of gangsters. And much of that pressure needs to come from Mexico itself.

For their part, Mexican politicians have tried repeatedly to pressure the United States to stop the illegal guns flowing south. But they run into an impervious barrier: American gun culture.

Gun Nuts

———

As the coronavirus tore around the planet in 2020, and governments imposed unprecedented lockdowns, hundreds went to protest at the Michigan state capitol on April 30. Many carried guns.

The Democratic governor, Gretchen Whitmer, had instituted some of the strongest lockdown measures in the United States, which were supported by some but infuriated others. The protesters were backing a Republican legislature to symbolically strip the governor of her executive powers (an action she could veto). Among them were members of various militias, the hard-core Second Amendment groups that do military-style training in the countryside. Many were dressed in camouflage and baseball caps, showing off loaded AR-15s and other firearms. More than a hundred decided to take the protest inside the state capitol building, many taking their rifles with them.

At the scene was a twenty-two-year-old student reporter, Anna Liz Nichols, just shy of graduating. Gun-toting protesters filled the gallery of the Senate, so she was unable to get in and cover the session. She heard shouting from across the building by the floor of the House and rushed over.

"There was maybe ten, fifteen people at the floor, and it soon became like a hundred. It happened really fast," she told me. "There was screaming at the police officers. There was calls to 'Let us in,' calls of 'Heil Whitmer.' They called the police 'bastards,' 'pigs.' Many of them were turning back and forth in the crowd, having their guns slung at a weird angle that let the gun hang really long."

The crowd was asphyxiating, and at five feet four, Anna was below the shoulders of many. Her facemask to protect against the virus was wet, making it difficult to breathe. And then a gun barrel whacked her in the side of the head.

"It hit me around the outside of my eye socket on my left side about as hard as a basketball," she said. It was likely an accident, she said. But there could have been a worse accident swinging loaded guns in a crowded building. Part of the tactic could be "to intimidate journalists and make us not want to go to work," she said. However, it was more intimidating for politicians.

Democratic state senator Dayna Polehanki looked up from the floor to see armed protesters on the balcony shouting down. She took a photo and put it in a tweet with the caption: "Directly above me, men with rifles yelling at us. Some of my own colleagues who own bullet proof vests are wearing them."[1] The pictures went viral, and the story hit front pages around the globe. Outside the United States, people found it mindboggling that this was allowed to happen.

The flashpoint cuts multiple ways. It recalls the Black Panthers going into the Sacramento state capitol with guns in 1967, but in the culture war of 2020, the protesters were white and supporting President Trump. They were also more directly harassing the lawmakers during a time of tough and contested political choices. In some countries, it recalls dark moments in history in which armed thugs have gone into parliaments to intimidate representatives as governments loom toward authoritarianism. It recalls coups.

Yet there is a very American twist. The protesters went through security to get into the building. They had to hand in their protest placards, which had been banned from the state capitol, but were allowed to keep their guns. It was perfectly legal for the protesters to stand above the lawmakers with loaded AR-15s.

The same is not true in all of the United States. In most state capitols, guns are banned, just like they are in airplanes and prisons. But Michigan is one of the few states that has not specifically prohibited them.

Phil Robinson, a founder of the Michigan Liberty Militia, said in a follow-up video that they were precisely demonstrating the liberties of the Second Amendment. "If you have a problem with us exercising our rights and are concerned that by doing so we are going to lose our rights, our rights were an illusion in the first place," he said. "Without the Second Amendment, you are a subject, not a citizen. Period."

This all illustrates the core arguments over gun rights and their limits in America. Hard-liners like the militiamen go back to that well-argued idea of needing rifles to rise against tyranny. And this can be no better shown than by waving AR-15s at lawmakers during a lockdown. For many others, the action does the opposite. Like too much gun proliferation, it is a threat to the democratic process itself.

This threat looked very real in October 2020 when thirteen men, including some of those who protested at the state capitol, were arrested and charged on terrorism and conspiracy counts for an alleged plot to kidnap Governor Whitmer.

The suspects were alleged to be in a militia known as the Wolverine Watchmen and one of them is accused of discussing the plot with the words, "Snatch and grab, man. Grab the fuckin' governor."

We have been following the iron river to inner-city Baltimore and over the border to Mexico. Now we are going to step back and look more deeply at the environment that allows the river to flow. Because there would be no private-sale loophole and there would be no laws banning the Tracing Center from using technology if it were not for the politics of American gun culture.

There is a massive caveat here. American gun culture incorporates the hundred million people who own guns and the many more who have shot them. Huge numbers enjoy hunting, shooting, and self-defense, and don't endorse waving rifles at lawmakers. But the politics of the gun culture are dominated by the radical positions.

These politics have two key manifestations: the gun lobby, especially the NRA, and the grassroots Second Amendment movement. They play off each other but are quite different beings.

The NRA is an organization in Washington, D.C., with a revenue that tops $300 million a year. It has individual executives worth millions at the heart of power. They justify their lucrative careers by arguing that they have delivered for their members.

The gun movement is made up of men, and some women, scattered around the United States, often in small towns, some with little money, some more wealthy. On one end are extreme hobbyists. On the other are extremists who spill over into right-wing terrorists.

———

David Arieno has about two hundred guns in the basement of his home in Alaska. I say "about two hundred," as he is not sure of the exact number. The sixty-three-year-old financial adviser has been collecting firearms for close to half a century, and keeps buying. His favorites are machine guns, not the semiautomatics that people can mistake for them, but the real-deal, bullet-regurgitating automatics. Wealthy from his finance work, he pays the machine gun tax, owns pre-ban models, and heads the Alaska Machine Gun Association (AMGA). Along with other wealthy members, including doctors and lawyers, he sprays caps on the icy plains of Alaska. They are ready for grizzly bears.

"Some people collect paintings. Some collect books. I collect guns," he tells me by phone from his home in the town of Chugiak.

David is friendly and open and talks about guns and rights and Alaska for two hours. His views reflect the big themes I find at shops and shows driving the gun culture: collecting, sport, self-defense, and politics. This is the NRA that Harlon Carter built.

I was introduced to David by veteran war correspondent Mike Kirsch, who shot a story on guns in Alaska and filmed in David's basement. It shows David with rows of firearms on racks, his house looking like a well-stocked armory.

Serving overseas in the air force, David became interested in gun technology, and we discuss the evolution of automatic fire. "I want to know the history of the guns, to keep that history alive," he says.

David and other gun collectors are profound hobbyists. Their motives in this sense are not unlike those of friends I have with vinyl records or Lego bricks crowding out bedrooms—the obsession of the collector creating a fight for space. Guns are durable goods that don't disappear, so if you buy a new one every couple of months, then the arsenal just gets bigger. And U.S. law puts no limit on the number of firearms you can own.

This point of collectors with their arsenals is often missed when analyzing the statistics. While having two hundred guns is a lot, it's not uncommon to find collectors with fifty firearms. This is a big factor making the total number of guns in civilian hands in the United States just keep rising, approaching 400 million. Meanwhile, the actual percentage of Americans who own guns has gone down, from more than half in the seventies to 30 percent of American adults saying they personally own a firearm in 2018, according to a Pew survey.[2]

David also enjoys the sport of shooting and directs me to videos on the AMGA website of members spraying over earthy ranges. I'd shot at targets myself a handful of times before I worked on this book, and did it a few more times while researching. I fired Glocks and H&Ks and AR-15s in ranges in California and Texas, and shot an AK-47 in a gun club hidden in a nuclear bunker in Serbia. It's undeniably fun pulling the trigger and seeing the hole blasted in the metal as the odor of the gunpowder fills your nostrils.

Writer Osha Gray Davidson describes the thrill in an article:

I was 10 years old the first time I fired a gun. It was love at first shot.

I loved the heft of the well-made .22-caliber bolt-action rifle. I loved the loud crack of the explosion when I squeezed the trigger, and the puff of smoke from the muzzle. I even grew to love the acrid smell of the spent gunpowder.

But most of all, I loved that I was able to hit the target dead center nearly every time.[3]

By dedicating time to it, anyone can get better, providing the buzz of mastering a technique. The dose of dopamine from hitting targets is akin to that of scoring in computer games and sports. And shooting doesn't rely too much on your fitness, so people who no longer play football can keep on firing guns, still shooting into their eighties. Older men are one of the biggest groups driving gun ownership, and the culture.

For hunters, the sport takes them into nature and, in their view, gives them a primeval connection to the hunting pursued by our ancestors. But while some of the animal killing takes skill, some not so much. The hustler Billyjack described bear shooting in Maine as throwing out a box of doughnuts and mowing down the furry friends. (To shrieks from animal lovers.)

The AMGA videos show little of outwitting prey and lots of blowing bricks to smithereens. One has them blowing up cars with explosives on Memorial Day. I found this desire to tear shit up with big guns from various enthusiasts. At the SHOT Show, I asked a collector why he owned a .50 caliber, especially considering how the bullets can cost four bucks a round. "The sheer power of the thing," he said. "I shot one of my neighbor's silos down one time. The whole thing just fell over like a tree." (The neighbor had asked him to do it.)

The AMGA videos also show men firing with their children and grandchildren. In one clip, a very young girl sprays with a mounted machine gun with an older man by her side.[4] Such images spark outrage from gun critics. And when a nine-year-old girl accidentally killed a gun instructor with an

Uzi at an Arizona gun range in 2014, it shocked people on both sides of the gun debate.[5]

Enthusiasts retort, however, that guns build special bonds among families. The father giving his child their first firearm on a memorable birthday is a common theme. As is a gun being passed down since the nineteenth century. They view their guns as a link to their family history as well as the history of the country.

Chris Waltz, a fifty-seven-year-old ex-marine, saw action on the streets of Panama when the U.S. military invaded to take out General Manuel Noriega in 1989. He now heads the AR-15 Gun Owners of America, a Georgia-based group for people who, as the name suggests, love their ArmaLite-style rifles and Second Amendment. Chris started the group in 2013 amid calls to ban AR-15s after Sandy Hook. As soon as he launched, it exploded in popularity.

"We started getting like thousands and thousands of people on our Facebook page," he tells me. "It was crazy how many people were just flocking . . . And within months we had hundreds of thousands of people."

The popularity of the AR-15 complicates hopes of a new ban. When Clinton passed his in 1994, the guns were relatively niche, but now millions of Americans have them.

The name AR-15 Gun Owners of America might sound like a radical group, especially after so many have been used in mass shootings. But Chris says he is prepared to compromise on some points. "I'm human. I've got a heart," he says, referring to the mass shootings. "We have to be able to keep guns out of mentally ill people's hands." Of course, this doesn't extend to a full prohibition.

Chris is another extreme hobbyist, but his hobby is super focused on his favorite gun. "The AR-15 is known as 'the man's Barbie.' Because just like Barbie, it has so many different outfits and things," he says. "Literally, I think there's a million different accessories for the AR-15 rifle."

This so-called scalability is a key reason for the popularity of the AR. Chris says that younger shooters also like the rifle because of computer games.

"They are playing *Call of Duty: Modern Warfare*, and these are the types of guns that they are using on there. They feel comfortable with that on the video, and the videos are pretty darn real-looking these days, and they learn how to handle them and accessorize them." This idea of boys graduating from computer guns to the real thing is of course terrifying to many.

Chris says his main reason for having firearms is self-defense. This lines with the top reason that 67 percent of Americans told a Pew survey that they own a gun.

"You go to any room in my house and you can find a gun," he says. "So if somebody comes through the door, you got a gun right there. You don't got to go halfway across the room or upstairs or downstairs to find a gun, and my family's comfortable with it because we've taught them how to shoot."

He adds a line repeated by many enthusiasts: "By the time somebody is in your house and he's in your face, calling 911 is not an option. It's too late."

Self-defense is an especially contentious issue between the gun rights and gun safety sides. There are certainly times when gun owners justifiably and successfully defend themselves with their firearms. However, guns can also hurt their owners: in 2017, guns were used in 505 accidental deaths and over 21,000 suicides in the United States.

The number of times that guns are actually used in self-defense is itself disputed, ranging from tens of thousands of incidents to millions per year. One issue is that definitions vary, ranging from flashing a gun as a deterrent to firing it on target. And if a criminal is injured by a homeowner defending themselves in a robbery, they aren't going to the police.

The figures are more solid for self-defense killings, known as "justifiable homicides." In 2018, there were 353 killings ruled as justifiable homicides by private citizens in the United States, the vast majority with guns. But this pales in comparison with the 14,123 murders recorded that year, of which

72 percent were with firearms. And there are plenty of questions about the claims of self-defense shootings by private citizens, especially when those killed are unarmed. The infamous case of George Zimmerman shooting dead the seventeen-year-old Trayvon Martin is the tip of the iceberg—and it was an incident that wrenched the heart of the nation.

Neither David nor Chris see themselves as political activists. But they do see their defense of the Second Amendment in clearly political terms.

"If you're not happy with the government, and they are repressing you, this gives you the ability to fight back," David said in Mike Kirsch's news report. "I'm not fomenting revolution. I'm not saying that. But much like we broke off from Great Britain in the 1770s, the first thing they did was they tried to confiscate weapons at Lexington. And that's what started the Revolutionary War."[6]

Most gun owners don't have as many weapons as David does, or the combat experience of Chris, and they come from a range of states and social classes. But these four elements of loving guns for hobby, sport, self-defense, and political belief are common, mixing together to form a formidable conviction.

The NRA claims to have nearly five million members like David and Chris driving it to victory, a number it has upheld publicly since 2014. Some investigative journalists believe this is an exaggeration.[7] The magazine *Mother Jones* reported how members all get a free edition of one of the NRA's magazines, *American Rifleman, American Hunter, America's First Freedom*, and *Shooting Illustrated*, yet the combined circulation of all these was 3.7 million in 2018. Back in the 1990s, an NRA board member admitted to writer Osha Gray Davidson that a significant number of the life members had died. "There just isn't that much incentive to go find out when someone passes away," the board member said.[8]

Yet even if the NRA had half the claimed members, that would still make it a well-supported group. And some members are very dedicated. Their active letter-writing and online presence can hit anyone who tries to stand up to them with a storm of criticism they quickly run from. The members also talk with their wallets, not only with membership fees but also with extra donations. According to NRA data published by CNN, a computer programmer in Houston gave $5,000 a year for a decade. Other top donors include a ranch manager, an airline pilot, and a geologist.[9]

In other words, to write off the NRA as just a stooge for the gun companies is to ignore the genuine grassroots movement giving it cash and support. On the other side, the company cash is crucial.

There is debate on how to value the U.S. gun industry. IBISWorld put the combined worth of manufacturing and sales at $28 billion in 2018, while the National Shooting Sports Foundation claimed an overall economic impact of $52 billion.[10] While this sounds a lot of money, it's not as big as various other industries. Americans spent $398 billion on consumer electronics that year and $482 billion on pharmaceuticals, and are estimated to shell out $150 billion a year on illegal drugs.[11]

However, gun companies are more generous to their lobby. Some give rates for every gun sold, while certain executives make big splashes through the "Golden Ring of Freedom," a donation scheme in which those who give over a million dollars get to ring the "freedom bell." They also advertise their products in NRA magazines, reaching the most dedicated collectors.

A big motive for giving to the NRA is precisely that the gun business is not so profitable. Gun companies often suffer hard times financially. A gun can last you all your life, which makes it hard to keep selling them without big contracts from security forces. Various firearms companies have declared Chapter 11 bankruptcy in recent years, including Colt and Remington. The NRA drive to keep fighting the threat of gun legislation, to sell the lifestyle, helps keep the sales up.

In hard times, gangsters become valued customers. And in this environment, companies need the NRA to protect them from legal consequences. As they handle a lethal product, they also face other potential court challenges. So the NRA works to secure laws such as the 2005 Protection of Lawful

Commerce in Arms Act, making it much harder to sue anyone in the gun business, even when there is corruption or faulty products that cause death.

Even considering the NRA is loaded, it's stunning how it has been able to shape American laws and put severe restrictions on a major federal agency. It's a case study in exerting influence in modern world politics.

It's notable that Wayne LaPierre, who has been chief executive and executive vice president of the NRA since 1991, is more of a politics guy than a gun guy. He comes from a wealthy family in upstate New York and did a master's degree in government before going into lobbying and quickly finding a home in the NRA. The writer Davidson describes him from an interview as soft-spoken, wearing hand-tailored suits, and knowing less about firearms than kids at his camp. Yet he understands politics as well as anyone in Washington.

A tool that LaPierre exploits is the power of focused gun voters who will punish politicians. "Some of them are just single-issue gun voters, and they will not forgive a politician who votes against their gun rights, their extremist gun rights position," says Jonathan Lowy, the chief counsel of Brady. "And there are very few single-issue voting blocs left in America."

The cold calculation that politicians make, Lowy says, is that going against gun rights will always lose these voters, while many concerned with gun safety can be won on other issues. In other words, pro-gun people are more dedicated to their cause than anti-gun people are to theirs. In this environment, the NRA system of grading politicians with scores from A to F is so effective.

Another prominent gun control activist, Richard Aborn, put it succinctly: "Although those opposed to gun control represented a minority view, they were a zealous single issue constituency that represented a political threat to any member who might support gun laws."[12] It's the old truth that an organized minority will win against a disorganized majority.

The NRA also dovetailed so well with the modern conservative movement. It grew right as the Democrats lost chunks of their white working-class base and the Republicans capitalized on cultural issues, especially guns and abortion. The top fifty receivers of NRA money are all Republicans, with those getting millions including Marco Rubio, Richard Burr, and the late John McCain.[13]

*   *   *

In the last decade, the political behemoth of the NRA has mutated yet again. When Trump took over the Republican message with the rhetoric of populism, and "the people" against "the elites," the NRA lapped it up. In February 2018, eight days after the Parkland shooting, LaPierre told the Conservative Political Action Conference that it was "the elites" who wanted to take people's guns.

"They hate the NRA. They hate the Second Amendment. They hate individual freedom. In the rush of calls for more government, they've also revealed their true selves. The elites don't care, not one whit, about America's school system, and schoolchildren . . . Their goal is to eliminate the Second Amendment and our firearms freedoms. So they can eradicate all individual freedoms."[14]

The NRA broadcast this message through its increasingly extensive media empire, including NRA TV. Stars on NRA TV included the spokeswoman Dana Loesch and an African American lawyer and gun enthusiast who takes the artistic name of Colion Noir. Loesch was especially scathing of mainstream media outlets, infamously saying of journalists, "They are the rat bastards of the earth. They are the boil on the backside of American politics."[15]

The wealth of the NRA cheerleaders didn't stop them from claiming to be the voice of the people. For several years, LaPierre made more than a million dollars annually,[16] and the others who reached the top, including Loesch and lobbyist Chris Cox, also became millionaires.

Some of the money was delivered in complex arrangements involving the decades-long advertising partner Ackerman McQueen, which the NRA was paying $40 million annually. The labyrinthine setup is described in a *Trace–New Yorker* piece by Mike Spies, who dug through tax forms and charity records to map out an intricate web of finances between the NRA, Ackerman McQueen, and other contractors.

Spies describes how the TV channel and magazines were crucial to keeping the money coming in and selling an identity in the culture war. "The NRA is now mainly a media company, promoting a lifestyle built around loving guns and hating anyone who might take them away," Spies writes.[17]

Other corners of the NRA were also making money in schemes that had strayed beyond those of a shooting organization and lobby. The NRA sold insurance policies for self-defense shootings, until the scheme was stopped after two years of state investigation and lawsuits.[18] And in 2015, NRA affiliates went on a paid junket to Moscow organized by Russian gun rights activist Maria Butina.

But while individuals in the NRA got rich, the lobby was struggling. Membership revenue was declining, down from 58 percent of its finances in 2008 to 40 percent by 2017,[19] according to NRA records, raising more questions over its true number of members. It spent heavily on Trump, giving him $30 million for the 2016 campaign, over twice what it spent on Mitt Romney in 2012. One ad showed a startled woman in her home with the words, "Don't let Hillary leave you defenseless."[20] But while Trump was delivering for the NRA politically, he didn't raise money. The NRA had been able to use Obama in calls to get donations, saying he was coming for their guns, but supporters felt comfortable with The Donald. Paradoxically, Obama was a bigger NRA fundraiser than Trump.

The deep problems of the NRA were exposed to the world in 2019, when internal conflicts blew up into simultaneous crises. Oliver North, the veteran of the Iran-Contra secret arms deal, had become NRA president and then resigned after less than a year, amid a spat with LaPierre. Chief lobbyist Cox quit amid the kerfuffle. LaPierre himself was accused of lavishly spending NRA donations on clothes and holidays. The NRA severed its ties with Ackerman McQueen. And Senate Democrats inquired into Russian infiltration into the lobby.

The conflicts reached a boiling point at the NRA's 2019 convention. Minutes before Trump addressed it, a court sentenced Butina, who had taken the affiliates to Moscow, to eighteen months in prison for being an undeclared Russian agent reporting to the Kremlin.[21] "She provided key information about Americans who were in a position to influence United States politics," the Justice Department said. Her role appeared to be part of the Kremlin's bigger game plan of making Washington more acquiescent to Moscow.

But the most important development was when New York attorney general Letitia James revealed that her office was examining the NRA's nonprofit status. Still registered in New York since it was founded by the Civil War veterans a century and a half ago, the NRA was vulnerable to the institutions of the Democrat-governed state. In the midst of the pandemic in August 2020, James struck the NRA with a lawsuit, arguing it should be dissolved "in its entirety" because it had thoroughly abused its role as a charity.

"The NRA diverted millions and millions away from its charitable mission for personal use by senior leadership," James said. "It's clear that the NRA has been failing to carry out its stated mission for many, many years. And instead has operated as a breeding ground for greed, abuse, and brazen illegality."[22]

The NRA fired back with a countersuit against James. "The NYAG's motive is nothing more than a gross misuse of regulatory power to undermine us as a political adversary," LaPierre said in a letter to members.[23]

The New York lawsuit has the potential to be a knockout blow to the whole structure of the organization. However, the NRA has been around a long time and changed with the eras. The pandemic and protests of 2020 helped massively boost gun sales. Even if it were run out of New York, the NRA could reemerge in a more friendly state in the South. It would be foolish to write off its ability to adapt yet again as the turmoil of U.S. politics burns into a new era.

Millions of Americans are frustrated by the hard-line positions of the NRA and its refusal to bend on measures such as universal background checks. But others believe its positions aren't extreme enough.

Among them is Phil Robinson, the founder of the Michigan Liberty Militia, whose members took their guns to the state capitol. A few weeks after the capitol protest, I got in touch with him through his Facebook page, on which he called himself "The Heathen" and displayed a photo with a bushy beard, a bulletproof jacket, and an AR-15 slung across his chest. We chat by phone, and then video, while he is sitting in his car in a white vest in his home of Barry County, a rural part of western Michigan. Phil is friendly if guarded on some details about himself and the militia tactics. But he's happy to let rip on the NRA, angry that it has made the tiniest compromises, such as on banning bump stocks, the accessories used by the Vegas shooter.

"They [the NRA] don't really understand what the 2A is and what it truly represents and stands for," Phil says. "There should be no compromise when it comes to the Second Amendment. It says very clearly, 'Shall not be infringed.'"

He also reprimands Trump for passing the bump stock ban. This makes The Donald weak on firearms in the view of hard-liners.

While the militia movement is a fringe phenomenon, it strikes at key points of the American identity and its relationship to guns. Its ideas also reach, and reflect, those of many more people. And the armed militias added to the violent turmoil of 2020—and could help the nation's seething tensions boil over into something worse.

Still, it doesn't help to overly hype what all the militias are now. Many have seen images of them running through forests, camping out in camo, and shooting targets. They are often referred to as paramilitaries, because they do some military-style training as well as give themselves warrior nicknames and ranks. But the term "paramilitary" can be overstating their reach. Many are more like clubs of (mostly) men getting outdoors for the weekend and playing guerrilla games. A *Vice* documentary on a militia in Georgia showed overweight, aging gents struggling with their push-ups. A comment on the video said, "The only real enemy they're up against, is diabetes and high blood pressure."[24] However, there are more serious elements in the movement that do have paramilitary potential—and there is a fringe linked to right-wing terror.

At the core of the militia is what can best be described as a fundamentalist interpretation of the Second Amendment. The "2A," as Phil calls it, is seen as sanctifying a natural (God-given) right that is fundamental to freedom and that allows people to defend their other rights.

"Without the Second Amendment, none of your rights are guaranteed," Phil tells me. "With the Second Amendment, you at least have a chance to protect your other amendments. Like I said before, it makes you a citizen, not a subject, because we see where every other country has banned guns, the pure tyranny that runs rampant."

The role of the militias in the Revolutionary War and the framing of the Second Amendment with the phrase "a well regulated militia" are of course key to inspiring the movement. But while jurists long interpreted the phrase as to limit gun rights to a regulated few, they flip it and see the opposite.

"Everybody is militia here in the United States," Phil says. "But some of us just wear the patch, and we express ourselves, and we are not afraid to let people know who we are."

While the movement is inspired by militias from the eighteenth century, its current manifestation is only a few decades old. Following Ruby Ridge and Waco, a former U.S. Air Force officer called Norman Olson formed the original Michigan Militia around 1994, laying down the ideological framework. As willing recruits flocked to his calls of resisting "a New World Order," he set up dozens of militias across Michigan and then toured the country, forming them from the southern border to the forests of Alaska.

This rapid rise floundered in the smoke of the Oklahoma bombing in 1995. When McVeigh and his cohort Terry Nichols were alleged to have attended meetings of a Michigan Militia chapter, it drew scrutiny from the press and federal agents. Police arrested members of various militias over the following years, hitting them with charges from illegal weapons to serious plots to carry out violence. Under pressure, many members dropped out, and Olson disbanded his group and went to Alaska. In a 2012 *Vice* interview, he said the government probably plotted Oklahoma to discredit the movement. "We think it did," he said. "We think they had to stop the militia because we were growing so fast across the country that we were threatening to take the power away from the federal government."[25]

Even with the ideologue spouting a batshit conspiracy, the movement survived, and returned to grow with the help of Facebook groups and the rhetoric that Obama was "coming for our guns." The true figures are hard to pin down, but the Southern Poverty Law Center claims that what it calls "Antigovernment 'Patriot' Groups" rebounded from a low of 131 groups across the United States in 2007 to reach 576 in 2019. Phil got together with two friends to found his Michigan Liberty Militia around 2016.

Like most militiamen, Phil's views on gun rights are for no compromise whatsoever. He says that all the gun laws back to the 1934 machine gun tax and 1968 Gun Control Act were bad. "Any law-abiding citizen is not going to commit a crime. Whether it's a semiautomatic or a fully automatic, I don't really see the difference," he says. It's a purist idea of a totally unregulated gun world.

I ask what he would do in the event of a new assault rifle ban. "I would probably pay it no attention, no mind," he says. "No, I would not comply." This makes me fear a new assault rifle ban could trigger a perilous confrontation.

Despite the public perception, militias claim they are not part of the racist hard right, and even play to the language of diversity. "Let's put these rumors to rest," Phil tells me. "First of all, we are not a right-wing group. None of us are any white supremacist [which he pronounces white "su-prem-ist"] . . . We have a Black man in our militia. We have a Puerto Rican man in our militia. We have women in our militia. And that goes throughout all the militias here in Michigan. They are all like that. We're diverse. We're patriots. As long as it's defending the flag, the Constitution, that's all that matters to us."

These affirmations are yet to be tested, but those studying the movement have found that militias do come from a different tradition and with different membership than the explicit white-power groups.

*   *   *

While it's not accurate to label the entire militia movement as far-right racist terrorists, we can't ignore the extremists on the edges. The thirteen alleged members of the Wolverine Watchmen were by no means the first militiamen to be charged with heinous crimes. In 2000, a Florida court sentenced militia "general" Donald Beauregard to five years for plotting to blow up a nuclear power station.[26] "He was clearly contemplating crimes of terrorism. There is no question he was engaged in activity that posed a serious threat of violence," the judge said. Then thirty-two, Beauregard was the manager of a farm store when he wasn't fantasizing about revolution. His militia was affiliated with the Southeastern States Alliance, which incorporated chapters from Alabama to Kentucky before it went defunct after Beauregard was locked up.

More recently, a group called the Boogaloo Bois emerged from the militia fringe. From about 2017, discussions on militia websites and pages talked of the "boogaloo," a weird code for civil war bizarrely inspired by the eighties breakdance movie *Electric Boogaloo*. (The movie was a sequel, so their boogaloo would be a sequel to the American Civil War.)

An analysis of Boogaloo chat boards by media outlet Bellingcat showed mixed messages.[27] Some white nationalists came in with their white genocide paranoia. But others focused on the radical Second Amendment message, taking it to the extreme of wanting to rise up against the police. They focused on police shootings, putting Ruby Ridge alongside African American victims. They also moved from pure camo to wearing Hawaiian shirts as accessories to their ARs.

In March 2020, the group found a martyr in twenty-one-year-old Duncan Lemp in the town of Montgomery, Maryland. Because of a juvenile criminal record, Lemp was banned from owning a firearm. Police came for his guns in a no-knock raid and shot him dead, claiming he fired first; his parents said they shot him in bed. "His name was Duncan Lemp" became a Boogaloo slogan.

As the year went on, their presence got picked up by the media, making them a recognizable name. Photos from the anti-lockdown protests showed various guys with guns and Hawaiian shirts, including one at the Michigan capitol wearing a Joker facemask.

But the Boogaloo Bois really hit the news when the protests over the murder of George Floyd lit up. Some of the Bois took to the street, seeing it as an opportunity to go against the police. Among them was a twenty-year-old in Denver who was stopped while driving to a protest with three rifles, handguns, and bulletproof vests. They were not illegal, so he complained to a TV station that police had "stolen" his guns.[28]

In a more tragic case, an alleged Boogaloo sympathizer was indicted by a grand jury for the ambush murders of a police sergeant and a federal security officer during Black Lives Matter protests in California in June. Steven Carrillo, thirty-two, was a U.S. Air Force sergeant on the rampage, according to the charges. The FBI claims he wrote the word "Boog" with his own blood on a stolen car.[29]

Other militia members have stood against the demonstrators. Seventeen-year-old Kyle Rittenhouse took an AR-15 to Kenosha, Wisconsin, during the protests and burning buildings that followed the police shooting of Jacob Blake in August 2020. Amid chaotic scenes, he was shown on video shooting dead two protesters and was charged with double homicide. Rittenhouse had reportedly responded to a call on the Facebook page of a group calling itself "Kenosha Guard." Facebook subsequently took down that page and those of various militias across the United States.

Some left-wing activists also take up arms. Days after the Kenosha killings, a member of the right-wing Patriot Prayer group was shot dead in Portland, by an affiliate of the antifascist movement antifa. Days later that shooter was himself shot dead by police.

America's abundance of guns means the political street fighting can so easily become lethal.

Militias represent only a tiny fraction of the gun enthusiasts. But their extreme interpretation of the Second Amendment is held by many more.

This creates a polarized climate in which gun owners or companies that call for compromise are booed down.

A typical case was in 2014 when a Maryland gun shop owner said he would sell so-called smart guns. These respond only to the fingerprints of their owners, in theory stopping them from going to gangsters. But hard-liners see them as a form of control. He received death threats and gave up.

In 2017, the gun maker Springfield Armory supported a bill in Illinois that required additional licensing for firearms sellers at the state level. Activists called the company a "sellout" and boycotted it.

In this environment, it's difficult for a figure in the gun world to support measures such as universal background checks. We are in a place where the extremes define the arguments. And this means basic measures that could slow the iron river have not come into play.

Many gun enthusiasts retort that authorities are failing to enforce the current laws because of corruption and conspiracies. When I ask Phil about the traffic of guns to Mexico, he concedes it is a problem but questions why it is permitted. "We're in a day and age where there's no hiding anything anymore. If they really wanted to stop it, my personal belief, they could stop it," he says.

In this conspiratorial view, elements of the hated U.S. government have been complicit in gun trafficking. Tragically, this is true. Which brings us squarely into Fast and Furious. We have looked at gangsters driving over borders, loopholes at gun shows, corrupt gun shops, and murderous Mexican soldiers. But the moment the ATF became complicit in arming cartels is the most controversial case of all.

8

Fast and Furious

Drugs are consumable; they go away. Guns don't go away.

—Steve Barborini, former ATF agent

Show me a hero and I will write you a tragedy.

—F. Scott Fitzgerald

The Peck Canyon cuts through the Sonoran Desert in Arizona just north of the border at Nogales, providing the respite of a stream and a little greenery amid the red, rocky landscape. Its name hails from bloodshed. In 1886, a band of Apaches, angry at being forced from their land, raided a ranch and killed Petra Peck and her daughter, the family of a New Yorker called Artemus Peck.[1] That killing was remembered locally. A nearby killing a century later would reverberate across the United States.

Brian Terry is perfectly cast as the all-American hero. Growing up in the Lincoln Park suburb of Detroit, he was one of four children of a worker at the Ford car factory. He played with a crew of kids called the Dead End

Gang, watched the Detroit Lions and Tigers, and dreamed of being a policeman like his Uncle Bob.[2]

Boasting a commanding physique, Terry served in the Marine Corps before going to college, joining his hometown police, and then joining the Border Patrol. When a chance opened to enter the elite BORTAC unit, he jumped. He was the oldest in his class at thirty-eight, facing punishing training that tested those half his age. Terry finished at the top, living up to his nickname "Superman," at one point fireman-carrying his partner three times around the training course.

"Brian always felt training should be real and to him he was mentally carrying a downed buddy," wrote police trainer Dan Marcou.[3]

Headquartered out of Biggs Army Airfield in El Paso, BORTAC stands for Border Patrol Tactical Unit, the equivalent of a SWAT team. It was formed in 1984 to deal with "riots" in Florida immigration lockups, and since then it has worked on everything from Operation Snowcap against cartels in Colombia to raiding a Miami house to pull out the Cuban boy Elián González. In 2020, it was controversially used to police protests outside the federal courthouse in Portland, Oregon. On the night of December 14, 2010, a BORTAC unit was operating in the Peck Canyon.

Considering the killing of Terry would have such repercussions, the coverage of the incident is surprisingly scattered. Official sources gave key facts years after, and there are still gaps in the details. Which speaks to a wider fog surrounding Fast and Furious.

The background was a series of shootings and robberies throughout 2009 and 2010[4] in the area a local journalist dubbed the "Peck Canyon corridor." The region is a crossing point for undocumented migrants and drug traffickers, close to where Flaco smuggled for the Sinaloa Cartel. Most of the victims of these robberies were themselves undocumented migrants, or *burros*, lugging marijuana.

The Border Patrol blamed the attacks on what it calls "rip crews" of bandits. Drug dealers robbing other drug dealers can be found from Baltimore to London, so it is unsurprising it happens in the desert, where smugglers are vulnerable. It's cheaper to steal drugs than to buy them.

Still, there are questions about who these rip crews really were. Robbing from the Sinaloa Cartel is hazardous. And while the Border Patrol would say the rip crews robbed cartels, it also identified them as members of a cartel.

The answer could lie in the intrigues of the Mexican Drug War. Since 2008, the Sinaloa Cartel had erupted into a civil war that pitted El Chapo against rival factions. El Chapo came out on top, but loyalists of other capos reformed into scattered bands. This may have been the case in Arizona, as former cartel thugs are the best suited to stealing from the cartel.

BORTAC agents were sent in and tracked a rip crew that had been operating for a year. Terry and five other agents began their stakeout on December 12 and had been two days at a location called Mesquite Seep, eleven miles north of the border. The seep is a choke point that smugglers will go through to get to Interstate 19 after trekking overland from Mexico.

Four of the agents, including Terry, were positioned on a small hill overlooking a wash, the other two at an observation point farther out. The night was dry, the moon two-thirds full. They were due to be relieved by another team at midnight, and Terry was to begin his Christmas holidays and go home to his family in Lincoln Park.

At 11:08 P.M., one of the lookouts radioed the agents on the hill to say a ground sensor was triggered, indicating people heading in their direction. The agents deployed in a line: Gabriel Fragoza on the right, William Castano to his left, followed by Terry and then Timothy Keller. Castano looked through night-vision goggles until he spotted five men, walking in single file, several carrying rifles.

"They were carrying their guns at the 'low ready' position," a position that made it easy for them to fire," Castano said.[5]

The gunmen were also lugging backpacks with tortillas, cans of beans, sardines, noodles, ammo, and gun lubricant, to make sure their rifles would fire in the desert. Castano allowed the first three gunmen to walk past, and as the other two approached, he shouted, "Police, police, *policia.*"

"Some of the individuals turned and faced us as if they were going to shoot at us," Castano said. "Others turned to run."

A defense lawyer would later claim the gunmen heard yelling in the dark and didn't know who it was. It could have been other bandits, so they didn't lower their guns. Castano and Fragoza fired first, but using "beanbag" rounds—big plastic shells used to stun people, often in riots. Castano lost his footing on the hill as he shot.

There was later debate as to why they shot nonlethal rounds. Border Patrol agents said that after the deaths of unarmed suspects, they'd been encouraged to use nonlethal force. But any U.S. policeman is permitted to fire live rounds at someone with a raised AK. And in the dark, the gunmen would have thought they were lethal bullets anyway.

The gunmen fired back, Fragoza seeing muzzle flashes in three different places. He pulled out his pistol and shot.

The muzzle flashes caused Keller's night vision to go out. When it returned, he saw a gunman with his Kalashnikov raised, scanning for a target. He shot with his rifle. "I was in fear of my life," he said.

Castano regained his footing and heard the cry from Terry.

"I'm hit," Terry said.

Castano rushed over to give first aid.

"I can't feel my legs," Terry said. "I'm paralyzed."

Castano asked where he had been shot, but Terry said he didn't know. In fact, a single Kalashnikov bullet had cut into Terry's lower back, severing his spinal cord and a main artery to his heart.

Terry lost consciousness. Soon after, his life left him as he lay on the hill in the desert, his fellow agents said.

There are conflicting reports about how exactly Terry's body was taken from the scene. But he was pronounced dead at 1:06 A.M. on the morning of December 15, 2010.

The aftermath of Terry's killing unwound rapidly. Police and FBI agents arrived at the scene and captured the wounded gunman, who was identified as Manuel Osorio Arellanes, originally from the town of Choix in northern Sinaloa. Moreover, they found at least two firearms, both

Kalashnikov WASR-10s from the Cugir factory, the serial numbers 1983AH3977 and 1971CZ3775.

The agents zapped the serial numbers to Martinsburg, where the team did a rapid trace to the Lone Wolf Trading Company in Glendale, Arizona, which reported it had sold them to a Jaime Avila Jr. When this data was shot back to the ATF in Phoenix, the agents shuddered. They knew Avila was a straw buyer for Mexican gangsters they were monitoring under Fast and Furious.

Within twenty-four hours, ATF agents arrested Avila, but initially charged him on a different straw buy. They appeared to be covering up a connection between Terry's death and Fast and Furious.

However, talk of a connection oozed out on blogs, including CleanUpATF .org, a site by disgruntled agents, and a militant pro-gun site called Sipsey Street Irregulars. ATF agent John Dodson blew the whistle in January, reaching out to Republican senator Chuck Grassley, an NRA loyalist. On January 27, Grassley wrote to the ATF acting director Kenneth Melson with the claims, following with a second letter, warning him not to go after whistleblowers.

As pressure built, the Zetas killed Jaime Zapata in Mexico, and Attorney General Eric Holder attended his funeral. Days later, on February 28, Holder ordered the Department of Justice's inspector general to do a report on Fast and Furious.

The story steadily gained steam in the media and was broken wide open on March 3, when CBS aired reporter Sharyl Attkisson interviewing agent Dodson nervously describing the operation. "A lot of people are going to get hurt with those firearms between the time we let them go and the time they are recovered again in a crime," Dodson said.

The Fast and Furious scandal was out of the bottle and rapidly ripped through the popular imagination of the United States and Mexico.

Terry himself became a hero for many, the symbol of a patriot falling to defend America. A foundation was set up in his name, his photo in uniform widely circulated, looking focused, strong, *iconic*. A supporter recorded a country song about his death, and Terry's sister wrote a children's book in his honor, *You Are My Hero*.[6] At the Border Patrol station in Bisbee, a memorial was built, a bronze statue showing Terry fireman-carrying a companion, his back straight, his muscles flexed, his head tilted down.

———

In Mexico, Fast and Furious reinforced the idea the United States was a bad ally that sowed destruction on its neighbor. Among gun rights activists, it reinforced the idea the ATF was a conspiratorial gang of gun grabbers. And among a broader section of America, it reinforced the idea of a corrupt elite failing to protect the dangerous southern border, a notion that would be central to the Trump campaign.

Steve Bannon talked about this when he visited Tucson in November 2017, shortly after he was pushed out as White House chief strategist. His speech was met with rowdy protests and rowdy supporters. As a reporter wrote:

"The groups were separated by a street, metal barriers and police officers. On one side, a man shouted into his megaphone. 'The people united will never be defeated!' On the other side, a woman yelled into her megaphone. 'The people united, are gonna be deported!' "[7]

Bannon reminisced to his crowd about Trump's election campaign, saying that he had told Trump that if he focused on the southern border, he would win the presidency.

"This is still the central issue in America. It's our sovereignty," Bannon said.

"I told the candidate that if you stick with this plan, to compare and contrast yourself as an agent of change, focus on southern border security, focus on these criminal cartels, focus on the issue of illegal immigration and legal immigration. Focus on this, you have a one hundred percent metaphysical certitude that you'll win."[8]

Bannon went on to say that waking up to border problems began right there in Arizona with the murder of Brian Terry.

"President Trump has, I think, done a tremendous job in his first year. But I can tell you, he wouldn't be president of the United States, if [it weren't for] the incident that happened here. Brian Terry will live in history as a historical figure. And the reason was he brought to the attention of the American people, put a human face on it, he put a hero's face on it, of what is exactly at risk on the southern border of our country."

I strongly disagree with the politics of Bannon. But when he says that Terry's death and Fast and Furious contributed to the rise of Trump, I think he is probably right.

My dad once told me, You have the conspiracy theory, you have the cock-up theory (which you might translate as the "screw-up theory"), and you have the cocked-up conspiracy theory.

I don't think all conspiracy theories are bunk. The conspiracy of the CIA working with drug traffickers turned out to be true. The sinking of the *Titanic,* meanwhile, was a giant cock-up. The creation of the Islamic State was a cocked-up conspiracy; the neocons had a plan to reshape the Middle East, but it went horribly wrong.

Fast and Furious spawned at least three conspiracy theories.

The first is the most familiar to Americans: Fast and Furious was a plot by Obama to create a scandal around guns in order to carry out gun control. Adherents of this idea look to the fact that Obama promised in his campaign to reinstate the assault rifle ban, but when he took office, he struggled to get support for it. The conspiracy theory was articulated by Republican Darrell Issa, then a representative from California and another big NRA loyalist.

"Could it be," Issa said on NRA TV, "that what they really were thinking of was in fact to use this walking of guns in order to promote an assault weapons ban? Many think so. And they haven't come up with an explanation that would cause any of us not to agree."

Adherents of the "Obama conspiracy" point to the failure of Holder to release all the documents, for which he was held in contempt of Congress. They add that documents that were released were covered in black ink.

"The suspicion is under all those black lines is proof that the largest gunrunning operation in history into the hands of the Mexican drug cartels has been conducted by the Obama administration's justice department," NRA president LaPierre told an interviewer.[9]

They also point to Obama administration links to Arizona. These include the former governor Janet Napolitano and her old chief of staff Dennis K. Burke, who became a top U.S. attorney in Arizona and was involved in Fast and Furious.

The fact that Obama didn't carry out significant gun reform is put down to the plot being foiled after the death of Terry. The ATF also issued a new regulation in 2011 following Fast and Furious to make stores in the border states report multiple buys of rifles. While this may seem a tiny deal, gun rights activists claim it's unconstitutional. And an email was uncovered of an ATF official asking for anecdotes of multiple gun sales from Fast and Furious to support the new rule.[10]

The second conspiracy theory is more popular south of the river. This holds that the U.S. government ran guns to cartels to make Mexico weak and unstable, and so easier to control. The theory was articulated in Mexican newspaper editorials, such as one after the case broke in 2011, headlined "Guns to Destabilize Mexico."[11] The movie *Miss Bala*, released late 2011, also showed an American agent personally running truckloads of guns to a cartel.

The third Fast and Furious conspiracy looks at where the guns went. Many of those captured were found in the hands of the Sinaloa Cartel, including the guns found in El Chapo's last safe house. The theory is that the U.S. government made a deal with the Sinaloa Cartel, letting it run drugs and supplying it weapons.

The theory gained steam in 2019 when Mexico's secretary of public security at the time, Genaro García Luna, was arrested for links to the Sinaloa Cartel. As of late 2020, the case against him was ongoing. Mexican president Andrés Manuel López Obrador then asked Washington for information on Fast and Furious. The implication was that the previous Mexican and

U.S. administrations had conspired together to support the biggest Mexican mob.

Conspiracy theories are important to understand because they color perceptions. But I personally don't subscribe to any of these Fast and Furious conspiracies. I believe in the cock-up theory, albeit with some foul play to cover up those cock-ups.

Saying that, I don't think it was simply a few rogue agents. The agents in Arizona certainly made grave mistakes, but Fast and Furious reflects wider troubles. The first is the dubious tactics that various federal agencies use to make cases against organized crime. The second is the utter failure to stop the colossal volume of firearms trafficked over the southern border.

"Walking guns" is a funny term. It's like saying that gangsters run guns, but governments walk guns.

It means different things to different people. When the Department of Justice did its review of Fast and Furious, it asked ATF agents about the expression. Some claimed they had never heard it before the scandal broke. Others thought it meant two things.

The first meaning is when agents pose as black market gun sellers and supply weapons to criminals. This is another tactic borrowed from narcs, a twist on the "buy and bust" tactic. When the agent becomes the seller, they call it the "reverse buy." They should seize the guns right away, but if they don't, they say they are "letting them walk." This is something that all agents agree is problematic—the government becoming the direct supplier of guns to gangsters.

The second is when agents know about guns being moved on the black market but don't act right away. Agents were more mixed on this tactic, with the ATF rulebook ambiguous. As it says in what is called the Firearms Enforcement Program Order: "Immediate intervention may not be needed or desirable, and the special agent may choose to allow the transfer of firearms to take place in order to further an investigation."[12]

So what does this mean in the real world? Say an agent is watching a woman go to a shop to straw-purchase five AKs. He can confront her, but even if she confesses, she might get only probation. Or he can follow her to the delivery and get the person ordering the sales. Or, alternatively, he could "flip her" and get her to deliver the guns while agents watch.

This last tactic is known as a controlled delivery, and is yet another tool from the narc box. When customs agents find someone bringing drugs over the southern border, they will often tell them they can deliver the dope while agents watch, so they can bust the stash house. The same works with guns.

This discussion was largely lost in the coverage of Fast and Furious. This is not to say that the agents didn't badly mess up. It's that it didn't happen in a vacuum.

"Gunwalking" has been going on a long time. Carson Carroll, a ranking ATF supervisor in Washington, said in one email that there were agents "who have been with ATF 30 years, say they can remember a couple of attempts of a controlled delivery back in the early 80's."[13]

Then there is the undercover work by agents like Koz. When he infiltrated biker gangs, he witnessed felons with guns but did not bust them right away, sometimes waiting years. In the meantime, the bikers could have used those guns to murder. Is there an ethical difference between seeing a criminal with a gun and not acting, and seeing a gun be trafficked to a criminal and not acting? But the former undercover tactic has not been especially controversial.

This is bigger than the ATF and stretches to all the major federal agencies. Look at the famous case of FBI agent Donnie Brasco infiltrating the New York mob (and the great film version of it with Al Pacino and Johnny Depp). Real name Joe Pistone, he conned his way into the Bonanno crime family and the Colombo crime family and witnessed countless crimes for six years. Finally, his evidence led to two hundred indictments and over a hundred convictions of Cosa Nostra gangsters. Again, he was allowing crime to take place, but federal agents saw this as the only way to take down the mob. (Pistone himself got the reward of five hundred dollars and a price on his head.)

This plays big in the war on drugs. Narcs put wires on dealers and hear them sell dope. But they wait to pounce until they can build a stronger case. In the meantime, heroin is sold, is injected, and kills. The difference is that there are no serial numbers on bags of heroin. Or as the former ATF agent Steve Barborini tells me, "Drugs are consumable—they go away. Guns don't go away."

The fight against organized crime is a dirty game, and the rules are blurry. This is not to justify Fast and Furious but to explain how the hell the agents got into the mindset of doing what they did.

While gunwalking goes back decades, it's foggy as to how much went on and where. But there is documentation of a major case called Operation Wide Receiver, which agents ran out of Tucson, Arizona, in 2006 and 2007, two years before Fast and Furious launched in Phoenix in 2009.

The fact that Wide Receiver happened under President George W. Bush weakens the argument that gunwalking was an Obama conspiracy, and Holder would raise this point in his defense. There was also a separate operation called the Hernandez Case in 2007 in which the ATF followed a "controlled delivery" of hundreds of guns into Mexico before losing sight of them.

There are links between Wide Receiver and Fast and Furious, and both ops involved guns from Arizona going to cartels. But there are also differences. In Wide Receiver, agents watched close to five hundred guns walk, as opposed to the nearly two thousand in Fast and Furious. And Wide Receiver had a more active role played by an informant firearms seller, the competitive shooter and gun magazine writer Mike Detty.

Detty detailed his life as a confidential informant for the ATF in the book *Guns Across the Border*, helped by a methodical mind and a journal. He elaborated on it in a long conversation with me, in which he was admirably open with his feelings. His story is of a gun dealer who wanted to do the right thing and take down the gangsters but got pulled into a dangerous web.

Detty was in a tough place when the ATF found him, which made him a keen recruit. Hailing from Philadelphia, he had longed for a career in the military but was cursed with arthritic ankles that wore away, leaving bone-on-bone contact. Trying to defy his "broken body," he completed the punishing Marine Corps training, only to get a medical discharge, which broke his heart.

Detty was hurt again when he got pushed out of his family business, leading him to go to Tucson, write for gun magazines, and sell AR-15s. Standing at shows with arthritic ankles was torturous, and he blames a loss of self-confidence on his wife leaving. Depressed, divorced, and close to fifty, the idea of secretly recording gangsters to bust a cartel was appealing.

"I was in a unique position. I was already divorced, I didn't have any kids, I lived here by myself," he says. "Every day I'd have that conversation with myself, 'Is this the day I'm going to put a bullet in my head?' Because I was so freaking miserable . . . So doing something dangerous and doing something reckless didn't bother me a bit . . . Maybe one of these kids will save me the effort and shoot me."

I'm struck by Detty's desire to want to stop guns going to cartels. While some gun enthusiasts deny there is a problem, Detty said the traffic bothered him. "I had no wish to see my guns being used in the savagery across the border," he writes. "Mexico was a country I enjoyed and whose people I'd come to love."

Furthermore, Detty condemns the shady gun dealers who take advantage of the private-sale loophole. He describes one of them who dressed in camo, claimed he had worked with Israeli special forces, and would usually have a hundred guns for sale.

"He was in the business of dealing firearms, but unlike me and many of the other dealers, he had no federal license to do so and did all his transactions without background checks," he writes. "I was disgusted—that was the kind of crap that gave gun shows and honest dealers like me a bad rap."[14]

Detty sold some guns in parts, such as lower receivers, which have a serial number and are considered a firearm. The cartels often buy the weapons this way and reassemble them south of the border, hence the code name Wide Receiver.

Even before Wide Receiver, Detty gave info to the ATF. In one case, he informed on an Arizona cop taking AR-15 lowers into Mexico, which led to the cop's resignation. In another, an elderly customer ordered seventy-five lowers, and agents followed him to a trailer, where he confessed. The man was straw-buying to pay for dialysis and died soon after. (This raises the issue of why an old man had to traffic weapons to pay for his health care.)

But those cases took little time or risk, while Wide Receiver would have Detty spending long hours spying on cartel affiliates. It was like he became a character in a movie.

"Not a feel-good movie by any means," he says. "Bad movie? Yes, absolutely . . . Bad movie all the way around. Still is. You come to see me and you'll see my security system. You'll see my dogs. And no matter where I'm at in the house, I've got a gun."

Wide Receiver kick-started when a man called Greg turned up at a gun show in February 2006 to buy all six of Detty's AR-15 lower receivers and order twenty more. Greg was in his early twenties, chubby in baggy shorts and a sideways cap, and Detty was surprised he passed the check and alerted the ATF. The agents came to the next show to watch Greg pick up the twenty lowers and order fifty more.

The agents told Detty to go through with the deal and gave him a cop recorder called a Hawk. Detty hid it in his pocket and met Greg at a McDonald's to get a deposit on the new order. As Greg handed over a fat envelope with $2,500, he blurted out that he worked with a guy who converted the guns to fully automatic, and Detty got it on tape.

"You know how the AR-15s shoot kind of fast but not real fast?" Greg said. "Well, we have a guy that machines them so they go real fast."[15]

Detty went to the ATF office and signed up as a confidential informant, getting photographed and fingerprinted. They handed him his first payment of $200. When he went in to see the ATF supervisor, he said he was concerned about the guns being used in murders. The supervisor told him not to worry, that they would work with Mexican colleagues to seize the arms and use the info to take down a cartel. Neither of those promises came true.

Detty got a mysterious call to say Greg was being relieved of his duties and others would pick up the guns. An ATF surveillance team watched two cartel affiliates go to Detty's home and hand over the remaining $10,700 in small bills for the fifty lowers. The agents put a tracker on the car.

When the gangsters left, an agent gave Detty another payment of $200. Detty was annoyed it was so low, as he'd spent days organizing the setup. The agent reminded him he was also making money on the gun deals. This is an uncomfortable element of Wide Receiver and Fast and Furious. Whether they liked it or not, the gun sellers profited off the op. In any case, the ATF agent later apologized and gave Detty another $300 for that job, and more payments dribbled in.

The cartel goons soon came back for another fifty receivers and asked for a grenade launcher. When Detty told the ATF, agents considered offering one from the Tucson Air Force base but decided that if they did, they would have to bust them right away, and they wanted to keep the case going.

The pattern carried on through 2006 and 2007. Detty sold to colorful characters coming to his home, including an older guy in ostrich-skin boots with a menacing bodyguard, and a guy with missing fingers. Detty recorded the deals and coordinated with ATF to mount surveillance. He cultivated a character as the shady gun dealer.

"I'd make them feel I was that friendly uncle that they had," he says. "I treated them each as a person, not as a gangbanger or cartel member or whatever."

He had close shaves. One time he was showing guns to the crew when the recorder started playing back aloud in his pocket. He must have nudged it. He pretended to take a phone call and none of them seemed to notice. Another time, the gangsters spotted an ATF tail from his house. Detty had to flip the script and pretend he was angry.

"I tried to turn it around and said, 'Hey. Who knows that you have money and you have guns? This could be one of the people you know trying to rip you off. I don't need that shit around here.'"

Another time he had six crooks in his house when an ATF agent used a flashlight to look at license plates and it shone in the window. "How in the world do you fuck that up so bad?" Detty says.

He had tense exchanges with the gangsters over money and saw a suspicious van parked outside his home. Detty started having nightmares and keeping loaded rifles around his house. He went to pick up the newspaper with a pistol in his pocket.

One of the guys he was dealing with got shot in Mexico. Another was arrested in Tucson for holding a gun to his girlfriend's head in a restaurant.

But the ATF kept paying Detty, giving him a total of $15,000 in informant fees over the years. And he kept on selling his weapons. He sold the goons more AR-15s, along with Kalashnikovs, Dracos, and .38 Super pistols. It went from dozens of guns to hundreds. The ATF would finally tally it up at 474 weapons for a total of $265,000.

Years later, only 64 of those guns had been seized.

A Department of Justice report gives insight into what the agents were playing at as Detty sold all these guns. They were trying to build a bigger case by gathering evidence on the trafficking network to put on a flowchart and bust the bosses. They used the tracking device to follow the car from Tucson to San Diego. They dug through the guy's trash and found a bank receipt showing a withdrawal of $8,000 just before he had bought guns. They got records of phone calls from Arizona to Mexico.

It is notable that during this time, the case was discussed by various ATF superiors and U.S. attorneys, and they never heavily questioned the tactic of letting the guns walk. Prosecutor Jennifer Maldonado, who first signed off on Detty recording the conversations, would later say she "compared the investigation to a drug case in which she understood that law enforcement officers can elect not to seize smaller quantities of drugs so that they can build a larger case."[16]

But the investigation stumbled. The agents believed the guns were going to two different cartels, the Arellano Félix Organization in Tijuana and a faction of the Sinaloa Cartel in Sonora. But while they got phone numbers in Mexico, they struggled to get names.

They decided to arrest Greg and flip him, signing him up as another informant. But Greg suddenly got cut out of deals and didn't come up with any info. The agents planned to go through with a reverse buy with a grenade launcher. But the gangsters shied away at the last moment. The agents gave license plate info and phone numbers to the Mexican attorney general's office. But it didn't come back with anything useful in return.

Moreover, they tried to put a tracking device in the stock of a Serbian AK. But it ran out of batteries and the antenna wouldn't work through the stock. And when they followed the traffickers by car or helicopter, they kept on losing them.

A problem was that the agents seemed to misunderstand the nature of Mexican organized crime. The Sinaloa Cartel does not operate like a regular corporation with a clear hierarchy. It is more like a federation of gangsters who work together on different jobs, and the different cells have a lot of autonomy. The kingpins like El Chapo are protected by many layers.

From Detty's description, the straw buyers were only associates of the cartel. They were buying guns on orders as well as making money on the side with their own deals. The ATF agents in Wide Receiver struggled to get off first base.

When agents finally gave up operational work on Wide Receiver in late 2007, they passed it on to prosecutors. Who sat on it. For years.

At this point, questions about walking so many guns came up, and prosecutors were hesitant about touching the mess. Prosecutor Thomas Ferraro had the case throughout 2008 and didn't issue any indictments before he left to become a magistrate. It was reassigned to Assistant U.S. Attorney Serra Tsethlikai, who raised doubts in an email in December 2008. "I don't like the case. I think it is wrong for us to allow 100s of guns to go into Mexico to drug people." She made no indictments before she accepted another detail in August 2009, and the case was shunted over to the gang unit.

In 2010, prosecutors finally indicted ten people on Wide Receiver. They were all low-level straw buyers charged for lying on the 4473s. Two of them remained fugitives. The highest sentence was thirty-three months.

While they prepared the prosecutions, Deputy Assistant Attorney General Jason Weinstein wrote in an email, "Been thinking about 'Wide Receiver I.' ATF HQ should / will be embarrassed that they let this many guns walk—I'm stunned."

While he wrote that, over four times as many guns were being walked under Fast and Furious.

As Wide Receiver faded to its inglorious end, Detty's relationship with the feds broke down. He had put his life on the line and was frustrated that they took years to indict and that he had to keep dealing with different prosecutors. Even worse, he says, the feds exposed him as an informant to reporters, putting his life in danger.

Rather than offer protection, a prosecutor asked him to hand over his journal. When he refused, as it had personal info, she threatened to subpoena it. The agents read his personal thoughts, even details of meeting an old flame.

The prosecutor questioned Detty about cooperating only for the money and exaggerating the dangers. Another prosecutor refused to give him intelligence on whether the gangsters were discussing revenge.

"All my life I had nothing but the greatest respect for federal agents and those who worked in the Department of Justice," he wrote. "Now, for the first time I was seeing them for what they were—lazy, sloppy, self-protecting civil servants who cared more about self-preservation and collecting a paycheck than doing the right thing."[17]

When Brian Terry was killed, Detty was furious to see agents trying to underplay the gunwalking. He subscribed to the idea it must be a plot to ban assault rifles.

"They just wanted as many American guns to show up at crime scenes in Mexico as possible," he tells me. "There's just no other explanation for it."

Detty paid a price for his efforts, not knowing if the gangsters might take revenge. One time, he was at the movies and saw a girlfriend of a straw buyer he had dealt with. He got up in the middle of the movie and walked out.

He's still looking over his shoulder.

———

While agents let guns walk in Arizona, bigger forces were at work in Washington and Mexico City. There is a popular perception that the Mexican Drug War began in 2006, when President Felipe Calderón launched his military offensive against cartels. But the violence actually began escalating in 2004, especially in the border city of Nuevo Laredo, where the Sinaloa Cartel battled the Zetas for the lucrative trafficking route. Over the next two years, the fighting spread to Sonora, Acapulco, and Michoacán, and Calderón reacted to this bloodshed with his crackdown. Which threw oil on the fire.

As noted, 2004 was the year the Clinton assault rifle ban expired. I don't think this expiry caused the Mexican Drug War. The forces were already in place: a weaker Mexican government losing power to control cartels, which battled it out for themselves with private armies. But it exacerbated the conflict, as cartels stocked up on the widely available rifles.

President Calderón enlisted U.S. help for his crackdown from 2007. He went on to address a joint session of U.S. Congress in 2010, where he condemned gun trafficking to Mexico, and he was in power when Fast and Furious broke. He is key to understanding the politics around the scandal, and he gave me a frank interview about it for an hour and a half in his office in Mexico City.

I covered the bloodshed under Calderón and was fairly critical of him. I believe his strategy against cartels failed and made Mexico more violent. For some in Mexico, he became a hate figure like certain other former presidents. Furthermore, one of El Chapo's lawyers at the trial accused Calderón of working for the Sinaloa Cartel, which many in Mexico jumped to believe. The denunciations grew louder when his former security secretary was charged with drug trafficking. However, when Calderón spoke to me, he refuted the accusations and I was impressed by his openness.

"[The lawyer] was unable to sustain such accusations, and actually all the witnesses he called, not one of them sustained that I had received any single cent from the criminals," Calderón told me.

Our conversation began with Calderón arguing against the idea that he waged a war on drugs. His fight, he said, was against the capture of the state by organized crime.

"We realized it was not only small villages or towns. It was complete cities and even states," he said. "And that was a real problem, a real threat, to the Mexican state, the Mexican nation."

He went on that the Mérida Initiative, in which Washington bankrolled the offensive against cartels, began as Mexico's idea. This goes against another common perception that Washington bullied Calderón into the drug war. The truth is that while the United States used to pressure Latin American countries to combat trafficking, Calderón's offensive was his own project.

"We needed the support, the real support of the American government, and also we needed to change the statement," Calderón said. "The issue is not about Mexican certification. It's not about the American supervision. It's about co-responsibility."

Bush and Calderón met in Mérida in March 2007 to agree on the plan, which would give Mexico almost $3 billion worth of support over the following decade. This came in hardware, including Black Hawk helicopters and high-tech wiretap gear.[18]

"I tried to explain what exactly we were looking for, in particular the technical support," Calderón said. "And I said, 'Well, have you ever seen this TV show *24* with Jack Bauer and so on?' He said yes. 'Well, I want all the instruments of this guy.' And we got it."

Calderón didn't bring American guns into the conversation right away. It wasn't until 2008, when Bush was on his way out, that Calderón realized the importance of the U.S. market in arming the cartels.

"[The guns] created an incredible disequilibrium between the Mexican law enforcement agencies and organized crime," he said. "Suddenly the old police forces in Durango, in Mier, Tamaulipas, like twelve policemen carrying revolver .38s, [were] against four or five Suburbans, plenty of AR-15s or AK-47s."

In this era, police in several towns fled their posts en masse, with one female police chief near Juárez running to the United States. Calderón got increasingly frustrated over the lack of action from Washington. When he got the historic opportunity to address the joint session of Congress in May 2010, he asked his cabinet about bringing up guns. Many said it was a bad idea.

"One part of my own cabinet was trying to persuade me to be very polite. To not address such kind of issues—'It's not the place. It's not the moment.' And I say I had no other opportunity to say that. In the name of the Mexican people, I decided to address the issue."

When he took the stand and talked about guns, he got cold stares from many lawmakers. But he felt he was doing the right thing.

"I am telling you the weapons you are selling are not going to the hands of the good American citizens to protect their family," he told them. "They are going to the hands of the criminals. And maybe one day those weapons will aim at the American citizens."

A few months later, the guns were used by the killers of Agent Terry and of Agent Zapata.

As Calderón put pressure on Washington, American officials told him they had a big operation in the works. This would turn out to be Fast and Furious.

"I was told the government was going to do something really serious about prosecuting gun traffickers. And then we started to understand there was some kind of cover operation to do so . . . At that time, it sounds very good for us. But we never realized it was going to be a complete disorder."

This backs up the ATF claim that it told Mexico about the op. Emails released on Fast and Furious also show there was a meeting in Mexico City in late 2010 with a U.S. team, including ATF head Kenneth Melson.[19]

However, Calderón said he began to realize something was amiss when a Zeta leader called Flavio "Yellow" Mendez was captured in January 2011. Yellow had knowledge that the U.S. government was letting guns walk into Mexico, Calderón told me. He even said agents were openly working with traffickers. This would later be backed up by another Zeta commander, Jesús "El Mamito" Rejón, captured in mid-2011.

"The buyers on the other side said the very U.S. government sold them the guns," Mamito said in an interrogation video.[20]

This is tricky information to interpret. But if gun traffickers were actually telling the Zetas that the U.S. government helped them, it would show how supremely messed up the operations were.

* * *

When the news of Fast and Furious broke, Calderón said *he* was furious. But when he saw the NRA-supporting Republicans use it to attack Obama, he chose not to rage publicly.

"There was an incredible attack of the Republicans. And the people who were involved the most with the American rifle association, they were the most aggressive people against the attorney general," Calderón said. "So we decided, we protest in private with the American government. But we decided not to be part of the campaign against the attorney general . . . It was completely an NRA operation."

Looking back, Calderón doesn't believe Fast and Furious was a conspiracy but a cock-up. "It was a good idea, but it was horribly implemented," he said.

After seeing the failure to stop gun trafficking under his government, Calderón is not optimistic about it being stopped in the future. The money going into the U.S. gun industry is too much of an incentive, he said.

"Private money, profits, is the name of this game," he said. "If they can organize a civil war in Africa, it would sell."

The developments take a different light from Washington. In his campaign, President Obama indeed talked about reinstating the assault rifle ban. Which led to a surge in sales, with people stocking up while they still could.[21] In the month of November 2008, gun sales shot up to 1.1 million.

When Holder became attorney general in February 2009, he also promised to bring back the ban. "There are just a few gun-related changes that we would like to make, and among them would be to reinstitute the ban," he said in his first press conference.

However, the Obama administration quickly backed away. When a reporter asked Holder about it two months later, he said, "I think what we're going to do is to try to, obviously, enforce the laws on the books."[22]

It seems that faced with the reality of power, Obama focused on a few concrete objectives, including health care, getting out of recession, and the

Iran nuclear deal. He saw the numbers were not there in Congress for the assault rifle ban and put it on the back burner.

In April 2009, three months into his presidency, Obama made his first trip to Mexico to meet Calderón. It was during an escalation in cartel violence, and there was a lot of security and few events. Among them was a news conference in the old presidential palace of Los Pinos, which I went to with the usual press corps.[23]

The presidents took only four questions, and the first was about guns, a U.S. reporter asking what happened to the promise on the assault rifle ban.

"Well, first of all, we did discuss this extensively in our meetings. I have not backed off at all from my belief that the gun—the Assault Weapons Ban made sense," Obama said. "Now, having said that, I think none of us are under any illusion that reinstating that ban would be easy. And so, what we've focused on is how we can improve our enforcement of existing laws, because even under current law, trafficking illegal firearms, sending them across a border, is illegal. That's something that we can stop.

"And so our focus is to work with Secretary Napolitano, Attorney General Holder, our entire Homeland Security team, ATF, border security, everybody who is involved in this, to coordinate with our counterparts in Mexico to significantly ramp up our enforcement."

Again, this shows Obama backing away from the ban. But he also emphasized there *would* be major efforts to stop gun trafficking over the border.

This is important background to Fast and Furious, a few months before it was launched. From the president to the attorney general on down, there was pressure on the ATF to fight the trafficking into Mexico. In the field offices, they faced this directive with limited resources and an enormous flow of weapons.

In August 2009, a few months before Fast and Furious started, I visited the ATF offices in Phoenix and looked at their stash of seized guns. The agent

Peter Forcelli took me down in the elevator to the vault. The room shone with Kalashnikovs, AR-15s, FN "cop killers," and .50 calibers, laid out on racks and filling buckets. It was one of the biggest arsenals of captured weapons in America.

Forcelli comes from New York and has a broad accent. ("Can I speak Spanish?" he said. "No, I can't even speak English.") He said that when he moved to Arizona, he was astounded by the sheer volume of illegal weapons. "I saw more Kalashnikovs here in my first week than in fifteen years in the New York police."

Forcelli would not be on the Fast and Furious team, and his testimony was critical of it. But he gave me good background information. He explained they had fewer than twenty agents looking at thousands of gun shops, and many didn't get inspected for years. Their usual tactic was to get sellers like Detty to report suspicious buyers. They would follow these buyers and try to bust them and the people they were delivering to. This added a lot of guns to the bulging piles in the vault. But Forcelli conceded they were stopping only a fraction of the guns going to Mexico. Facing this challenge, agents came up with Fast and Furious.

As well as thousands of released emails and letters, there are two key accounts of the day-to-day of the Fast and Furious operation. The first is the Department of Justice report. This is packed with info and interviews with most officials involved. But it must be considered that the DOJ is investigating itself.

The second is a book by ATF agent John Dodson, who blew the whistle to Senator Grassley. Dodson provides a systematic account with some colorful phrases. "No one likes the prick who says, 'I told you so,'" he begins.[24] But by his own account, he was blocked out of many discussions of his supervisors and not privy to their conversations with Washington.[25]

The case begins in October 2009, with the creation of "Group VII," one of four ATF strike forces investigating firearms trafficking in the Phoenix territory. Group VII would eventually be headed by Special Agent David

Voth, a former marine who worked street gangs in Minneapolis. Hope MacAllister, who had ten years in the Phoenix Field Division, was there from the start. Dodson would move over from Virginia, and there were some inexperienced agents, one still on probationary status. Bill Newell oversaw them as head of the bureau.

On October 31, a Phoenix gun shop alerted MacAllister that four young men had bought nineteen Kalashnikovs. Group VII found that two of the buyers had the same address on their Arizona driver's licenses and saw they that were getting weapons from various shops. One personally bought seventy-five guns in six weeks.

The agents followed the buyers to a house owned by a man in his twenties named Manuel Celis-Acosta, and they identified him as a primary target, the one they hoped would link them to the cartel. Very quickly, the agents got confirmation that the "Celis-Acosta gang" was delivering the guns to Mexico; on November 20, Mexican soldiers busted a truck in Naco, Sonora, and seized forty-two firearms. The weapons were traced to straw buyers they had watched, alongside others they added into the probe.

MacAllister told her bosses they should hold off on busts as they went after bigger fish. As she wrote in an email on November 27: "We are actively identifying much larger players in the organization and contacting any of the purchasers at this point in time will adversely affect the success of this investigation."[26]

As Voth took charge of Group VII, agents carried on watching the straw buyers get hundreds of guns and take them to stash houses. By the end of the year, they had bought over nine hundred firearms, mostly from five stores. Dodson claims that he and some other agents saw this was problematic right away.

"As the weeks went on, it was the same routine," Dodson writes. "Hope would get a call from a gun dealer advising that one of our low-level knuckleheads was in the store or on their way there, and purchasing high quantities of the same make and model weapons all at one time. We'd rush out to the respective gun shop, set up in the parking lot, and watch, taking pictures or video as they exited the store, arms full of boxes containing weapons.

Sometimes there would be so many they would have to wheel them out on a store cart . . . Our coping mechanism was to joke about it."[27]

Group VII tried to build a bigger case. They finally got a techie from the El Paso Intelligence Center (a multiagency hub) to put a tracking device into an AK-47 and fed it to the gun shop. Unfortunately, Dodson writes, it was the wrong variant of AK-47, and the straw buyers didn't want it. The ATF had to get the shop owner to pitch the rifle until one of the straws eventually took it.

They were finally tracking the guns. For less than an hour. The agents lost the signal; maybe because it went into a warehouse; maybe the battery died; maybe the bad guys found it.

"Back at the office, the only concern expressed was for the loss of the GPS equipment and their having to account for that," Dodson writes. "The guns getting away . . . well, that was business as usual."[28]

The next tracker worked better. It was placed in a gun sold to a straw, and the ATF followed it to the Tohono O'odham reservation, an area used for smuggling. Agents stopped the truck and seized forty-one guns. Two women were in the vehicle: a driver who was a convicted drug smuggler and confessed, and a passenger who claimed she was going over to Mexico to buy chimichangas.

It was the biggest gun bust that came directly from Fast and Furious intel. Dodson claims it was more to get the tracker back.

The agents switched focus to a wiretap. Voth was keen on getting a wire from the start, Dodson claims, as he had used one successfully in a gun trafficking case in Minnesota, winning him an Agent of the Year award.

However, getting a wire takes time and paperwork. The agents have to gather evidence and work on a complicated affidavit. And Voth complained that the prosecutor was especially slow. While the affidavit was being fine-tuned, the straws were on a voracious binge of gun buying. By the time it was filed on March 4, they had bought more than 1,400 weapons.

By then, tensions in Group VII were boiling over. It was not just about the tactics but also personality clashes. Dodson doesn't hide his disdain for Voth. ("He didn't have an ounce of initiative and could seldom muster an original thought."[29]) But Dodson also conceded he could be blunt himself. ("I'm the guy with the broken Kanuter valve."[30]) When Voth finally got the wire, agents complained about the unsociable hours having to listen to the bugged phones. Voth replied with an irate email.

"It has been brought to my attention that there may be a schism developing amongst the group," he wrote. **"If you don't think this is fun you're in the wrong line of work—period!** . . . Maybe the Maricopa County jail is hiring detention officers and you can get paid $30,000 (instead of $100,000) to serve lunch to inmates all day."[31]

The problems that Group VII ran into in Fast and Furious were the same ones that agents faced in Wide Receiver. The cartel smugglers kept switching phones and were careful whom they called and what they said. They were not as easy prey as a gang in Minnesota or Brooklyn. And Celis-Acosta was a rather mysterious affiliate who was on the edges of the mob.

The agents waited, hoping more evidence would beckon. In May 2010, the Border Patrol stopped Celis-Acosta in the town of Lukeville, and when they saw he was under investigation, they took him in, discovering a few dozen bullets and nine cell phones in his truck. MacAllister drove down, pretended to be an ICE agent, and questioned him. After conferring with her bosses and the prosecutor, she decided not to hold him, as they wanted to keep looking up the chain—another action that would come back to haunt them.

The ATF agents may have hoped they would get Celis-Acosta on the phone to a cartel boss and be heroes writing their own books. But their investigation just got them to moneymen buying guns from Celis-Acosta, including another mysterious figure called Jesus Miramontes-Varela.

The story of Miramontes-Varela was later uncovered by Richard Serrano at the *Los Angeles Times*, citing days of interviews that Miramontes-Varela gave to FBI agents.[32] According to the testimony, Miramontes-Varela was a cartel affiliate from northern Mexico who collected money off marijuana growers for the Juárez Cartel. After the cartel wars scorched his town, he moved stateside, distributing drugs around Texas, Colorado, and New Mexico and moving guns south.

While Fast and Furious was in action, Miramontes-Varela and his brother bought a quarter of a million dollars' worth of guns through Celis-Acosta, according to Serrano's story. He had links to the Sinaloa, Zetas, and Juárez cartels, appearing to follow the classic gunrunner playbook of selling to rivals in a war.

But before the ATF got to Miramontes-Varela, the FBI was on his case, and they arrested him and flipped him. He gave them the location of a mass grave in Palomas, Mexico, which the FBI passed to Mexican police, who discovered twenty corpses, including those of two U.S. residents.

The ATF finally arrested Celis-Acosta in February 2011. But by then Miramontes-Varela was unindictable because he was an FBI informant. In other words, Group VII's main target was working with a guy working for the FBI. One of the problems in trying to decipher Fast and Furious is there are overlapping fuckups in multiple directions.

To understand the actions of Group VII in Fast and Furious, it is useful to think about playing poker. You have a hand that looks promising, and you bet big. But as more cards are dealt, you realize the hand is not as good as it looked. Yet you are in deep, so you throw in more money to avoid a loss—only to get thoroughly busted in the end.

Fast and Furious looked promising at the beginning, and the hopes went up the chain of command to the brass, who were desperate for a big case on gunrunning to Mexico. But as time went on, the case soured. Yet it was hard to walk away, knowing how many guns had been smuggled. The agents wanted to connect the trafficking to big names. Yet the more time they took, the more guns were trafficked, and the bigger the final fall would be.

*   *   *

At the end of August 2010, agents finally questioned a straw buyer. A gun shop alerted the ATF that a suspicious man had just purchased a .50 caliber for $9,000. When an agent confronted him, he gave up the rifle and said he had been recruited by a childhood friend, Jaime Avila. The straw purchasers were paid $70 per pistol, $100 per rifle, and $500 for each .50 caliber, he said.

This questioning seemed to trigger the Celis-Acosta gang to virtually cease buying guns. So the ATF finally moved to indict. But it took months. The prosecutor handled the case alone, while occupied by several other cases, and the Fast and Furious materials detailed over three thousand pages.

On December 14, when Agent Terry was shot in Peck Canyon, the case had still not been indicted. It was not for another month, on January 19, 2011, that a federal grand jury finally indicted twenty members of the "Celis-Acosta Organization," mostly straw purchasers. It hit them with lying on the forms as well as conspiracy and money laundering (for buying the guns with drug money). Jaime Avila, who bought the guns found at the murder scene of Agent Terry, would get fifty-seven months; others, similar sentences.

One of the most damning documents the Justice Department released had the names of the straw purchasers with the amount of guns each one had bought. The biggest was Uriel Patino. He purchased 723 guns for a total of $575,000.

That is so nuts I have to say it again. A man working for Mexican drug cartels walked into gun shops in Phoenix and personally bought more than seven hundred guns for half a million dollars without being stopped. In total, according to the official numbers, the straws spent $1.47 million buying 1,961 guns.

Most are still out there.

On June 28, 2012, the U.S. lower house voted to hold Holder in contempt of Congress, the first time in history the action was taken against an attorney general. His crime was refusing to hand over all the Fast and

Furious documents after they had been subpoenaed by the Oversight Committee. To complicate it further, Obama at the eleventh hour declared executive privilege to not release the files.

The vote was 255–67 in favor, with the Republicans controlling the House and all but two voting for it. They were supported by seventeen Democrats from conservative districts, with the NRA saying that it was rating lawmakers on whether they supported the motion. More than a hundred Democrats walked out in protest, led by the Congressional Black Caucus. The drama of border violence, weapons trafficking, and shady ATF tactics had shot up to drama in the halls of power.

Holder claimed he was the victim of a witch hunt as he tried to stop voter suppression during Obama's reelection. "Today's vote may make for good political theater in the minds of some, but it is at base both a crass effort and a grave disservice to the American people," he said.

Darrell Issa, the Oversight Committee chairman, insisted they were trying to find the truth. "A year and a half later, the Terry family is still searching for answers," he said when presenting the motion.[33] He went on to lead a civil suit to get the documents, which would drag on for years.

Was it inevitable that the investigation into Fast and Furious would become so politicized? Could there have been a more methodical weighing of the evidence and its implications supported by both sides?

Maybe years ago. But long before Trump, Washington became dominated by partisan politicians pursuing political points. The investigation into Fast and Furious fell into the same cauldron that swallowed Iran-Contra, Bill Clinton's "high crimes and misdemeanors," and Trump's collusion with Russia. Holder became one in a line of administration figures held in contempt without consequences. Under Bush, it was White House chief of staff Joshua Bolten and White House counsel Harriet Miers; under Obama, it was Holder; under Trump, it was Attorney General Bill Barr. Contempt of Congress doesn't mean what it used to.

But beneath the white noise, was there a cover-up?

The accusations start with a letter going back to February 4, 2011, in which Assistant Attorney General Ronald Weich denied there was gunwalking. "That ATF 'sanctioned' or otherwise knowingly allowed the sale of assault weapons to a straw purchaser who then transported to Mexico—is false," Weich wrote. Nine months later, Weich conceded that was untrue and said he had been given bad information.

The next flashpoint was Holder's testimony to Congress in May 2011. When asked when he first heard about the operation, he replied, "I'm not sure of the exact date, but I probably heard about Fast and Furious for the first time over the last few weeks."

However, CBS reporter Sharyl Attkisson dug up a memorandum that Holder had been sent briefs about it since at least July 2010. Holder's response, in turn, was that he receives hundreds of memos and hadn't read or remembered them.

For what it's worth, the Justice Department report cleared Holder. It said he was "not aware of allegations of 'gun walking' in the investigation," and "did not personally review these reports at the time."[34]

This culminates in the refusal to hand over thousands of documents. The Justice Department said that it had given 7,500 files by June and others could compromise prosecutions. But for many, it looked like it was hiding something.

Over the years, more documents have trickled out, some from a Freedom of Information request by Attkisson, but they have not revealed much that's new. Meanwhile, the legal wrangling over Issa's lawsuit plodded on through 2020.

None of the officials involved in the gunwalking were fired, let alone prosecuted. Voth went back to Minnesota, Newell to Washington; MacAllister stayed in Phoenix. The whistleblower Dodson stayed on at ATF but said he was isolated and harassed, even blocked out of computers.

So was there a government op to traffic guns for political gains?

It could well be that there are embarrassing emails from officials. After Fast and Furious, anybody near it claimed they knew little, or were just following protocol. The documents could contradict their testimonies, show more involvement, or perhaps have them criticizing their political enemies. The tactic could be to delay for years until people don't care anymore.

But the bigger conspiracy doesn't add up.

The first point is that a huge number of guns were already being trafficked to Mexico. The Obama administration wouldn't need to allow AKs to go south to make a point. They could simply cite the trace information on the thousands of guns that already had been captured in Mexico and linked to U.S. stores.

The second thing is that, tragically, gun deaths in Mexico don't swing politics in the United States. Especially when even the shooting of six-year-old American children could not muster support for an assault rifle ban.

The third point is that we have ample evidence of agents genuinely messing up. If the whole thing were a plan to flood Mexico with guns, these leaked emails of blunder would have had to have been concocted.

The whistleblower Dodson, who is a fierce critic of the administration and praised as a hero by gun hard-liners, himself points away from the conspiracy.

"Fast and Furious is not a grand conspiracy or cover-up—or at least it didn't start that way," he writes. "Quite the contrary, it started as an all too normal occurrence in federal government, another example of the self-licking ice-cream cone. It was the result of good people, patriotic people, smart people even, trying to get credit for the big takedown."[35]

Fast and Furious came out of two big and connected problems. The first was the questionable tactics developed by federal agencies to go after organized crime. The second was the scope of organized crime, and especially its enormous gun trafficking over the southern border.

After the scandal, in March 2011, Holder ordered an end to all gunwalking. Now if agents have knowledge of any guns being sold to straw buyers, they have to step in right away. It was a solid move. But it won't stop gun trafficking. The reason that so many guns were moved in Fast and Furious so quickly is because the traffic over the southern border is so massive. But the ATF did not create this problem. It existed anyway.

This gets into the deceptive arguments by the gun lobby. It was angry that ATF agents did not seize guns more quickly. But it is against empowering agents to seize more guns, or even know when there are multiple sales of rifles. It was furious about the ATF having knowledge about guns that went to Mexico and were used to kill. But it denies that generally there is a problem of guns going to Mexico and being used to kill.

In other words, it doesn't mind if there is trafficking to Mexico. As long as the ATF doesn't know about it.

And this is one of the tragic outcomes of Fast and Furious. Since it happened, the ATF has been terrified of going near the cases of gunrunning over the border. But weapons keep flowing over in ridiculous numbers. And these guns are being used in brutal violence that is destabilizing the region, not only in Mexico but throughout Central America and into Colombia, contributing to a crisis building up on the U.S. border at the end of the decade.

9

Refugees

i want to go home,
but home is the mouth of a shark
home is the barrel of the gun

—Warsan Shire, "Home"

———

I met Fresa in February 2015.

I was reporting for my book *Gangster Warlords* and went down to Honduras to talk to gang members. The journalist Orlin Castro worked with me on getting the interviews, as he has the connections from growing up in the rugged barrios of San Pedro Sula, for several years the most homicidal city on the planet. Fresa, his friend, was driving us and was carrying a handgun to provide security, as Orlin had suffered threats.

We spent a week on the humid roads of Honduras, amid the gaping leaves of banana trees, going into prisons and towns to talk to gangsters. I got on easily with Fresa, who was friendly and charismatic, just turning thirty. When we finished the interviews, Fresa and I went to a club in San Pedro, with blaring reggaeton and buckets of beers. He's a muscular, good-looking guy, and a girl approached to give him her phone number when they hadn't even chatted. That made him laugh, and he had this funny smile that enveloped his whole face.

As we talked and drank, Fresa mentioned that he had been in a *banda*. I didn't know too much about these bandas at the time, but I would learn more over the following years. They are groups of criminals in the Honduran neighborhoods that club together for activities like drug selling, armed robberies, and hits for money.

A lot has been written about gangs in Central America, especially the MS-13. But in Honduras, these bandas are also a potent force, with better connections to cartels. They portray themselves as self-defense squads protecting neighborhoods from the MS-13, but the bandas themselves drive a lot of violence.

I didn't ask Fresa more about his past that night. I had been inter-viewing criminals all week, and I was enjoying drinking beer and talking crap. I had no idea how deep he was in it, how much blood he had on his hands.

Up until now, I have focused on the iron river flowing around the United States and over the southern border into Mexico. Now the river takes us farther afield into Central America and Colombia. Here, the guns reach conflicts that have unleashed thousands of refugees, many of whom arrive at the Rio Grande. But a key city to understanding this traffic is in the Sunshine State of Florida.

———

The ATF center in Martinsburg has a map on the wall titled "International Firearms Trafficking," with lines to all the countries where guns have been traced. The lines cluster over the Caribbean, shooting to Central America and South America. But they also zoom over to Africa, Europe, Asia, and Australia. In fact, they cover most the world.

Every year, guns are traced to between 75 and 90 different countries, says program coordinator Neil Troppman. And over five years, this makes a total of 136 countries where guns have been recovered that were made or sold in the United States. (Considering there are 195 countries in the world, this is an impressive number!)

In some cases, guns are legally exported to security forces, from where they are pilfered and end up in the hands of gangsters and guerrillas. A notorious case is Iraq, where the Pentagon supplied M16s, and some found their way to the Islamic State.

But an incredible number of guns are smuggled from the U.S. civilian market, sometimes over great distances. Police on the southern Philippine island of Mindanao cracked open a box at a cargo terminal to find a Glock, a Ruger, and an STI that had been stolen stateside.[1] The port was 7,384 miles from the western coast of the United States.

Former ATF agent Steve Barborini explains how the guns reach so many countries. Barborini specialized in gunrunning for decades, and now teaches firearms trafficking courses at the ATF academy. His probes took him to nutty spots. He foiled a plot to sell stinger rockets to the IRA, busted weapons destined for Iraq, and went undercover in Germany to buy a grenade launcher.

Barborini is one of the ATF agents who is himself a gun enthusiast and keeps his own collection of about fifty weapons. This helped him go undercover among the "gun nuts" (his words), and when he infiltrated a militia selling machine guns, some of these "whack-jobs" (his words again) threatened to kill him.

He has lived most his life in Florida, an ideal place for his focus, as it sits on the vast gun-smuggling corridor of the Caribbean Sea. The warm water beloved for cruises links the United States to over three hundred ports in dozens of countries, including Jamaica, Haiti, Honduras, Colombia, and Venezuela. Millions of tons of cargo float over the waves every day. The sea that was once the favorite haunt of pirates is now replete with gunmetal.

This region counts for some of the most common foreign traces after Mexico. In 2018, the ATF successfully traced over 2,800 crime guns to the United States from five of the Caribbean and five of the Central American nations.

Barborini explains the modus operandi for getting them there. Smugglers acquire weapons through the tried and tested ways: straw purchasing, the private-sale loophole, theft. They send the weapons through one of many shipping companies in Florida that offer consumer freight. With big communities from all over Latin America, it's easy to hide guns among the goods that people send home: cameras, fridges, TVs, furniture.

"You go to the shipper, and you drop off a box, and you say what's in there, 'household goods.' They don't care," he says. "You sign a form saying there are no explosives or guns in there, a customs declaration. And then they ship 'em. And then on the other side, they pick up the box. And maybe, one or two pots or pans in there . . . It's pretty simple because nobody checks. There's no X-rays."

Another way to smuggle guns is to put them in cars, which are shipped over the sea stuffed with consumer goods.

"You look at these vehicles and you can't see inside," Barborini says. "It's filled to the roof with blankets, towels, pots and pans, clothing. But in there are five or six handguns you don't know about."

One man who knows firsthand about this gunrunning is Jermaine Cohen, alias Cowboy, a former member of the notorious Jamaican Shower Posse. Cohen testified in a New York trial against his old boss Christopher "Dudus" Coke, but then later faced deportation proceedings and was in jail in New Jersey, where I talked to him.

"Sending a firearm to Jamaica is one of the easiest things. It's like sending rice or sending corned beef," Jermaine told me. "You send it in microwave. It's just how you design to send it . . . It don't get random checked. The screening cannot pick it up."

To help with the smuggling, Jermaine describes how Shower Posse affiliates work in the Jamaican docks. "They know everything coming in," he said. "They take it off in the nighttime."

Ships leaving Florida also reach the southern cone of the Americas. One case was broken open when customs inspectors in Doral checked in boxes of sporting goods to find a hundred AR-15 receivers. In the subsequent Operation Patagonia Express, they followed them to Argentina and worked with local police to seize 2,500 guns. Argentine police found houses with bunkers used as workshops to assemble the AR-15s.[2] Police blamed the traffic on the Brazilian PCC, a powerful mob in South America.

So why doesn't the ATF do more to stop this Florida traffic? The agents complain about the same factors that overwhelm Arizona. The ATF bureaus in Florida are understaffed and have to deal with over 7,000 FFLs in the state as well as local gun crime.

They look for clumsy straw buyers, but it doesn't get them far. Even when the straw buyers confess, Barborini says, it's hard to get overworked federal prosecutors to take a case that will likely end in probation. "The sentencing guidelines are very low," he says. "They're not going to get any jail time. What's the deterrent factor?"

So ATF agents try to make the straw buyers rat on their bosses so that they can build a bigger case. Which leads back to the espionage game to bust trafficking rings. One such Florida ring followed in so-called Operation Castaway featured an especially prolific illegal gun seller.

Hugh Crumpler III was an upstanding citizen in Palm Beach, Florida, a Vietnam vet, a champion bass fisherman, and a guide taking tourists through the Stick Marsh. He also liked to collect guns and go to shows to buy and sell them.

When he hit his sixties, his hobby drifted into dodgy waters. With customers at the shows hungry for guns using the private-sale loophole, he saw the opportunity to make money. He would go to shops to buy new guns and resell them for a markup, even though he didn't have a license. It was just like the private sellers I saw in Dallas do.

Some of the customers would ask for specific weapons, which he would then buy, effectively being a straw purchaser for them. He purchased 529 guns in sixty-two multiple-sales transactions in less than a year. In total, he would sell about one thousand firearms during the spree, according to his confession.

Some of the guns ended up in Honduras, Colombia, and Puerto Rico, where they were definitively traced to five shootings. In Colombia, a gun was used in a murder by a *sicario* for the Medellín cartel. The so-called time to crime (length of time between the sale and when the gun was used in a crime) in the Medellín murder was sixty-six days. In Puerto Rico it was just nine days.

It's startling how Crumpler thought he could get away with it. And how he indeed could get away with buying a thousand guns and selling them before he was caught. The story is revealed in court documents and an interview that Crumpler gave from prison to Univision.

Crumpler sold his arsenal in 2009 and 2010 for hundreds of thousands of dollars. An ATF agent captured the way Crumpler did business by posing as a buyer and making a hidden recording.

The agent asked if a Glock that Crumpler had was "cash-and-carry."

"Yes," Crumpler replied. "All my business is cash-and-carry."

The agent asked if he would have to fill out a 4473.

"No, Obama won't know that you have it," Crumpler replied.

The agent said he wouldn't pass the background check.

"Don't tell me that, don't tell me that," Crumpler responded, and sold him the gun.

Later, the agent and an informant went to Crumpler's house. The informant said he was a felon and wanted to buy a gun.

"Don't shoot anybody with it," Crumpler joked. "I appreciate you being honest with me . . . Most people are afraid that Obama is going to come take their guns away."

*   *   *

During his selling spree, Crumpler got mixed up with a group of Hondurans linked to cartels and corrupt politicians. In August 2009, the Honduran military carried out a coup against President Manuel Zelaya, marching him in his pajamas onto a plane to Costa Rica. Crumpler said he believed the Hondurans were using the weapons to defend the new right-wing government and he thought the U.S. government would be okay with that.

"These people were wanting more guns, and they were indicating to me that it was to support the new government," he told Univision. "Which I believed. And, I wanted to believe. And at the same time, I'm asking myself, 'I've bought a lot of guns. I've not hidden the fact that I've bought a lot of guns. And I've sold a lot of guns. And I've not hidden the fact that I've sold a lot of guns. Why hasn't the ATF contacted me?' That's what I asked myself. And the only thing I could come up [with] was they wanted me to sell these guns to these people. Well, I thought they wanted it because the guns were going to support an American type of government."[3]

Eventually, ATF agents did contact Crumpler, told him the guns were going to gangsters, and got him to cooperate. He passed the ATF information until a shipment of the weapons heading to Honduras was busted. Police nabbed several of the traffickers although, Crumpler says, some got away.

After the arrests, the ATF seized crates of Crumpler's guns and wads of his money. Crumpler made an agreement and pleaded guilty to dealing in firearms without a license, and got thirty months. This again indicates the shorter sentencing on gun crimes compared with drug crimes. He sold a thousand guns, some of which were used in murders, although he did cooperate.

While Crumpler was in prison, news of Fast and Furious broke, and in a court filing he claimed to be the victim of a similar sting.

"I was the pawn of the government in an unconstitutional operation," Crumpler said. "I was allowed to perform illegal activities after I should have been contacted by the ATF . . . This was done so that the Obama Administration could enact stricter gun laws based on crimes and evidence in which they participated and created."[4]

A spokesman for Florida's U.S. Attorney's Office denied the charge, saying they hadn't let any guns walk. Crumpler was released from prison and died in 2017, at age seventy.

There are differences between Castaway and Fast and Furious. The gun dealers in Fast and Furious did not commit crimes but contacted the ATF. Crumpler broke the law and informed as part of a deal. To label any investigation into gun trafficking as a corrupt government op is to muddy the waters.

Still, there are legitimate questions about how long the ATF agents took to act. And it's notable that Crumpler said that he thought the U.S. government was sanctioning his support of the right-wing coup. Those were not mad ravings. Because the United States does indeed have a history of shipping guns to authoritarian right-wing forces. Especially when they are at war.

In 2009, I covered the Honduras coup from the streets of Tegucigalpa. It was a surreal scene when Zelaya tried to fly back to the capital on a Venezuelan jet, but the army blocked the airfield, and he did circles and left. The soldiers fired at protesters and literally blew the brains out of an eighteen-year-old kid; I saw his corpse and twenty yards down the road saw the tissue from his brain. As the tests on the AR-15 showed, that is what rifle blasts do to human heads.

The coup was tragic, smashing a period of democratic hope. But worse was to come. Violence soared, bodies littered the streets, gangs multiplied, and government corruption was endemic. In 2012, I returned to cover a prison fire that killed 360 inmates, many roasted in their cells while guards shot to stop them from escaping. I was shocked how the country had deteriorated, how people were so on edge. That year, Honduras was classified as the most murderous country on earth, with 86 murders per 100,000, seventeen times the rate in the United States.

As it is in Mexico, it's impossible to know the exact breakdown of where the guns in Honduras come from. But between 2014 and 2017, almost half, or 45 percent, of the firearms that Honduras submitted to the ATF for tracing were confirmed to be made or sold in the United States. Also as in Mexico, the other 55 percent of firearms were not definitively traced, so more could have been sold in U.S. shops. And as in Mexico, more guns were captured and never made it into the eTrace system.

We can argue about percentages again. But we can't argue with the fact that a significant number of firearms are trafficked from the United States to gangs in Honduras, who carry out brutal crimes.

While rifles rule in Mexico, the most common firearms in Honduras are handguns. Fresa had a Glock. Back in Honduras in 2017, I met up with him again, and he posed with it for photos as he told me his hellish story.

I was in San Pedro with Orlin and the photographer Patrick Tombola documenting the relentless violence. The murder rate had officially gone down since its peak, although it was still sky high, and residents of poor neighborhoods described a wave of disappearances.

We spent a lot of time in a slum called La Planeta, controlled by the Barrio 18 gang. A woman Orlin knew did home cooking, including a mouthwatering chicken soup, and we would eat at her house for a few lempiras. Orlin knew a girl in the barrio who had survived a shooting, so one afternoon as the sun was going down, we went to meet her on a scrubby field at the end of the street.

Katery Ramos is fourteen, slim and pretty, sitting in a wheelchair being pushed by her mom. She was shot when she was twelve years old, hit by a stray bullet while she was playing in the street. She says she has no idea who fired. But then she wouldn't snitch for the good of herself and her family.

I hear a version of the story from others. This is gang turf, and members of a rival gang came in and shot at her brother. But a bullet missed and hit his twelve-year-old sister.

This is another reason guns are worse than knives. Knives don't normally injure bystanders.

When I question Katery, she is shy and gives short answers. I ask her about the moment the bullet hit. "I was standing up for a moment, and afterwards I fell down," she says.

I ask her if it hurt. "No, no," she says.

The bullet went in just above her waist and cut through her spine. She was taken to the public hospital, where she found she had lost the use of legs. They said she wouldn't walk again and sent her away in a flimsy wheelchair, and she has been living in it the past two years.

I am flabbergasted that a pistol bullet can paralyze someone like this. I have met various people who survived shootings without terrible injuries. How come this poor girl is confined to a wheelchair? If growing up in one of the most violent neighborhoods in the world is already hard, imagine doing it semi-paralyzed.

I think that a rundown public hospital can't have given her the best attention, that there has to be a better treatment. I blurt out that I will look further into it. "There must be a way to cure this," I say. "I am a journalist, but if you let me investigate a little, maybe I could find a foundation that could offer support."

The faces of Katery and her mom light up. But I am stupid to offer hope. I find out later that when a bullet cuts through the spinal cord, it can often leave people paralyzed from the waist down. If the injury is complete, and the spinal cord has been totally severed, there is no way to repair it. Thousands of people around the world, including many Americans, live with paralysis because one cursed bullet cut through their spines.

I ask Katery how school is, but she says she doesn't go because there is no special track for wheelchairs. I ask if she has friends, and she says there is one girl and they sit around and listen to music. I ask her what she does all day. "I just lay down," she says.

When she tells me this, I am holding back tears and can hardly speak. We go back to the house, and I am struck by the image of this beautiful girl lying on a mattress paralyzed as the world goes by, and I cry into the chicken soup.

* * *

Bullet wounds can be real fuckers.

Iain Overton, of the charity Action on Armed Violence, writes about the history of treating them in his book *Gun Baby Gun*.

"Gunpowder's arrival onto the battlefield made the treatment of trauma wounds far more complex," he writes. "No longer the splice of a sword or the pierce of an arrow. Rather, embedded bullets, gunpowder burns and gaping holes in flesh changed forever the nature of wounds."[5]

He describes the evolution. In the sixteenth century, a French surgeon used egg yolk and rose oil on bullet injuries. In the American War of Independence, a surgeon advised putting onion into the wounds. The Crimean War saw Florence Nightingale radicalize sanitation, which greatly reduced deaths.

X-rays revolutionized treatment, along with the effective use of amputations. In Vietnam, the U.S. Army learned to treat gunshot victims quickly in mobile units. In Iraq and Afghanistan, the casualty rate from bullets was reduced even further. But as Overton concludes, with many gunshot victims, "dragged back from the edges of death by the medic's steady hand," there are now more walking wounded.[6]

The battlefield techniques in Iraq filter down to the harried medics in Latin America. I have driven around with ambulances in several of the most violent cities. In Juárez, they are professional paramedics paid by the council. But over in Culiacán, they are student volunteers. All have vast experience because they have treated so many wounds. Caps in the chest, in the leg, the arm, the lungs, the buttocks, the head. A medic from Juárez told me about when he went to a conference in the United States on bullet wounds. They went around the room, and medics from various U.S. cities described the handful of gunshot wounds they had treated. He blushed when he said he was treating them every night.

Bullets can be merciful. A doctor in Mexico City described an obese man who was shot twelve times as he drove a truck but survived. The X-ray showed all twelve bullets floating in his fat. But bullets, especially from high-powered rifles, can also pummel through flesh, tearing up organs and shattering spinal cords.

Fresa got shot in 2016. He was hospitalized for many weeks, his cohorts spending a million lempiras, or about forty thousand dollars, to bring him back to life. Yet it is not enough payback for what he has done to others.

When Orlin suggests we speak to Fresa about murders, I'm surprised. When we'd hung out in the club, he'd told me he'd been in a banda, but I didn't know he'd done hits. Orlin says he has risen in the crime world.

We drive to Fresa's home, in a middle-class neighborhood rather than the sprawling slums. It's good to see him, and we hug and chat. He reveals that he was shot and pulls up his T-shirt to show his stomach. Four bullets ripped through it, and he has a gaping wound down the entire front of his torso with the thick marks of stitches on either side and bulbous holes and lumps.

He sticks on a ski mask, and we sit him down on the bed and roll the camera. He tells his story from the beginning. It reveals hard truths about the gun murder epidemic in Latin America.

Fresa was abandoned as a baby of eight months, his mother going to the United States. He grew up in an orphanage in San Pedro until he was five, and a woman looked after him until he was twelve, and then he was on his own, living on the street. "I really had a childhood of suffering," Fresa says.

Fresa references this abandonment as a source of the dark things he does. It's like the thug from the Barrio Azteca said: you look for kids who are neglected and have hate inside.

When he was thirteen, another street kid said he knew a house where there was a man with money they could rob. A bunch of street kids took knives and stormed it. They found a woman with four abandoned children she looked after, ten to twelve years old. The kid who brought them there said they had to kill them. It wasn't really an assault. It was an act of revenge. The kid had lived there too, and been bullied, and he wanted payback.

"In the beginning, I wasn't in favor of killing them, because they were children," Fresa says. "But something got inside me, and I said, 'Let's do it,' and that night we killed five people."

They didn't massacre them all in one go. Instead, they isolated them and took care of them one at a time.

"We had a strategy, even at that young age. We had one in a room, and we said, 'If you move, something bad will happen to your family,' and they didn't move. And we killed them one by one," Fresa says. "We suffocated them with an iron, cut off heads."

I feel cramps in my stomach. While I've covered violence for two decades, this is psychologically one of the most violent acts I have heard. Homeless children butchering a woman and children. While guns are used to kill more people, there is something more terrifying about slaughter with a blade. But perhaps the most horrifying thing is the thought of thirteen-year-olds doing this. It's the revelation of the monster inside us.

After the slaughter, Fresa had nightmares. "There is a reaction in the mind. Fear. But not fear of being hurt, which I have never had, but the thought of what you have done and what you have imagined and what was driving you on that night. It filled me, and gave me two days of night-mares, so I couldn't sleep. And from there I got into the question of sicariato."

Fresa quickly graduated to guns. He and his crew of killer kids used them to hold up buses and were happy they no longer suffered the aches of hunger.

"When you kill for the first time, you get a different attitude. You see the street like a game . . . My mind was evolving in this way, this bad and direct way. I didn't regret it, not anymore, because I had money in my pocket, because I felt the street was the only thing that would look after me."

The first time Fresa did a hit, he got paid three hundred dollars. That is relatively high. I talked to an MS-13 member who did his first hit for less than fifty. Fresa had caught the eye of a local gangster who hired him for the job, to take out a man who owed money. Fresa followed his target onto a bus and blasted the victim in the head at point-blank range.

"The brains blew out, and I was covered in blood, and I ran for two hours. The police were looking for me, but I went into markets and places where I could hide."

Fresa joined the banda, an organization of about a hundred men, linked to a wider network of bandas across Honduras. As he got older, he provided security for drug traffickers, including locals working with the Sinaloa Cartel. The Sinaloans use Honduras as a base to receive cocaine from Colombians and take it north to Mexico. At one point, Fresa met a lieutenant of El Chapo's, who was later shot by police in Sinaloa.

Fresa makes most of his money with hits. His crew became experienced, armed and organized, and could charge more money for taking lives. He will do some hits for $2,000, he tells me, if it is an easy target he can blast on a quiet street. But he will take bounties of up to half a million lempiras, or $20,000. The big money is for high-profile targets, drug traffickers with armed bodyguards, powerful businessmen, politicians. Up to ten men attack, using AK-47s and AR-15s.

They have taken courses on long-distance shooting to be more effective. When they attack in force, one or two people are assigned to carry out the kill, the rest to protect them. They will often attack in cars, using vehicles to block in the victims, like the Zetas did to Agent Zapata.

"If I am the leader, I will get out, and I have to finish the job, and the rest are just there for security," he says. "At that moment the police don't matter or anything. We have to be ready to die in those moments."

Drug traffickers are often the ones paying for hits. But it can also be businessmen or politicians. In fact, drug traffickers and politicians are often one and the same. In October 2019, a court in New York convicted the brother of the Honduran president, Juan Antonio Hernández, of cocaine trafficking.

I ask how many people Fresa has killed personally. He admits slowly that it is forty-five.

In most countries, he would be one of the worst mass murderers. But such a kill count is tragically common in the hot spots of Latin America. I have interviewed others who have killed more—although I have not been out drinking in a nightclub with them.

Fresa shot the majority of his victims. But he decapitated nine of them. In these cases, the banda abducts its prey and takes them to a safe house to carry out the mutilation. Decapitation sends a more cutting message and ends the victim's life in more pain.

"It's often because the target has betrayed someone. It's in the contract. The contract always says what you have to do. The client might want a video so they can send it to the organization. They are sending a message that says, 'Look, you are not going to betray me. Look, I have strong people. Look, they will cut off heads because a bullet isn't enough.' A bullet hits and the person dies, while cutting off a head makes the person suffer. They have to suffer."

I ask Fresa how the victims react when they know they are going to lose their head.

"The first thing they do is shout. But we always put tape on their mouths. Even with the tape, you still hear the shouts the first time, like when you are hitting someone with a machete," Fresa says. "Until the last moment, the person does not die, because his nerve is still alive. So the person still has the nerve and with the head being cut off, he still says, 'Don't kill me.'"

I don't take writing these words lightly. Real people are suffering this brutality. But this is what such a level of violence means. It's pain, misery, broken bodies, and tortured souls.

The money Fresa makes from this butchery provides a middle-class life for his family, one far better than how he'd grown up on the streets. But he fears for the future of his children.

I ask him about religion. Priests in Latin America agonize about how people commit such acts, how it shows a failure in their teachings. There is also a growing evangelical Christian movement in Honduras battling for souls. Fresa says that he has been to both churches but struggles to give his heart to God.

"I don't know if there is forgiveness," he says, "for the things I have done and all I have been through."

———

While nobody doubts that the violence in Honduras is devastating, there is debate as to whether it is really an armed conflict, like a war, or just a horrendous crime problem. A thousand miles to the south, however, almost all agree there has been an armed conflict in Colombia, involving guerrilla groups and paramilitaries. It's been referred to as "the world's longest war."

The start date most look to is 1964, the year the Revolutionary Armed Forces of Colombia (FARC) were formed. Paramilitaries rose to fight them, and the drug traffickers worked with both sides and formed their own private armies. The United States designated the FARC as terrorists in 1997 and an umbrella of paramilitaries known as the United Self-Defense Forces of Colombia (AUC) as terrorists in 2001. A government estimate put the conflict's death toll at 218,000 people over a half a century.[7] A peace deal signed in 2016 aimed to end the conflict, but various squads of dissident guerrillas, paramilitaries, and traffickers keep on killing.

The guns arrived by various routes during various eras. When the Central American wars ended by the early nineties, there was a sucking motion, pulling many guns south into Colombia. The Brazilian Red Commando gang was caught buying guns from corrupt soldiers around South America and exchanging them with the FARC for cocaine. And in a case straight from a John le Carré novel, the spy chief of Peru, Vladimiro Montesinos, was found diverting surplus Kalashnikovs from Jordan to the FARC.[8]

However, a significant stream of guns has also been from the U.S. black market to this war and its designated terrorists. There are two main routes.

The first is through Miami, as the guns Crumpler sold showed. In another case, in 2012, a Colombian network in Florida run by a former paramilitary commander was hiding guns in car batteries.

The other route is through Mexico. In the Chapo trial, the prosecution played a recording of Guzmán negotiating the price of cocaine directly with the FARC. This may be where the FARC got some of the .50-caliber rifles they have been found with. And Mexican cartels have been flying planes with guns to Colombia since the 1980s, as the pilot Blengio described.

Another piece of evidence is Fast and Furious. The weapons linked to the op had originally been bought in Arizona and trafficked into Mexico, mostly to the Sinaloa Cartel. But in 2012, Colombian police discovered a stash belonging to the Medellín cartel that was traced to the botched operation. It included two rifles and fourteen Belgium FN pistols, a captain of the Colombian national police said.[9]

In the 2000s, Colombia cracked down on planes flying from Mexico. However, the Mexicans and Colombians adapted to do their deals in Honduras and Panama, smuggling the guns south over the lawless rim known as the Darién Gap.

The Darién Gap dividing Colombia and Panama is one of the rare places on the planet without roads. This makes the sixty miles of rain forest some of the most unspoiled terrain on earth.

Standing on a high path and looking over, I think this is how the world would have been thousands of years ago. Abundant nature. Thick woodlands. Animals galore.

And highly hazardous. I see a funny little frog and am about to pick it up when Oliver Schmieg, a photographer friend with me, warns that Darién is home to rare poisonous frogs. I turn to some giant ants, but he points out that the ants here can give you a poisonous bite like a scorpion's. He signals to some leaves that are also poisonous enough to leave blisters. In fact, the whole place is perilous.

This savage nature and stories of drug traffickers make it an attractive spot for macho adventurers. Crossing the Darién is on the bucket list for those wanting to go to the toughest places.

To be honest, though, the risk is not that great anymore. The presence of entire armed columns of paramilitaries marching though Darién is a thing of the past, the kidnapping threat waned. On the edge of the gap, there is a funky beach town you can reach by boat, and you can find a guide to take you through the jungle. A steady stream of African migrants head through it on their mammoth journey to the United States.

As Darién is a corridor for undocumented migrants, it is also favored by smugglers. And just as on the U.S. border, cocaine goes north through Darién while guns go south.

The Caribbean feeds into the Gulf of Darién, which in turn feeds into a smaller sea called the Gulf of Urabá. Across Urabá from the Gap sits a wild smuggling town called Turbo.

The area is controlled by a crime group called the Gulf Clan. While most people may have never heard of it, or may confuse it with Mexico's Gulf Cartel, the Clan has become the biggest mob in Colombia. In 2018, the U.S. Attorney General's Office created task forces against the five most threatening transnational criminal organizations, and the Clan was on the list.

The Clan is a descendent of the paramilitaries that rose to fight the FARC but themselves became mass murderers and cocaine traffickers. With two decades working in Colombia, Oliver has built sources among the Clan, and we meet them over several days. Among them, we talk to Cesar, a thirty-two-year-old who has smuggled in guns through Darién.

Cesar is wanted on an arrest warrant for weapons charges and murder, and this makes him nervous and keeping an eye out for cameras. We finally find an empty café where we can lurk in the back, and over coffee and Colombian sweet bread, he tells his story. He describes his work bringing in guns but claims he didn't do the murder and says he wants out.

*   *   *

Like many in the region, Cesar is Afro-Colombian, his father scraping by with cutting wood and fishing. Cesar finished only elementary school in Turbo before he was guarding motorcycles and washing cars for tips. By fifteen, he was also running errands for the traffickers. It was never about the thrill but always the money, he says. He believes in God, "*demasiado*," a great deal, and respects his mother, but he was in need, and the gangsters were the only ones in his barrio who had cash. He refers to the Clan simply as *la Empresa*, or the Company.

While many friends became gunmen, Cesar prefers boats, and he took to the waves to move the Company's merchandise. He began as the number two on a boat, but moved up within a year to be captain. They used fishing boats that the men crafted in Turbo, vessels made of fiberglass with motors that they call *panguitas*.

Cesar and his companion would pack the boat with fishing gear and catch some on the way, a mix of fish and shrimps. They sailed over the south of the Gulf of Urabá into a river called the Río Sucio, which threads through the wild territory below the Darién Gap. Arriving at a rendezvous point, they coordinated with radios to meet the cohorts, who came from Panama.

Cesar would collect over a hundred guns in a shipment, a mix including Kalashnikovs, AR-15s, and Berettas. The weapons were new and semiautomatic, signaling they were from the retail rather than the military market. Cesar and his companion worked rapidly, packing the guns underneath the tackle and fish. They would take the boat back under the cover of darkness to a point where the guns were loaded into a truck.

Other cohorts watched out for soldiers. If all was clear, they radioed, "The water is sweet." If they saw soldiers, they said, "The water is salty."

Cesar never got arrested on his missions. One time, police stopped the boat, but he told them that they just had fish, and the officer took a glance and let him go. Another time, they were loading the guns when a handful of soldiers stumbled upon them. The traffickers exchanged fire with the soldiers from a distance, but the troops were too few and retreated. The smugglers hid the guns and disappeared into the jungle.

The jobs were every few months, when guns had come through in Central America and there was demand for them in the Clan. Cesar got paid three million Colombian pesos for a trip, or about nine hundred dollars. Given the poverty he'd grown up in, it seemed a small fortune. After a job, he would go with his companion to a brothel. "You are exhausted and you want to relax, have a good time, with the *putas*, with your companions," he says.

In between trips, he worked construction, making a hundred dollars a week. With the boosts from trafficking, he bought a shack in his barrio, gave money to his mother, and supported a girlfriend and two children.

Smuggled guns are the main source of weapons for the Clan, he says. While soldiers armed the paramilitaries in the nineties, he says that is no longer the case. Colombian security forces are overly violent but not quite as money-hungry as those in Mexico.

Cesar says that the guns are exclusively for Clan members and they don't sell them elsewhere. The weapons aren't a business, but a tool to help its main business of cocaine. The Clan bans other people from selling guns in Turbo, he says. It operates its own form of gun control, and only its hit men can be armed, so they have a monopoly on criminal force.

"It's very difficult to get a gun if you are not part of the Company," he says. "Maybe you'll get a knife."

The Clan claims to use its guns to keep the barrios safe, and if someone steals or commits rape, they may execute them. On one occasion, an eighteen-year-old robbed a shop close to Cesar's house. The gunmen found him two days later, shot him dead, and left his corpse on the street as a warning. "They keep the pueblo clean," Cesar says. The Clan doesn't carry out this service for free, however, but charges for "protection." All the businesses in Turbo have to pay, he says, especially bars, restaurants, and grocery stores.

Cesar does not consider himself as a Clan member but rather as a contractor. This is true of many criminals on the edges of crime families.

But this did not stop him from being indicted in a sweep on the mob. A woman in his barrio went to the police as an informant, or *sapo*, and fingered various men.

When the arrest warrant was issued, the police turned up at Cesar's house, but only his girlfriend was there. Cesar fled to the mountains and then to Medellín. When we meet him, he has just returned, trying to figure out his next move. He says he'd like to get out of the Clan, but his boss said that is problematic because he knows too much. And he could need its help if he goes to prison or faces the case in court.

Cesar says that the informant did it for the money, as Colombian police give *sapos* significant rewards. However, the police failed to protect her. The Clan found out and she turned up dead. At least that was the story; cartels often kill the wrong people.

Both the paramilitaries and the FARC have carried out many brutal massacres, driving people from their homes. The United Nations estimates the war in Colombia has displaced more than seven million people, the most in the hemisphere.[10] Many ran to makeshift camps and slums on the edge of cities, while others fled the country to join refugee communities around the globe.

Millions have also run from the poverty and violence in neighboring Venezuela. But the refugee crisis that caused the most noise in the United States came from back in Central America.

———

Signs of a rising tide of refugees from across Central America became apparent throughout 2018. That summer I went to the southern Mexican border to find out what was happening.

Undocumented migrants cross into Mexico from Guatemala at many points but especially near the town of Tapachula, where they float over a river on rafts, and near Tenosique, where they walk along a dirt path in the hills. Both crossing points and shelters were packed.

There is debate over the difference between migrants and refugees. The word "migrant" usually refers to those who move country for economic reasons, which can be to escape desperate poverty. A refugee is someone who flees home because their life or freedom is in danger. But in reality, the distinction is blurred, with some fleeing both hunger and bullets.

In the shelters, I met some who said they were going for economic reasons. A drought linked to rising temperatures was ravaging farmers in Central America and adding to woes. But many Salvadorans, Guatemalans, and especially Hondurans told me stories I had been hearing increasingly for years. Gang members had threatened them, murdered their families, shot them, burned down their houses, raped them. Police offered no protection and sometimes worked with the gangs.

In Tenosique, I met Francis Gusmán, a thirty-two-year-old from Yoro, Honduras, sitting in a wheelchair outside a shelter. Despite her injury, she was confident and outspoken, traveling with her husband, twelve-year-old son, orphaned thirteen-year-old niece, and a family friend. Francis had been shot in 2016 by a stray round during a gang fight and lost the use of her legs. But unlike Katery, Francis had some feeling in her lower body and could wriggle her toes. Apparently, the spinal cord was only partially severed. The gangsters went on to murder her sister for witnessing a shooting, causing Francis to flee.

It's tough being crippled on the migrant trail. When Francis crossed into Mexico, her husband and friend took turns carrying her as they trekked along a thirty-six-mile road.

Francis had applied for asylum in Mexico. "I pray to God we will be approved," she said. "Because there is no way we can turn back." Many other Hondurans were heading right through Mexico in the hope of finding refuge in the United States.

Getting into this refugee stream may seem off topic. But it is important to see the broader effects of gun violence: the way it destabilizes countries, which in turn creates refugees, which in turn stirs up politics in the United States and Europe. It's the butterfly effect in full motion. Refugee surges in recent years have come from Syria, Iraq, Somalia, and Libya, caused by guns and bombs. But the migrant caravans of Central Americans were the first to bring refugee camps to the U.S. border.

After World War II, the men and women trying to build a new world were concerned about the plight of refugees. The problem was in plain view with millions of displaced people in camps across Europe. And the unveiling of the Holocaust revealed how many Jews died who had tried to flee but been refused entry by country after country.

In 1951, delegates to the young United Nations signed the Refugee Convention promoting the principle that those who flee their country because of serious threats to their life or freedom should not be forced to return. The following year, the United States passed the Immigration and Nationality Act, incorporating the idea into U.S. law.

As gangster violence ravaged Latin America, increasing numbers applied for asylum. They didn't do this only in the United States. The applications in Mexico skyrocketed, from 2,000 in 2014 to 48,000 in the first eight months of 2019.[11] But the largest number would try for U.S. soil, with asylum applications surging from 21,000 in 2010 to almost 140,000 in 2017. Latin America counted for five of their six top countries of origin.[12]

U.S. courts usually rejected Mexican and Central American applicants. The judges ruled that people were fleeing crime and were not targeted because of their ethnicity or an authoritarian government. The judges were also cautious about opening the floodgates, a lawyer told me. Between 2012 and 2017, courts denied 88 percent of asylum applications from Mexicans, 79 percent of those from El Salvador, and 78 percent of those from Honduras. In contrast, only 20 percent of applications from China were rejected.[13]

But some refugees presented damning evidence of cartels linked to governments going after them. And despite the rejections, more refugees kept coming.

In April 2018, Trump announced his zero-tolerance policy at the border, largely in response to the rising number of refugees, who often came as families. The harshest measure was to step up the enforcement of the laws to separate the families, taking children away from their parents. The sight of young kids being wrenched from their mothers provoked some of the most visceral reactions to the Trump administration, and polls showed it was rejected by two-thirds of Americans.[14] By the time Trump signed the executive order to end family separation in June 2018, more than two thousand children had been taken from their parents. A year on, some were still not reunited.

The first "migrant caravans" emerged in Mexico in 2011. They were in response to migrants suffering abuse at the hands of cartels, including mass kidnappings for ransom. Travelers banded together for security, encouraged by a growing network of activists.

The first sign of a "mega caravan" was a flyer shared in Honduras on social media in October 2018. It had a picture of a man in a hat with a backpack, his arms raised making a symbol like a cross. "We don't go because we want to. The violence and poverty expels us," it said. It told people to meet at the San Pedro bus station a week later and had an arrow saying "Mexico."

Orlin hit the bus station, reporting for a local TV station. People told him their stories of violence and hunger, and the station broadcast it live in blanket coverage. Many watched it and decided within hours to join in, showing the level of desperation. By the time the caravan set off at five-thirty A.M. on the morning of October 13, there were about 1,200 people. As they marched through Honduras and Guatemala toward Mexico, the numbers swelled to over 7,000.

The news dropped with a bang in the run-up to the U.S. midterm elections, and Trump seized it, ordering active military troops to the border. He painted it as an invading army marching on the gates.

When the caravan was massing on the Guatemala-Mexico border, I rushed down. The refugees and migrants gathered in a rustic Guatemalan town called Tecún Umán, which has a bridge over the Suchiate River to the Mexican town of Hidalgo. As I was traveling, the caravan pushed past the Guatemalan border guards onto the bridge. They got to the Mexican side and met a throng of federal police, and a standoff turned into pushes and shoves, with rocks thrown at officers, who fired back tear gas.

I arrived to see the stunning scene of the bridge barricaded, with thousands of migrants squatting on it. Below the bridge, people crossed the river illegally on rafts made of tractor tires. It wasn't very clandestine. From a concrete landing dock, the oarsmen charge twenty-five pesos a head—about a dollar thirty. It's used by residents in Tecún Umán who travel to Mexico to buy cheaper goods, as well as by migrants.

Just before midnight, I found an oarsman to take me across to Guatemala. The river was beautiful in the night, reflecting the light of an almost-full moon. I stepped onto the shore of Tecún Umán and found migrants filling the streets, families sprawled on the sidewalks, mothers coddling babies, groups of men gathered in circles.

I walked onto the bridge, thick with people. Amid the multitude, I found a migrant activist called Rubén Figueroa. We talked about the scale of the march. "This is not a normal action," he said. "It's an exodus." This word, "exodus," was repeated by many, giving a dramatic tone to the surreal scene.

The caravan fired up emotions in the United States. Conservative media covered it incessantly, highlighting Trump's mobilizing of the troops. In contrast, liberals were concerned it was being overhyped and would help Trump in the midterms.

I think it was genuinely big news. There was a humanitarian tragedy in Central America. And the fact that thousands march on a border gate is significant; it shakes at the structures of nation-states that define our world. Seeing the refugees and migrants occupying the bridge under the bright moon, I seemed to be witnessing a revolutionary moment.

As day broke, thousands went from the bridge to the riverbank, some crossing on rafts, others using a rope to wade through the water (which is risky because the river can sweep people away). By late afternoon, the Mexican town of Hidalgo was filled with migrants, and there was a triumphant feeling that borders could not stop them. Rumors floated that the federal police would smash the caravan. But the Mexican government backed down, and thousands marched on to Tapachula amid a festive atmosphere.

Over the next two months, several more caravans followed, and by the end of the year, tens of thousands would have traveled in them. In 2019, the total numbers flowing into Mexico would reach the high hundreds of thousands—a river of people heading north while the river of guns flowed south. The exodus comparison rang louder.

The caravans plodded north through Mexico, with people marching, jumping on trucks, sleeping in parks and in churches. On the road, I heard countless tales of tragedy and hope. There were teenagers alone, single mothers, groups of lads, weathered old men, and a huge presence of families. Unlike migrants I had interviewed over the years, many on the caravan had no solid plans, nobody they were going to meet, no place to head, no money. Many were evangelical Christians putting their hope in God to guide them forward. Preachers held services in town squares, the faithful reaching their hands out, pulling their heads back and staring to the heavens.

The stories of violence abounded. David Maldonado, thirty-one, from the Honduran city of Progreso, had worked as a builder. When he labored in a different barrio, thugs held him down, shot him in both legs, and said that they never wanted to see him again.

Violeta Monterroso and her husband, Candido Calderón, both forty-two, came with their three young children. In their hometown of Suchitepéquez in Guatemala, they had a stall selling juices, making eight dollars a day, enough to scrape by. But men from a gang came flashing guns and demanding an extortion payment of over a thousand dollars, saying they would murder the children if they didn't pay. They left in the dead of night and headed for the caravan.

"There is nobody that can protect us there. We have seen in the other cases they kill the people and kill their children," Violeta said. "Sometimes the kids ask to go home, but I say we can't turn back, and they are sad."

When the caravan reached Tijuana, the city government stuck six thousand people in a cramped sports park that sits on the border, with the view of a road in San Diego. December was cold and wet, and the conditions deteriorated, with feces from the portable toilets spreading into expanding puddles, the mud turning into a swamp. The wretched atmosphere was a world away from the festive feeling in the south.

One day, the rain turned into a storm, and the puddles of shit-infested water soaked the tents and left families filthy and shivering. I saw people in soaked clothes crammed under tarps, mothers trying in vain to keep babies dry. Above it, they could watch the cars cruising along the most southern road of San Diego, a glimpse of the land that they had seen before only on television, that they believed offered peace and prosperity. In the night, the Tijuana government shut down the camp and moved them to another center in one of Tijuana's most violent barrios.

The caravans of 2018 took the tribulations that migrants had long gone through and made them highly visible for a moment, causing virulent reactions—some of sympathy, some of fear or anger. They provided sharp images that can be seen alongside iconic moments in U.S. immigration history, from the lines at Ellis Island to the Mariel boatlift.

Some lucky refugees in the caravan won asylum. Some sneaked in over the border. Many spent long months in detention centers on the U.S. side, where terrible conditions would be exposed.

When Mexican president López Obrador took power in December 2018, he said he welcomed the Central Americans and would provide work for them. But as 2019 rolled on, the numbers kept rising, and there were no clear government plans to help. Under pressure from Trump, López

Obrador used a new National Guard to round up and deport them by the tens of thousands.

Meanwhile, the Trump administration ruled that the asylum seekers would have to wait in Mexico, making refugee camps swell, and a string of the refugees were murdered in border cities. In August 2019, the White House announced that any asylum seeker who had passed through another country would not be accepted. This counted out the Central Americans going through Mexico, as well as those from many other countries. It threw seven decades of U.S. asylum tradition on its head.

The border crisis was officially over. Until the next one.

In Honduras, the violence raged on.

As I covered the caravan, Orlin called me on a Sunday. I answered to hear a sober voice.

Fresa was dead, he said. His body was found riddled with bullets in an SUV. There was a rumor the MS-13 was behind it. But who knows. Fresa's two children were left fatherless.

"I'll pray for his soul," I said.

Those were my words. But I also struggle to find my religion. And after the crimes Fresa committed, after what all the killers in the Americas have done, I am not sure we should pray for their souls. But I still think about him.

10

Terrorists

Terrorists stage a terrifying spectacle of violence that captures our imagination and turns it against us. By killing a handful of people the terrorists cause millions to fear for their lives.

—Yuval Noah Harari, *21 Questions for the 21st Century*

———

On a summer Saturday morning in August 2019, Dr. Alejandro Rios Tovar finished a typical thirty-hour shift, in which he conducted a routine gall bladder surgery at El Paso's University Medical Center.[1] Driving home, the bearded thirty-four-year-old picked up food at a McDonald's and was looking forward to eating and crashing out until Sunday, when he would have to do it all again. But just after getting in the door at 10:55 A.M., he received a text from his chairman of surgery. "Active shooter. Walmart. Unknown number of victims," it said.

"Honestly, I didn't think much of it," Rios Tovar would tell a House Judiciary Committee. "I had an active shooter alert a month earlier, and the

SWAT team only brought in one victim." He thought the trauma surgeon at the hospital, his mentor, could handle it.

Another text arrived two minutes later, sent to multiple surgeons. "If anyone is in El Paso go to the hospital. There is an active shooter and we will get at least four or five victims."

Rios Tovar jumped in his car and ran red lights. When he got to the hospital, the shooting in Walmart was over, the pain and loss just beginning. Rios Tovar found the trauma bays full; fourteen gunshot victims were bought into the University Medical Center in thirty-four minutes, with another eleven sent to the nearby Del Sol Medical Center.

The scene was his worst nightmare: victims with gaping bullet holes in their flesh. "I am not a military surgeon, but what I saw looked like a war zone," he said. "Small gunshot wounds in the legs amounted to huge areas of cavitation and exit wounds larger than a grapefruit. I had never seen anything like this before. How could a firearm create this type of destruction?"

He had treated many patients with wounds from handguns, but these were different. "Sometimes it's even difficult to find the holes [from hand-guns] because of how small they are. And the clean-cut appearance looks like a pencil made them. Here it was not so." He treated a woman with a third of her pelvis shattered into dozens of pieces and multiple holes in her intestines.

The surgeons at University Medical Center saved thirteen of the fourteen patients. But not the first victim that Rios Tovar had turned to.

Jordan Anchondo was a twenty-four-year-old mother of three, beautiful and jokey. Two months earlier, she gave birth to her first boy, whom she called Baby Paul. Four days before, she celebrated her wedding anniversary to Andre, an entrepreneur who'd just finished renovating their house.

They had a hectic day planned: taking her daughter, Skylin, to cheer-leading practice; going to Walmart to buy pens for the new school term; and having family and friends over for a party. The fiesta would celebrate the triple whammy of their anniversary, their renovated house, and Skylin's birthday.[2] After they dropped Skylin off, they went to the Walmart on the eastside for the school supplies.

Each of the victims had their own story of why they'd popped into the store. Elsa Mendoza de la Mora, a fifty-seven-year-old school principal from Juárez, was on her way to visit family and stopped for refreshments. Javier Rodriguez, fifteen, was waiting in line with his uncle, who was going to cash a check. Angelina Silva Englisbee, eighty-six, was on her cell phone in line to the checkout.

The shooter used a WASR-10 from Cugir to blast for six minutes, hitting forty-six people. Andre stood in front of him, shielding his wife and baby, and was cut down with bullets. Jordan cradled Baby Paul, turning her back on the shooter. Bullets tore through her shoulder and she fell, breaking Baby Paul's fingers. When the shooting finished, the paramedics took the baby from her arms and rushed them to the University Medical Center. Skylin asked why her parents didn't pick her up from cheerleading practice.

Jordan grabbed Rios Tovar's attention as soon as he got to the hospital. She had been talking but suddenly went lifeless, and they tried chest compressions and ventilation to bring her back. It was to no avail. Rios Tovar quickly and methodically cut open her chest to begin what he calls "manual cardiac compression." Three liters of blood immediately spilled to the floor. He tried frantically to stop her from dying, but there was no hope.

"I had to pronounce the time of death just ten minutes after I had arrived to the hospital," Rios Tovar said. "The look of disappointment in my resident's eyes ate at me, but I couldn't process that now. We had more to do."

Jordan was one of twenty-two victims who died that day. Her husband, Andre, was another. Baby Paul would survive, to be looked after by Jordan's parents.

Rios Tovar studied Jordan's autopsy to see if he could have saved her, if he had made a mistake. He discovered the wounds were too deep.

"She had this hole the size of a baseball at the top of her lung. Her subclavian vessels were essentially nonexistent. If this injury had been caused by a small firearm, she may have had a chance of survival. But there is absolutely nothing I could do to fix that kind of devastating injury. I hope that she died knowing that she protected her child from the same fate."

Rios Tovar was tormented by his powerlessness. "That first patient haunts me every night. I wish I could have done more, and I blame myself for her death."

Guilt is curious. Some people who should feel bad about what they have done are walking around happy. Others who shouldn't feel guilty are haunted.

We now trace the iron river back to one of the darkest waterways: the scourge of terrorism and mass shootings. This is a bit tangential to our main story, as many of the guns used, including the one in El Paso, are not from the gun black market but are bought legally. However, others are acquired using the same techniques of straw buys and the loophole. And many of the same weapons are wielded.

The shootings also rhyme with the cartel violence in other ways. There is a tragedy to the death of innocents on both sides of the border. And while the cartel bloodshed speaks to institutional failures in Latin America, the mass shootings speak to a psychosis of the United States in how certain disturbed individuals act out with such destruction.

There are attempts to classify both mass shootings and cartel killings as acts of terrorism. What "terrorism" really means is heavily debated. But one definition is the killing of innocent people to create a story in the media that furthers a political agenda. The massacre in El Paso certainly fulfilled this characterization.

Outside Walmart, a makeshift memorial sprung up and was soon overflowing with flowers, candles, teddy bears, balloons, paintings, and photos.

People planted twenty-two white wooden crosses that had been made by carpenter Greg Zanis of the charity Crosses for Losses. Zanis lost his father-in-law to gunshots in 1986 and had been making crosses ever since, totaling twenty-six thousand by the time of the El Paso shooting.

"Today is the worst day," Zanis said to reporters as he finished laying the crosses. "I'm going to have to go to Dayton, Ohio, right now. I don't know how I can handle this."[3] He was referring to the other mass shooting that happened that weekend, killing ten.

A painting in the El Paso memorial asked, "How Many More?" The names of the victims were written on the crosses.[4]

Andre Anchondo, 23, and Jordan Anchondo, 24

Arturo Benavides, 60

Leonardo Campos Jr., 41, and Maribel Campos, 56

Angelina Silva Englisbee, 86

Maria Flores, 77, and Raul Flores, 77

Jorge Calvillo Garcia, 61

Adolfo Cerros Hernández, 68

Alexander Gerhard Hoffman, 66

David Johnson, 63

Luis Alfonso Juarez, 90

María Eugenia Legarreta Rothe, 58

Elsa Mendoza de la Mora, 57

Iván Filiberto Manzano, 46

Gloria Irma Marquez, 61

Margie Reckard, 63

Sara Esther Regalado Moriel, 66

Javier Rodriguez, 15

Teresa Sanchez, 82

Juan de Dios Velázquez Chairez, 77

They joined a list of 745 victims of the ninety biggest mass shootings since Columbine. El Paso was the seventh most fatal mass shooting and one of the nation's worst racist attacks. It was also part of a dangerous trend: the convergence of mass shootings by disturbed individuals and terrorists turning increasingly to the gun.

———

Anyone who saw the bombardment of news knows the suspected shooter was identified as twenty-one-year-old Patrick Wood Crusius. He was accused of driving from Dallas to El Paso to commit the atrocity, ten hours to murder *the other*.

It's that same route the gun trafficker Jorge drove to take AR-15s from gun shows into Mexico. The same route that we drove to track him, through the nothingness for miles. What were Crusius's thoughts as he sped through the desert?

Some say we should not publish the names of mass shooters, that it adds to their cult, encourages others to follow in their path. I respect that opinion. Mass shootings do seem to be contagious, and acts of terror are designed to seek media coverage. I think we need to be careful of sensationalist reporting. But to black out names would require a blanket attempt involving authorities, media, and search engines. And that might create more intrigue, elevate myths. Plus, journalists do need to ask questions about these killers. Like where they get their guns.

In any case, the censuring didn't happen. Many of you already have a mental image of the face of Crusius from news bulletins: awkward-looking, geeky, but otherwise fairly normal. This normality is disturbing: the monsters are among us, and we can't distinguish them.

The reports of Crusius's life are somewhat contradictory. He has a twin sister but he was considered a loner. His father left home when Crusius was twelve because of alcohol and drug abuse, but then became a therapist to others with alcohol problems.[5] Some schoolmates described Crusius as reclusive and bullied, others as a nice kid.

Crusius graduated from Plano Senior High School in 2017. His yearbook shows a photo of him in a crime investigation class with a quote underneath:

"It is interesting to learn about how the world of law enforcement works." Another contradiction.

He moved in with his grandparents to attend Collin County College and worked as a bagger in a supermarket. "Working in general sucks," he wrote in a LinkedIn profile. He dropped out of college and moved out of his grandparents' house six weeks before the shooting.

After he drove to El Paso, he told the police, he was hungry, so he went to Walmart and then decided it would be his target. He posted a manifesto to the website 4Chan saying the attack was for political, not personal, reasons: "defending my country from cultural and ethnic replacement."

He got out of his car wearing dark clothing, earmuffs, and thick glasses, his WASR-10 raised chest-high. He started firing in the parking lot and carried on into the store. One witness said he was letting white and Black shoppers pass, aiming for Hispanics. But white people were among his victims, including a German man. Video shows people running, crouching, bodies sprawled on the floor in pools of blood. A man livestreamed as he ran: "He's got an AK. I got no shot in my pocket." No security guards could be seen.

El Paso police arrived at 10:39 A.M. to find the dead bodies scattered. But Crusius managed to get into his car and drive out of the parking lot. Texas Department of Public Safety rangers in an unmarked vehicle came up behind Crusius on Viscount and Sunmount with the siren blaring. Crusius got out with his hands raised and shouted, "I'm the shooter."

The officers drove Crusius to El Paso police headquarters, where two detectives interviewed him. He waived his Miranda rights and told them he had shot multiple victims and his targets were "Mexicans." The detectives hearing this were both of Mexican descent.

The use of firearms in mass shootings is among the most emotive issues in the gun debate. Bombs make bigger bangs and have been a terrorist worry for decades. But most of the lone wolves don't have the skills to build them, and many describe a fascination with firearms.

In his manifesto rant, Crusius talks about the WASR-10. "Main gun: AK47 (WASR 10)—I realized pretty quickly that this isn't a great choice since it's the civilian version of the ak47. It's not designed to shoot rounds quickly, so it overheats massively after about 100 shots fired in quick succession. I'll have to use a heat-resistant glove to get around this."

Crusius told detectives he had ordered the Romanian gun and gotten it delivered to a local dealer to pick up.[6] When you order guns online commercially, you still have to pass the background check. This contrasts with the online private market that uses the loophole. Crusius passed, so it was a legal buy. He didn't have a felony, wasn't in a gang, wasn't a member of a designated terrorist group. He didn't use the black market, because he didn't need to. And this is the most common method that mass shooters in the United States use to get their guns. Again, this underlines the problem that they are "normal people" walking among us. How do you level the right to bear arms with people with no records committing massacres?

After every mass shooting, the ATF comes in to see if there are crimes they can prosecute, offenses committed to get the weapons. But in El Paso, there were none.

This is obvious to those who have studied the issue, but many, including journalists, get confused about it. After Las Vegas, reporters berated an agent with questions about why the ATF didn't stop the shooter, Stephen Paddock, from getting so many rifles. The answer is that it couldn't. He bought his arsenal of fifty-five firearms legally, and used fourteen of them in the biggest mass shooting in recent U.S. history.

In the Vegas case, the ATF did finally file a charge against a man from Arizona who sold Paddock some ammunition (although not the bullets used in the attack). They said the man had illegally manufactured rounds, which he finally pleaded guilty to.[7] But it was somewhat scraping the barrel to find someone accountable in the Las Vegas shooting.

This underlines a central problem after mass shootings: when the murderers kill themselves. There is nobody to prosecute. The families of the victims want justice. But how?

There are similar stories of other mass shooters buying guns. The killers in the Orlando nightclub (forty-nine victims), at Virginia Tech (thirty-two victims), and in Parkland's Marjory Stoneman Douglas High School (seventeen victims) all passed background checks and bought weapons legally. This raises very valid questions about the laws themselves, getting back to that ferocious debate.

However, in other cases, shooters did get weapons using the same techniques of traffickers: straw buys and private sales.

Straw buying was used in Columbine in 1999. The killers, Eric Harris and Dylan Klebold, had pleaded guilty to a felony theft and were underage. (Harris would turn eighteen just before the shooting; Klebold was seventeen.) A friend, Robyn Anderson, went to a gun show and bought two shotguns and a carbine rifle for them. In return, Klebold went to the prom with Anderson three days before the massacre. Anderson bought the guns from a private seller, so she didn't fill out a 4473. Prosecutors thus declined to prosecute her, as she hadn't lied on a form.

A co-worker at a pizza restaurant where the killers worked also helped them arm up. Philip Duran went to a gun show with Harris and Klebold and bought a TEC-9 handgun for five hundred dollars from a man called Mark Manes. Manes would later confess that he suspected the gun was going to the killers and that they were underage. He got six years for selling a gun to a juvenile, while Duran got four and a half for his involvement.[8]

Parents of victims complained that these were short sentences, considering they had lost their children. The defense lawyer replied that in normal circumstances they wouldn't have gotten any prison time at all. Again, there is a hunt to find someone accountable when the killers kill themselves.

More recently, straw purchasing was used for the San Bernardino shooting. Enrique Marquez Jr. bought two AR-15s for his neighbor Syed Rizwan Farook. Farook and his wife used them in December 2015 to kill fourteen people and injure twenty-four before police shot them dead. That case was different in that prosecutors charged Marquez with providing material support for terrorists—meaning he could face decades in prison.[9] When Islamic terrorism is involved, the prosecutions suddenly become tougher. The law allows it.

More shooters have used the private-sale loophole. Radcliffe Haughton of Wisconsin was prohibited from buying guns because of domestic violence. But in 2012, he posted a message on ArmsList.com sounding desperate, the kind of distressed buyer that makes gun sellers hike the price.

"Looking to buy ASAP," his message said. "Prefer full size, any caliber. Email ASAP. I constantly check my emails. Hoping it has a high mag capacity with the handgun, ammo, accessories. I am a serious buyer. Email me ASAP. Have cash now and looking to buy now. I am mobile."[10]

A man replied, met Haughton, and sold him a Glock .40 in a private sale with no background check. The next day Haughton dressed in camo, walked into a spa, and shot dead his ex-wife and two other women, injured another four people, and then committed suicide.

The tragedy was repeated in Harris County, Texas, near Houston, in 2015. David Ray Conley had served prison stretches and violently abused women. He set up a deal online to buy a 9 mm from a private seller. Storming his ex-girlfriend's house, he shot his son, her five other children, and her husband. Conley chained his ex-girlfriend to the bed and made her witness the other killings before he killed her too.

The cases go on. Dylann Roof should have been prohibited from buying a gun because of a drug offense. But when he did a background check, the FBI failed to find it within the three-day limit (the other loophole). He bought a Glock 41 and used it to murder nine African Americans as they prayed at an Episcopal church in Charleston, South Carolina.

Seth Aaron Ator failed a background check to buy a gun in 2014 because of mental health issues. So he turned to the private-sale loophole to buy an AR-15. In August 2019, after losing his trucking job, Ator went on a shooting rampage in Odessa, Texas. Victims of his bullets included a postal worker about to finish her shift, a father at a stoplight, and a seventeen-month old baby.[11]

*　*　*

Many mass shootings have happened in states where a lot of guns are trafficked. Texas has the highest number of licensed dealers in the country and is major a state for trafficking to Mexico. Florida is the top state for trafficking to the Caribbean. Virginia is a significant source of trafficking to Baltimore, New York, and Washington. Nevada is a source of trafficking to California as well as the home of the biggest firearms trade show in the world. Is the presence of more gun stores and more of a black market influential to a mass murderer? Maybe.

Another link to trafficking is the type of firearm. It was the same WASR-10 variant of the Kalashnikov used by the Zetas who killed ICE agent Jaime Zapata, by the bandits who killed border agent Brian Terry, and by Crusius to massacre shoppers in Walmart. AR-15s are smuggled in huge numbers into Mexico and used in dozens of mass shootings.

This gets to a raging debate in gun politics. How much difference does the power of these weapons make to the lethality of the massacres? In other words, would the assault rifle ban reduce the body count? To analyze this, we need to look in detail at the way the guns are used in the killings. Breaking down the logistics of such tragedies can sound dehumanizing. But these cold facts give us a better sense of how guns thread through crime, terror, and war.

In May 1981, the Zastava factory in Yugoslavia churned out one of its many M-70 Kalashnikov-style rifles and delivered it to the Yugoslavian Territorial Defense Forces. After civil war broke out in 1991, the gun made its way to a unit in Bosnia, to later fall into the hands of a Serbian militia. Where it fell off the map. And reappeared on the night of Friday, November 13, 2015, in the Paris nightclub Bataclan, wielded by a man pledging allegiance to the Islamic State.[12]

The three assailants in the Bataclan shot security staff and stood on a mezzanine in front of the bar spraying bullets at the heavy metal fans. They killed ninety people in the club, while another forty died that night in other attacks in Paris—the biggest mass shooting in Europe since World War II. A survivor from the Bataclan committed suicide shortly before the second anniversary of the massacre.

Mikhail Kalashnikov died two years before the Paris attacks, so he did not see this horrific use of his gun. But tragically, the fully automatic Kalashnikov was an ideal weapon for such a massacre. The killers were facing unarmed civilians crowded into a theater. They did not need to aim, just to fire as many bullets as they could to get the maximum number of casualties.

On today's battlefields, such automatic fire is not very effective. Most combatants have machine guns at their fingertips. But as they know that their enemies do too, they don't expose themselves like the old colonial redcoat regiments. Instead, they use cover, fire from a distance, and often rely on airstrikes. Spraying wildly isn't an economic use of ammo. They want to hit a target.

A cruel paradox, then, is that fully automatic guns are ideal for massacring unarmed civilians but are rarely used in that function in combat.

The Las Vegas shooting on October 1, 2017, had eerie similarities to Paris, if apparently without the political motive. As at the Bataclan, random people were gunned down at a concert: the Route 91 Harvest music festival in the Vegas Village. When bullets were first fired in both Paris and Vegas, revelers thought they were firecrackers.

In Vegas, they interrupted country star Jason Aldean while he played his hit "When She Says Baby." Video shows people screaming with nowhere to escape, the crowds blocking the exits. Fifty-eight people lost their lives before the shooter turned a gun on himself.

Among the many stories of pain and heroism was that of Rosemarie Melanson, who was then fifty-four and came with her two adult daughters. A bullet struck Melanson in the upper chest and traveled sideways through her body, breaking ribs, severing her esophagus, and tearing her intestine, liver, and spleen. Unconscious, she felt like she was floating out of her body and looking down from above.

"I could see my own body laying down there. The next thing I know I was in heaven," Melanson told ABC News. "And I saw my dad and my two brothers, and my uncle. And it was so beautiful. It was so beautiful you didn't want to come back. They just told me, 'It's not your time, Rosemarie. You've got to go back.'"[13]

Melanson woke briefly as she was being dragged to the ambulance by retired fireman Don Matthews. She spent six months in the hospital and underwent twelve surgeries but ultimately survived. She had an emotional reunion with Matthews and thanked him for saving her life.

As at the Bataclan, the shooter was firing into a thick crowd of people in a confined space. He just needed to unload as many bullets as possible. Most were unarmed. But even if some were armed in Vegas, they couldn't see where the shots were coming from. Even the police were confused, thinking there were several shooters. And if anyone had known, it would be extremely hard to return fire to a hotel window 1,100 feet away, and if they did, they could have killed other hotel guests.

A sixty-four-year-old millionaire, Paddock had rented two adjoining rooms in the Mandalay Bay hotel, numbers 134 and 135, on the thirty-second floor. The rooms are still there, but it is hard to find them because the hotel has changed the floor numbers. The thirty-second floor officially no longer exists, as casino guests could get upset if they knew where they were.

When police finally stormed the suite, they found Paddock had fired from fourteen guns, spewing out 1,057 shell casings.[14] Paddock had some weapons on bipods and switched between them as they heated up, shooting out a broken window with a line of sight into the venue. Beyond the fifty-eight dead, another 413 people suffered gunshot or shrapnel injuries. Another testament to the destructiveness of such weapons in crowds is that the same bullets often travel through several people.

Paddock fired the thousand bullets between 10:05 and 10:16 P.M., which makes an overall rate of close to a hundred rounds a minute. However, he fired in bursts that analysis showed reached ninety bullets in ten seconds. As was widely publicized, he achieved this speed by using bump stocks. These are add-ons that cost about four hundred dollars and that replace the rifle stock (the part that sits against the shooter's shoulder) with one the rifle can slide into back and forth. This allows the recoil to push the rifle back into the shooter's finger so that he doesn't need to move the finger. Paddock used it to achieve a rate of firing that is two-thirds the speed of a fully automatic AR-15.

In this sense, the Vegas massacre was atypical of mass shootings in the United States. Paddock was effectively firing with machine guns, again similar to the shooters at the Bataclan.

Despite their capacity to unleash such a torrent of bullets, the ATF had approved bump stocks in 2010 as an unregulated accessory. After Vegas, the Trump administration banned them in 2018, citing the National Firearms Act restrictions of machine guns. This was one of the few regulations that the NRA did not launch a campaign against. As Tim Dickinson wrote for *Rolling Stone*, bump stocks undermined the NRA arguments about a radical difference between semiautomatic and automatic weapons.

"Why is the NRA not kicking and screaming—or suing? The organization has long touted the distinction between civilian semi-automatic rifles and military guns with fully-automatic capability as the reason civilians should be able to own weapons like the AR-15."[15]

The massacre at the Pulse nightclub in Orlando was the deadliest mass shooting in the United States for only fifteen months, until Vegas. At Pulse, the killer Omar Mateen used two semiautomatic weapons, a SIG Sauer MCX and a 9-mm Glock 17.

Like the killers in Paris and San Bernardino, Mateen pledged allegiance to the Islamic State. But like the shooters in El Paso and Charleston, Mateen was targeting a minority, hitting a gay nightclub; it was an attack of hate *and* terror.

Mateen pushed past security and fired more than two hundred bullets into another packed room of revelers. He was shooting slower than Paddock or the Bataclan attackers did. But he was still shooting fast. Analysis of one recording finds that he fired twenty-four bullets in nine seconds. Mateen was frighteningly accurate with his shots, killing forty-nine and injuring another fifty-three.

So Mateen used only a fifth of the bullets of Paddock in Vegas but killed four-fifths the number of people. The fact he was firing on semiautomatic likely made him shoot more accurately, and he might have killed no more with a full automatic. Either way, the massacre shows without a doubt that a semiautomatic rifle with large magazines can be a devastating weapon.

On the Norwegian island of Utøya on July 22, 2011, Anders Behring Breivik attacked youngsters at a Labour Party camp. He posted a manifesto of more than 1,500 pages ranting about "patriotic Europeans" fighting "cultural Marxism" and "Islamic colonization." Breivik used a Ruger Mini-14 rifle with magazines of thirty rounds and a Glock that he had bought legally. The massacre would lead to a change in gun laws in Norway, as mass shootings did in Britain, Australia, New Zealand, and Canada.

Like Mateen, Breivik was firing with a semiautomatic. But unlike those who attacked nightclubs, he attacked targets in a wider space, hunting unarmed teenagers on a small island. Using a semiautomatic was more efficient to strike at the victims one at a time. He shot dead sixty-seven—more victims than in Vegas—and his gunshots injured another thirty-two.

Again, the atrocity confirms the devastating effect of a semiautomatic rifle in carrying out a mass killing. And it brings up another issue. The rifle he was using did not have enough features to classify it as an assault rifle under the U.S. bans. It had a wooden stock and no pistol grip. Yet it proved extremely lethal. It fired the same powerful ammunition as AR-15s, had large detachable magazines, and could shoot fast and accurately.

Second Amendment advocates claim that the AR-15 is not that different from other rifles now. Such a claim is true to an extent. Many semiautomatic rifles on today's market can do most of what an AR-15 can do. Which opens up hard questions about how to legislate guns to stop the massacres.

One last tragedy to break down. Virginia Tech, on April 16, 2007, was in its time the biggest U.S. mass shooting in the recent wave, and as of this writing has become the third biggest. Seung-Hui Cho killed thirty-two people and injured seventeen with gunshots. And he didn't use a rifle at all, but two pistols: a Glock 19 and a Walther P22.

Cho first killed two students in a dorm, then went back to his room, wrote a note with the words "You caused me to do this," and mailed a letter, photos, and videos to NBC. He then went into a building called Norris Hall, where he fired 174 bullets in nine minutes. His victims included twenty-five students and five faculty members.

The area was not as packed as the nightclubs, but his victims were cornered. Would he have murdered more with a semiautomatic rifle? Probably. As Dr. Rios Tovar testified, the wounds from Kalashnikovs are more devastating than those from pistols. But the two pistols wielded by Cho were still tragically effective.

These shootings all have distinct factors that show how the lethality of a weapon can be relative to its environment. No simple ban on one type of gun would make the problem disappear. That is not to say that measures cannot be taken to reduce this terrible loss of life. It is just that those measures are not as simple as one might hope.

Another conclusion is that *tactically*, there is no big distinction between so-called terrorist attacks and those by "nonpolitical" individuals. If bullets fly toward you, it doesn't change things if the shooter is a radical Islamist, a white supremacist, or was just bullied in school. The labels come from the motivation. But even when you look at the individuals, there are similarities between Crusius and Cho, between Mateen and Paddock, between Breivik and Harris.

A lot of policy wonks want a clear line between the terror of extremists and the terror of supposed madmen. Having them in separate boxes is more orderly. But that line is, at best, blurry.

———

Are mass shooters mad? This question touches a range of issues. Some certainly have mental health problems. But at what point does this qualify as insanity? And how should stopping mass shootings be matched with not unduly locking up the one in five Americans with mental health issues? Meanwhile, the defense of insanity alleviates the punishment. And the families of victims want justice.

How about when killers have political manifestos? Can you have an insane terrorist? Or at least a mentally ill one?

A starting point is to look at who mass shooters are. They are over-whelmingly men. Many are white, including the killers in El Paso, Vegas, Columbine, and Sandy Hook. But not all. The perpetrator of Virginia Tech was Asian, of Orlando was second-generation Afghani, of San Bernardino was second-generation Pakistani, of Harris County was African American.

Journalist Derek Thomson sums up a common trait that threads through them. "Mass shootings are often committed by lonely and unrooted men, suffering from both grandiose aspirations and petty grievances," he writes in the *Atlantic*.[16] That makes sense. But it also applies to many people who are not mass shooters. And loneliness does not equal mental illness.

Some mass shooters have certainly had mental health problems. Cho of Virginia Tech received psychiatric help for depression and social anxiety. He got a gun through a loophole in Virginia's reporting of mental health issues to the background check system, which has since been closed.

But Paddock of Las Vegas was never diagnosed with mental illness, and a brain scan found no abnormalities. One doctor said after the fact that he suspected Paddock might have been bipolar. But that is a far cry from certified insanity. Mateen of Orlando was never diagnosed as mentally ill either. His wife would later say he was abusive and unstable, but again that is a tenuous link.

Doctors are highly cautious of presuming mass killers are mad. Rosie Phillips Davis, the president of the American Psychological Association, made this point in a statement following El Paso.

"Routinely blaming mass shootings on mental illness is unfounded and stigmatizing," she said. "Research has shown that only a very small percentage of violent acts are committed by people who are diagnosed with, or in treatment for, mental illness. The rates of mental illness are roughly the same around the world, yet other countries are not experiencing these traumatic events as often as we face them. One critical factor is access to, and the lethality of, the weapons that are being used in these crimes. Adding racism, intolerance and bigotry to the mix is a recipe for disaster."[17]

A famous list of mental disorders is released by the American Psychiatric Association. It includes everything from pyromania to bibliomania (the collecting and hoarding of books) to caffeine-induced anxiety disorder. But there is no "mass shooter syndrome." Not yet.

In 2015, Malcolm Gladwell wrote a piece in the *New Yorker* headlined "Thresholds of Violence" about the rise of school shootings. He dates the beginning of their upswing to a shooting in Moses Lake, Washington, in 1996 and follows through Columbine, Virginia Tech, and Sandy Hook to the many smaller shootings that don't dominate front pages.

Gladwell looks at the stark differences between shooters, citing one who was abused, one who was delusional, and one (Harris from Columbine) who, he says, was psychopathic. "A school shooter, it appears, could be someone who had been brutally abused by the world or someone who imagined that the world brutally abused him or someone who wanted to brutally abuse the world himself," Gladwell writes.

Amid the lack of a common mental condition, he turns to another explanation: a theory that shootings are like a "slow-motion, ever-evolving riot."

He cites Stanford University sociologist Mark Granovetter, who wrote in the seventies how riots sweep people up in mass hysteria. If a hundred people are smashing windows and stealing flat-screens, even the timid kid will do it. The same phenomenon can be found in much group behavior, Granovetter observed.

Gladwell applies this to the evolution of school shooters. Many cite and emulate those before them, like the perpetrators of Columbine. This illustrates how the riot spreads and newcomers emulate those already smashing windows. The kids may not themselves be psychopaths but may copy the psychopathic behavior of Harris.

"The problem is not that there is an endless supply of deeply disturbed young men who are willing to contemplate horrific acts," he concludes. "It's worse. It's that young men no longer need to be deeply disturbed to contemplate horrific acts."

Critics dismiss Gladwell's big ideas as pop psychology. But I think there is something in his "Thresholds of Violence." I am not totally convinced by the riot analogy, however. I have witnessed riots and looting in London, Berlin, Mexico City, Haiti, and Venezuela. People certainly get spurred on by others, and this makes legal sense: if everyone is looting, you are less likely to get arrested. But rioters are not generally doing things they think are abhorrent. Many would justify throwing bricks at police or stealing from stores even before everyone else did it.

A behavior that might be closer to school shooting is cartel violence. I watched the turf wars escalate in Mexico. Beheading was not common before 2006. In the first instance, gangsters cut off the heads of two policemen and put them on a wall. A few months later, mobsters rolled five heads onto a disco dance floor. By 2012, this had reached forty-nine decapitated corpses. The gangsters copied the other atrocities and took them further, as with the escalation of mass shootings.

Some mass shooters emulate gangsters: Harris and Klebold of Columbine made a video for a school project called "Hitmen for Hire." An accompanying text talks about a fantasy business plan in which they would be hired to shoot bullies.

Still, there are big differences. Gangsters claim most of their victims are other gangsters. And they have a clear motivation for what they do: money. They justify their actions by the fact that crime is their only way out of poverty.

Mass shooters aren't getting paid and are guaranteed to end up dead or in jail. So what is their motivation?

Psychologist Jillian Peterson and sociologist James Densley studied all the mass shootings in America since 1966 and analyzed the data systematically. Like Gladwell, they observe that mass shooting is contagious. However, they say most of the killers have suffered trauma in the form of bullying, abuse, or exposure to violence. They add that the shooters have the means to carry out the attacks, the access to firearms. And they say shooters often have a triggering incident, which can be a relationship breakup or job loss.[18]

Their grievances, they say, lead to grabbing on to political justifications. "Many are radicalized online in their search for validation from others that their will to murder is justified," they write. In other words, they have the will first and then seek the radical framework. It is in these twisted ideologies that mass shooters find their vindication; the deluded idea their bloodshed helps a greater cause.

———

Humans have unleashed terror throughout history. The Achaean Greeks sacked Troy, massacring civilians and desecrating temples to terrify those who stood against them. When the Romans defeated the slave leader Spartacus, they crucified six thousand of his fighters along hundreds of miles of road. It wasn't just about murdering them, but about making a spectacle of their deaths.

The actual word "terrorism" emerged in the French Revolution. *Terrorisme* was used to describe Robespierre and his Jacobins putting

thousands to the guillotine in the heart of Paris. This was the same murder
on public display as that of the Romans.

Over the next century and a half, the word morphed to something closer
to its current usage. It was applied to rebels from Ireland to Serbia, killing
with blades and dynamite. They struck like ghosts and made big bangs,
which spread more fear than actual death.

Historians date the modern age of terrorism to 1968. That year, three
Palestinians hijacked an Israeli airliner and flew it to Algeria. They were
from a group led by George "the Doctor" Habash, who was no Islamic
radical but a Marxist from a Christian family. He described how he used the
tactic to make a splash in the newspapers. "When we hijack a plane it has
more effect than if we kill a hundred Israelis in battle," Habash told the
German magazine *Der Stern* in 1970.

Habash had the vision to see how the media broadcast violence against
civilians so that suddenly anyone getting on a plane would be worried. He
was fighting asymmetrical warfare. His band of Palestinian guerrillas could
not defeat Israel militarily. But he put immense pressure on Israel with
public violence against noncombatants. Since then, terrorism has been tied
to the media coverage it garners.

Extremist nationalists and Communists followed. The Japanese Red
Army called for worldwide revolution when it took over a plane with
samurai swords in 1970. The Irish Republican Army called for a united
Ireland as it blew up a British pub where soldiers got drunk in 1974.

By the 1990s, Islamic radicals became the principal purveyors of terror
tactics. When al-Qaeda crashed planes into the World Trade Center, they
took Habash's idea of a media splash to a level he could scarcely have imagined, creating the biggest news event since World War II.

An effect of September 11 was to tighten security at airports around the
entire world. Since then, we have all been getting our bags screened and
pulling out laptops, and it is tough to get a tube of toothpaste on a plane, let
alone a bomb. So the extremists turned to hotels and bars, buses and concerts.

Bombs blew up commuter trains in Madrid in 2004 and London subway
trains in 2005. Then in November 2008, militants in Mumbai mixed bombs

with gunfire, and it was bullets that claimed most of the 174 lives lost over four days. Terrorists all took note.

Adherents of the Islamic State took these mass shootings to Europe in a campaign from 2014 to 2016. Targets included the Jewish Museum of Belgium, the Great Synagogue in Copenhagen, the offices of *Charlie Hebdo* in Paris, and the Bataclan.

Bombings carried on, as did terror attacks with knives and with vehicles. But bullets were making the most noise. And they led to a tactical convergence between the mass shootings by Islamist extremists, those by white supremacists, and those by men without an apparent ideology.

Thinkers including Noam Chomsky argue against this narrow use of the word "terrorism." He says it should also refer to the violence by governments against civilians. The U.S. bombing of Baghdad or Syria nerve-gassing city centers could be called terrorist attacks. That is more similar to the violence of Robespierre and Rome.

Chomsky makes a salient point. But there still is, at least, a type of terrorism by insurgent groups and lone wolves. And this is the one that most legal codes refer to. In the United States, the definition of "terrorism" varies somewhat over different laws, but in a section of code requiring annual reports on terrorism to Congress, it says: "The term 'terrorism' means premeditated, politically motivated violence perpetrated against noncombatant targets by subnational groups or clandestine agents."[19]

In other words, a nonstate actor murdering innocent civilians for a political justification is terrorism. Which is exactly what Crusius did in El Paso. And what Dylann Roof did in Charleston. And what Robert Gregory Bowers did in the Pittsburgh synagogue shooting. Except they weren't charged with terrorist offenses.

The reason comes down to the way U.S. terrorism laws are framed. The most important list of terrorist groups is compiled by the State Department and is specific to foreign organizations. Terrorism is seen as a foreign threat, one from a hostile world that the United States has to defend against.

In contrast, "domestic terrorism" is a term that can be used in investigations such as El Paso. But prosecutors say it provides a framework rather than a chargeable offense.

Crusius could still get the death penalty for "capital murder of multiple persons." But there are wider implications. Some see a skewed agenda to charge Islamic radicals with terrorism and not white power fanatics. And it affects the gun crimes. Currently, a straw buyer for a domestic terrorist could be charged only with lying on the form, which would be a hard pill to swallow for the families of victims.

Journalists have analyzed the words of mass shooters since at least the eighties. After Columbine, the writings of Harris were given particular coverage. Harris espoused beliefs that look confused and contradictory. On a webpage, he said he hated racists. "Don't let me catch you making fun of someone just because they are a different color because I will come in and break your f*ck*ng legs with a plastic spoon," he wrote. However, in the same piece he made disparaging remarks about African Americans and said, "Foreigners! Get out of my country." He also wrote an essay on Nazism, which shows admiration: "Germany needed a leader and Hitler was the best leader Germany had." Despite that, the attack was largely reported as apolitical.

Since then, mass shooters have released writings and videos that reference Columbine. They commonly talk about rejection, including by women, and mix it with violent misogyny and race hate. This reflects the blurred line between political and nonpolitical terror.

On one end of the spectrum, though, is a clear ideological framework for terrorism. Both Islamic extremists and white supremacists have political theories to justify their mass murder, and they have striking similarities.

The white supremacist mass shooters reference each other in their manifestos. Brenton Tarrant, the killer of fifty-one worshipers at two mosques in New Zealand, pays tribute to Breivik of Norway and Roof of Charleston.

Crusius of El Paso, in turn, begins his own rant by saying, "I support the Christchurch shooter and his manifesto."

An idea that threads through is the white genocide conspiracy: the myth of a plot to wipe out the white race through immigration, racial mixing, and lower birth rates. Tarrant says his attack aimed to drive a further wedge between races and force nonwhite people out of white-majority countries. This is strikingly similar to al-Qaeda's line that it will sow division between religions and force nonbelievers out of Muslim lands.

Tarrant also says he wants to create more division over the gun issue in the United States. The conflict over the Second Amendment, he says, will lead to civil war. Obviously, the vast majority of gun owners abhor terrorism. But many mass shooters are obsessed with guns. This creates the paradox that while they are against gun control, their actions provide a reason for it.

———

There is one more thing linking the iron river of guns to gangsters and to terrorism: the phantom of the narco-terrorist.

This gained attention in November 2019 when cartel gunmen in Mexico massacred nine women and children who were U.S. citizens from a cross-border Mormon community. Family members sent a petition to the White House to classify Mexican cartels as terrorist groups, a motion that two Republican representatives had submitted a bill on. In an interview with Bill O'Reilly, Trump said he would indeed designate them. This would empower the U.S. military to carry out strikes over the southern border, an action advocated by Republican senator Tom Cotton. However, Trump subsequently backed away from the designation, citing objections from the Mexican government.

While this "narco-terrorist" label may sound Trumpian, it has been around for decades. Peruvian president Fernando Belaúnde Terry coined the term in the early eighties to describe an alliance between coca growers and guerrillas from the Shining Path, an army of Communist revolutionaries who made the U.S. terror list after they blew up truck bombs in Lima.

The terror tactics and the label spread to neighboring Colombia, where Pablo Escobar masterminded the bombing of an Avianca jet in 1989, killing all 107 people on board, including two Americans. Like Habash, Escobar was fighting asymmetrical warfare. He couldn't defeat the Colombian government militarily but could put huge pressure on it by killing plane passengers. A federal court in New York tried the Medellín *sicario* Dandeny Muñoz Mosquera for the bombing, convicting him on terrorism charges from a 1986 statute on killing Americans abroad, and he was given ten life sentences. Colombia's FARC guerrillas and AUC paramilitaries then made the U.S. terrorist list.[20]

Mexican cartel violence clearly spreads terror. When the first severed heads appeared, the chief of Mexico's federal investigative agency said *sicarios* had been inspired by the decapitation videos of al-Qaeda. In 2008, cartel thugs threw grenades into a plaza where people were celebrating Independence Day, killing eight random civilians. In 2012, the Taliban decapitated seventeen people at a wedding in a shocking story—but that same year cartel thugs in Mexico dumped the forty-nine headless bodies.

However, the case for naming these cartels as terrorist groups gets tricky. The FARC, Shining Path, and AUC are all political groups, so their terror falls easily into that U.S. legal definition of "politically motivated violence." Mexico's cartels don't care about Marx or Islam and just want to make sacks of cash.

A counterargument is that the Mexican Drug War is not only about drugs. Cartels attack politicians and have links with politicians. They control aspects of a territory, including all criminal rackets and who enters and leaves. Their motivation to kill people has thus become political.

Mexico has in fact been using its own terrorist charges against cartel thugs for several years. In a 2015 case, those prosecuted were cartel foot soldiers who blockaded dozens of roads with burning trucks and torched gas stations while their cohorts shot down an army helicopter with an RPG.[21]

So should the United States step into the cartel-terrorist cauldron in Mexico? While some on the right cheer it on, it could have unintended consequences for causes favored by the left. If the Sinaloa Cartel were on the terror list, then the people getting its guns could be slapped with the charges of providing material to a foreign terrorist organization. This could be used on straw buyers or a corrupt firearms dealer, and instead of a slap on the wrist, they could go to jail for decades.

It would also have positive implications for the refugees fleeing these cartels. If an asylum seeker had their life threatened by a designated foreign terrorist organization, a U.S. judge would have to look more favorably on their case. And Mexicans can still file for asylum in the United States, as they are not passing through third countries. Perhaps a lawyer in the Trump administration pointed this out, which was why he backed off.

The idea of terrorism as chiefly a threat from outside has a psychological impact. People fear incursion. After September 11, the United States was on high alert for another radical Islamic attack. There were various scares of terrorists coming over the southern border, but they did not pan out.

Two decades later, the problems of foreign terrorist attacks appeared overstated, although this is partly due to security services foiling plots. Meanwhile the worst wave of terror has been homegrown, from the men who attacked El Paso, Pittsburgh, Charleston, Las Vegas, and Parkland. And while the attacks in Orlando and San Bernardino may have been inspired by foreign groups, the perpetrators were born in the United States.

In short, after 9/11, the nation effectively defended itself from terrorists from abroad. But then Americans became the terrorists themselves.

11

Ghosts

Monsters are real, and ghosts are real, too. They live inside us, and sometimes they win.

—STEPHEN KING, INTRODUCTION TO *THE SHINING*

———

A man in his living room crouches over a 3D printer, feeding in plastics coded by funny arrangements of letters: PLA, ABS, PETG. He zaps a design into the printer from his computer. And boom. Out pops a gun. A verifiable killing machine. He is ready to go murder people. It's all over. Everything we've talked about. The cartels, the corner crews, the mass shooters—everyone can print up all the firepower they want at home. The ATF may as well shut down. And the gun companies. And the gun smugglers are out of business. Guns will be everywhere. The dreams of a completely armed society will come true.

For many that is a terrifying idea. For others it is liberating.

But it is a fantasy. At least right now.

Or is it?

Guns from 3D printers made a splash in 2013 with a firearm called the Liberator, a weird-looking weapon that resembles a gas pump nozzle. A group called Defense Distributed popped it out, fronted by a young Arkansan living in Austin called Cody Wilson. Defense Distributed put the plans for the Liberator free on the internet, where they were reportedly downloaded a hundred thousand times before the State Department shut them down, citing arms export control regulations.[1] A series of suits and countersuits followed that are ongoing, while the plans are on the dark web.

Cody gave a ton of media interviews and became a popular subject for features, starring in four documentaries. While gun enthusiasts come in different shapes and sizes, Cody was unusual. He didn't have a background in the military or hunting, but was a preppy law-school dropout who mused on libertarian theory and quoted Foucault.

The media portrayed him as a threatening radical, with *Wired* famously putting him on a list of the most dangerous people in the world. Which all seemed to play well for Cody. He gained an adoring online following, who made comments on videos like "This dude has a massive intellect that obliviously exceeds the interviewers," and "I'm so glad that Cody knows how to deal with fake news." Silicon Valley heavyweights wined and dined him, including PayPal founder Peter Thiel.[2] All this helped boost Wilson's Defense Distributed while he launched a cryptocurrency platform called Dark Wallet.

In 2016, Cody released a book telling the story of the Liberator and offering more musings against the global order. In 2017, he founded Hatreon, which briefly crowd-sourced people who had been booted out of the mainstream, including white supremacists. He looked like an ascending digital entrepreneur.

Things crashed in 2018, however, when Cody paid to have relations with a sixteen-year-old girl he met through a "sugar daddy" dating site. When the affidavit was filed accusing him of sexual assault, he fled to Taiwan, where he was arrested and sent home. He stepped away from Defense Distributed, made a deal to plead guilty to "injury to a child," got seven years' probation, and had to register as a sex offender.

His fans online were suddenly mum. Except for in a few chat boards, where they muttered about the government catching him in a honey trap.

In the videos, Cody comes across as telegenic, and you can see why so many filmmakers put cameras on him. He gives red meat to gun nuts, hits back at journalists, and rails against governments and corporations, which is all appealing in the populist era. But underneath the surface, I struggle to find a coherent concept of the world he wants to build.

On the other hand, he did have the vision that printing a 3D gun would be a big deal. It propelled him to fame and helped him make a bundle of cash in other ventures, if also to face legal challenges. And it stirred up the debate about how you can and can't police guns in the digital revolution.

His action is reminiscent of the punk group the Sex Pistols provoking a reaction by screaming "Anarchy in the U.K." Cody indeed spoke of his gun-printing project as an anarchistic provocation.

"Really it's a kind of blunt way of demonstrating the anarchist potentialities of distributed manufacturing, digital manufacturing," he told RT. "We're interested in pushing at the margins of technology, at the margins of politics, in this environment that we believe is somewhat post-political."[3]

The Liberator, however, has a big catch. The gun is largely useless. It not only looks ugly. An ATF agent in Los Angeles told me he had seen the tests, and agents were not worried, because criminals wouldn't use it. It is inaccurate, fires a very short distance, and can easily blow up, potentially hurting the shooter.

The British National Ballistics Intelligence Service also printed up some Liberators, and its tests were shown on the BBC. "All of them have failed catastrophically," said the ballistics investigator Tony Gallagher. "These guns are of no use to anyone. They are too unpredictable and pose probably the greatest danger to the user."

This is a central point that most media missed. Headlines said things like "3D Printed Guns Are Easy to Make and Impossible to Stop." That was plain wrong, and Cody did not actually make an effective 3D-printed firearm. He created a gimmick gun that made him famous and got him into business selling other products.

The distortion of the news stems from two sources. Many reporters didn't understand or didn't want to understand that the gun was useless. It was a sexier story that anyone could print killer guns. And Second Amendment enthusiasts knew that the gun was useless but loved the narrative that 3D-printed guns would kill gun control.

The problems of the Liberator aren't because the design is bad, but because the technology itself is not there. Cheap 3D printers, even the ones that cost a few thousand dollars, work with plastic that is relatively soft. Firing a gun creates a lot of friction and heat. A gun frame printed with this plastic can't handle the pressure. There is no simple design solution to this.

But Cody did get the ball rolling. In the years since, a network of those making 3D-printed guns have connected digitally. You can find chats on Reddit, YouTube, and Twitter, while the serious swapping of designs is on closed systems. One group calling itself Deterrence Dispensed (a twist on Defense Distributed) put a video out in 2019 showing a Glock being printed. Along with funky house music, the designer adds metal parts and then fires it in a field. Subtitles flash up saying: "GO AHEAD TRY TO STOP THIS YOU FILTHY STATISTS."[4]

Yet there are caveats. The metal in the gun includes what is called a Glock upper receiver, which you still need to buy commercially. The idea that the Glock is pure plastic is a myth. It was spread by a scene in *Die Hard* in which Bruce Willis says, "That punk pulled a Glock 7 on me. You do know what that is? It's a porcelain gun made in Germany. Doesn't show up on your airport X-ray machines." In reality, various parts of the Glock are metal, including the barrel, and you won't get them on a plane. Plus Glock is Austrian, not German.

Moreover, while the man in the Deterrence Dispensed video fired off a few shots, that does not mean the gun wouldn't fracture or blow up if used a lot. Chances are the plastic parts wouldn't be much stronger than the Liberator's. The lower-range 3D printers use softer plastics. The commercial

Glocks use a special high-tech polymer with a secretly guarded formula and industrial machines to cast it. And its guns go through painstaking tests.

Criminals are not going to use cheap 3D-printed guns at this point. Especially when there are so many other guns around. This problem may be solved in the future. But it may not be. The challenge is not with the digital printing, which is rapidly evolving, but with the industrial processes of casting plastic. Thankfully.

There have been efforts to print guns from stronger materials. An engineer at a company called Solid Concepts printed a .45-caliber pistol with a process called "direct metal laser sintering," in which metal is put into a powder and then rebuilt.[5] But this was made with a printer that costs half a million dollars. At that price, you could buy an industrial machine to make a gun using the traditional process.

Some people may be scratching their heads here, because they have heard ghost guns are a real problem. And they are. But these are not 3D-printed guns; rather, they're weapons assembled in homes or workshops from parts bought off the internet that do not have serial numbers. To confuse things, media reports often mix up the two, talking about 3D-printed guns and showing pictures of home-assembled guns. In reality, they are different things. And the assembled guns really are being used by gangsters, in both the United States and Mexico.

———

Amateurs have been knocking up homemade firearms for centuries. In World War II, Philippine rebels made pipe guns, which use a thin piece of plumbing pipe pushing into a fatter pipe with a firing pin that ejects the bullet. The idea spread round the world. Others made pen guns, while amateur gunsmiths made more elaborate homemade contraptions. But factory guns still account for the vast majority of firearms.

In the 1980s, people in the United States started selling guns in kits. Companies on the fringes of the gun industry did this by getting the firearms parts and selling them in a way that circumvented gun regulations.

They were not legally selling guns, just pieces of metal, so they didn't need to be licensed dealers, and they didn't need to ask for 4473 forms. The buyers, who could include felons, made guns without serial numbers, and these are the ghost guns.

One was used in a terror attack on the Brooklyn Bridge in 1994.[6] A Lebanese immigrant struck in revenge for the Hebron massacre of Palestinians by a Jewish settler. The attacker fired at a van of Hasidic students returning from Manhattan, killing a sixteen-year-old and leaving another with a bullet in his brain. Parents of the victim, and the survivor, sued the gun-parts makers, but a jury ruled against them in 1998.

The phenomenon of ghost guns raised the legal question of at what stage a gun becomes a gun. Citing the Gun Control Act, the ATF ruled that the lower receiver—the part that has the serial number—is a firearm. So people buying these had to abide by the laws of any other gun sale.

But the fringe merchants got around this again. They began selling receivers, especially for AR-15s, that were missing holes, known as "80 percent lowers." These are not considered firearms until the holes are drilled in. So the merchants sell them as unregulated machine parts, and people can take them home, drill them, and build ghost guns.

The weakness of regulation on these firearm kits is another testament to the power of the gun lobby. In most countries, it is simply illegal to build your own guns. Many upper receivers are as integral to the gun as lowers, so it is inconsistent that one is regulated and one isn't. And 80 percent lowers are sometimes advertised for the very fact they circumvent laws.

While the internet did not create this making of ghost guns, it has massively boosted it. With a few taps of the keyboard and a credit card, you can find gun kits and get them mailed. A slew of shady companies make money off this cottage industry.

In the ATF offices in Los Angeles, I talk to agents who just busted gang-bangers assembling ghost guns. The agents found a garage with machinery and rifles that were being assembled with black and red parts. A gang member denied they were his. But he had red ink all over his hands. He was literally caught red-handed.

Ginger Colbrun, the regional ATF spokesperson, says they make such hauls all the time. Back in the eighties, ghost guns used to count for a negligible amount of those seized from criminals. But that has radically changed.

"Right now, what we're seeing in Southern California is approximately thirty percent of the firearms that we seize or buy off the street are non-serialized homemade guns," she says. "These guys are making them hand over fist."

Until recently, they mostly seized ghosts of AR-15s. But now they are seeing an increasing number of pistols, she says, the standard for gangbangers who want weapons they can conceal. She hits back against the argument that only amateur gunsmiths want kits.

"It's fine if you're a hobbyist and you want to go make your gun, and that's your thing, but it's prohibited people who are taking these," she says. "It's not really cheaper, but people are doing this because they're untraceable."

Ghost guns now count as a fourth major source of guns for criminals, she says, alongside straw buyers, theft, and private sales. A review of California police records by the *Trace* shows that ghosts have been recovered in "homicides, robberies, active shooter incidents, and domestic violence cases."[7] Some of the worst cases in which there have been at least one ghost gun used include a bank robbery in Stockton, in which a hostage was killed; a man in Walnut Creek who shot dead a nineteen-year-old woman before committing suicide; the Santa Monica mass shooting, in which a man who was prohibited from buying a gun used a ghost to kill five people; and the Rancho Tehama Reserve shooting, in which a man on bail for multiple felonies killed five people.

Amid such overwhelming evidence, it is untenable to say that ghost guns are not being used in murder. So defenders of ghosts revert to the old argument that it's not the fault of the guns; it's the fault of the criminals.

The fact that ghost guns don't have serial numbers can be a blow to an investigation. If a regular gun is recovered at a crime scene, police call up the trace center and at least have a chance of a lead. For this reason, ghost guns are desirable to criminals, and it's profitable for people to make and sell them. Some are quadrupling their investment, according to an ATF agent cited by the *Trace*.

It's relatively low risk for a ghost-gun seller. If he is not a felon, then he is not breaking the law by building a gun. And he is allowed to sell a weapon he has made by claiming it as a private deal. Only if prosecutors can prove that he is selling weapons to make a living can they convict him of being engaged in the business without a license. In most cases, people are convicted with ghost guns only because they are felons or also have drugs.

Still, when I bring up ghosts during my tour at the ATF National Tracing Center, Scott Curley gives me some room for hope. He starts off by telling me the official ATF name for them is "self-manufactured unserialized firearms," or SMUFs.

"I think we're still going to use 'ghost guns' in the newspapers," I say.

"But that is an inaccurate thing," Curley says. "Because ghost guns aren't actually invisible. You can sit there and do a variety of things between NIBIN [National Integrated Ballistic Information Network]and other crime gun intelligence."

He points out that if such a gun is used in crimes, they can still identify the "ballistic fingerprint" from the markings on the shells. So if someone is caught with the weapon, they can still be convicted of the crime. Furthermore, if they find a gun, they could still potentially identify where the parts have been manufactured, and the sellers might give them information. It is similar to how those investigating a homemade bomb will look at the pipes and materials and may be able to trace them to a hardware store and see who has been shopping.

"Would you call that a 'ghost bomb'?" Curley says.

"But 'ghost gun' has that alliteration," I say.

Smugglers are also running ghosts. In most of Latin America, it is illegal to build your own guns, and you can't buy parts off the internet. As a result, the ghost-gun companies are not allowed to mail outside the United States. But criminals can simply get them sent to a U.S. address and smuggle them out. In Operation Patagonia Express, in which thousands of weapons were seized in Argentina, agents traced pallet loads of parts being smuggled from Miami. Boxes of bits also make their way over the Rio Grande.

In 2014, police in the Mexican state of Jalisco raided a pair of workshops where they found cartel goons assembling AR-15s. The police released video showing they were using 80 percent lowers, which they had in crates, and were milling them with a machine called a Hardinge VMC 600 II, which can be found for about nineteen thousand dollars. The gangsters had assembled about a hundred guns, the state attorney general said, with police seizing thirty-two complete weapons as well as crates of receivers.[8]

The guns were going to the Jalisco New Generation Cartel, the AG said. This is the same cartel that Republican lawmakers wanted to put on the terrorist list, whose foot soldiers shot down a Mexican army helicopter. Among their many atrocities was a mass grave of seventy-four corpses.

It is unclear if the cartel affiliates had bought the AR parts in a vast job lot or had made the effort to buy them a few at a time. If someone is ordering one hundred 80 percent receivers, there has to be a suspicion they are in a drug cartel. Some producers might care. Some don't. They argue that the more ghost guns in circulation, the better, that it will all help shatter gun control.

———————

The debate over ghost guns gets into what role governments should have in dealing with firearms. And it cuts into the philosophy of libertarianism, an idea that is at the heart of U.S. culture and has gained steam in the digital era.

Some libertarians go further than the NRA. The lobby defends firearms companies and resists any gun safety legislation. The ghost fringe argues that everybody should be printing their own guns, even criminals, which would undermine the companies.

Still, the NRA supported Cody Wilson, giving him airtime. This is probably because the NRA understood that 3D-printed guns are not a threat to the companies at the moment, but Cody worked well to threaten gun control. Until he got arrested.

While Cody is out of the spotlight (for now), his ideas have plenty of support. Libertarians, mostly from the right but some from the left, are growing in number and guns are a pet issue. For many, gun control is the apotheosis of state tyranny and an armed populace the expression of individual freedom.

Libertarian ideas are so broad it's impossible to sum up exactly what their vision of a future looks like and how guns fit in. Some still accept forms of gun regulation, such as convicted murderers not being allowed firearms. Others believe guns should be as ubiquitous as cell phones. Many have a notion of empowered individuals with guns and a weaker government that does not have the monopoly of force. "I want to see a gay couple defending their marijuana plantation with automatic rifles" is a repeated catchphrase.

Peace would be upheld, they argue, by the nonaggression principle. People have their guns for defense, which makes criminals less likely to harm them. Carjackings would be "assisted suicides" because the driver would always have a gun for self-defense. It's an idea that chimes with the game theory of mutually assured destruction.

The argument that gun control, even for narcos and terrorists, is a lost cause comes from various directions. There is the notion of there being too many guns, the billion on the planet, the 393 million among American civilians. There is the phantom of ghost guns changing the game. There is the long history of failure to stop gangs from getting guns. Meanwhile, the voices in support of gun rights are strong and many. And central to their argument is that if criminals have guns, then it is better to have them to defend yourself, or as the mantra goes, "The only way to stop a bad guy with a gun is with a good guy with a gun."

There are authentic cases of armed citizens defending themselves. In Sutherland Springs, Texas, a mass shooter killed twenty-six people before a former NRA firearms instructor shot and injured him. In Mexico, self-defense militias have risen up against cartels. In some towns, they can claim success, although in others, the militia members have themselves become violent criminals. And there are plenty of individual stories of people shooting muggers, rapists, and burglars, and many more of guns being used as deterrents.

There are also cases of armed defense going wrong. I was in the Condesa, a trendy middle-class neighborhood in Mexico City, with a friend and our families when we got news of a shooting a few blocks away. It turned out that a thief had held up a restaurant, and a man at a table drew a gun and fired at him. But the hero missed and shot a woman at another table in the head. This is not a wild exception. The accuracy rate of New York police in real situations is infamously about 17 percent.[9]

It is easier to assassinate someone or shoot into a crowd of civilians than to accurately hit a threat in a confrontational situation. This is one reason that self-defense killings pale in comparison to murders. In 2015, there was one "justifiable homicide" in the United States using a gun for every thirty-four criminal homicides using them. Police don't get the upper hand on criminals because they are sharpshooters. They do it with overwhelming force and the use of incarceration.

This leads to a major factor that is so blatant it can be overlooked. The United States has commanding law enforcement. This is despite the immense problems of corrupt and racist police murdering unarmed suspects. It is despite the fact that it fails in pockets of the country. It is despite the fact that there are messed-up operations like Fast and Furious. It is despite the fact that U.S. gun law is all over the map. Despite all this, police and federal agencies hit certain criminals hard, and law enforcement is well funded and takes few casualties. For many, including myself, the system is too repressive, the police shoot too many civilians, the prisons lock up too many. But this doesn't alter the fact that the United States has potent police agencies.

The police operate in a United States awash with illegal drugs and guns and billions of dollars in drug money. They don't seriously challenge this.

But they take down many of the most violent criminals, and especially any gangsters who want to shoot it out with police. They set down lines such as stopping criminals from getting away with kidnapping for ransom.

This strikes me after covering crime for two decades in Latin America, and hearing the stories of women like María de Lourdes, whose son was abducted. In much of the continent, law enforcement cannot cope with the crime wave, which is itself linked to the gun and drug markets of the United States. This creates violent societies that people run from. Gun murder is a reality that people face every day, and most do not see a societal path out of this, just a daily struggle. Some of that reality is shared in Baltimore, St. Louis, and Detroit, but not in most of America.

I respect law-abiding Americans having guns to defend themselves. But it is not those guns in civilian hands that make the difference between the United States and Latin America—it is institutions. Most Americans are not safe from a cartel storming their home to kidnap them because they have an AR-15. They are safe because the police and federal agencies have been hammering organized crime for decades. In Mexico, you see what a cartel hit squad looks like, and it is not something that you can stop on your own if they come for you, even if you have a bunch of guns.

Some gun advocates have genuinely seen a lot of violence in their lives. But others haven't, and some of their ideas about it are based on fantasy. Perhaps if they saw what gun violence really looks like—the bodies, the injuries, the tears—it would change their views. Perhaps not.

This reflects the big paradox at the center of this story. The United States churns out millions of guns but has the institutions to withhold the criminality, while having hot spots of violence and the terror of mass shootings. Latin America receives the flow of guns but does not have the institutions to withstand the violence. And drowns in blood.

A friend and science journalist, Erik Vance, made a comparison that sums up the difference in institutions and how they are viewed. In one year, he was in four countries: the United States, Mexico, China, and Sweden. Sweden has strong institutions, and its people believe in them, he said. China has weak institutions, but its people still have faith in them. Mexico has weak institutions, and its people don't believe in them. The United States has strong institutions, but Americans have little faith in them.

This is worth bearing in mind for what the future will look like. If the U.S. government does become weaker, and criminals can openly switch from handguns to automatic rifles and .50 calibers, it might not be the libertarian paradise some imagine. It might look more like Latin America.

On the other hand, some embrace the vision of a dystopian future, of a breakdown of society, as inevitable. They see rising crime, terror, racial violence, refugees, environmental destruction, and stumbling governments. And in this situation, guns are the best way to defend yourself. Iain Overton, of Action on Armed Violence, says a cultural manifestation of these fears is the cult of zombie fiction: the fight for survival against ravenous undead horrors.

"There's lots and lots of zombie films, apocalypse films being watched," he told me. "If you go to the logical end game of that—global warming will bring profound social disruption—then actually a gun is quite useful to have because then it will protect you against the marauding zombie hordes."

That's grim tonic to go to bed with. But there is another vision of the future. A vision of collectivist action to stop violence, of young people correcting the mistakes of their parents, of freedom meaning not only the power of the individual but also the freedom to come together to create a better world. This may sound overly optimistic. But it is a reality in the hearts of millions.

12

Day of the Dead

I say "family" because of all the pain that I see in the crowd. And that pain is another reason why we are here. Our pain makes us family. Us hurting together brings us closer together to fight for something better.

—ALEX KING, CHICAGO'S PEACE WARRIORS,
MARCH FOR OUR LIVES, 2018

I met Javier Valdez in 2008 in the cantina near his newspaper, where he was sitting at a table by himself with a bottle of whiskey and a glass. It was during a long, hot, bloody summer in Culiacán, the state capital of Sinaloa. El Chapo was locked in a brutal turf war against his old friend Arturo "the Beard" Beltrán Leyva, unleashing shootouts over the city. This was the year the Mexican Drug War really escalated, going from a crime problem to a crime war. I traveled from Mexico City to Culiacán six times that summer, and a friend gave me the number of the journalist Javier. When I called, he told me to find him in the cantina, El Guayabo.

Javier oozed charisma and was a great listener, which was how he soaked up people's stories and regurgitated them in his *cronicas*, or journalistic essays. His face was warm and welcoming beneath his goatee, thick-rimmed glasses, and Panama hat, which would become iconic in his portraits. But what I remember most about him is his voice, a lilting Sinaloan accent mixing barrio slang with literary color.

We talked and drank into the morning, the conversation flowing from drug cartels to social class to punk rock. He described how he had been a hippie student and stood as a political candidate when he was underage. His slogan: *Cholos si, chota no*—Homeboys yes, cops no. When he gave me a ride to my hotel, he blasted Amy Winehouse and we had a drunken sing-along to "Back to Black."

Javier had been reporting for two decades then and was about to hit his most prolific period. He published his first major book, *Miss Narco*, in 2009, with profiles of women in the cartel life: beauty-queen girlfriends, drug mules, money launderers. "The skin of the Western Sierra Madre has blood in its pores," Javier wrote. "There is pain and shouting. The memory of villages burned, families running terrified, men robbed, mutilated, and killed, women of all ages submitted to sexual abuse."

Miss Narco made Javier a national literary figure, and he poured out a book every year: *Orphans of El Narco, The Taken, With a Grenade in the Mouth, Narco Journalism.* At the same time, he mentored young journalists at the newspaper he cofounded, *Ríodoce*, which means "twelfth river"; there are eleven rivers in Sinaloa, and they wanted a river of information. He didn't sensationalize the violence. His work was a love letter to the people he had grown up with: their pride, their ambitions, their vulnerabilities. As he went on, he focused more on the victims, the orphans, the mothers searching. He wrote like he spoke, blending Sinaloan argot with metaphors and allegories, a voice akin to a Gabriel García Márquez or a Hunter S. Thompson. His work is a glimpse into the soul of Mexico in this bloody period.

I saw Javier sporadically over the years, often at gatherings of the small circle of journalists who cover the drug war in Latin America. In a group bursting with larger-than-life characters, Javier was the biggest of them all. At a seminar on journalism and trafficking in Mexico City in 2009, he described how his son Francisco, then ten, had asked if he was scared. " 'I *am* scared,' I told my son. 'But I feel what I do has value.' "

It wasn't just that Javier accepted the risks and tolerated the fears. He felt he didn't have a choice. As he told an interviewer in 2011, "To die would be to stop writing."

El Chapo was extradited to New York on January 20, 2017, hours before Trump was sworn in as president. There was debate about whether the extradition was a last-minute gift to Obama or an early gift to Trump. I think the latter, and the Mexican government wanted to throw Trump a bone in the hope he wouldn't go too hard on building the wall and deporting Mexicans.

El Chapo's vacuum led to yet another turf war in Sinaloa, as his sons, known as Los Chapitos, fought with a lieutenant, El Dámaso López, for the empire. The shootouts returned to Culiacán. In the midst of the fighting, Javier interviewed Dámaso on the phone and wrote it up for *Ríodoce*. Just before it hit the stands, an envoy of the Chapitos warned him not to publish it. When Javier said it was too late, Chapitos affiliates followed the delivery trucks, buying every copy.

Javier thought about fleeing but decided that would unfairly displace his wife and children. As weeks passed, the threat seemed to dissipate. In a video from his fiftieth-birthday party, Javier joyfully plays drums in a rock band. His shirt reads LIFE BEGINS AT FIFTY.

On May 2, Dámaso was arrested in Mexico City, and parts of Javier's interview with him ran again, in a national newspaper. On the morning of May 15, 2017, Javier went to his office and talked with fellow editor Ismael Bojórquez. Javier left to buy chicken for lunch, and Ismael went to the bank. As Ismael returned, he spotted a crowd around a body on the street. At first he thought it was the victim of a hit-and-run. Then, as he told me, "I saw the hat and the shoes, and I thought, *Oh, fuck . . . it's Javier.*"

Close to noon, Javier had been shot twelve times near the offices of *Ríodoce.*

The systematic murder of journalists is another tragedy of the Mexican Drug War. The numbers are brutal. More than 150 journalists killed since 2000. More than 300 in a government protection program because of threats. Mexico ranking alongside the war zones of Syria, Afghanistan, and Iraq as the most perilous countries for the trade.

That not only means 150 tragedies for the individuals and their loved ones. It limits reporting, turning chunks of the country into black holes.

But other journalists fight on despite the deaths. They dig up scoops about politicians working with gangsters, tell the human stories amid the crime war. Standing against all the money, all the killers, *all the guns*, with nothing but words can seem foolhardy. Or heroic.

Most murders of Mexican journalists are never solved. However, a year after Javier's death, federal police in Tijuana arrested the getaway driver, who would be sentenced to fourteen years, and prosecutors indicted a shooter, already in prison on firearms charges.[1] Another suspect was murdered. At the trial of El Chapo, Dámaso took the stand and blamed the Chapitos for ordering the killing. However, in 2020, Mexican federal prosecutors issued an arrest warrant for the son of Dámaso, known as El Mini Lic, for being the mastermind of the hit. Mini Lic was in U.S. custody, and as of late 2020 remained north of the border.

The murder weapon used to kill Javier has not been found, but the numbers make it likely it was another gun sold in the United States. Seven weeks before Javier was slain, his colleague Miroslava Breach was also shot dead, after uncovering corruption in Chihuahua. In that case, the weapon was identified as a Colt .38 Super, serial number 0049EZS. It was from a limited edition of two hundred pistols with engravings of Mexican revolutionary Emiliano Zapata made by the iconic American gun company. It was sadly ironic. An American gun with a picture of a Mexican freedom fighter was used to try to silence Mexico's freedom of speech.

Days after his death, Javier's son Francisco wrote a letter to his dad. "Where are you, father?" he wrote. "I look for you everywhere, in every space, in every object you touched. I look for you in my dreams but I don't see you. I don't see your face, your big and worn body, half a century old. Half a century that you fought for many, gave what you had, delivered the most human of you to us." He finished, "Don't doubt that I will talk to my children about you, I will tell them how brave and badass you were."

Painters drew murals of Javier across Mexico. In one in Culiacán, he is smiling in his hat and glasses on a bright blue background. "Let the walls speak *vato* [homie]," he says, "because the citizens have shut up."

Reporters in Mexico opened Twitter accounts for Javier, Miroslava, and other murdered journalists. "They killed me for investigating and condemning," says a tweet from Javier's account. "They wanted to shut us up but we go on speaking."

The idea that the dead are still present, that they go on talking, denouncing, drinking, laughing with us, is reflected in other aspects of Mexican culture. On the Day of the Dead, on November 1 and 2, families traditionally make *ofrendas* for their loved ones who have passed away. They give them their favorite food, drinks, cigarettes. And spend time with them.

Death is not the end in this tradition, as the dead exist in people's hearts. And so the many who have died from gun violence still exist in our hearts. And we can ask ourselves what we can do to honor them, and stop others from sharing their fate.

On November 4, 2019, three cars of women and children drove along a rugged dirt path through the Sonoran mountains, seventy miles south of the U.S. border. They were U.S. citizens as well as having residency in Mexico, from a cross-border community of Mormons that has thrived for a century and a half. The gunmen ambushed from two points, spraying them with AR-15s and a Minimi machine gun.

The bullets tore through the vehicles, piercing cushions, dashboards, and windows. The men torched one of the cars, a Suburban carrying a mother and four of her children, reducing its frame to a charred husk of metal. They shot another woman dead after she climbed out of her car, reportedly to plead for mercy. In all, three women and six children were murdered.

But amid the great brutality, fortune showed flashes of mercy. Five children survived bullets to the back, jaw, leg, wrist, and chest and hid terrified for hours on the freezing mountainside. The fusillade also missed Faith Marie Johnson, a seven-month-old baby who sat in a car seat in the back. With her head nicked by a fragment of shrapnel, she survived more than nine hours without food, water, or milk. Finally, a group of relatives arrived to rescue her, including Julian LeBaron, a carpenter and anticrime activist from a sprawling Mormon family. "She opened her eyes, like, 'What's up?'" he said. "I think she had been crying all day."

This time the massacre garnered blanket coverage from Fox News and angry tweets from Trump demanding justice. The FBI crossed the border to help with the crime scene, which the Mexican government justified by saying that the bullets were U.S. made, and most likely the guns were too. President López Obrador met with the families and went to the Mormon village in Sonora.

Yet even in this high-profile case, Mexican prosecutors couldn't seem to solve it. A Mexican general claimed that the Juárez Cartel carried out the atrocity, mistaking the victims for *sicarios*. Federal police and soldiers arrested some men in Chihuahua but struggled to find evidence linking them to the crime.

In January 2020, the families of the victims joined a four-day march from the city of Cuernavaca to the Mexican capital calling for truth, justice, and peace. The widow and children of Javier Valdez were also there, as was Javier Sicilia, a poet whose son was killed by gangsters, and the families of people murdered and disappeared across Mexico, holding photos of their loved ones.

"We can blame and complain about what the government does all day long, but that will never fix our problem. We have to act," Julian LeBaron told me as we trudged along the highway. "Any society that allows their people to be murdered with impunity eventually ends up losing all of their freedom."

The march forms part of a wider wave of protests against the violence in Mexico. The disappearance of the forty-three students, at the hands of a police force implicated in the Hechler & Koch case, provoked huge demonstrations, and people still march on the anniversary of the atrocity. Citizens keep taking to the streets in cities such as Guanajuato, Celaya, Monterrey, Victoria, and Veracruz to call for peace and safety.

The demand for less gun violence is clear. But how do we get there?

Marches can be emotional and inspiring. And they can be frustrating. The right to protest is a cornerstone of democracy. It is fulfilling to take to the street to express your outrage. And protesting together with others provides a sense of unity, of being part of something bigger than yourself. But they can be frustrating because they don't change policy by themselves. They can feel like banging your head against a wall.

On March 24, 2018, hundreds of thousands felt the unity on Pennsylvania Avenue, in Washington, D.C. The Crowd Counting Consortium estimated that there were 470,000 in the nation's capital and 1.4 to 2.1 million across the United States, and there were eighty-four marches abroad.[2] It was likely the fourth-biggest march in the history of the United States. And it was organized by high school students.

Like the protests in Mexico, the March for Our Lives reflected the spirit of honoring those who have died of gun violence and trying to stop others from meeting the same fate. But it was on a bigger scale. After covering the bloodshed for so many years, I was inspired to see a generation redefine the gun issue so fearlessly. This same feeling swept many—a moment of hope.

How the school massacre in Parkland led in six weeks to such a momentous event can seem in retrospect like it was inevitable. But as Dave Cullen recounts in his book *Parkland*, in which he followed the students through the turbulent year, there was a combination of circumstances, and the leaders were driven and talented at turning from tragedy to protest. The use of social media was crucial. And people responded. The time was right.

Among the speeches televised to millions, the silence of Emma González for the six minutes and twenty seconds it took to shoot dead the seventeen students of Parkland was the most memorable. Silence speaks to humanity in the face of senseless massacre. But words also inspired. The March for Our Lives did well to connect the school shootings to the gang killings that haunt inner cities. A group called the Peace Warriors from Chicago's North Lawndale College Prep High School met with Parkland students in the weeks leading up to the march. The Peace Warriors were formed to support students whose family members die from gun violence, helping in the vulnerable period after the loss. Seventeen-year-old Alex King took to the stage and recounted how his nephew had been shot dead less than a year before.

"The day I lost my nephew was a huge turning point in my life. I started doing a lot of bad things, hanging around a bad crowd. I started to really give up," Alex said. "Our community has been affected by gun violence for so long and will continue to be affected by it if we don't do something. But through my friends and colleagues I found help to come out of the dark place."

The hatred spewed by some hard-liners against the Parkland kids speaks again to the extremist side of the gun movement. But the numbers of protesters speaks for itself. As does the inspiration they gave to many more, a feeling articulated by Bruce Springsteen when he played a concert soon after.

"That weekend of the March for Our Lives, we saw those young people in Washington, and citizens all around the world, remind us of what faith in America and real faith in American democracy looks and feels like," Springsteen said. "It was just encouraging to see all those people out on the street and all that righteous passion in the service of something good."

A pitfall was perhaps too much of a culture of celebrity around the organizers. Young people have taken part in protests for decades, from the schoolchildren of Soweto to the 1960s student protests in Europe. But they did not have their lives thrown into the maelstrom of social media and the twenty-four-hour news cycle. That force amplified the message of March for Our Lives. But it also put awesome pressure on its organizers.

Still, March for Our Lives continues to echo years after Parkland. And the organizers have the potential to grow in their political visions. They have already made their moment in history.

A year and a half after Parkland, I talk with campaigners from Brady, the prominent gun safety group, in its Washington offices a few blocks from the U.S. Capitol building. Kyleanne Hunter is a former marine who served in Iraq and Afghanistan and is now Brady's vice president of programs. Jonathan Lowy, the chief counsel, is considered one of the best legal minds on American gun law.

Kyleanne had just come from the Senate with disappointing if predictable news. A few months earlier, the House had passed H.R. 8, the Bipartisan Background Checks Act to kill the private-sale loophole, with a vote of 240–190, including the support of eight Republicans and all but two Democrats. The following day, the House passed a bill to expand the maximum time for a check from three days to ten days, to kill the other loophole that allowed Dylann Roof to arm up. It opened the possibility of the most important federal gun reform since the Brady Bill. But as Kyleanne witnessed in the Senate, majority leader Mitch McConnell refused to bring the bill before the floor.

Despite that, Kyelanne and Jonathan are upbeat and think it shows progress. A few years ago, they say, the Republicans would have wanted to bring the bill to a vote to make the Democrats look bad among pro-gun constituents. But now they prefer not to talk about guns. This shows a profound shift in the politics, they say, with voters seeing gun safety as a priority issue, spurred on by the mass shootings and peace marches.

"We are seeing a swing and a change," Kyleanne says. "People on our side of the aisle are ranking gun violence as one of their top three issues."

This has helped gun safety groups get more funding, outspending the gun-rights groups in the 2018 midterms for the first time. Kyleanne is also finding moderate gun owners more open to talking about issues such as background checks. She touts the idea that you can't have strict gun regulations in the military but then none at home.

"There are more and more reasonable gun owners who think the NRA is ridiculous," she says. "We are not saying the enemy is guns. We are saying the enemy is irresponsibility."

They also cheered the financial scandals of the NRA, which make the invincible gun lobby machine suddenly look vulnerable. "I'm more optimistic than ever that we are going to see real significant change very soon. No question in my lifetime," Jonathan says. "Even without the NRA in the death spiral that it's going through now, the politics have changed, and more people are caring about preventing gun violence."

Maybe they are right, and we are on the cusp of another major moment of gun reform. And even if it isn't right away, it could come in the following years. But if it happens, will it reduce America's iron river?

———

Gun safety advocates are not all on the same page. Some focus only on the simplest measures such as universal background checks, others on buyback programs of "assault rifles," others on creating a license system for gun owners. The center of gravity is in moderate reform, the idea of respecting people's right to have arms to defend themselves and hunt while keeping weapons away from killers. But some want to repeal the Second Amendment itself, arguing that only then can gun safety reform be upheld in the Supreme Court after the case of *District of Columbia v. Heller*.

Here, I do not wade too deeply into this fundamental discussion or all the measures on the table. They are outside the scope of this story on gun trafficking. I focus on using the information from this investigation to analyze the areas that could specifically reduce gunrunning, which affects the United States and many other countries. If gun reform is achieved, architects need to contemplate this trafficking and the simple measures that could reduce the iron river. This is the part of our story that has not happened yet.

There are four main methods by which guns go into the black market or are directly acquired by criminals: the private-sale loophole, straw buying, theft, and ghost guns. Simple measures can be taken in all four that would have a substantial effect while respecting the rights of gun owners.

Universal background checks have been called the low-hanging fruit, the easiest measure to get through, as they gain the most unified support. While that is true, they would also be genuinely important, dealing a knockout blow to this method of criminals acquiring guns, as the loophole simply would not exist. The argument that universal checks could not be enforced is nonsense, as various states already apply them, allowing them to go through licensed gun dealers. This also provides revenue for struggling stores.

Straw buying may be the most important way that gangsters get guns, and this could not be totally eliminated. But it could be massively reduced without even changing the law by raising the sentencing guidelines for straw purchasers. Under the law, people can in theory do years in prison for lying on Form 4473. But the guideline is probation, which is what most straw buyers get, and by definition, they do not have previous felonies.

If they were to get a greater punishment, including prison time, it could dramatically change the situation. Why would someone straw-buy for a hundred dollars if they were facing jail? A campaign could accompany it, so that people better know what they would be getting into. There is a misperception that straw buying is victimless crime, but the guns are used to murder. The men who provided the guns that were used in Columbine, the guns used by the criminals who killed border agent Brian Terry, and the rifles used in San Bernardino all got prison sentences. So why are others allowed to walk when there are victims, including innocent children, killed by stray bullets in inner cities? How much money would people want to be paid to risk prison? Thousands of dollars? Which would completely change the game for acquiring weapons.

Giving prison sentences to straw purchasers would also make the ATF field operations worthwhile. They would have a real impact by arresting straws rather than just treading water. And this would reduce the incentive of getting into twisted espionage cases such as Fast and Furious.

Another element is to reduce the number of guns people can buy at one time, something that various states already have. Anyone who walks in and buys ten identical Kalashnikovs, like the man getting the gun that killed Agent Zapata, should raise a flag. And it's nuts that a gangster could buy eighty-five handguns in a single purchase. This also means getting the ATF to take its policing of gun shops more seriously, and to take away the licenses from the criminal ones, without fear of repercussions. It's the few rotten shops providing most of the traffickers.

The gun stores also need to be serious about stopping theft, but that would require a law change. The video in North Carolina of robbers sliding open the unlocked cabinets underlines the problem. The stores could stop this by simply having better alarms and locked cabinets. This has been proposed in the SECURE Firearm Storage Act, drafted by Representative Bradley Scott Schneider of Illinois, which would mandate that gun stores keep firearms in secure places. Those who fail would be fined, and repeat offenders would have their license revoked. This is another measure that should be easy to convince the public of and does not affect the rights of regular gun owners. But it could make a big difference in the trafficking to criminals, especially those in the inner cities.

In any major effort to hit the firearm black market, it is important to go after ghost guns. They have already become a significant problem in California. And if it were difficult to acquire guns by other methods, the traffickers to Mexico and Baltimore would switch to the ghosts. A bill proposed by Representative Adriano Espaillat of New York, which he calls the Ghost Guns Are Guns Act,[3] would make all the kits and the core parts be treated as firearms and require background checks. It incorporates the upper and lower receivers by using the wording "any combination of parts designed or intended for use in converting any device into a firearm and from which a firearm may be readily assembled."

People can still make artisanal guns. But there is nothing artisanal about drilling a hole in an 80 percent lower. The measure would be opposed by the libertarians wanting guns to be absolutely everywhere. But the majority of people wouldn't care if you need to pass a background check to buy an unfinished receiver, which they have never heard of. And the argument that ghost guns cannot be stopped is untrue; 3D printing is not there yet.

Those four measures could be game changers in themselves, but there are other questions. One is on .50-caliber rifles. They are a fringe hobby in the United States for gun aficionados who are willing to spend big cash but cannot be practically used in self-defense or hunting. In Mexico, however, they are an important factor in giving the cartels insurgent capabilities.

Banning them wouldn't even be necessary. All it would require is for gun shops to report to the ATF the sale of all .50 calibers, and possibly have an extended background check. The agents can check out the buyer. If it is a hobbyist, fine; but if not, they catch a straw buyer or perhaps get to bigger fish and stop a .50 caliber from going to the Mexican Drug War. The .50 calibers may be used in a small percentage of attacks in Mexico, but they have a big psychological impact.

The question of "assault rifle" bans or buybacks gets into trickier territory. A ban would reduce the firepower available to the crime armies of Mexico and to the mass shooters in the United States, though it would have less impact on the U.S. gang shootings. But there is a more fervent mobilized opposition against it. Millions of Americans now have the weapons and are opposed to a ban, which would set off a visceral reaction from hard-liners.

There were also issues with the 1994 ban about exactly how to define "assault rifles" and how to confront the fact that a wooden Ruger rifle like the one used in Norway can also be used in a massacre.

Another option could be to have more extensive background checks for semiautomatic rifles so that people could still buy them but with a further investigation into their history, to look for straw buyers or potential mass shooters. Again, this is something many gun enthusiasts would rally against, but some could find it acceptable. Gun owners themselves complain about the Parkland shooter being able to buy the rifle despite red flags. So would they be prepared to give law enforcement the teeth to stop such scenarios?

A challenge to all this is the division cutting through our societies. The gun hard-liners turned this into an issue of "us versus them." Some on the left embrace this culture war and call for seizing the guns of old white men. That rhetoric doesn't help reach a compromise. When talking to gun enthusiasts, I have been surprised by how many are open to measures when you really lay them out. But the broken politics has not been able to do this. It would help to separate the concerns of the grassroots gun owners from the corruption of the NRA.

However, there are other problems ensnared in the issue. Among these is the poverty connected to crime and guns. And entwined with this is the scourge of drug addiction.

The entangled weeds of the drug and gun black markets need to be challenged at the same time. One reason for the failure to combat cartels is the separate focus on each of these problems. A goal would be to craft more comprehensive policies that take the dual rackets into account and look at larger solutions. In both instances, it is a case of harm reduction.

The idea of a war on drugs is mostly out of vogue, the phrase now used by critics but not often by the actual proponents of drug enforcement. Yet we are still stuck with the effects of the "drug war" on the ground, from Baltimore to Sinaloa.

Drug policy reform is the broader effort to shift the way we deal with the drug problem. It does not mean pressing a button to legalize all drugs and the disease will be cured. It's about facing up to the fact that prohibition policies did not stop people from taking drugs while they financed violent criminals. Harm reduction means reducing both the bad effects of drug addiction and the cash going to cartels.

In our societies, we already allow alcohol and tobacco while we have health campaigns to discourage their abuse, and these have borne fruit. Smoking in the United States has hit record lows. Drinking worldwide has dropped by 5 percentage points since 2000.[4]

We could move further forward with marijuana legalization and get away from the halfway house we are in right now. While it is fully legal in eleven U.S. states, and legal for medicinal use in thirty-three, cannabis is still banned federally. This creates a gray market where it is smuggled across state lines, and millions of pounds are still trafficked from Mexico, giving cash to super-violent cartels. It's ludicrous when marijuana is legal in half the country that green dollars fund hit men in the Zetas and kids shooting up the corners of Baltimore. The fully legal market could be regulated across North America, helping the economy amid the depression. It's coming to terms with the reality of the situation.

However, we need to fight harder against the most noxious drugs such as heroin and crystal meth. While efforts are needed to stop the traffic, there is a huge space for improvement in rehab work. The American Medical Association found in 2019 that while 20 million Americans live with a substance abuse disorder, an incredible 90 percent do not get the necessary treatment.[5] Effective help includes full rehab so that people give up drugs completely. But various medicines now have been found to be effective substitutes for dependency. Treatment will not work on every addict. But it can work on millions, and as they each consume large amounts of drugs, this can mean taking billions of dollars away from violent criminals. Investment in rehabilitation also reduces the criminality of the addicts themselves, gets them out the prison system, and saves untold anguish in families.

* * *

Reducing the drug-money flow is key to reducing the bloodshed. Jelly Roll dropped out of high school to sell dope on the corner in Baltimore because he could make $3,500 a week. Such an offer in a city with high youth unemployment is hard to compete with. But as young men are lured to unleash gun violence, it only undermines the legitimate opportunities for everyone to get out of poverty.

The same is true south of the border. Fresa got paid by drug traffickers to commit horrific murders, which seemed like his only way to get off the street and to give his children a middle-class life. Yet he ended up full of bullets and left his children fatherless.

Again, it's a question of harm reduction. The United Nations claims the illegal drug trade is worth more than $300 billion a year. If marijuana legalization and rehab for hard drugs reduced that by a third, the gangs would have less money to buy off youngsters and rotten police officers. If it managed to reduce it by half, then crime power would really be diminished. Claiming we can abolish the entire drug trade through enforcement is an unhelpful fantasy. But it is realistic to try to substantially reduce the drug money flowing to the most ruthless villains and give others a chance to compete for the lives of the recruits.

Governments and independent organizations need to step into these marginalized spaces. Improved jobs and resources are of course needed, although this depends on broader economic policies. But even in the current economy, social work projects can go a long way. Mentors offering guidance to the potential recruits of gangs and cartels can have remarkable success. Many of those I have talked to who fell into the gangster life said they were offered no hope as kids. Yet I have also witnessed social workers in the hardest areas who steer vulnerable youths onto a better path. It's not only crime prevention. It's winning the hearts and minds, before they go to those who will turn them to commit heinous crimes.

Gun violence is the Herculean challenge facing governments across Latin America. Again, reducing the power of cartel finances is key. If they have less money to bribe cops and train killers, then there is more chance of turning the tables. Across the region, measures can be taken to reform police, work with young people being recruited into the crime armies, and legalize chunks of the drug market such as marijuana. And on the issue of guns, there is particular room for progress.

Stopping the "leakage" is crucial. Arms inventories need to be checked on a regular basis and people detained when guns are missing. The pressure can come from within governments and the civil society groups that lobby them. But it could also come from the arms-exporting countries. Germany and the United States can insist that if the weapons disappear into the hands of criminals, they won't be sold.

Dedicated firearms units could help in Latin America, with elements of police forces specifically cracking down on gun-trafficking rings. Again, they need to be vetted heavily for corruption. And Mexico could check its northern border more, with technology that looks for guns in vehicles.

Unlike in the United States, there is no political cost in cracking down on illegal guns in Mexico. There is a huge clamor in the population calling for it. Investment in it could pay off in the long term. Right now Mexico is caught in a hazardous feedback loop. Criminals are armed to the teeth; so criminals overwhelm police; law and order breaks down; criminals become more powerful; they make money; and they arm up to the teeth. If there were a substantial reduction of guns in Mexico, it could create a positive feedback loop. Police could get the upper hand on criminals, which would reduce the level of crime, which would reduce the money in the hands of gangs, which would allow them to buy fewer guns, which would mean police could get the upper hand. When there are thirty-five thousand murders a year, it is tough to even begin to solve them. If the murder numbers are reduced, the clear-up rate could improve exponentially. And people could stop fleeing the violence as refugees.

Some may sigh that these changes will never happen. They are indeed tough challenges. But human beings have solved tougher. Nations across the world have radically reduced violence before. There is no reason this can't happen again in San Salvador, Ciudad Juárez, and St. Louis. People do not need to live with this suffering and bloodshed. Change is possible.

———

Two museums. Two countries. Two realities.

The first one is in Las Vegas. The Museum of Organized Crime and Law Enforcement, better known as the Mob Museum, is one of my favorite museums anywhere. In Vegas's historic downtown, around the corner from the casinos, it tells the story of the Mafia in the United States, especially in its golden age during Prohibition, narrated with interactive technology and original artifacts. There is the very wall from the St. Valentine's Day Massacre, the bricks shipped over from Chicago. It's a relic important to the history of machine guns, the ATF, and Al Capone, the El Chapo of the twenties.

And there are the guns. One of Capone's revolvers, a .38 Smith & Wesson, hangs on the wall. His friend Parker Henderson Jr. bought it and gave it to Capone in Miami. When Capone was arrested for tax evasion in 1931, the gun went missing, turning up seven decades later in a 2004 raid on a Kentucky illegal gambling den. Guns are durable goods.

Next hangs an original tommy gun alongside a quote from Vegas sheriff Sam Gay, who ran the city police during Prohibition. "You can't deal with these new gunmen with a single action .45," Gay said. "Need a machine gun. I'm too old to learn to run one, so I quit."

These stories are fun because they are historical. Al Capone is not killing people anymore—the loved ones of his victims are all gone. I spoke at the museum about Latin America, was invited to join its advisory board, and helped with an exhibit on the drug wars. But they are not the main feature. Everyone loves the stories of the Mafia, the truth behind *The Godfather*.

America can enjoy the mythology of the Mafia because it's largely history, its worst violence in the United States in the past. You can put the guns of Al Capone on display alongside the bricks of the St. Valentine's Day Massacre from 1929. But not the guns of Paddock, who massacred many more people, nine miles away in 2017. That would be an act of profound disrespect. Likewise, it would be hard for Baltimore to have a museum of its heroin kingpins and their guns. It would be seen as glorifying the violence that goes on destroying lives.

The second museum is in Mexico City. It's also got a technical title and a popular one; it's officially called the *Museo del Enervante*, but most call it the Narco Museum. It sits in the Defense Department headquarters, close to Mexico's only gun store, and has a collection of artifacts that soldiers have seized from drug traffickers. It's not open to the public, only to journalists, investigators, and politicians.

It's as fascinating as the Mob Museum and more surreal. The drugs themselves fill vials: marijuana, crystal meth, heroin, cocaine, even black cocaine. Pieces from the trap cars of the kind that Flaco built are on display, with secret compartments in their gas tanks and seats. Glass cases hold medals given to gunmen by the Zetas; one medallion has a *Z* on one side and a picture of gangster soldiers on the other. The items get weirder: a cowboy waistcoat, which is really a bulletproof vest; a cell phone bathed in gold; a four-foot statue of a drug lord in the image of a saint.

And as in the Mob Museum, there are guns. The Narco Museum doesn't bother with the regular piles of AKs and AR-15s, which are shown off by the army at press conferences. It has guns that stand out. Heavier weapons fill a cabinet: .50 calibers, shoulder-held rocket launchers, including an RPG-29, known as a Vampire. Next come dozens of weapons that the narcos have bathed in silver, gold, and precious stones.

The AK-47s form a series, the celebrated Goat Horns, glimmering in their golden coats. Pistols have gems that form words and pictures, images of Jesus, the Virgin of Guadalupe, the revolutionary Zapata. Guns boast the initials of their owners, one with *ACF*, standing for Amado Carrillo Fuentes, the "Lord of the Skies," who carried cocaine in Boeing airplanes. It's strikingly similar to the golden gun of El Chapo's that New York prosecutors showed a photo of at the trial. The narcos decorate their guns like they are sacred items; they are the source of their power; the tool that has elevated them from paupers to billionaires; the weapons that have soaked their homeland in blood.

Opening this museum to the Mexican public would be tricky. It would be seen as glorifying the narcos in the midst of a war that rages fiercely. It has tributes to fallen soldiers who died fighting traffickers and a mural showing them in heroic poses against a demonic enemy. But it lacks a tribute to the fallen civilians, to the disappeared, to the refugees.

We can hope one day the Narco Museum will be opened up. Because the violence will be history, a past story of bloodshed that can be studied like the museums of the Mexican Revolution, the American Civil War, the violence of Al Capone. There will no longer be mass graves of 250 corpses, refugees in camps drowning in feces on the U.S. border, mothers scouring the earth for a sign of their sons and daughters.

We can hope there can be a museum for the violence of Baltimore, remembering those bad old days when children were killed with stray bullets. We can hope that the era of mass shootings will be a phenomenon to study in the history books.

Someday this will come to pass. Our efforts could make it happen sooner. But perhaps, there is worse to come first.

ACKNOWLEDGMENTS

My editor, Anton Mueller, was a huge part of *Blood Gun Money*. He got the ball rolling and steered me toward the goal line. It couldn't have happened without you, feller. And thanks to the whole Bloomsbury team, including Morgan Jones, Laura Phillips, Maureen Klier, Tara Kennedy, Marie Coolman, and my agent, Katherine Fausset.

As always, it's the sources that make the book. Thanks to everybody who lights up these pages for sharing their stories and often coffees, food, beers, and friendship. I also conducted dozens more long interviews that I didn't finally include in the text because of space, but they all helped immensely in understanding these issues of guns and crime and conflict. Thanks so much for everyone's time and knowledge, including Robert Bunker, Robert Muggah, Nic Marsh, Jonah Leff, Doug Farah, Nils Duquet, Alex Yablon, Matt Schroeder, R. T. Naylor, Wendy Cukier, Alejandro Hope, and many more.

Cheers to journalist partners in crime for sharing contacts, materials, and thoughts, including Michel Marizco, Sean Glynn, Mike Kirsch, Nick Quested, Tristan McConnell, Danny Gold, Matt Cipollone, Amy Lee Jones, Noah Hurowitz, and Luca "Fluker" Baratti. Props to those who helped me in the field, including Ricardo Torres-Cortez (Las Vegas), Jelly Roll (Baltimore), Addie (New York), Tilo López (Los Angeles), Misha Pantovic (Serbia), Trayan Velev (Bulgaria), Miguel Perea, Jose Luis, and Joel Gonzalez (Ciudad Juárez), Miguel Ángel Vega (Sinaloa), Lev García (Veracruz), Orlin Castro (Honduras), Oliver Schmieg (Colombia), and my check-in man,

Jan-Albert Hootsen of the CPJ. And special big up to the photographers who shared great pictures: Oliver, Patrick Tombola, and Ross McDonnell; to my brainstorming partner, Andrew Paxman, and my web man, Ryan Cresswell. Cheers to the *NYT* crew, including Boris Muñoz, Clay Risen, Jenée Desmond-Harris, and Azam Ahmed, and the CR crew, including Gavin Strong, Alan Zamayoa, Eduardo Arcos, Zoe Phillips, Francisco Garcia, and Adriana Thomas. And you can't make old friends, like Luigi Loizides, Kelly, Mel, Rob, Sarah, Thads "Duncan," Frank Jack, Nubia, the Johns (Dickie, Hecht, and Roeder), Laura, Ana Maria, Alejandra, Adam Saytanides, Nancy, and Oscar "y los 50 varos?"

The biggest inspiration of all comes from my family. Thanks, Mum and Dad, who have always been there, my sisters and the next gen, Charlie and Jack, my *suegros* and *cuñados*, and, above all, my beloved Myri and Amalia. Thank you for being you.

APPENDIX: THE TEN RULES OF CRIME GUN-ONOMICS

1) A gun on the black market goes for about two to six times the price it costs in a shop, depending on location and circumstances.
2) When it is a ghost gun, with no serial number, it increases the value of the weapon.
3) A gun that is "burned" (used in a murder) is a *devalued product* and will sell much cheaper.
4) If a buyer is beefing (i.e., somebody wants to hurt them), they are a *distressed buyer* and the price shoots up drastically.
5) Guns can be bartered, especially for drugs.
6) Guns and bullets can be used as currency.
7) A big criminal organization can utilize its manpower to acquire guns more cheaply than buying from gunrunners.
8) Having a cause that a government agency wants to sponsor is a way to get cheap or free guns.
9) It's cheaper to steal a gun than to buy a gun.
10) Having lots of guns allows you to seize more guns.

SELECTED BIBLIOGRAPHY

Barrett, Paul, *Glock: The Rise of America's Gun*. New York: Broadway Books, 2012.

Barger, Ralph "Sonny," with Keith and Kent Zimmerman, *Hell's Angel: The Life and Times of Sonny Barger and the Hell's Angels Motorcycle Club*. New York: HarperCollins, 2011.

Chivers, C. J., *The Gun*. New York: Simon & Schuster, 2010.

Cullen, Dave, *Parkland: Birth of a Movement*. New York: HarperCollins, 2019.

Davidson, Osha Gray, *Under Fire: The NRA and the Battle for Gun Control*. Iowa City: University of Iowa Press, 1998.

Detty, Mike, *Guns across the Border: How and Why the U.S. Government Smuggled Guns into Mexico*. New York: Skyhorse, 2013.

Dodson, John, *The Unarmed Truth: My Fight to Blow the Whistle and Expose Fast and Furious*. New York: Threshold Editions, 2013.

Knox, Neal. Compiled, edited, and annotated by Chris Knox, *Neal Knox—The Gun Rights War: Dispatches from the Front Lines, 1966 through 2000*. Phoenix: MacFarlane Press, 2009.

Hartmann, Thom, *The Hidden History of Guns and the Second Amendment*. Oakland: Berret-Koehler Publishers, 2019.

Lawson, Guy, *War Dogs: The True Story of How Three Stoners from Miami Beach Became the Most Unlikely Gunrunners in History*. London: Viking, 2016.

Moore, James, *Very Special Agents: The Inside Story of America's Most Controversial Law Enforcement Agency—the Bureau of Alcohol, Tobacco and Firearms.* New York: Pocket Books, 1997.

Overton, Iain, *Gun Baby Gun: A Bloody Journey into the World of the Gun.* Edinburgh: Canongate Books, 2015.

Rottman, Gordon, *The Book of Gun Trivia: Essential Firepower Facts.* Oxford: Osprey Publishing, 2013.

Satia, Priya, *Empire of Guns: The Violent Making of the Industrial Revolution.* New York: Penguin Random House, 2018.

Stohl, Rachel, Matt Schroeder, and Dan Smith, *The Small Arms Trade: A Beginners Guide.* Oxford: One World Publications, 2007.

Winkler, Adam, *Gunfight: The Battle over the Right to Bear Arms in America.* New York: W. W. Norton & Company, 2011.

NOTES

CHAPTER 1: THE GUNS OF EL CHAPO

1. From a speech at a presentation of the documentary *No Se Mata La Verdad* in Mexico City, May 18, 2018.

2. The estimate is from the Small Arms Survey published in 2018. A summary can be found at: www.smallarmssurvey.org/fileadmin/docs/Weapons_and _Markets/Tools/Firearms_holdings/SAS-Press-release-global-firearms -holdings.pdf.

3. Topher McDougal, David A. Shirk, Robert Muggah, and John H. Patterson, *The Way of the Gun: Estimating Firearms Traffic across the U.S.–Mexico Border* (Igarape Institute and University of San Diego Trans-Border Institute, March 2013).

4. The ATF trace statistics are on www.atf.gov. An ATF record with specific reference to this figure is at: www.atf.gov/file/135106/download.

5. Office of the Inspector General, *A Review of ATF's Operation Fast and Furious and Related Matters* (U.S. Department of Justice, September 2012), 17.

6. Office of Public Affairs, "Viktor Bout Extradited to the United States to Stand Trial on Terrorism Charges," U.S. Department of Justice, November 17, 2010.

7. The government motion can be found at: www.documentcloud.org/docu ments/5485206-Government-letter-to-block-mentions-of-Operation.html.

8. T. Jefferson Parker, *Iron River* (New American Library, 2011).

9. John Gramlich and Katherine Schaeffer, "7 Facts about Guns in the U.S.," Pew Research Center, October 22, 2019.

CHAPTER 2: THE DRACO

1. Steve Rosenberg, "Kalashnikov 'Feared He Was to Blame' for AK-47 Rifle Deaths," BBC, January 13, 2014.

2. I conducted a detailed interview with Victor Avila on the events. The attack was also described in various court cases of the perpetrators, and there were great details on the case in: Spencer S. Hsu, "'We Are Shot! We Are Shot!' An ICE Agent's Final Moments Resound in U.S. Court," *Washington Post*, July 25, 2017; and in: Mary Cuddehe, "Agent Zapata," *Atavist Magazine*, No. 19, November 2012.

3. Among reports are those by Impunidad Cero, www.impunidadcero.org. Its brief on 2019 report is: Guillermo Raul Zepeda and Paola Jimenez Rodriguez, "Impunidad en Homicidio Doloso en Mexico: Reporte 2019," *Impunidad Cero*, December 2019.

4. Wesley Pergament, "Boom! The Story hehind Gunpowder," *Daily China*, September 10, 2017.

5. Donald E. Worcester and Thomas F. Schilz, "The Spread of Firearms among the Indians on the Anglo-French Frontiers," *American Indian Quarterly*, University of Nebraska Press, 1984.

6. John Pilger, *Hidden Agendas* (Vintage, 1998), 118.

7. Adam Winkler, *Gunfight: The Battle over the Right to Bear Arms in America* (W. W. Norton & Company, 2011), 193.

8. C. J. Chivers, *The Gun* (Simon & Schuster, 2010), 5.

9. Rick Schmitt and Rick Young, "Romanian Weapons Modified in the U.S. Become Scourge of Mexican Drug War," Center for Public Integrity, February 3, 2011, updated May 19, 2014.

10. Mike O'Connor, "Albanian Village Finds Boom in Gun-Running," *New York Times*, April 24, 1997.

11. Data on the countries under various arms embargoes is compiled by the Stockholm International Peace Research Institute, available at: www.sipri.org /databases/embargoes.

12. Nima Albagir, Salma Abdelaziz, Mohamed Abo El Gheit, and Laura Smith-Spark, "Sold to an Ally, Lost to an Enemy," CNN, February 2019, and "Arms Supplied by U.S., Saudi Ended Up with Islamic State, Researchers Say," Reuters, December 14, 2017.

13. Winkler, 102.

14. Winkler, 8.

15. Surveys include: "Strong Voter Support for Second Amendment Doesn't Extend to Assault Rifles," Rasmussen Reports, November 26, 2019.

16. Chivers, 236.

17. Miles Kohrman and Jennifer Mascia, "Everything You Need to Know about Federal Background Checks," *The Trace*, July 11, 2015, updated April 9, 2020.

18. Paul Barrett, *Glock: The Rise of America's Gun* (Broadway Books, 2012), 82.

19. Ibid., 68

20. The Wikileaks cable is entitled, "Guatemalan Response on Potential Sale of Map-Origin Firearms." It can be found at: wikileaks.org/plusd/cables /08GUATEMALA482_a.html.

21. Ken Picard, "In Franklin County, a Global Arms Dealer Quietly Makes a Killing," *Seven Days*, January 23, 2013.

22. Stories include: "WikiLeaks Secret Cables Detail Delray Firm's Role in Arms Trade," *Palm Beach Post*, September 11, 2011, and Schmitt and Young, "Romanian Weapons."

23. Lawrence Walsh, "Final Report of the Independent Counsel for Iran/Contra Matters," Chapter 8, fas.org/irp/offdocs/walsh/chap_08.htm.

24. Office of the Inspector General, *A Review of Investigations of the Osorio and Barba Firearms Trafficking Rings* (Department of Justice, March 2017), 116.

CHAPTER 3: GUN POLICE

1. As cited in: Fox Butterfield, "Terror in Oklahoma: Echoes of the N.R.A.; Rifle Association Has Long Practice in Railing Against Federal Agents," *New York Times*, May 8, 1995.

2. James Moore, *Very Special Agents: The Inside Story of America's Most Controversial Law Enforcement Agency—The Bureau of Alcohol, Tobacco and Firearms* (Pocket Books, 1997), xiv.

3. Lily Rothman, "The Original Reason the NRA Was Founded," *Time*, November 17, 2015.

4. Col. William C. Church in *The United States Army and Navy Journal and Gazette of the Regular and Volunteer Forces*, vol. 8, Army and Navy Journal Incorporated, 1871, as digitized by Cornell University.

5. As cited in: The Week Staff, "The Surprising History of the NRA," *The Week*, March 18, 2018.

6. As cited in: Arica L. Coleman, "When the NRA Supported Gun Control," *Time*, July 29, 2016.

7. This is part of the description displayed under the bust of Carter in the NRA National Firearms Museum.

8. John M. Crewdson, "Hard-Line Opponent of Gun Laws Wins New Term at Helm of Rifle Association," *New York Times*, May 4, 1981.

9. Laura Smith, "The Man Responsible for the Modern NRA Killed a Hispanic Teenager, before Becoming a Border Agent," *Timeline*, July 6, 2017.

10. Crewdson, "Hard-Line."

11. Cited in: Osha Gray Davidson, *Under Fire: The NRA and the Battle for Gun Control* (University of Iowa Press, 1998), 46.

12. Adam Winkler, *Gunfight: The Battle over the Right to Bear Arms in America* (W. W. Norton & Company, 2011), 66–67.

13. Cited in Davidson, 36.

14. Victor Cohn, "Bullet Lodged an Inch from Reagan's Heart," *Washington Post*, April 16, 1981.

15. Ralph "Sonny" Barger, with Keith and Kent Zimmerman, *Hell's Angel: The Life and Times of Sonny Barger and the Hell's Angels Motorcycle Club* (HarperCollins, 2011), 65.

16. Ibid., 166

17. Ibid., 125

18. U.S. Code § 926 can be found at: www.law.cornell.edu/uscode/text/18/926.

19. Joe Sommerlad, "How Was the NRA Founded and How Did a Gun Lobby Become So Influential in American Politics?" *Independent*, April 26, 2010

20. Neal Knox, compiled, edited, and annotated by Chris Knox, *Neal Knox—The Gun Rights War: Dispatches from the Front Lines, 1966 through 2000* (MacFarlane Press, 2009), Editor's Note.

21. Sara Rimer with Sam Howe Verhovek, "Growing Up Under Koresh: Cult Children Tell of Abuses," *New York Times*, May 4, 1993.

22. The letter was first reported by the *Washington Post* on April 28, 1995, and can be found in full on Congressional records at: www.govinfo.gov/content/pkg /CREC-1995-05-09/html/CREC-1995-05-09-pt1-PgS6294.htm.

23. Sarah Pruitt, "How Ruby Ridge and Waco Led to the Oklahoma City Bombing," *History*, May 22, 2018.

24. Phil Helsel and Andrew Blankstein, "Judge Refuses to Strip Mongols Motorcycle Club of Its Trademark," NBC, February 28, 2019.

CHAPTER 4: BODY MORE

1. Jayne Miller, "Baltimore Ends 2018 with 309 Homicides; I-Team Breaks Out Statistics," WBALTV, January 2, 2019.

2. The ranking of homicidal cities is compiled annually by Mexico's Citizens Council for Public Security, or El Consejo Ciudadano para la Seguridad Pública y la Justicia Penal. They can be found at: www.seguridadjusticiaypaz .org.mx.

3. Justin George, "Some Baltimore Neighborhoods Condemned to Endure a Shocking Degree of Violence," *Baltimore Sun*, October 6, 2016.

4. Chelsea Bailey, "Baltimore Activists Hold Second Cease-Fire as City Reaches 300 Homicides," NBC News, November 3, 2017.

5. Fred P. Graham, "Handgun Imports Held Up by U.S.," *New York Times*, August 17, 1968.

6. "Maryland Gun Ban Is Hotly Debated," *New York Times*, October 9, 1988.

7. Brian Freskos, "Easy Targets," *New Yorker*, in partnership with *The Trace*, February 2019.

8. The Trump speech can be seen at: www.youtube.com/watch?v=aHIB_VteLAU.

9. "Medieval London's Murder Hotspots Revealed," BBC, November 28, 2018.

10. The shooting that Colion was responding to was also detailed in: Kevin Rector, "Baltimore Police: Two People Killed, Seven Injured—Including 15-Year-Old—in Weekend Violence," *Baltimore Sun*, April 30, 2018.

11. These are from CompStat figures of the New York City Police Department. They can be found at: www1.nyc.gov/assets/nypd/downloads/pdf/crime_statis tics/cs-en-us-city.pdf.

12. A good account of the case is by Jessica Lussenhop, "When Cops Become Robbers," BBC, April 3, 2018.

13. Justin Fenton, "Freddie Gray Alleged Back Injury Detailed in Unsealed Report," *Baltimore Sun*, December 31, 2015.

14. Justin Fenton, "Witness: Baltimore Gun Trace Task Force Officer Brought Him Trash Bags Full of Looted Drugs amid 2015 Riot," *Baltimore Sun*, February 1, 2018.

15. I refer to drug overdose deaths compiled by the CDC, which can be found at: www.cdc.gov/drugoverdose/data/statedeaths.html.

CHAPTER 5: THE BORDER

1. Rachel St. John, *Line in the Sand: A History of the Western U.S.–Mexico Border* (Princeton University Press, 2012).

2. The vote count can be found at: clerk.house.gov/evs/2006/roll446.xml.

3. Douglas S. Massey, "The Mexico-U.S. Border in the American Imagination," *Proceedings of the American Philosophical Society*, June 2016.

4. From the history unit of Mexico's navy. The piece can be found at: 2006-2012 .semar.gob.mx/unidad-de-historia-y-cultura-naval/independencia/morelos .html#_ftnref5.

5. J. David Truby, "Guns of the Mexican Revolution," *Small Arms Review*, V14N11, August 2011.

6. Seth Mydans, "The Assassination in Mexico; Man Who Shot Colosio Recalled as a Loner Who Said Little," *New York Times*, March 25, 1994.

7. Ali Vitali, "Trump Likens Border Crossers to Professional Mountain Climbers, Bashes California During Wall Tour," NBC News, March 13, 2018.

8. Seizures are reported by CBP. A sample can be found at: www.cbp.gov/sites /default/files/assets/documents/2019-Mar/CBP-Border-Security-Report -FY2018.pdf.

9. Figures from the shop's sales were released by Mexico's Defense Department and are detailed in: Alonso Urrutia, "Entre 2010 y 2015 Sedena Vendió 255 Mil 712 Armas," *La Jornada*, February 2, 2016. (The figures also include sales to Mexican police forces.)

10. Ashley Meeks, "Border Police Chief Pleads Guilty to Running Guns to Mexico," Reuters, August 25, 2011.

11. A report by the FBI's National Gang Intelligence Center that also alleges links between the Bandidos and Mexican cartel members can be found at: https:// www.fbi.gov/file-repository/stats-services-publications-national-gang- report-2013/view

12. There is a news release on the case by the U.S. Attorney's Office Southern District of Texas, entitled "Attempted Firearms and Ammunition Smuggling to Zeta Cartel Lands Two Men in Federal Prison," August 1, 2012.

13. Estimates of U.S. rifle production can be found at: news.guns.com/wp-content /uploads/2018/09/NSSF-MSR-Production-Estimates-2017.pdf.

14. Parmy Olson and Zusha Elinson, "Gun Sellers Are Sneaking onto Facebook's Booming Secondhand Marketplace," *Wall Street Journal*, August 20, 2019.

15. Rob Milford, "Mesquite Texas—The Gun Show Capital of America," Breitbart, April 7, 2015.

16. A summary of the survey can be found in: www.ncbi.nlm.nih.gov/pubmed /28055050.

17. A report on the study can be found at: www.bjs.gov/content/pub/pdf/suficspi16 .pdf.

18. "Texas Shooter Evaded Background Check by Purchasing Weapon in Private Sale," CBS/Associated Press, September 3, 2019.

19. Essay by Richard M. Aborn, "The Brady Bill," in Al Smith, *American Cultures: Readings in Social and Cultural History* (Kendall/Hunt Publishing Company, 2006), 157.

20. Jennifer Mascia, "How America Wound Up with a Gun Background Check System Built More for Speed than Certainty," *The Trace*, July 21, 2015.

21. Results of the poll can be found at: news.gallup.com/poll/1645/guns.aspx.

22. The Editors, "Against Universal Background Checks," *National Review*, August 9, 2019.

23. ATF reports on gun traces to Mexico can be found at: www.atf.gov/resource -center/data-statistics.

24. A government statement on the size of the Mexican armed forces can be found at: sedena.gob.mx/pdf/ifai/2011/julio-2011.pdf.

25. Ali Watkins, "When Guns Are Sold Illegally, A.T.F. Is Lenient on Punishment," *New York Times*, June 3, 2018.

26. In 2019, a court found that the Ohio gun dealer had not committed a crime in selling the guns and was not liable for injuries caused by them. "Court: New York Man Shot in 2003 Can't Sue Ohio Gun Dealer," Associated Press, May 11, 2019.

CHAPTER 6: LEAKAGE

1. Bill Chappell, "Heckler & Koch Fined $4.2 Million Over Assault Rifle Sales in Mexico," NPR, February 21, 2019.

2. Lucy Perkins, "Firearms Company Colt Defense Files for Bankruptcy Protection," NPR, June 15, 2015.

3. The press statement can be found in German at: www.heckler-koch.com/de /presse/detail/article/heckler-koch-wird-die-heutige-entscheidung-des -stuttgarter-landgerichts-sorgfaeltig-pruefen-einzieh.html.

4. As of late 2020, the cases against the former presidents of Argentina, Guatemala, Peru, Bolivia, and El Salvador were yet to be resolved.

5. "U.S. Returns Moon Rock to Honduras," BBC, September 23, 2003.

6. Héctor Molina, "Robadas o Extraviadas, 15,592 Armas de Instituciones," *El Economista*, April 24, 2019.

7. Blanca Cortés Martínez, "Pistola Usada en Tiroteo de Cuernavaca Habría Sido de un Policía," *Radio Formula*, May 10, 2019.

8. "Un Policía es Asesinado en México Cada Día, en lo que Va del Año ya Suman 107," *Infobae*, April 21, 2019.

9. The SIPRI arms transfer database can be found at: www.sipri.org/databases /armstransfers.

10. "El Salvador Prisoner Caught with Grenade up Backside," Reuters, March 1, 2007.

11. A release from the El Salvador national police on the seizure is entitled "Policía Descubre Arsenal de Guerra en Santa Ana."

12. Cited in: Nick Miroff and William Booth, "Mexican Cartels' Familiar Weapons: U.S.-Made Grenades Sent to Fight Communism Turn Up Again, with Different Targets," *Washington Post*, July 17, 2010.

CHAPTER 7: GUN NUTS

1. The photo could be seen at: twitter.com/SenPolehanki/status/1255899318210 314241.

2. John Gramlich and Katherine Schaeffer, "7 Facts about Guns in the U.S.," Pew Research Center, October 22, 2019.

3. Osha Gray Davidson, "All Fired Up," *Washington Post*, June 4, 2000.

4. These clips are on the Mike Kirsch report, which can be seen at: www.youtube .com/watch?v=FWJ62QBzpeI&t=211s.

5. The incident was widely covered, including in: Kimberley McGee and Fernanda Santos, "A 9-Year-Old at a Shooting Range, a Spraying Uzi and Outrage," *New York Times*, August 27, 2014.

6. From clip of Kirsch video, as above.

7. Dave Gilson, "The NRA Says It Has 5 Million Members. Its Magazines Tell Another Story," *Mother Jones*, March 7, 2018.

8. Davidson, "All Fired Up."

9. Blake Ellis and Melanie Hicken, "The Money Powering the NRA," CNN, October 2015.

10. The IBISWorld reports can found on www.ibisworld.com. The NSSF report can be found at: d3aya7xwz8momx.cloudfront.net/wp-content/uploads/2019 /02/2019-Economic-Impact.pdf.

11. This figure comes the report *What America's Users Spend on Illegal Drugs, 2006–2016*, commissioned by the Office of National Drug Control Policy using methodology developed by the RAND Corporation, www.rand.org /pubs/research_reports/RR3140.html.

12. Richard M. Aborn, "The Brady Bill," in Al Smith, *American Cultures: Readings in Social and Cultural History* (Kendall/Hunt Publishing Company, 2006).

13. David Leonhardt, Ian Prasad Philbrick, and Stuart A. Thompson, "Thoughts and Prayers and NRA Funding," *New York Times*, October 4, 2017.

14. The clip can be seen at: www.youtube.com/watch?v=sBEQnBueres.

15. Dana Loesch said this on NRA TV in 2016, as cited in Jenni Fink, "Video of NRA's Dana Loesch 'Happy' over Media Being 'Curb Stomped' Resurfaces after Capital Gazette Shooting," *Newsweek*, June 29, 2018.

16. Katie Warren, "NRA Head Wayne LaPierre Made $1.4 million in 2017," *Business Insider*, August 21, 2019.

17. Mike Spies, "Secrecy, Self Dealing, and Greed at the N.R.A.," *New Yorker*, in partnership with *The Trace*, April 17, 2019.

18. "The NRA Ends Its Carry Guard Insurance Program," *The Trace*, July 19, 2020.

19. John Cook, "NRA Membership Dues Tumbled Last Year," *The Trace*, September 20, 2018.

20. The ad can be seen at: www.youtube.com/watch?v=hPM8e_DauUw.

21. Described in news release: "Russian National Sentenced to 18 Months in Prison for Conspiring to Act as an Agent of the Russian Federation within the United States," U.S. Department of Justice, April 26, 2019.

22. A video of the statement can be seen at: www.nytimes.com/2020/08/06/us/ny -nra-lawsuit-letitia-james.html.

23. Wayne LaPierre, "The Forces against Freedom," NRA, August 14, 2020.

24. The *Vice* video of the militia can be seen at: www.youtube.com/watch?v=FWJ 62QBzpeI&t=732s.

25. The *Vice* interview with Norman Olson can be seen at: www.youtube.com /watch?v=ky49ltgeXRU&t=761s.

26. Pat Leisner, "Florida Militia Leader Sentenced," Associated Press, July 28, 2000.

27. Robert Evans and Jason Wilson, "The Boogaloo Movement Is Not What You Think," *Bellingcat*, May 27, 2020.

28. Jeremy Jojola, "Police Seize Assault Rifles, Handguns from Anti-Government Member at Denver Protest," 9News, June 1, 2020.

29. Melanie Woodrow, "Steven Carrillo Charged in Oakland, Santa Cruz Co. Officer Killings Linked to Boogaloo Movement, Federal Investigators Say," ABC, June 21, 2020.

CHAPTER 8: FAST AND FURIOUS

1. A history of Peck Canyon is at: www.gvrhc.org/Library/PeckCanyon.pdf.

2. Many details of Terry's early life are found in a lawsuit, of which documents can be found at: big.assets.huffingtonpost.com/4f2a000c8f517.pdf.pdf.

3. Lt. Dan Marcou, "Police History: Brian Terry Is a Hero Gone too Soon," *Police1*, March 24, 2014.

4. Leo W. Banks, "Smugglers' Paradise," *Tucson Weekly*, November 25, 2010.

5. The statements of the agents from this scene were taken from the affidavits released by federal prosecutors in 2014.

6. Wendy Colburn-Blanco and Kelly Terry-Willis, *You Are My Hero* (CreateSpace Independent Publishing Platform, 2015).

7. Fortesa Latifi, "Steve Bannon Comes to Tucson, Hundreds Protest," *Cronkite News* (Arizona PBS), November 20, 2017.

8. Audio from Bannon speech courtesy of Michel Marizco.

9. From interview with *Newsmax*, also detailed in: Martin Gould and Ashley Martella, "NRA's LaPierre: 'Fast and Furious' Was Plot against Second Amendment," *Newsmax*, October 12, 2011.

10. Sharyl Attkisson, "Documents: ATF Used 'Fast and Furious' to Make the Case for Gun Regulations," CBS, December 11, 2011.

11. Jorge Fernández Menéndez, "Armas para Desestabilizar a México," Excelsior, November 7, 2011.

12. Office of the Inspector General, *A Review of ATF's Operation Fast and Furious and Related Matters* (U.S. Department of Justice, September 2012), 15.

13. Inspector General, *A Review of Fast and Furious*, 96.

14. Mike Detty, *Guns Across the Border: How and Why the U.S. Government Smuggled Guns into Mexico* (Skyhorse, 2013), 58–59.

15. Ibid., 10.

16. Inspector General, *A Review of Fast and Furious*.

17. Detty, 233.

18. A detailed Congressional report on the Mérida Initiative, 2007 to 2020 can be found at: fas.org/sgp/crs/row/IF10578.pdf.

19. Sharyl Attkisson, "Newly-released Fast and Furious Documents (. . . Still Keeping Government Secrets)," sharylattkisson.com, August 22, 2019.

20. The interrogation was conducted by Mexico's controversial Public Security Department. The quote can be seen on: www.youtube.com/watch?v=YUD5 Tcq9NIw.

21. Gregor Aisch and Josh Keller, "What Happens after Calls for New Gun Restrictions? Sales Go Up," *New York Times*, updated version, June 13, 2016.

22. Pete Williams, "First 100 Days: Assault Weapons Ban," NBC, April 24, 2009.

23. The transcript of the news conference can be found at: latimesblogs.latimes .com/washington/2009/04/text-obama-calderone-news-conference.html.

24. John Dodson, *The Unarmed Truth: My Fight to Blow the Whistle and Expose Fast and Furious* (Threshold Editions, 2013), 1.

25. Among other materials on the operation, there is also a book by Katie Pavlich, *Fast and Furious: Barack Obama's Bloodiest Scandal and Its Shameless Cover-Up* (Regnery Publishing, 2012).

26. Inspector General, *A Review of Fast and Furious*, 113.

27. Dodson, 53.

28. Ibid., 65.

29. Ibid., 79.

30. Ibid., 77.

31. Cited from: Inspector General, *A Review of Fast and Furious*, 173, with punctuation as shown.

32. Richard A. Serrano, "From a Mexican Kingpin to an FBI Informant," *Los Angeles Times*, April 21, 2012.

33. Video of Issa presenting the motion is at: www.youtube.com/watch?v=YtcQ -LCoRd0.

34. Inspector General, *A Review of Fast and Furious*, 453.

35. Dodson, 6–7.

CHAPTER 9: REFUGEES

1. "PH Seeks US Help in Tracing Source of Smuggled Guns," *Rappler*, March 3, 2016.

2. Daniel Politi, Ernesto Londoño, and Patricia Mazzei, "Grenades, Land Mines and U.S. Weapons Parts: Argentina Foils Huge Smuggling Operation," *New York Times*, June 28, 2019.

3. An audio of the interview is at: soundcloud.com/univisionnews/exclusive -interview-with-hugh.

4. Cited in "Before Fast & Furious, Florida had Operation Castaway," *Miami Herald*, October 5, 2012.

5. Iain Overton, *Gun Baby Gun: A Bloody Journey into the World of the Gun* (Canongate Books, 2015), 50.

6. Ibid., 52.

7. The estimate is from the Centro Nacional de Memoria Histórica, counting 218,094 deaths from the armed conflict between 1958 and 2012.

8. Simon Romero, "Peru: New Conviction for Ex-Spy Chief," *New York Times*, September 23, 2006.

9. "Armas que EE. UU. Infiltró en la Mafia Aparecen en Medellín," *El Tiempo*, September 9, 2012.

10. The UN Refugee Agency stated that as of March 2018, there were 7.6 million internally displaced people in Colombia.

11. The asylum figures in Mexico are collected by the UN Refugee Agency, whose Mexico website is: www.acnur.org/mexico.html.

12. U.S. data on refugees on Homeland Security site is found at: www.dhs.gov/sites /default/files/publications/Refugees_Asylees_2017.pdf.

13. Holly Yan, "Which Nationalities Get Rejected the Most for US Asylum?" CNN, May 3, 2018.

14. An example poll was carried out by University of Maryland with Nielsen Scarborough, from March to April 2019. It found 65 percent of respondents said family separation was unacceptable compared to 25 percent who said it was acceptable.

CHAPTER 10: TERRORISTS

1. You can see a video of Dr. Alejandro Rios Tovar's testimony at: www.rollcall
    .com/news/video/watch-el-paso-surgeons-graphic-testimony-treating
    -walmart-shooting-victims.

2. Among reporting on Jordan and Andre Anchondo is: Sarah Mervosh, "They Died Shielding Their Baby in El Paso. Their Family's Anguish Was Only Beginning," *New York Times*, August 12, 2019.

3. Daniel Trotta, "His Cross to Bear: Carpenter Creates Memorial for Yet Another Shooting," Reuters, August 6, 2019.

4. Nick Siano, "El Paso Shooting Victims List Update: What We Know about the Walmart Victims as of Monday," *El Paso Times*, August 5, 2019.

5. Lia Eustachewich, "Dad of Accused El Paso Shooter Is a Licensed Counselor Who Battled Addiction," *New York Post*, August 7, 2019.

6. Jolie McCullough, "El Paso Shooting Suspect Said He Ordered His AK-47 and Ammo from Overseas," *Texas Tribune*, August 28, 2019.

7. The Justice Department news release on a guilty plea in the case is entitled "Arizona Man Pleads Guilty to Engaging in the Business of Manufacturing Ammunition Without a License," November 19, 2019.

8. Michael Janofsky, "Columbine Killers, on Tape, Thanked 2 for Gun," *New York Times*, November 13, 1999.

9. Martinez pleaded guilty to conspiring to provide material support to terrorists in 2017. The Justice Department news release is entitled "Enrique Marquez Jr. Agrees to Plead Guilty to Plotting Violent Attacks and Buying Firearms for

Shooter in San Bernardino Terrorist Attack," February 14, 2017. Martinez later attempted to withdraw his guilty plea but a judge ruled against it.

10. Tom Barrett, "Gun and Security Expert Says He Would Not Have Sold to Radcliffe Haughton," Fox6 Milwaukee, October 25, 2012.

11. "Odessa Mass Shooting Debunks Argument against Universal Background Checks," *USA Today*, September 9, 2019.

12. Von Stefan Candea, Jürgen Dahlkamp, Jörg Schmitt, Andreas Ulrich, and Wolf Wiedmann-Schmidt, "How EU Failures Helped Paris Terrorists Obtain Weapons," *Der Spiegel*, March 24, 2016.

13. "The Anatomy of the Las Vegas Mass Shooting, the Deadliest in Modern US History," ABC News, December 23, 2018.

14. Data from LVMPD, *Criminal Investigative Report of the 1 October Mass Casualty Shooting*, released in July 2019.

15. Tim Dickinson, "Why Isn't the NRA Screaming about the Bump Stock Ban?" *Rolling Stone*, December 19, 2018.

16. Derek Thompson, "Mass Shootings in America Are Spreading Like a Disease," *Atlantic*, November 6, 2017.

17. News release from the American Psychological Association, "Statement of APA President in Response to Mass Shootings in Texas, Ohio," August 4, 2019.

18. Jillian Peterson and sociologist James Densley, "We Have Studied Every Mass Shooting Since 1966. Here's What We've Learned about the Shooters," *Los Angeles Times*, August 4, 2019.

19. U.S. Code § 2656f as cited from www.law.cornell.edu/uscode/text/22/2656f.

20. Michael Cooper, "For Medellín Assassin, 10 Life Sentences," *New York Times*, May 6, 1995.

21. Luis Herrera, "Un Día de Terror," *Reporte Indigo*, May 1, 2016.

CHAPTER 11: GHOSTS

1. Andy Greenberg, "State Department Demands Takedown of 3D-Printable Gun Files for Possible Export Control Violations," *Forbes*, May 9, 2013.

2. Danny Yadron, "Tech Renegade: From Print-at-Home Guns to Untraceable Currency," *Wall Street Journal*, December 31, 2013.

3. Interview on RT can be seen at: www.youtube.com/watch?v=-mBFI56FkR0.

4. Video of homemade Glock can be seen at: www.youtube.com/watch?v=aTW7 OF4k55Q.

5. Coverage of the gun includes: John Newman, "Solid Concepts Uses Metal Additive Manufacturing to Build a Gun," *Digital Engineering*, November 8, 2013.

6. Nichole M. Christian, "Makers of Pistol Are Sued in Brooklyn Bridge Attack," *New York Times*, March 14, 1998, and Robert D. McFadden, "Jury Clears Gun Makers of Culpability in a Shooting," *New York Times*, March 28, 1998.

7. Alain Stephens, "Ghost Guns Are Everywhere in California," *The Trace*, May 17, 2019.

8. Police video of the raided gun workshops can be seen at: www.youtube.com /watch?v=XVCfGsOgLkc.

9. Al Baker, "A Hail of Bullets, a Heap of Uncertainty," *New York Times*, December 9, 2007.

CHAPTER 12: DAY OF THE DEAD

1. As of September 2020, neither the indicted shooter nor "Mini Lic" had been tried. Stories on arrests include: "CPJ Welcomes Conviction in Murder of Mexican Journalist Javier Valdez," Committee to Protect Journalists, February 28, 2020, and "2nd Suspect Arrested in Killing of Respected Mexican Reporter Javier Valdez," Associated Press, June 11, 2018.

2. Dave Cullen, *Parkland: Birth of a Movement* (HarperCollins, 2019), 207.

3. The Ghost Guns Are Guns Act was introduced on February 14, 2019.

4. Sara Miller Llana and Courtney Traub, "Culture Shift: What's behind a Decline in Drinking Worldwide," *Christian Science Monitor*, October 3, 2018.

5. A brief on the study: Kevin B. O'Reilly, "90% Who Need Substance-Use Disorder Treatment Don't Get It," American Medical Association, October 22, 2019.

INDEX

A NOTE ON THE AUTHOR

Ioan Grillo is a contributing writer at the *New York Times*, specializing in crime and drugs. Based in Mexico City, he has also worked for *Time* magazine, the History Channel, CNN, Reuters, the Associated Press, and *Esquire*. He is the author of *El Narco*, a finalist for the Los Angeles Times Book Award, and *Gangster Warlords*, a *New York Times Book Review* Editors' Choice and a *Guardian* Book of the Year.